Teaching Literature in
Grades Ten Through Twelve

Published for the
Indiana University English Curriculum Study Center
EDWARD B. JENKINSON, *Director*

Previously Published

On Teaching Literature: Essays for Secondary School
    Teachers
Teaching Literature in Grades Seven Through Nine
On Teaching the Bible as Literature: A Guide to
    Selected Biblical Narratives for Secondary Schools
Two Approaches to Teaching Syntax
What Is Language? and Other Teaching Units for
    Grades Seven Through Twelve

Forthcoming Volumes

Theme Assignments for Grades Seven Through Twelve
Books for Junior and Senior High School Teachers of
    English: An Annotated Bibliography

Teaching Literature in

Grades Ten

Through Twelve

EDITED BY

EDWARD B. JENKINSON
Coordinator for School English Language Arts;
Director of the Indiana University
English Curriculum Study Center

and

PHILIP B. DAGHLIAN
Professor of English
Indiana University

BLOOMINGTON   *Indiana University Press*   LONDON

ACKNOWLEDGMENTS

The portion of the project of the Indiana University English Curriculum Study Center reported herein was supported through the Cooperative Research Program of the Office of Education, U.S. Department of Health, Education, and Welfare.

The IU Center received additional financial support from the Cummins Engine Foundation, which awarded Indiana University a grant providing funds for meetings and equipment that could not be financed by the grant from the U.S. Office of Education.

The staff of the Indiana University English Curriculum Study Center wishes to thank William E. Wilson, former State Superintendent of Public Instruction, for launching this project in 1962 by appointing teachers to committees to help develop the courses of study and by appointing Edward B. Jenkinson, Coordinator for School English Language Arts at Indiana University, chairman of the committees. The staff further wishes to thank the State Department of Public Instruction, under the direction of Richard D. Wells, Superintendent, for distributing this volume to all senior high school teachers of English in Indiana's public schools.

Many teachers played important roles in shaping this volume by contributing ideas, by making suggestions for revisions of various units, and by experimenting with the materials in their classrooms. They painstakingly helped to eliminate errors from the various drafts; the staff of the English Curriculum Study Center accepts responsibility for the errors that remain.

Members of the state-appointed Committee on Literature that helped formulate plans for this volume include:

Dr. Dorothy Bucks, Professor of English, Hanover College; Mrs. Margaret Elam, Chairman of the Department of English, Central High School, Corydon; Dr. Cary Graham, Head of the English Department, Butler University; Mrs. Ruth Herin, Chairman of the Department of English, Broad Ripple High School, Indianapolis; Miss Catharine Howard, Chairman of the Department of English, Mt. Vernon High School, Mt. Vernon; Mrs. Norma Kelly, Teacher of English, Oliver P. Morton High School, Hammond; Mrs. Helen Lee, Teacher of English, Central High School, Fort Wayne; Dr. Terence Martin, Professor of

English, Indiana University; Mrs. Katheryn Offutt, Chairman of the Department of English, Noblesville High School, Noblesville; Dr. Josephine Spear, Chairman of the Department of English, University High School, Bloomington; Miss Ruth Sinks, formerly Chairman of the Department of English, West Lafayette High School, West Lafayette; and Thomas Walker, Teacher of English, Culver Military Academy, Culver.

The staff of the English Curriculum Study Center also wishes to thank these teachers for writing invaluable comments on one or more of the units that they taught in their classes or studied carefully and for helping the staff decide which units should not be included in this volume:

John Alexander, Teacher of English, Portage High School, Portage; Mrs. Margaret Beeman, Teacher of English, Mt. Vernon High School, Mt. Vernon; Charles Billiard, English Supervisor, Fort Wayne Community Schools, Fort Wayne; Mrs. Frances Blake, Chairman of the Department of English, Franklin Community High School, Franklin; Mrs. Madonna Bright, Teacher of English, Southside High School, Muncie; Mrs. Emma J. Cagle, Chairman of the Department of English, Brazil Senior High School, Brazil; Mrs. Jeanne Campbell, formerly Teacher of English, Noblesville High School, Noblesville; Robert Crawl, Teacher of English, Garfield High School, Terre Haute; James Daugherty, formerly Teacher of English, Central Junior-Senior High School, South Bend; Sister Francis de Sales, C.S.C., Teacher of English, Bishop Noll Institute, Hammond; Mrs. Betty DeVol, Teacher of English, Warren Central High School, Indianapolis; and Mrs. Susie Dewey, Supervisor of English, Terre Haute Public Schools.

Mrs. Margaret Dillard, Teacher of English, Franklin Community High School, Franklin; Mrs. Mary Dold, Chairman of the Department of English, Portage High School, Portage; Mrs. Faye Donald, Teacher of English, Wiley High School, Terre Haute; Miles D. Eley, Teacher of English, Warren Central High School, Indianapolis; Mrs. Joann R. Fisher, Teacher of English, Huntington County Community High School, Huntington; Mrs. Mary Ruth Fowler, Teacher of English, Warren Central High School, Indianapolis; Mrs. Doris Grant, Teacher of English, Gerstmeyer High School, Terre Haute; James S. Hedges, Teacher of English, Mt. Vernon High School, Mt. Vernon; Mrs. Edna Houze, Teacher of English, Columbus Senior High School, Columbus; Mrs. Olive Hughey, Teacher of English, Franklin Community High School, Franklin; Miss Mabel Hunter, Chairman of the Department of English, Oliver P. Morton High School, Hammond; and Miss Catherine

Jackson, Chairman of the Department of English, Central High School, Fort Wayne.

Miss Edith Jones, Chairman of the Department of English, Wiley High School, Terre Haute; Malcolm Julian, Supervisor of English and Foreign Languages, Muncie Public Schools; Fred J. Kepler, Teacher of English, Oliver P. Morton High School, Hammond; Miss Judith Kuban, Teacher of English, Bishop Noll Institute, Hammond; Mrs. Hope Lawrence, Teacher of English, Franklin Community High School, Franklin; Miss Betty Major, formerly Teacher of English, River Forest High School, Hobart; Mrs. Harriet McGuire, Teacher of English, Warren Central High School, Indianapolis; Mrs. Barbara McKown, Teacher of English, Noblesville High School, Noblesville; Mrs. Mary Ann McQuillan, Teacher of English, Honey Creek High School, Terre Haute; Miss Arlene Miller, formerly Teacher of Engish, River Forest High School, Hobart; Warren D. Munro, Teacher of English, Portage High School, Portage; and Fredrick Preston, formerly Teacher of English, Central High School, Muncie.

Mrs. Elizabeth Reilly, Chairman of the Department of English, West Vigo High School, West Terre Haute; Donald Seybold, Teacher of English, Franklin Community High School, Franklin; Mrs. Juanita Shearer, Teacher of English, Brazil High School, Brazil; Neal Shortz, Teacher of English, Warren Central High School, Indianapolis; Mrs. Betty M. Smith, Teacher of English, Penn High School, Mishawaka; Mrs. Viola Soderstrom, Teacher of English, River Forest High School, Hobart; Mrs. Mary Tunmer, Chairman of the Department of English, Tipton High School, Tipton; Mrs. Edith Voges, Teacher of English, Honey Creek High School, Terre Haute; Mrs. Margaret Walker, Coordinator of Language Arts and Reading, Hammond; Mrs. Elizabeth Weddle, formerly Teacher of English, Franklin Community High School, Franklin; Larry B. Wray, Teacher of English, D. E. Gavit Junior-Senior High School, Hammond; Sister M. Xavier Therese, C.S.C., Teacher of English, Bishop Noll Institute, Hammond; and Mrs. Juanita Young, Chairman of the Department of English, Huntington County Community High School, Huntington.

The staff of the IU Center is also grateful to Brother Thomas Corbett and Sister Mary Xavier, Supervisors of English for the Archdiocese of Cincinnati, and to the teachers of English in the Middletown, Ohio, parochial schools who are experimenting with these materials at various grade levels and commenting on the new materials in this volume.

The units in this volume have undergone many revisions, each of which had to be typed, mimeographed, collated, and mailed to pilot-school teachers. Three secretaries—Mrs. Robert Spencer, Mrs. James Louden, and Miss Donna Holtel—cheerfully accepted the tasks of re-typing the many revisions and of proofreading the final volume.

CONTENTS

x   *Contents*

Teaching Literature in
Grades Ten Through Twelve

Introduction

EDWARD B. JENKINSON

The study of literature as we present it in the several volumes in this English Curriculum Study Series is the careful study of individual literary works. Like Professor Paul Zietlow, who designed the poetry sequence for grades ten through twelve, the writers of the essays on the novels and of the various genre sequences focus attention on each work "as a human statement conveying in words someone's thoughts and feelings." The writers are not concerned with giving students the sometimes interesting, but frequently extraneous, biographical material on each author. Nor are they unduly concerned with presenting a history of the period as background for the study of a specific work. (Occasionally a brief comment on the history of the times helps a reader fit a work into its proper context, but usually only a brief comment—not a two- or three-period lecture—is necessary.) Nor are the writers unduly concerned with what has come to be, in many English classes, a stultifying preoccupation with critical terminology. (Professor Zietlow uses only four critical terms, imagery, metaphor, irony, and sonnet, in his revolutionary poetry sequence.) The primary concern of these writers, then, is to teach students how to read.

Perhaps all teachers of English should pause to consider what kind of student should ideally emerge from English class. Professor Philip B. Daghlian once asked curriculum designers the following challenging question and then answered it:

> Do we strive to produce college matriculants, or literary critics, or cultivated captains of industry, or what? Perhaps the teacher's task would be easier and more clearly defined if he aimed for two things in his classes in literature: 1) to teach his students how to

1

read; and 2) to leave with them some ability to judge and evaluate what they have read. These goals are inclusive enough to cover all levels of literary interest, from the hard-working slow learner to the potential PTA president to the eventual Ph.D. candidate.

To teach students how to read and to respond to literature, a teacher need not have students memorize critical terms, fill in the blanks on a hundred test questions on each novel, or write the traditional book report that kills student interest in literature and/or leads a student to the false belief that he understands what he has read simply because he can respond to the superficial questions common as aids to the preparation of book reports. Nor need a teacher of English apologize for the class study of literary works by offering his course as source material for studies in history, sociology, psychology, linguistics, or arts and crafts.

For years American literature "had to be taught" in grade eleven. Why? "Because students study American history then." And students traditionally waded through American literature, plodding from Jonathan Edwards to Washington Irving to Henry Wadsworth Longfellow with the enthusiasm of Huck Finn on his way to school. The sequences that follow are not based on the traditional course marriage of American literature to American history. Instead, American literature is studied in grade ten; English literature in eleven; and world literature in twelve. Why? The rationale is simple: most tenth graders can respond intelligently to the best of American literature if they are properly guided by a perceptive teacher. This, of course, does not mean that they will respond with brilliant critical essays on each work, but we are not attempting to turn them into literary critics. Instead, our goals are simply to teach students how to read and to leave with them some ability to judge and to evaluate what they read. And tenth grade students can read and evaluate such works as *The Member of the Wedding, The Red Badge of Courage, Adventures of Huckleberry Finn, The Crucible, The Emperor Jones,* "The Egg," "My Kinsman, Major Molineux," and selected poems of Emily Dickinson. But relatively few tenth graders can read and respond intelligently to *Antigone, Crime and Punishment, Rosmersholm,* and *Siddhartha.* Yet we believe that important works should be included in the high school English curriculum. We have learned that most seniors can read and respond to such works of world literature, whereas most sophomores cannot. We have assigned English literature to grade eleven since we want all students to study English literature and since we know that all students enroll in English class in grade eleven but not all take English in grade twelve. Hence, our sequence of American literature in ten, English literature in eleven, and world literature in twelve.

Throughout the sequences presented in this and other volumes on literature in this English Curriculum Study Series, the writers underscore these obvious facts—the first three of which I included in the Introduction to *On Teaching Literature: Essays for Secondary School Teachers:*

1. The able teacher of literature champions no single method of teaching novels, short stories, poems, plays, essays, or biographies but, instead, carefully studies each work, both in terms of its genre and as an individual work of art, before deciding how to present it to his students.

2. The conscientious teacher of literature reads not just one essay on teaching the novel, for example, but books of essays that give him fresh insights into novels and how to approach them in his classroom.

3. The successful teacher of literature realizes that good teaching demands a great deal of time, hard work, and intelligence.

4. The prudent teacher of literature does not kill student interest by following the study of each work with a hundred true-or-false test questions, or fifty multiple-choice questions, or ten questions painstakingly devised to trap the unwary student, who did not practically memorize the book as he plodded through it and who may not recognize the irrelevant details asked for on the test, thus proving to himself and the teacher that he does not read well and deserves a low grade.

5. The humanistic teacher of literature realizes that literature cannot be measured like science, that student understanding of literary works cannot be evaluated by objective testing, and that students can be led to understand and appreciate literature only through careful questioning. Framing challenging questions takes time, the prudent teacher knows, but he also realizes that he must

take that time if he intends to have his students come to grips with the work at hand. He further realizes that challenging questions asked on essay examinations take a great deal of time to evaluate but that he can use no other test method if he intends to discover how well his students understand the work.

The writers of the essays on the novels and the genre sequences in this volume have carefully prepared challenging questions for students. They all know how much time the framing of such questions takes, but they are willing to spend the time because they realize that they must if they plan to lead students to an understanding of the work. Each writer offers the teacher a number of sample questions that should enliven class discussion, and each writer also offers many questions that could readily be asked on essay examinations. And each writer hopes that every teacher of literature will take as much time as he did to restudy the work and to frame questions so that students will learn how to read and how to evaluate what they have read.

The teaching of literature takes time. And since it takes more time than most administrators, parents, and teachers of other disciplines realize, it seems appropriate to end this Introduction with the same last three paragraphs with which I ended the Introduction to *On Teaching Literature: Essays for Secondary School Teachers:*

> Much has been written about the reduction of class loads for teachers of English. The National Council of Teachers of English, the Modern Language Association, the Commission on English of the College Entrance Examination Board, and other national and state organizations have suggested that no teacher of English be assigned more than four classes with a total of 100 students. Most of the arguments for class-load reduction are based on the paper-grading load of the teacher, which is formidable.
>
> Like the close reading of literature, the evaluation of themes is time-consuming. Carefully read and evaluated, a theme of 250 words takes at least ten minutes of a teacher's time. Give him 150 themes to read outside class each week and the teacher spends at least 25 hours at that task alone. He has precious little time left for reading literature as carefully as the essayists in this volume suggest that he must if he is to perform successfully in the classroom.
>
> The essayists in this volume are concerned with the superior teaching of literature. Future volumes in this series will be con-

cerned with the superior teaching of composition, syntax, usage, semantics, dialects, phonemes, morphemes, logic, and lexicography as well as literature. To teach these subjects well requires a great deal of time, and it therefore seems appropriate to make a plea now for the reduction of class loads. The reading, paper-grading, and preparation loads of a good teacher of English are so great that he cannot possibly perform well in a classroom if he has a crippling load of five classes with 125 students a day, or, worse, an inhuman load of five, six, or seven classes with 150 to 225 students a day. New curriculum materials, new textbooks, new books of criticism, new audio-visual aids, and new books like this one, will be of little value to the teacher if he does not have time to read, to think, and to prepare. Quality education depends upon good teachers who have the time to strive for excellence.

Part I
POETRY

▨▨

Properly presented, Professor Paul Zietlow's sequence on poetry should do much to dispel the notion, still all too prevalent in the land, that poetry is a kind of salutary experience, like castor oil perhaps, which is "good for" teachers and students alike, but is not much fun for anyone. By reducing technical terminology to a minimum, by focusing attention on the poem itself rather than on a vague and frightening abstraction called poetry, by concentrating on the concrete expression of experience in the poem, Professor Zietlow forces teacher and student alike to see that a poem is an artistically ordered version of human talk. By reminding both teacher and student of the importance of the communication of experience, he demonstrates the centrality of poetry to the entire culture of a people.

The choice of selections by national origins follows essentially the pattern of this volume: poems for the tenth grade are primarily American; for the eleventh grade they are primarily English. For the twelfth grade the poems are American and English rather than from world literature in translation, as is the case in the sequences for drama and the short story. Reasons for this deviation may readily be found in the unit on translation* which we recommend for the beginning of the twelfth grade. And of course there is nothing to prevent a teacher from presenting a few poems in translation, provided he exercises caution.

* See Edward B. Jenkinson's "Nothing Moves Without Translation," a unit in *What Is Language? and Other Teaching Units for Grades Seven Through Twelve,* a volume in this English Curriculum Study Series.

Poetry Sequence for Grades Ten Through Twelve

PAUL ZIETLOW

Assistant Professor of English
Indiana University

The following sequences of poems illustrate how one might teach poetry to high school students. The general emphasis throughout the three sequences is on poetry as *human talk*—on the poem as a human statement conveying in words someone's thoughts and feelings. The interest is not primarily in poetic technique and specialized critical terminology, but in the humanity, the range of awareness, the sense of value and meaningfulness expressed in the individual poems. The goal is to help students see a poem as something spoken by someone who grasps an important meaning and feels strongly about it, and whose words can, if properly examined and understood, increase the reader's sense of what is important and what is worth feeling strongly about.

That poetry is *human talk* can hardly be overemphasized. Poetry *is* an appropriate and fascinating subject for academic study, and it has challenged the particular interests and specialized skills of brilliant, sensitive, knowledgeable men who have devoted their lives to its examination. These men have developed several competing and contradictory systems of complex and useful critical theory, and have established a vast specialized vocabulary for talking about poetry. But few high school students are going to devote their lives to the examination of poetry, and those who are ought to begin at the beginning: poems are human statements on what are for the poets compelling subjects, arising out of situations which, for the poets, can be dealt with only in words. Various critical theories enable us to differentiate between poetry and prose, poetry and "poetic language" in fiction, poetry and drama, and so on. But these theories are irrelevant at the beginning: poems are like all other examples of carefully selected, highly structured uses of language in that they are informed by a sense of value—the words and their arrangement are chosen to the exclusion of all other words and arrangements because to the poet they seem *better*; they express a point of view, a way of looking at things, a sense of what counts and what doesn't count. And poetry, seen from this angle, is like any unified utterance any of us makes, whether written or spoken, if that utterance is at all worth paying attention to. A student who wants to break up with his girl friend has to decide how to do it; he may decide to say something to her, and he may decide not to—it's a matter of *choice*. If he does say something, and probably he will, he'll pay some attention to what he says and how he says it, and he will doubtless reject alternatives and commit himself to one way of doing it, either consciously or unconsciously—he'll make *choices*. His girl friend will doubtless pay careful attention to everything he says, to the way he begins and the way he ends, to his tone of voice and the expression on his face. A poem is similar: a poet has something to say; his saying it is the assertion of a complex system of careful choices—conscious or unconscious—and the reader must pay careful attention to every choice, every word, every nuance. The goal of these sequences is to teach students how to pay that kind of attention.

Several corollaries follow from this emphasis on poetry as *human talk*. Although the poems in the sequences are arranged to allow for a great deal of comparison and contrast, the questions asked about them are designed primarily to illuminate the *uniqueness* of each poem. Each poem is *something said* with a value and importance of its very own; in certain important ways *it is unlike anything else ever said*. A student, having gone through these sequences, should end with a thorough knowledge of important, interesting, unique *things said,* and with a clear understanding of why they are important, interesting, and unique. The satisfaction of these goals requires *time*. A teacher ought usually to spend at least an entire class hour on each poem dealt with, and *often more.* It may seem a waste of time to spend an hour or two on, for example, Emily Dickinson's "The morns are meeker than they were" —on eight brief lines, on forty-five words—but time lavished on an individual poem *is the most efficient way* to introduce students to poetry. Ruskin once wrote, in an essay on reading: "You might read all the books in the British Museum (if you could live long enough), and remain an utterly 'illiterate,' uneducated person; but if you read ten pages of a good book, letter by letter,—that is to say, with real accuracy,—you are for evermore in some measure an educated person." The assumptions about education implied in Ruskin's statement underlie these sequences. Let us reduce our students' reading, and teach them to read what they read well, lest they remain illiterates.

Another corollary: because of the emphasis on poems in particular rather than on poetry in general, and because of the emphasis on poems as human talk rather than subjects of specialized academic study, *there is no requirement for the teacher to present critical terms unless the need for critical terms arises.* The tenth grade sequence introduces no special vocabulary. As the eleventh grade sequence is structured, there is a need for students to learn how to use only two critical terms: *image* and *metaphor.* The only special word students must learn how to use in working through the twelfth grade sequence is *irony,* and it's not such a special word at that. The goal is to get students to feel that poetry is worth reading because it makes a direct appeal to what is central in human experience, rather than to the special knowledge of a handful of people—that we can talk about poetry intelligently with the language we use when we talk intelligently about almost anything else.

Each of the sequences, however, is designed to illustrate a general point. In the tenth grade, the emphasis is on the poem as choice; the poems in the eleventh grade sequence illustrate various uses of comparisons, and the kinds of intensity and complexity which result from skillful use of comparisons; in the twelfth grade the focus is on the character of the speaker (who, in that sequence, is distinguished from the author), and on the irony which so often results from the limitations, the flaws, the weaknesses in the speaker. Any of the three sequences could be expanded to include more poems; and, of course, all teachers will have their own good ideas for substitutions for the poems suggested here. The teacher using this document is to see the sequences as examples of how it might be done, rather than as prescriptions for how one ought to do it.

A few more comments on the choice of poems: most of the poems included in the tenth grade unit were written by Americans; most of the poems in the eleventh grade unit are English; and the twelfth grade selections are fairly evenly distributed between English and American poets. One could easily make substitutions, for example, of American poems for the English ones if one wished to teach only American literature in the tenth grade. The poems for the tenth grade almost all deal with nature, for the eleventh with love and religion; the twelfth grade sequence contains a large number of dramatic monologues and poems arising out of dramatic situations. One could easily develop thematic relationships between the tenth and eleventh grade poems and the other kinds of literature being taught, and the twelfth grade poems could easily be related to work with drama. Certain poets are represented by more than one poem. Poems by Emily Dickinson appear again and again on the grounds that it would be desirable for high school students to develop, over a period of time, a fairly extensive knowledge of the work of a single poet; Emily Dickinson is a good one to know because she is one of our finest American writers, and her poems are brief and, on the surface at least, immediately accessible.

Finally, there are two activities which, in my judgment, ought to go on during the teaching of any poem; I seldom mention them in the sequences themselves, because I assume they will always occur:

1. *Reading aloud.* Every poem ought to be read aloud more than once before it is discussed, and, as often as possible, students ought to do the reading. A teacher can tell a great deal about where the difficulties in understanding lie when the students read aloud; and students, over a period of time, can learn to find real pleasure in working up their understanding of the poem to the

point that they can perform an interpretation of it by reading it aloud.

2. *Elucidation of the difficult phrases and unfamiliar words.* Fairly early in the discussion of a poem the teacher ought to get the students to identify, look up, and talk about new words, and to straighten out difficult syntax. Often these two activities can work together: a student's stumbling over a word or a phrase can help the teacher see where the most immediate problems in understanding are, and these immediate problems ought to be dealt with immediately.

Here, then, are the sequences. Some of the poems are fairly thoroughly explicated; others are followed by what amounts to a list of leading questions. In either case, the intention is to *illustrate* the kind of discussion that might take place on the basis of the poem, and the kinds of questions the teacher might ask.

Poetry for Grade Ten

The goal of this sequence is to help students see poems more clearly as meaningful human statements—as coherent, ordered responses to some aspect of human experience. The unit emphasizes none of the techniques of expression *peculiar* to poetry; instead, it requires the teacher and the students to regard a poem primarily as a piece of writing to be talked about in much the same way as one would talk about any human statement composed in words. The major emphasis is on broadening the student's awareness that a poem results from a conscious or unconscious *choice* or system of choices; the student should come to see each poem as a unique response, felt and expressed to the exclusion of all other possible responses to a given situation. Except for the first poem, "The Ballad of Sir Patrick Spens," the unit is composed of groups of poems on similar subjects; all these poems, in a general way, express responses to nature, and they permit frequent and useful comparison and contrast. The questions that appear most frequently are: Why did the poet *choose* (to describe what he describes; to include this detail; to use this word), and how else could be have done it?

The unit begins with a form presented in the junior high school sequence—the ballad—as a way of establishing a new emphasis in a familiar context. The point has already been made in grade seven that a ballad tells a story by "leaping and lingering"—by jumping from crucial moment to crucial moment in the action, and by condensing or ignoring what comes in between. The new emphasis is on the poem as a result of choice: Why has the ballad teller chosen the moments over which he lingers? Why has he left out other moments? What makes the moments he dwells on so crucial? The version of "Sir Patrick Spens" given here (later,

14

artistically inferior versions are longer) provides a particularly effective basis for considering such problems, because the teller ignores what from one point of view might appear to be a crucial moment: the shipwreck. For the purposes of this sequence, then, the major question is: Why does the teller of "Sir Patrick Spens" fail to include an account of the shipwreck?

Since the discussion is to deal with what is left out of the ballad, one should begin by establishing a clear understanding of what is included. Someone might read the poem aloud once or twice while the rest of the class, listening, attempts to divide it into episodes or scenes.

SIR PATRICK SPENS[1]
*(modernized)**

The king sits in Dumferline town,
    Drinking the blood-red wine:
"O where will I get a good sailor
    To sail this ship of mine?"

Up and spake an elder knight,
    Sat at the king's right knee:
"Sir Patrick Spens is the best sailor
    That sails upon the sea."

The king has written a broad letter
    And signed it with his hand,
And sent it to Sir Patrick Spens,
    Was walking on the sand.

The first line that Sir Patrick read,
    A loud laugh laughed he;
The next line that Sir Patrick read,
    The tear blinded his ee.[a]

"O who is this has done this deed,
    This ill deed done to me,
To send me out this time o' the year,
    To sail upon the sea?

"Make haste, make haste, my merry men all,
    Our good ship sails the morn."

* The spelling of some of the words in the poems in this unit has been modernized to help the students.

"O say not so, my master dear,
   For I fear a deadly storm.

"Late late yestre'en I saw the new moon
   With the old moon in her arm,
And I fear, I fear, my dear master,
   That we will come to harm."

O our Scots nobles were right loath
   To wet their cork-heeled shoon,[b]
But long ere all the play were played
   Their hats they swam aboon.[c]

O long, long may their ladies sit,
   With their fans into their hand,
Before they see Sir Patrick Spens
   Come sailing to the land.

O long, long may the ladies stand,
   With their gold combs in their hair,
Waiting for their own dear lords,
   For they'll see them no more.

Half o'er, half o'er to Aberdour
   It's fifty fathoms deep,
And there lies good Sir Patrick Spens,
   With the Scots lords at his feet.

[a] *ee*: eye   [b] *shoon*: shoes   [c] *aboon*: above

The divisions will look something like this: I. The king's council (the king needs a good sailor; the "elder knight" recommends Sir Patrick; the king writes his letter); II. Sir Patrick's reception of the letter (he laughs; he weeps; he wonders who is responsible for his ill fate); III. Sir Patrick's command to his men, and their reluctant response to it; IV. A shift in perspective: the Scots nobles (who drown) and the waiting ladies (whose husbands will never return); V. Sir Patrick and the Scots lords at the bottom of the sea.

   The next question is: What else might the teller have included? The goal is to get the students to use their imaginations to become aware of the wide range of possibilities from which the teller has selected and arranged his materials. He could have explained to us, for example, the mission of the king's ship. He could have developed the motives of the "elder knight" (is he treacherous? does he want Sir Patrick to die? or is he simply giving his king good, straight advice?). The teller could explain Sir Patrick's situation more fully (does he have enemies whom he suspects, or is his line "O who is this has done this deed" merely a rhetorical means for indicating his despair?). The teller could have Sir Patrick and his men debate on whether or not they should undertake the mission. And so on. But, most obviously, he could have described the shipwreck. Any of these possibilities is worth discussing, and the same general point could be made by discussing any of them. By way of illustration, let us examine the most obvious one.

The question is: What would the teller gain by including the shipwreck? What might the shipwreck scene be like? The goal again is to get the students' imaginations working, to get them to see the possibilities in the situation. We might see Sir Patrick heroically struggling against the wind and the sea, against natural elements. But is that an important point? Is there anything else in the poem to suggest that its subject is a man's heroic struggle against nature? There could be; the poet could use this situation to develop such a subject, but he doesn't. The shipwreck scene might be used to reveal Sir Patrick's skill as a sailor (he could be described giving commands, trimming the sails, handling the rudder). But his skill as a sailor is "given" at the very beginning of the poem; we are asked to assume it, and what is important about Sir Patrick is something else. Or the shipwreck scene might be used to develop Sir Patrick's ability to command loyalty from his men. Again, is this ability the important feature of his character in the poem? The more possibilities the students can be made to see in the situation, the more clearly they will see the poem as the teller's commitment to one set of possibilities to the exclusion of others; the more clearly they will see that the poem is a product of choice.

The final question is: What *does* the teller see in the situation? What choice has he made? The answer is that he sees something like Sir Patrick's ennobling loyalty—his willingness to serve at all cost, the way that willingness makes him more noble than the other "nobles" (who, at the end of the poem, lie at his feet), and the tragic consequences of that willingness. The important thing is his *decision* to risk death in the service of his king, and not the act itself. It is fairly easy to see how the teller's handling of the scenes illustrates this point. Sir Patrick immediately suspects the king's command means his death (he weeps when he reads the second line of the letter, perhaps because he has already made up his mind to obey the king's extreme, absurd—"laughable"—command). He seems to express suspicion of treachery, but the lines immediately following the stanza in which the hints of his suspicion appear contain his command to his men. The teller describes no wavering, no struggle to come to a decision. One of Sir Patrick's men reminds him of the probable consequences of his course of action, but we don't have to hear an argument between them: Sir Patrick has made up his mind, and it's probably safe to say that he commands the same kind of loyalty from them as the king commands from him. That is, in this ballad (as in all examples of good writing) the speaker's central purpose determines the selection and arrangement of what appears. He has omitted parts of the story either because he couldn't use them to develop his central purpose, or because the use he could make of them would be redundant; and he has included those parts of the story which he can make count best in developing his main theme.

The next two poems in this sequence deal with reactions to a season—autumn. The main point to be made in contrasting the two poems is that they represent two of an infinite number of possible reactions to autumn. Each represents a system of conscious or unconscious choices made to convey a response chosen or felt to the exclusion of all other possible responses. First, a poem by Gerard Manley Hopkins:

SPRING AND FALL:

TO A YOUNG CHILD*

Gerard Manley Hopkins[2]

Margarét, are you grieving
Over Goldengrove unleaving?
Leáves, líke the things of man, you
With your fresh thoughts care for, can you?

* From *Poems of Gerard Manley Hopkins*. London: Oxford University Press, 1948. Reprinted by permission of The Reverend J. Meskell, S. J.

Áh! ás the heart grows older
It will come to such sights colder
By and by, nor spare a sigh
Though worlds of wanwood leafmeal lie;
And yet you wíll weep and know why.
Now no matter, child, the name:
Sórrow's spríngs áre the same.
Nor mouth had, no nor mind, expressed
What heart heard of, ghost[a] guessed:
It ís the blight man was born for,
It is Margaret you mourn for.

[a] *ghost*: spirit, as in Father, Son, and Holy Ghost

What is the subject of this poem? The subject is Margaret's reaction to fall, which, roughly speaking, is described in the first nine
lines, and interpreted by the speaker in the last six lines. Unlike
"Sir Patrick Spens," here there are two levels of response: Margaret's reaction, and the speaker's attitude towards it. We must
keep the two separate, and consider each in its turn.

First, what is Margaret's response? Grief. How is that grief defined for us? (How can any feeling be defined?—an important
question, because the goal of many poems is to define a feeling.)
The poet here defines Margaret's grief in two ways: he lets us
know the immediate cause ("Goldengrove," a grove of trees, is
"unleaving") and the effect it has on Margaret (she weeps). That
is, one can define grief by specifying what makes one feel it (the
loss of something precious, the death of a loved one, the fall of
leaves in autumn), or by describing the effect of the feeling on
one's behavior (one mopes, one loses interest in other things, one
weeps). (Question: What other ways are there for defining a
feeling?) Is there anything in the poem that helps us see that the
falling of leaves is good and sufficient cause for grief? Let us
examine the line "Though worlds of wanwood leafmeal lie." The
students might be asked to define "wanwood" and "leafmeal";
they might begin by looking them up in the dictionary. They will
discover that the words are coinages, that Hopkins compresses into
a brief space a large range of meanings and associations. Wanwood suggests a grove of trees gone pale—trees which have lost
their color and vitality. Hopkins has coined leafmeal by analogy

with piecemeal; the word suggests leaves fallen and strewn piecemeal upon the ground. How do these words intensify Margaret's grief? Don't they suggest a world without color, a world without vitality, a disorderly world reigned over by chaos and death? The line itself is made particularly intense by the arrangements in stress and alliteration, and illustrates a common feature of good poetry: intensity created by means of compression and the skillful ordering of sounds. And it is clearly the product of conscious choice, for Hopkins has invented new words—the old ones available to him didn't suit his needs—to create the impression he wishes to convey.

The speaker, of course, puts a further twist on Margaret's sorrow by citing a different cause. One might call the students' attention to the distinction between "mouth" and "mind" on the one hand, and "heart" and "ghost" (spirit) on the other. Margaret's heart and spirit, according to the speaker, are aware of something that her mouth and mind are unable to comprehend and express—an awareness that becomes conscious and expressible only as one grows older (there are assumptions about growing up implied by this poem which superior students might be interested in exploring). Margaret, without knowing it, is mourning for herself, for she, like all men, was born for "blight." And what is that blight? The key lies in "wanwood leafmeal": the death and disorder to be seen in the fallen and falling autumn leaves threaten us all. Margaret is grieving for her own *fall*, of which her heart and spirit are dimly but surely aware. (And, one might add, her self-centered grief over her own condition is another kind of "blight.") It is worth calling the students' attention to the patterns of alliteration and stress in the last four lines; the brilliant compression and tricks with sound in "heart heard of, ghost guessed" (where there are two pairs of words distinguished by a change in only one sound) can be shown to have the same intensity, achieved by different means, as "wanwood leafmeal." A final question might be: Does anyone see any relation between the compression and patterning of sounds in this poem and the general theme of fall into death and disorder?

The main reason for using "Spring and Fall" is to show the profound and somber meaning that can be found in an autumn scene. Notice the contrast with this brief poem by Emily Dickinson:

THE MORNS ARE MEEKER THAN THEY WERE*

Emily Dickinson

The morns are meeker than they were—
The nuts are getting brown—
The berry's cheek is plumper—
The Rose is out of town.
The Maple wears a gayer scarf—
The field a scarlet gown—
Lest I should be old fashioned
I'll put a trinket on.

One might begin by asking the students to visualize what is described in each line: What does it mean to say the mornings are "meeker," that the "berry's cheek is plumper," that the "Maple wears a gayer scarf," and so on? Why does Emily Dickinson use language referring to garments in the earlier lines? How does this language relate to "Rose is out of town" (as if the rose has gone on vacation—fashionably left town for the "season")? Relate this vocabulary to the last line. Or one might ask the students to write substitute lines, and then to note the difference in effect (for example, "The dawn is breaking later" for the first line, or "The summer rose is fallen" for the fourth). What is the total effect of the first six lines? Certainly not grief, but what? The speaker doesn't give us a word for her response; instead she proposes an appropriate action. What is the meaning of that action? How does it define the poet's response? What does the choice of "old fashioned" reveal about the poet's response? Is fall seen as the end of something? Is it something to be feared? What is the most striking word in the last line? Is it a surprise, or have we been prepared for such a word? What would the effect of the last line be if it read "I'll put my jewelry on"?

Finally, the students might be asked to compare and contrast "Spring and Fall" and "The morns are meeker than they were" as responses to autumn. Which is the more valid response? Which is truer? Which makes more sense? The discussion should lead students to see that each of the poems has a validity, an accuracy,

* From *The Poems of Emily Dickinson*, Thomas H. Johnson, ed. Cambridge, Mass.: The Belknap Press. Copyright 1951, 1955 by The President and Fellows of Harvard College. Reprinted by permission.

a "truth" of its own. The next question might be: All along we have been assuming that these two poems were responses to the same thing—autumn; is that true? Is autumn the same thing in "Spring and Fall" as it is in "The morns are meeker than they were"? If it's not, how do you account for the disparity? Is autumn in reality more than one thing?

We have reached difficult and sophisticated questions. They are open questions—worth discussing even if they can't be conclusively answered; it's healthy for students to realize that such questions exist. Perhaps they can't be answered now (perhaps they can *never* be settled with certainty), but they are worth raising nevertheless. We shall return to similar questions later in any case.

Let us now examine two poems about flowers, both of which have something to do with fall.

TO THE FRINGED GENTIAN

William Cullen Bryant

Thou blossom bright with autumn dew,
And colored with the heaven's own blue,
That openest when the quiet light
Succeeds the keen and frosty night.

Thou comest not when violets lean
O'er wandering brooks and springs unseen,
Or columbines, in purple dressed,
Nod o'er the ground-bird's hidden nest.

Thou waitest late and com'st along,
When woods are bare and birds are flown,
And frosts and shortening days portend
The aged year is near his end.

Then doth thy sweet and quiet eye
Look through its fringes to the sky,
Blue—blue—as if that sky let fall
A flower from its cerulean wall.

I would that thus, when I shall see
The hour of death draw near to me,
Hope, blossoming within my heart,
May look to heaven as I depart.

The first line tells us clearly that the fringed gentian is an autumn flower. One might begin by asking what the view of autumn is in the poem: Is it more like that of "Spring and Fall" or that of "The morns are meeker than they were"? Obviously, more like "Spring and Fall." Why? Bryant tells us specifically that he sees autumn as the end of something, as the prelude to approaching death ("The aged year is near his end"). How does he make this general thought specific? By being questioned on specific points, the students should be led to see how Bryant arranges the details of the first three stanzas in order to give a sense of absence, barrenness, and isolation.

But is this sense the only impression the poem creates? What is the relationship between the last stanza and the first four stanzas? What is the most important word in the last stanza? "Hope," because hope is the human quality that the fringed gentian brings to the speaker's mind. Is it "hope" in general, or a specific kind of hope? It is the hope that looks to heaven; it *may* occur when the hour of death approaches. Why is it that the fringed gentian brings this kind of hope to the speaker's mind? Because it comes late in the year, after the other flowers are gone. It is "heaven's own color." It looks to heaven with its "sweet and quiet eye."

These are all obvious ways in which the fringed gentian is like hope, and a comparison between the last stanza and the previous four makes us see how carefully Bryant has arranged the description of the flower in order to make his point. The final question is: Does the flower help us see anything about hope that the last stanza doesn't make explicit? The last stanza shows us where hope will occur (in the heart), when (at the hour of death), how (it will blossom like a flower), and what it does once it's there (it looks to heaven). But it doesn't tell us what the source of hope is: Who causes it? Who "causes" the fringed gentian? Has it occurred haphazardly, or does it seem to be the result of some plan? The answer to these questions should not be "God causes it," for Bryant never gets that specific. But the students should be led to see the *hints* and *suggestions* implicit in "colored with the heaven's own blue" and "as if that sky *let fall*." Hope seems to be something that can blossom naturally, like the fringed gentian, as part of the natural scheme of things. One might at this point *contrast* the view of autumn in "To the Fringed Gentian" with that of "Spring and Fall." The latter poem sees only death and disorder, suggested by the falling leaves. "To the Fringed Gentian" calls attention to a late-blossoming, blue flower, looking upward towards the sky.

Looking at the fringed gentian, Bryant sees the meaning of a certain kind of hope. What does Philip Freneau see in "The Wild Honey Suckle"?

THE WILD HONEY SUCKLE

Philip Freneau

Fair flower, that dost so comely grow,
Hid in this silent, dull retreat,
Untouched thy honied blossoms blow,[a]
Unseen thy little branches greet:
 No roving foot shall crush thee here,
 No busy hand provoke a tear.

By Nature's self in white arrayed,
She bade thee shun the vulgar eye,
And planted here the guardian shade,
And sent soft waters murmuring by;
 Thus quietly thy summer goes,
 Thy days declining to repose.

Smit with those charms, that must decay,
I grieve to see your future doom;
They died—nor were those flowers more gay,
The flowers that did in Eden bloom;
 Unpitying frosts, and Autumn's power
 Shall leave no vestige of this flower.

From morning suns and evening dews
At first thy little being came:
If nothing once, you nothing lose,
For when you die you are the same;
 The space between, is but an hour,
 The frail duration of a flower.

[a] *blow*: bloom

What is the main quality of the honeysuckle? The first and last lines make it explicit: frailty. What details in the poem help create the impression of frailty? Look at the adjectives: Why "little

branches" and not simply "branches"? Why "vulgar eye" and not
simply "eye"? Why "guardian shade" and not simply "shade"? Why
"soft waters" and not simply "waters"? What is the point of the last
stanza? Look closely at the lines "If nothing once, you nothing
lose, / For when you die you are the same." In what sense was the
flower "nothing once"? (Its "little being" came from "morning suns
and evening dews" which themselves are frail and fleeting; also,
they are *elements*, not life, and are therefore "nothing." Hence,
arising from "nothing," the honeysuckle has nothing to lose, and
when it dies it returns to the elements, and is "the same" as it was
before.) How do the last lines define life? Obviously they minimize
it, turn it into "space between" ("space" suggests nothingness), a
mere "hour"; define it as "frail duration." But if life is *merely* this,
how do we account for the preciousness ascribed to the flower in
the second stanza? ("Nature's self" has "arrayed" the flower, has
put it in its proper place where it will be safely guarded.) Isn't
there a disparity between the subdued importance placed on the
flower's life in the first three stanzas (not even the flowers in Eden
were more gay) and the minimizing of life in the last stanza? The
flower does *not* have nothing to lose, but everything. And what is
the effect of this disparity? Might it not help us to see how precious
life is—even the life of a tiny flower? By telling us that life is
nothing because it is so frail and fleeting, doesn't the poem force
us to object, "No, life is everything—so precious precisely because
it *is* so frail and fleeting"? Unlike "To the Fringed Gentian," this
poem does not offer the flower to us as a kind of equivalent of a
moral quality, but it suggests to us, in a comparatively indirect
way, something about the qualities and preciousness of life.

The following poem has even less explicit meaning; it appears to
be merely a description, and the main question might be: *Is* it
mere description?

PEAR TREE[*]

H. D. (Hilda Doolittle)

Silver dust,
lifted from the earth,
higher than my arms reach,

[*] From *H. D. Selected Poems.* New York: Grove Press, Inc. Copyright
1957 by Norman Holmes Pearson. Reprinted by permission.

you have mounted,
O, silver,
higher than my arms reach,
you front us with great mass;

no flower ever opened
so staunch a white leaf,
no flower ever parted silver
from such rare silver;

O, white pear,
your flower-tufts
tuck on the branch
bring summer and ripe fruits
in their purple hearts.

"Let's begin by looking at the first line: Is it "mere description"? What does "Silver dust" refer to? (The petals of the flowers on the tree.) Why refer to the petals in that way? They are not silver, but white ("O, white pear"). Silver is not an accurate description of the color. What is it an accurate description of? Why does the poet choose that word? And why dust? Think of other words. For example, what would the effect be if one substituted "flakes" for "dust"? Why does the poet say the "dust" is "lifted from the earth, / *higher than my arms reach*"? Why not "eight feet high"? "as high as an elephant's eye"? That is, there are other ways of specifying the height of the blossoms; why choose this way? Why mention the height at all? What is the effect of "you have mounted," "you front us," "no flower ever parted"? The tree is seen almost as an active, wilful being that self-consciously displays itself for us to behold, and can be addressed ("O, white pear") as if it were capable of understanding. What new quality is introduced in the third stanza (fertility, fruitfulness)? Why is it appropriate to mention this quality? Finally, is this poem merely a description, or does it reveal for us a "meaning" in the tree? Notice that it makes us see something in the tree to the exclusion of other things: fragility on the one hand ("dust") and on the other strength ("mounted," "staunch"), abundance ("great mass," "thick on the branch"), and fruitfulness. All three of the poems on flowers describe, but the descriptions are quite different in character. Would it be accurate to say that "To the Fringed Gentian" *moralizes,* "The Wild Honey Suckle" *comments,* and "Pear Tree" *celebrates?* Or are there better words?

Let us examine three other responses to nature, this time to spring. I have again chosen poems by Hopkins and Emily Dickinson in order to illustrate the varieties of response individual poets are capable of.

AN ALTERED LOOK ABOUT THE HILLS*

Emily Dickinson

An altered look about the hills—
A Tyrian light the village fills—
A wider sunrise in the morn—
A deeper twilight on the lawn—
A print of a vermillion foot—
A purple finger on the slope—
A flippant fly upon the pane—
A spider at his trade again—
An added strut in Chanticleer—
A flower expected everywhere—
An axe shrill singing in the woods—
Fern odors on untravelled roads—
All this and more I cannot tell—
A furtive look you know as well—
And Nicodemus' Mystery
Receives its annual reply!

How do we know this is a poem about spring? The students should be led to see that while some of the lines (for example, "An altered look about the hills") merely suggest change of some sort, others ("A wider sunrise in the morn," "A flower expected everywhere") clearly specify spring. The students' attention might be called to specific words, and they might be asked to provide substitutions: Why "altered" rather than "changed"? Why "wider" rather than "earlier"? What does "Tyrian" mean? "flippant"? "furtive"? How can one justify the choice of these words? Next,

---

* From *The Poems of Emily Dickinson,* Thomas H. Johnson, ed. Cambridge, Mass.: The Belknap Press. Copyright 1951, 1955 by The President and Fellows of Harvard College. Reprinted by permission.

one might ask if the items listed appear haphazardly, or in an ordered sequence. The students should see that the first twelve lines can be divided into six couplets, five of which contain pairs of related items: look-light; sunrise-twilight; foot-finger; fly-spider; sound (singing)-odors. That is, this is an ordered, selected group of springtime occurrences. The rhyme scheme is also worth noting: does "morn" rhyme with "lawn"? "foot" with "slope"? and so on. The point to be made is that comparatively slender similarities in sound can be used as a basis for "rhyme."

The main question, of course, concerns what the description adds up to: it characterizes a "reply" to "Nicodemus' Mystery." The poem provides a good example of the power poets can derive from brief allusions to events, stories, other works of literature, and so on, that they assume the reader to be familiar with. Is anyone in the class familiar with Nicodemus? The students might be asked to look him up in the Bible, or the teacher might wish to save time by providing the relevant passage:

> There was a man of the Pharisees, named Nicodemus, a ruler of the Jews: the same came to Jesus by night, and said unto him, "Rabbi, we know that thou art a teacher come from God: for no man can do these miracles that thou doest, except God be with him." Jesus answered and said unto him, "Verily, verily, I say unto thee, Except a man be born again, he cannot see the kingdom of God." Nicodemus saith unto him, "How can a man be born when he is old? can he enter the second time into his mother's womb, and be born?" (*John* 3:1-4, King James Version)

What Nicodemus can't understand is how youth can spring from age, how new birth can arise out of approaching death. Spring, as Emily Dickinson describes it here, provides the reply. The expanding light, the intensified color, the lively fly and the spider at his trade "again," the new energy in Chanticleer, the renewed sounds and odors—all suggest a rebirth of natural vitality and energy. Question: Does spring really answer Nicodemus' question? Nicodemus confuses physical and spiritual rebirth. Isn't Emily Dickinson talking about physical rebirth in this poem? Or is she?

Hopkins' "Spring" also celebrates the vitality and energy of the rebirth of nature in spring, but with important qualifications:

SPRING[3]

*Gerard Manley Hopkins**

Nothing is so beautiful as spring—
  When weeds, in wheels, shoot long and lovely and lush;
  Thrush's eggs look little low heavens, and thrush
Through the echoing timber does so rinse and wring
The ear, it strikes like lightnings to hear him sing;
  The glassy peartree leaves and blooms, they brush
  The descending blue; that blue is all in a rush
With richness; the racing lambs too have fair their fling.

What is all this juice and all this joy?
  A strain of the earth's sweet being in the beginning
In Eden garden. —Have, get, before it cloy,
  Before it cloud, Christ, lord, and sour with sinning,
Innocent mind and Mayday in girl and boy,
  Most, O maid's child, thy choice and worthy the winning.

One might begin by asking what gives the sense of vitality and energy in the first eight lines of the poem. First of all, the poet describes living things: weeds (why weeds? why not flowers?), thrush's eggs and the thrush's song, a peartree, lambs. What about the sky, which we normally think of as being inanimate? Hopkins describes it "all in a rush"—in motion, almost as if it, too, were alive. What kinds of verbs does Hopkins use here? Is there any similarity between "shoot," "rinse and wring," "strikes like lightnings"? Are there such verbs in "An altered look about the hills"? No, the only verb not in a dependent clause is "Receives" in the last line. Which of these poems seems the more vital, energetic? Certainly Hopkins'. The verbs have something to do with it; is there anything else? Let's look at the word "fair" in "lambs too have fair their fling." What is its syntactic function? One can't be sure; there are at least two possibilities: adjectival (have their fair fling) and adverbial (have their fling fairly), and there may be more. And what possible meanings can "fair" have? The word seems almost to flicker between at least two meanings and at least

---

* From *Poems of Gerard Manley Hopkins*. London: Oxford University Press, 1958. Reprinted by permission of The Reverend J. Meskell, S. J.

two syntactic functions, and interpreting it requires a greater than normal exertion of energy on the part of the reader. Likewise, the line "Thrush's eggs look little low heavens" forces a readjustment in the reader's mind: he has to do something to make sense of the line—add a word perhaps (look *like* little low heavens). Are there any other places in the first eight lines of the sonnet which require this kind of extra interpretive energy on the part of the reader? Are there any such places in "An altered look about the hills"?

We have established that "Spring" creates a more vital, more energetic effect than "An altered look"; indeed, the latter poem seems almost subdued beside it. A close examination of Hopkins' last six lines reveals that he has intended to create the effect of a virtual *excess* of energy and vitality. One might begin by straightening out the syntax of the last three and a half lines (I've chosen this poem partly because it illustrates the difficulties of syntax which poets sometimes exploit; it seems to me that the last three and a half lines of this poem would reward a full class period devoted to them). First, what is the *mood* of "Have, get," the main verbs in these lines? (imperative) Who is being addressed? ("Christ") Who is Christ in these lines? (He is the "lord," the "maid's child.") What is Christ to "have, get"? ("Innocent mind and Mayday in girl and boy.") When is Christ to "have, get" the "innocent mind . . . ?" ("before it cloy, before it cloud," before it "sour with sinning") What does "it" refer to? (To "a strain of earth's sweet being. . . .") And where have we seen that "strain" described? (It is the vitality and energy of spring characterized in the first eight lines.) The last three and a half lines, then, could be rearranged in the following way:

> O Christ, lord, maid's child, have, get the innocent mind and Mayday in girl and boy (which are most thy choice and worthy the winning) before it (the strain) cloys and clouds and sours with sinning (the innocent mind, etc.).

The next question is: Why might this "strain" "cloy," "cloud," "sour with sinning"? Why is the mind innocent? Why the reference to Eden? Who else was innocent and then sinned? Why did Adam and Eve fall? Now let's return to the first line: "Nothing is so beautiful as spring." The poem shows the line to be true, but the poem shows us also that there is something higher or more important than beauty. Beauty is fine, but it must be placed in the proper perspective. That is, like Emily Dickinson's poem, this sonnet celebrates the vitality and energy of spring, but, unlike the other poem, it limits and qualifies that celebration.

A rather surprising attitude towards spring appears in the following poem by Emily Dickinson: not celebration, but dread.

I DREADED THAT FIRST ROBIN SO*

Emily Dickinson

I dreaded that first robin so,
But he is mastered now;
I'm some accustomed to him grown—
He hurts a little though.

I thought if I could only live
Till that first shout got by,
Not all pianos in the woods
Had power to mangle me.

I dared not meet the daffodils
For fear their yellow gown
Would pierce me with a fashion
So foreign to my own.

I wished the grass would hurry,
So, when 'twas time to see,
He'd be too tall; the tallest one
Could stretch to look at me.

I could not bear the bees should come;
I wished they'd stay away
In those dim countries where they go.
What word had they for me?

They're here, though; not a creature failed—
No blossom stayed away
In gentle deference to me,
The Queen of Calvary.

---

* From *The Poems of Emily Dickinson*, Thomas H. Johnson, ed. Cambridge, Mass.: The Belknap Press. Copyright 1951, 1955 by the President and Fellows of Harvard College. Reprinted by permission.

Each one salutes me, as he goes,
And I my childish plumes
Lift, in bereaved acknowledgment
Of their unthinking drums.

What are the important words in this poem which help characterize the speaker's feelings towards spring ("dreaded," "dared not,"
"fear," "could not bear," "bereaved," and so on)? What is the
source of the speaker's dread? Let's examine the robin in the first
two stanzas. Apparently the "shout" in line six refers to the song of
the robin. Why doesn't the poet say "song" instead of "shout"?
Obviously, robins don't shout; nor are the sounds of woods in
spring those of pianos having the power to "mangle" (and why
pianos? why not violins or trumpets?). Where else in the poem
are violent powers ascribed to nature? Does this deliberate distorting and exaggerating of the forces of nature tell us more about
springtime, or about the state of mind of the speaker when she
experienced the springtime?

Obviously, the poem *does* characterize the state of the speaker's
mind. At the onset of spring she was, for some reason, hyper-
sensitive, for some reason unprepared for the experience. But does
this mean that the fearful, violent power she senses exists in her
mind alone? What else does she see in spring besides this power?
What does she mean when she says that the daffodils wear a
"fashion / So foreign to my own"? What bothers her about the
bees? Apparently that they have no "word" for her. The speaker
seems to feel a gap between herself and nature; nature seems to
go on in its busy, inevitable way without paying any "gentle deference" to her or to anyone. She can *wish* the grass would grow
quickly, but she can't *make* it do so; no one can. And isn't there
something fearful in that? Spring may be beautiful, but we have
no control over it; it results from powerful, inevitable natural
forces, which work out their endlessly recurring cycles whether
we want them to or not. The speaker, then, sees in nature both
dreadful power and dreadful indifference to the human beholder.
Notice how the last two words of the poem ("unthinking drums")
unite these two perceptions.

The speaker calls herself "The Queen of Calvary." Why? Does
she mean that she is like Mary? If so, how might she be like Mary?
In what other sense might she be a "Queen of Calvary"? What state

of mind is she describing in this poem? Can you imagine someone in a state of mind in which what might ordinarily seem joyful causes great pain instead of delight? Compare the pain, the grief, the fear in this poem with the subdued and amused pleasure and hope in "An altered look about the hills." How do you account for such different views expressed in two poems by the same poet on the same subject? Or is the subject the same? If the subject is the same, does spring mean the same thing in both poems? Consider all three poems on spring. Which seems the more accurate—or are they all equally accurate? Which seems the most complex? Why?

We end this unit on nature poems with a poem by Longfellow called "Nature":

NATURE

Henry Wadsworth Longfellow

As a fond mother, when the day is o'er,
    Leads by the hand her little child to bed,
    Half willing, half reluctant to be led,
And leave his broken playthings on the floor,
Still gazing at them through the open door,
    Nor wholly reassured and comforted
    By promises of others in their stead,
Which, though more splendid, may not please him more;
So Nature deals with us, and takes away
    Our playthings one by one, and by the hand
    Leads us to rest so gently, that we go
Scarce knowing if we wish to go or stay,
    Being too full of sleep to understand
    How far the unknown transcends the what we know.

What are the two parts of this poem? What is the relation between them? The relation is something like equivalency: what equals what? Fond mother equals nature; child equals man; going to bed equals death; reluctance to go to bed equals reluctance to die—all this is fairly obvious. Does the equivalency ever break down? How do you account for the "playthings" in *both* parts of the poem? What might "playthings" in the second part of the poem refer to? Worldly possessions? Duties and obligations? Why doesn't Longfellow specify the reference for us instead of repeating "playthings"? In the first part of the poem he mentions "promises of others in their [the playthings'] stead"; is there an equivalent for these promises in the second part? What does "what we know" refer to in the last line? What does the child know in the first part? What does "the unknown" refer to? Is there an "unknown" in the first part? What does "transcends" mean? What is Longfellow suggesting about the "unknown" when he says it "transcends" the known? Having answered these last few questions, would you say that there is an equivalency in the last part for the "promises" of the first?

The poem is called "Nature." Wouldn't a better title be "Death"? In this poem, what is the relation between nature and death? Why is nature compared to a "fond mother" (rather than to a father? a nurse? a sister?)? What does this poem tell us about how we ought to regard death? the world we live in? Which of the other poems in this unit is this poem most like in its attitude towards nature? towards death? Which is it least like?

In discussing this poem, we have done something we have not explicitly done before: we have talked about an extended comparison. Do any of the other poems in this unit rely on similar extended comparisons? Find *parts* in the other poems which rely on comparisons. What does a poet gain by using comparisons?

We have arrived at the subject of the eleventh grade unit: figurative language; metaphor, simile, and other kinds of comparisons. The student should be aware at this point that poetry results from choice, and that each poem produces a unified total effect towards which all the poet's choices contribute. The interest in this sequence has been primarily in single meanings: what does this word mean? (usually one thing); what is the poet's choice here? (usually one thing); and so on. In the sequences which follow, students are led to watch for *double* meanings: *comparison* in the eleventh grade (What is being compared to what? What *two* things are going on? What is the relation between them?); in the twelfth grade *irony* (What are the *two meanings* implied by this word—this phrase—this situation? What is the difference between them? In what sense is that difference ironic?). If, as a result of the tenth grade sequence, the student has come to understand how to apprehend single meanings, he will be well prepared to deal with more complex double meanings.

Poetry for Grade Eleven

Since many (perhaps most) poems rely heavily on comparisons to achieve their effects, this unit is devoted to various kinds of comparisons. It follows logically the tenth grade unit: there the emphasis was on the poem as choice; here the narrowed focus is on one kind of choice—the comparisons the poet chooses to draw to the reader's attention. The movement is generally from simple poems, resting on single or at least rather obvious comparisons, to more complex poems, which rely on more difficult comparisons. The main question, whether the comparison is explicit or implied, always is: How are the two things compared appropriate to one another? A secondary major question is: How are they *inappropriate?*—for often poems invite readers to contrast as well as to compare.

The unit begins with a simple poem by the eighteenth century minor poet, William Oldys:

ON A FLY DRINKING OUT OF HIS CUP

William Oldys

Busy, curious, thirsty fly!
Drink with me and drink as I:
Freely welcome to my cup,
Couldst thou sip and sip it up:
Make the most of life you may,
Life is short and wears away.

Both alike are mine and thine
Hastening quick to their decline:
Thine's a summer, mine's no more,
Though repeated to threescore.
Threescore summers, when they're gone,
Will appear as short as one!

What is the speaker's situation in this poem, and what is his reaction to it? The speaker sees a fly drinking from his cup, and invites him to have more (lines 3–6 should be clarified: "You would be freely welcome to my cup even if you could drink it all; you may make the most of life—after all, life is short"). Is there anything strange about the speaker's reaction? How do you react when a fly settles on the rim of your cup?

How does the speaker justify his strange reaction? The answer lies in the second stanza: the fly's and the speaker's lives are "both alike." In what sense? In brevity. But the speaker himself points out that his life will be sixty times longer than the fly's. Isn't that a great difference? How can he say "mine's no more"? The answer is that once it is over, it "will appear" to be no more. What does he mean by that? The students might be asked to illustrate what the speaker says here from their own experience.

The speaker here sees something, and forms an attitude towards it on the basis of a comparison. In what direction does the comparison move? Is he comparing his life to a fly's, or a fly's to his? Perhaps the answer is neither—they are "both alike"; the speaker is expressing his community with this ugly parasitic insect, and its community with him. Question: What kind of man does the speaker seem to be? Congenial, generous, humane, friendly, good-natured, humorous. Why? How does the comparison he makes help one to sense his values and qualities? What difference would it make if the poem were addressed to a child who wanted to drink from his cup?

Let's contrast this poem with a quite different one by George Herbert:

VIRTUE

George Herbert

Sweet day, so cool, so calm, so bright,
   The bridal[a] of the earth and sky:
The dew shall weep thy fall tonight;
   For thou must die.

Sweet rose, whose hue, angry and brave,[b]
   Bids the rash gazer wipe his eye:
Thy root is ever in its grave,
   And thou must die.

Sweet spring, full of sweet days and roses,
A box where sweets compacted lie;
My music shows ye have your closes,[c]
And all must die.

Only a sweet and virtuous soul,
Like seasoned timber, never gives;
But though the whole world turn to coal,
Then chiefly lives.

[a] *bridal*: wedding celebration   [b] *brave*: splendid
[c] *closes*: concluding cadences, a term drawn from music

Why is this poem called "Virtue"? Why not "The Soul"? Because the poem defines virtue, by describing its effects on the soul: only the virtuous soul lives, and it lives *chiefly* when "the whole world turn to coal" (burns to cinders at the end of time). Why then the stanzas on "day," "rose," "spring"? What do they have to do with a "virtuous soul"? They *contrast* with it in that they are mortal—part of "the whole world" of stanza four. Why choose "day," "rose," and "spring" as illustrations of mortality? In "On a Fly Drinking Out of His Cup," William Oldys thinks of mortality while looking at a fly. Why doesn't Herbert use flies, spiders, and lizards here? What do "day," "rose," and "spring" have in common that make them particularly appropriate illustrations of mortality *in this poem?* Is there any reason for the order in which the three subjects are presented?

In Oldys' poem, the speaker looks at a fly and sees a similarity between the fly's life and his. In "Virtue," the main turn of the poem hinges on a *contrast*, rather than on a comparison. In the poems which follow, what is more important, comparison or contrast? Also, Oldys' poem is based on a dramatic situation. Is "Virtue"? That is, just as Oldys addresses a fly, Herbert addresses day, rose, spring; do we therefore have the sense that the speaker is standing near a rose on a springtime day? Or do we rather feel that Herbert has chosen day, rose, and spring out of the range of his general experience to *illustrate* mortality for the purposes of heightening the meaning of virtue? Finally, notice the brief comparisons in "Virtue." Why is day "The bridal of the earth and sky"? Why is the root in the "grave" instead of in the earth? Is there a comparison involved in "The dew shall weep thy fall tonight"?

Both the poems dealt with so far contain things described; a useful term for a "thing described" in a poem is *image*, although "thing described" might work just as well. The image in Oldys' poem is a fly drinking from a cup; Herbert's poem contains images of day, rose, and spring. Most of the questions asked so far can be reduced to: What is the image like? and What is the function of the image? In Oldys' poem the image is a description of an "actual" event; it induces the poet to see an important similarity on the basis of which he establishes an attitude towards the event. In Herbert's poem the images function as illustrations of mortality, particularly appropriate because of the kinds of images they are.

John Donne's "A Lecture Upon the Shadow" uses an image in a more complex way:

A LECTURE UPON THE SHADOW

John Donne

Stand still, and I will read to thee
A lecture, Love, in love's philosophy.
    These three hours that we have spent,
    Walking here, two shadows went
Along with us, which we ourselves produced;
But, now the sun is just above our head,
    We do those shadows tread;
    And to brave clearness all things are reduced.
  So whilst our infant loves did grow,
  Disguises did, and shadows, flow
From us, and our cares; but, now 'tis not so.
That love hath not attained the high'st degree,
Which is still diligent lest others see.

Except our loves at this noon stay,
We shall new shadows make the other way.
    As the first were made to blind
    Others, these which come behind
Will work upon our selves, and blind our eyes.
If our loves faint, and westwardly decline;
    To me thou, falsely, thine,
    And I to thee mine actions shall disguise.
  The morning shadows wear away,
  But these grow longer all the day,

But oh, love's day is short, if love decay.

Love is a growing, or full constant light;
And his first minute, after noon, is night.

In this poem what is the image—the thing described—the picture
the reader creates in his mind's eye? We picture a man addressing
his lover; they have been walking for three hours, and now it is
noon; the man talks about shadows and love as part of a "lecture"
on "love's philosophy." Why a "lecture"? Why do people usually
give lectures? Is the man trying to teach something to his lover?

Let's examine the comparison: Is it accurate to say that the
speaker is comparing *love* to *shadows*? Only in the most general
way; we must be more specific. The speaker is comparing the
growth and *decline* of love ("infant loves did *grow*," "love hath
not *attained*," "love *decay*," "Love is a *growing*, or full constant
light") to what happens to shadows as the day progresses from
morning to evening. What is the speaker saying about the growth
and decline of love? While love is growing, the lovers are self-
conscious about how they might appear to others—"disguises" and
"shadows" flow *from* them. (What does he mean by this? Do you
know people who seem to fall in love as part of an act—because
they aspire to the role of lover—because they want others to think
they are in love?) When love reaches its full constancy, there is
no deception; the lovers see each other clearly for what they are,
and others see them in the same way. As love declines, the lovers
begin to disguise themselves in order to deceive one another. The
next question is: How does the comparison with shadows clarify
what the speaker is saying about the progress of love? This is a
poem about the relation between love and deception: How are
shadows appropriate to the idea of deception? In the second
stanza, in what sense will the shadows thrown behind the lovers
"blind" their eyes? (They appear to be what they were before, at
noon, but now they cast shadows behind them, which can't be
clearly seen from the front. From the front one can't tell they are
casting shadows; hence their appearance is deceptive.) Let's return to the question of why the speaker gives a "lecture": At what
stage in love's development is the love between the speaker and
his lover? Their love has reached its full constancy, just as their

walk has reached its climax, just as the sun has reached its zenith: What must they beware of? Would you say that the speaker's willingness to speak this lecture indicates that his love has attained the "high'st degree"? Why, or why not? Finally, would you say that the image in this poem functions more like the image in "On a Fly Drinking Out of His Cup," or like the images in "Virtue"?

So far we have considered a poem in which the image is an occasion calling for reflection ("On a Fly Drinking Out of His Cup"), a poem in which the images act primarily as illustrations ("Virtue"), and a poem in which the image is both an occasion calling for reflection and a thoroughly worked out illustration ("A Lecture Upon the Shadow"). How do the images work in Keats' "On First Looking into Chapman's Homer"?

ON FIRST LOOKING INTO CHAPMAN'S HOMER

John Keats

Much have I traveled in the realms of gold,
    And many goodly states and kingdoms seen;
    Round many western islands have I been
Which bards in fealty to Apollo hold.
Oft of one wide expanse had I been told
    That deep-browed Homer ruled as his demesne;
    Yet did I never breathe its pure serene
Till I heard Chapman speak out loud and bold:
Then felt I like some watcher of the skies
    When a new planet swims into his ken;
Or like stout Cortez when with eagle eyes
    He stared at the Pacific—and all his men
Looked at each other with a wild surmise—
    Silent, upon a peak in Darien.

The first picture we get is of a man traveling. He has "traveled" in "realms of gold," "goodly states and kingdoms," "Round many western islands." But what does "bards in fealty to Apollo hold" mean? Bards are poets; Apollo is, among other things, the god of poetry; and "in fealty" means "in trust." In what sense do poets hold islands in trust for the god of poetry? Poets obviously aren't kings, viceroys, or real estate agents. Keats must mean that *in writing* about these islands, the poets somehow hold them in trust for Apollo. Homer, the next four lines tell us, "ruled as his demesne" (land he legally possesses) a "wide expanse." Does that mean that Homer somehow possessed merely that land on which the action of his epics takes place? Or does it suggest that Homer ruled over a "wide expanse" of human experience? Obviously the latter. Why? Let's look again at the first image. Our man traveling hasn't traveled physically over geographical realms; rather he has "traveled" by *reading*. The image is an image *for* reading. What is the difference between the function of this image and the function of the images in the other poems? Is this a real, dramatic situation? No. Does traveling *illustrate* reading? No. Does Keats compare traveling to reading explicitly, as Donne compared what happened to shadows on a sunlit day to the rise and decline of love? No. Rather Keats describes an image, and provides many obvious hints that it is a picture of *something else;* we are not to take it literally. And an image used in this way is called a *metaphor.* Traveling in this poem is a metaphor for reading.

The next question to ask about this poem is the important question to ask about any metaphor: Why is the image appropriate to the thing it represents? Why is traveling an appropriate representation for reading? What aspects of travel does Keats emphasize? It broadens one and provides variety (*"many* goodly states and kingdoms"; *"many* western islands"). What else? Is there a contrast in the kinds of images used in the first eight lines and the kinds used in the last six? Notice that the images in the last six are more specific: not generalized "realms of gold," "states and kingdoms," "western islands" but specific *watchers,* an astronomer and Cortez. And the "watcher of the skies" is not necessarily a traveler—an important clue. What does that watcher do? He sees *something new.* Is "newness" mentioned at all in the first eight lines? Who was Cortez? What happened to him on the "peak in Darien"?[4] Reading has its normal conventional pleasures (can the students be made to see the conventionality of the language in the first four lines?) but it also provides awe-filled, silent excitement—feelings like those of Cortez when he first saw the Pacific. That is, a reader is more than a traveler—he is an explorer, and his explorations can be rewarded with the thrill of *discovery.* Notice, Keats does not make this explicit; he tells us instead that on reading Chapman's translation of Homer he "felt . . . *like*" a watcher of the skies, *like* Cortez. The images help us understand what something *feels like:* what it feels like to read for the first time something grand and beautiful.

Now let's examine another poem in which the images are representations of what something *feels like:*

EXULTATION IS THE GOING*

Emily Dickinson

> Exultation is the going
> Of an inland soul to sea,
> Past the houses—past the headlands—
> Into deep Eternity—
>
> Bred as we, among the mountains,
> Can the sailor understand
> The divine intoxication
> Of the first league out from land?

The students should first be led to see that the poem is a metaphorical definition of exultation. The image is a ship going out to sea, and the poem sets up several implicit equations: soul (mentioned) equals ship (not mentioned); sea (mentioned) equals eternity (mentioned). What do "inland," "houses," and "headland" suggest? It must be *time* for they represent a direct contrast with eternity. That is, exultation is a movement from time into eternity. What is the meaning of "divine intoxication"? Is it another metaphor for "exultation"? Does it make sense to see "intoxication" as a kind of movement out of time towards eternity? Is the ship metaphor appropriate to the feeling? Have you ever gone out to sea in a ship? How did it feel as you drew away from land, headed out to sea?

Emily Dickinson in this poem finds a way of putting into words something that can hardly be expressed. We all may have *felt* exultation, but how can we make the meaning of the feeling clear

---

* From *The Poems of Emily Dickinson,* Thomas H. Johnson, ed. Cambridge, Mass.: The Belknap Press. Copyright 1951, 1955 by The President and Fellows of Harvard College. Reprinted by permission.

to ourselves and to others? Poems again and again are attempts to find equivalents in words for inner awarenesses that can hardly be expressed. Here Emily Dickinson creates a metaphor for hope:

HOPE IS THE THING WITH FEATHERS*

Emily Dickinson

Hope is the thing with feathers
That perches in the soul
And sings the tune without the words
And never stops at all.

And sweetest in the gale is heard—
And sore must be the storm
That could abash the little bird
That kept so many warm.

I've heard it in the chillest land
And on the strangest sea;
Yet never in extremity
It asked a crumb of me.

Why is it appropriate to see hope as a bird which sings most sweetly in a storm? In what sense can a song keep someone "warm"? (Notice that "warm" itself is a metaphor for the effects of hope.) What are "chillest land" and "strangest sea" metaphors for? Why is it so difficult to define the meaning of these metaphors? What significance do you see in hope's never asking for so much as a crumb?

Here is another, brief, metaphorical poem by Emily Dickinson:

Faith is a fine invention*
When gentlemen can *see*,
But *microscopes* are prudent
In an emergency.

What does the word "invention" say about the meaning of faith? How do inventions come into being, and why? What does "see" mean? What is "microscopes" a metaphor for, and what does the

* From *The Poems of Emily Dickinson*, Thomas H. Johnson, ed. Cambridge, Mass.: The Belknap Press. Copyright 1951, 1955 by The President and Fellows of Harvard College. Reprinted by permission.

poem mean by "emergency"? It's easy to imagine a situation in which "microscopes" aren't enough, and one has to take something on faith. Can you imagine a situation in which faith is useless, and a microscope "prudent"?

SUCCESS IS COUNTED SWEETEST*

Emily Dickinson

Success is counted sweetest
By those who ne'er succeed.
To comprehend a nectar
Requires sorest need.

Not one of all the purple host
Who took the flag today
Can tell the definition
So clear of victory

As he defeated, dying,
On whose forbidden ear
The distant strains of triumph
Burst agonized and clear!

This poem defines the situation in which success counts most. To what extent is the definition metaphorical? Is the battlefield scene in the last two stanzas a metaphor or an illustration? Do the lines "To comprehend a nectar / Requires sorest need" contain a metaphor, or do they provide an illustration?

Here Emily Dickinson creates a metaphor not to define a feeling or abstraction, but to convey a visual effect:

SHE SWEEPS WITH MANY-COLORED BROOMS*

Emily Dickinson

She sweeps with many-colored brooms,
And leaves the shreds behind.
Oh, Housewife in the Evening West,
Come back, and dust the pond!

* From *The Poems of Emily Dickinson*, Thomas H. Johnson, ed. Cambridge, Mass.: The Belknap Press. Copyright 1951, 1955 by The President and Fellows of Harvard College. Reprinted by permission.

You dropped a purple ravelling in—
You dropped an amber thread—
And now you've littered all the East
With duds of emerald!

And still she plies her spotted brooms,
And still the aprons fly,
Till brooms fade softly into stars,
And then I come away.

Who is the sweeper in this poem? Emily Dickinson never makes
her identity explicit, but there are plenty of hints. She is the
"Housewife in the Evening West" who has "many-colored brooms,"
drops purple ravelings and amber threads, and so on; her "brooms
fade softly into stars." The sweeper is the sun, which "sweeps" the
sky and landscape with many-colored rays; it is described as if it
were a busy housewife, ineffectually tidying things up in the
evening. In this poem we are given a metaphor for a *visual* effect,
rather than for an abstraction or feeling. What more can be said?
One might ask: Is this an appropriate metaphor? Whoever would
have thought of comparing the sun to a housewife? On the surface,
there seems to be a tremendous disparity between the two parts
of the metaphor; it's hard to imagine bringing two such different
things together successfully, and Emily Dickinson's wit in doing
so is one of the sources of our pleasure in the poem. And this disparity between the things compared is often a source of pleasure
in metaphor. This is an important point: in order to gauge the
meaning and effect of any comparison, one must often be aware
not only of the similarities inherent in the things compared, but
of the differences as well. Emily Dickinson's yoking two such
disparate things as the sun and a housewife seems almost audaciously to call our attention to her boldness and wit. Look back
over the other poems by Emily Dickinson in this unit. Do any of
them reveal a similar audacity?

Finally, let's consider what the choice of metaphor in this poem
suggests about the speaker's attitude towards the sunset. Does the
poet see in the sunset anything like awe-inspiring grandeur? At
first one might be tempted to say no, for the metaphor domesticates
nature, makes it seem entirely familiar and commonplace. But

what about phrases like "purple ravelling," "amber thread," and "duds of emerald"? Are they domestic and commonplace? The sunset litters these riches out of neglect—because it is just a little untidy and inefficient—yet they *are* incomparable riches. Now, what is the attitude towards the sunset in this poem? Is it a simple or complex one?

Here is an audacious poem, in which the speaker himself points out the disparities in his comparisons:

LONG-WHILE I SOUGHT TO WHAT I MIGHT COMPARE
(AMORETTI IX)

Edmund Spenser

Long-while I sought to what I might compare
Those powerful eyes which lighten my dark spright;[a]
Yet find I nought on earth to which I dare
Resemble th' image of their goodly light.
Not to the sun; for they do shine by night:
Nor to the moon; for they are changed never:
Nor to the stars; for they have purer sight:
Nor to the fire; for they consume not ever:
Nor to the lightning; for they still persever:
Nor to the diamond; for they are more tender:
Nor unto crystal; for nought may them sever:
Nor unto glass; such baseness mought offend her.
Then to the Maker self they likest be,
Whose light doth lighten all that here we see.

[a]*spright:* spirit

The first four lines state a problem: to what can the speaker compare the "powerful eyes" of his lover; the earth provides no suitable comparisons. He goes through a list of "earthly" things to which men often compare their lovers' eyes. He notes an important disparity between the eyes and each item on the list. Finally he compares them to the ultimate unearthly source of all earthly light, God himself, and confidently affirms that this is the appropriate comparison. But don't we see a crucial disparity here? What is that disparity? Why doesn't the speaker acknowledge it? Could it be that he doesn't see it? Is this a "serious" poem, or is the poet deliberately, audaciously exaggerating? Why might he exaggerate deliberately and audaciously? What is the purpose of the poem? Here is another poem which is merely a list of comparisons.

PRAYER

George Herbert

Prayer, the Church's banquet, angels' age,
　　God's breath in man returning to his birth,
The soul in paraphrase, heart in pilgrimage,
　　The Christian plummet sounding heaven and earth;

Engine against th' Almighty, sinner's tower,
　　Reversèd thunder, Christ-side-piercing spear,
The six-days' world transposing in an hour,
　　A kind of tune, which all things hear and fear;

Softness, and peace, and joy, and love, and bliss,
　　Exalted manna, gladness of the best,
Heaven in ordinary, man well dressed,
　　The Milky Way, the bird of Paradise,

Church bells beyond the stars heard, the soul's blood,
The land of spices; something understood.

In Spenser's poem the speaker seeks a suitable object with which to "liken" his lover's eyes; it is a poem about making comparisons, and the machinery for making comparisons is on the surface. It is fairly obvious why the speaker considers each item on his list, and he explicitly tells us why he rejects each item. Herbert's poem, on the other hand, is a list of metaphors for prayer. He never tells us why he has chosen an item to put on the list; we have to figure that out for ourselves, and sometimes it's not so easy. Let's examine some of the more difficult metaphors. Why is prayer "the Church's banquet"? The Church feasts on prayer; prayer is the food that nourishes it. But it's not an ordinary meal; it's a banquet, a grand, heightened, celebrational occasion. Why "angels' age"? The age of man is finite; angels' age is infinite: prayer puts men in contact with infinite life. "Soul in paraphrase": prayer is the soul's formula for condensing and interpreting its meaning. "Engine against th' Almighty": this, along with "sinner's tower" and "Christ-side-piercing spear," suggest that prayer is something of a weapon to be used against God. Prayers are effective; they get through to God, just as the spear reached Christ's heart. Men use prayers in their own defense: they pray to be forgiven for their sins. Also, the things men confess in prayer and the things men pray for might wound God by revealing to Him men's pettiness and inadequacy. "The six-days' world transposing in an hour": an hour of prayer can "transpose" the "six-days' world" (the world God created in six days which then fell as a result of Adam's sin) into something better. "Heaven in ordinary": prayer brings heaven into the ordinary life. And so on. This gloss of the difficult metaphors, of course, is one man's interpretation; it should illustrate the complexity and force of the metaphors in the poem, and show the compression poets achieve through the use of metaphor. Question: As we've come to understand metaphor, the last phrase in the poem ("something understood") is not a metaphor; it is therefore set off from the rest of the poem, and given a unique importance. Why might it be the most important phrase in the poem?

"Prayer" is a collection of metaphors. The next poem, "The Pilgrimage," is unified by a single, sustained metaphor:

THE PILGRIMAGE

George Herbert

I travelled on, seeing the hill, where lay
    My expectation.
A long it was and weary way:
    The gloomy cave of Desperation
I left on th' one, and on the other side
    The rock of Pride.

And so I came to Fancy's meadow strowed
    With many a flower:
Fain would I here have made abode,
    But I was quickened by my hour.
So to Care's copse I came, and there got through
    With much ado.

That led me to the wild of Passion, which
 Some call the wold;
A wasted place, but sometimes rich.
Here I was robbed of all my gold,
Save one good angel, which a friend had tied
 Close to my side.

At length I got unto the gladsome hill,
 Where lay my hope,
Where lay my heart; and climbing still,
When I had gained the brow and top,
A lake of brackish waters on the ground
 Was all I found.

With that abashed and struck with many a sting
 Of swarming fears,
I fell and cried, "Alas, my King,
Can both the way and end be tears?"
Yet taking heart I rose, and then perceived
 I was deceived;

My hill was further; so I flung away,
 Yet heard a cry,
Just as I went, "None goes that way
And lives." "If that be all," said I,
"After so foul a journey death is fair,
 And but a chair."ᵃ

ᵃ *chair*: chariot

What is a pilgrimage? Does this poem describe a real pilgrimage, or a metaphorical pilgrimage? How do you know it is the latter? What is the pilgrimage a metaphor for? What is the object of the pilgrimage? It is "the hill, where lay / My expectation." What does that mean? Let's examine the other geography along the way; everything else is given a specific meaning: the gloomy cave is Desperation, Pride is a rock, Fancy is a meadow strewn with flowers, Care is a copse, Passion a wilderness. How are the things described appropriate to the human traits and moral qualities they represent? How is desperation like a gloomy cave? passion like wilderness? and so on. The one item in the landscape that isn't given a specific meaning is the hill of expectation. Why? Why is it appropriate that the pilgrim finds "brackish water" at the top of the hill? What is his reaction when he sees it? He earlier avoided desperation: is he experiencing desperation now, or something higher and more significant? He sees his hill further. What does that hill represent? The poem seems to distinguish false from true expectation. What might false expectations be? What does the poet gain by not specifying what these expectations are? Why is it that the pilgrim must die in order to reach his hill? How does the poem help us see why he might be willing to die? Finally, once again, what is the pilgrimage a metaphor for? Life, yes, but what aspect of life?

"The Pilgrimage" is a fairly straightforward, obvious poem. Herbert's "Redemption," another poem based on an extended metaphor, is somewhat more difficult:

REDEMPTION

George Herbert

Having been tenant long to a rich Lord,
  Not thriving, I resolvèd to be bold,
And make a suit unto Him, to afford
  A new small-rented lease, and cancel th' old.

In heaven at His manor I Him sought:
  They told me there, that He was lately gone
About some land, which He had dearly bought
  Long since on Earth, to take possession.

I straight returned, and knowing His great birth,
  Sought Him accordingly in great resorts—
In cities, theatres, gardens, parks, and courts:
At length I heard a raggèd noise and mirth

  Of thieves and murderers; there I Him espied,
  Who straight, "Your suit is granted," said, and died.

The metaphor in "The Pilgrimage" is a rather simple story: a traveler traverses a difficult landscape to reach his destination, finds only disappointment there, and sets out again for something higher. The story in "Redemption" is somewhat more complicated, and its significance is less explicit. The speaker is a "tenant" (exactly what is a tenant?) to a "rich Lord," but he hasn't thrived; he wants to "make a suit" (exactly what is a "suit"?) to the lord to have his old lease canceled, and replaced by a "new small-rented lease" (exactly what is a lease?). In the second quatrain of the poem, when it becomes clear that the story is not a real one, but a metaphorical one (the speaker goes to his lord's—God's—manor house in Heaven), the reader realizes that he must reinterpret the key words in the first quatrain. In what sense is God "rich"? In what sense can a man be a "tenant" to God and pay rent to Him? And so on. (Notice that in "The Pilgrimage" the speaker does much of the interpreting for us: each item of the landscape is named.) Also, as the reader goes on, he must continue to translate the key words into other terms. What is the "land" on earth that God "dearly bought / Long since"? What are we to see in the Lord's returning to earth to "take possession" of the land He dearly bought? The speaker makes the mistake of looking for the lord in "great resorts." Exactly what kind of mistake is this? Who in the Bible makes the same kind of mistake? Who misunderstands the sense in which Christ is "king"? What does the last scene described in the poem remind us of? Why was Christ crucified? To *redeem* mankind. The title of the poem then has two meanings: a commercial sense (we still have it today—we redeem coupons, we redeem debts, we have trading stamp redemption centers), in that it refers to a commercial transaction between the tenant and his lord; and a spiritual sense, which in this poem is merely implied. How does the description of commercial redemption help us to understand the meaning of spiritual redemption? Why does the lord grant the speaker's suit before dying?

Here is an even more complicated poem, which has one central and several subsidiary comparisons:

HOLY SONNET XIV[5]

John Donne

Batter my heart, three-personed God; for You
As yet but knock, breathe, shine, and seek to mend;
That I may rise and stand, o'erthrow me, and bend
Your force to break, blow, burn, and make me new.
I, like an usurped town to another due,

Labor to admit You, but, Oh, to no end;
Reason, Your viceroy in me, me should defend,
But is captived, and proves weak or untrue.
Yet dearly I love You, and would be loved fain,
But am betrothed unto Your enemy:
Divorce me, untie, or break that knot again;
Take me to You, imprison me, for I,
Except You enthrall me, never shall be free,
Nor ever chaste, except You ravish me.

What are the two main comparisons in this poem, and what is the relationship between them? The speaker compares himself first to "an usurped town to another due," that is, to a town in which the control is in the hands of a person other than the one to whom the town owes its allegiance. The person to whom it owes allegiance has left a "viceroy" (reason) to control the town, but reason is either too weak or untrue. (Why both weak and untrue? Reason may be too weak to control, or rational processes applied to spiritual matters might lead to false conclusions or doubt.) Hence the poet calls upon God to "batter" his heart—to storm the walls by force, and take rightful command. The speaker also compares himself to a bride, who is betrothed to the wrong lover (God's enemy); hence he calls on God to rend asunder violently the ties that bind him to his false lover. What is the similarity between these two comparisons? In both cases we have worldly civil arrangements, which in the highest sense are unstable and false; they must be violently overthrown.

Notice the similarities between the phrases "That I may rise and stand, o'erthrow me," "Except You enthrall me, never shall be free, / Nor ever chaste, except You ravish me." These seem to violate normal expectations—to turn the world upside down. How can one stand by falling, achieve freedom by being enslaved and chastity by being ravished? This violent yoking of apparent opposites is called *paradox*. But our examination of the comparisons shows that they are only *apparent* paradoxes. The speaker calls for restoration that can result only from the violent destruction of the old, false ties. A man is free only when he pays due allegiance to his rightful superior; a bride is chaste only when she gives her love to her rightful groom.

What is the spiritual state of the speaker? Compare him with the speakers in the previous five poems. They seem to have achieved the reconciliation that this speaker seeks. This speaker knows rationally what he needs, but he is nevertheless rebellious. He calls upon God violently to subdue him because he cannot subdue himself. Can you think of similar situations from your own life— situations when your reason was weak or untrue, and you were somehow unable to pursue the ends you knew you ought to have pursued?

Finally, these last six poems express orthodox Christian views of human experience. Must one believe in orthodox Christianity to *like* these poems? to think they are *good* poems?

All of the poems we have dealt with so far rest on rather obvious comparisons. Many poems rely heavily on comparisons which are only hinted at in indirect and subtle ways. One such poem is Wordsworth's "I Wandered Lonely As a Cloud":

I WANDERED LONELY AS A CLOUD

William Wordsworth

I wandered lonely as a cloud
That floats on high o'er vales and hills,
When all at once I saw a crowd,
A host, of golden daffodils;
Beside the lake, beneath the trees,
Fluttering and dancing in the breeze.

Continuous as the stars that shine
And twinkle on the milky way,
They stretched in never-ending line
Along the margin of a bay:
Ten thousand saw I at a glance,
Tossing their heads in sprightly dance.

The waves beside them danced; but they
Outdid the sparkling waves in glee;
A poet could not but be gay,
In such a jocund company;
I gazed—and gazed—but little thought
What wealth the show to me had brought:

For oft, when on my couch I lie
In vacant or in pensive mood,

They flash upon that inward eye
Which is the bliss of solitude;
And then my heart with pleasure fills,
And dances with the daffodils.

There are explicit comparisons here ("as a cloud," "as the stars"), but the main comparison is implicit; what is it? Notice the words that are used to describe the daffodils: "crowd," "host," and "jocund company." What do these words usually refer to? Notice what the daffodils do; they flutter, yes, but they also "dance"; they toss "their heads in sprightly dance"; they outdo "the sparkling waves in glee." What do these actions remind us of? The daffodils are described as if they were a "crowd," a "jocund company" of dancing, gleeful people. And why is it important that the poet should emphasize the crowd-ness, the dancing (an activity we do in groups), the glee of the flowers? Notice he first presents himself as wandering (which is aimless, random, unlike dancing) like a cloud blown purposelessly by the wind. He is lonely. And when do the daffodils mean most to him? When he is in "vacant and pensive mood" (why vacant? why pensive?); when he is in solitude. Then his heart *dances* (a joyful, purposeful activity) *with* (in communion, as a part, no longer isolated) the daffodils. What does nature mean for this speaker? Notice how important his implied comparison is for answering this question.

We have examined a number of poems whose effects result chiefly from skillful use of images and comparisons; we have seen examples of several ways in which images and comparisons function, and we have arrived at some important definitions. Tennyson's complex and moving "Tears, Idle Tears" provides a good testing ground for what students have learned so far.

TEARS, IDLE TEARS[6]

Alfred, Lord Tennyson

Tears, idle tears, I know not what they mean,
Tears from the depth of some divine despair
Rise in the heart, and gather to the eyes,
In looking on the happy autumn-fields,
And thinking of the days that are no more.

Fresh as the first beam glittering on a sail,
That brings our friends up from the underworld,
Sad as the last which reddens over one
That sinks with all we love below the verge;
So sad, so fresh, the days that are no more.

Ah, sad and strange as in dark summer dawns
The earliest pipe of half-awakened birds
To dying ears, when unto dying eyes
The casement slowly grows a glimmering square;
So sad, so strange, the days that are no more.

Dear as remembered kisses after death,
And sweet as those by hopeless fancy feigned
On lips that are for others; deep as love,
Deep as first love, and wild with all regret;
O Death in Life, the days that are no more!

The first line establishes the problem dealt with in the poem: what is the "meaning" of the "tears, idle tears"? The first stanza tells us the source of the tears ("some divine despair"), and the occasion for their coming into being (*"looking* on the happy autumn-fields," and *"thinking* of the days that are no more"). The next three stanzas characterize the tears with adjectives referring to emotional qualities; they are "fresh," "sad," "sad and strange," "dear," "sweet," "deep," and "wild." Notice that Tennyson makes each of these qualities specific by associating a comparison with it. "The first beam glittering on a sail, / That brings our friends up from the underworld" is fresh, and the tears are equally fresh; the last beam "which reddens over one / That sinks . . ." is sad, and the tears are equally sad; and so on. The direct purpose which calls into being each of the images in this poem is to intensify and particularize an emotional quality. But is this direct purpose the only function of the images? Are there any important similarities between them?

Yes, there are. The image for "sad and strange" is obviously similar to the image for "dear." The one is of a dying person, hearing birds at dawn, perhaps for the last time, while seeing the light of the sun make the casement window "slowly grow to a glimmering square," perhaps for the last time. The other is of a live person remembering the kiss of a dead lover. Both yoke life and death, and make something vividly important crucially unattainable to a living person. What other of the images yoke life and death? Why does the first ship mentioned rise up from the "underworld"? Notice the subtle suggestions in the word. It could be simply a way of referring to the other side of the globe; as ships appear over the curve of the earth's surface they seem to arise from an "underworld." But the word also suggests the classical equivalent of hell, and recalls mythological figures who descended into the underworld only to return afresh. Likewise "sinks . . . over the verge" in the next image refers most obviously to the way a ship seems to descend over the earth's curvature; but the phrase so closely echoes some of the language we often use when referring to death, that we are reminded not only of the temporary loss of geographical departure, but also of the permanent loss of death. And why is it appropriate that the tears come while the speaker looks at an "*autumn*-field"? Notice that although each image arises to fill an immediate need (the need to specify an emotion that plays a part in the poem), together they point towards and prepare us for the conclusion: "O Death in Life, the days that are no more." What does "Death in Life" mean? How do the images help us to see what it means? Why does a sense of "Death in Life" provoke *idle* tears? (Notice that idle is no idle word.) Finally, notice that there is a great deal of evidence in the poem to suggest without making it explicit that the real cause for the idle tears is the loss of a loved one. What is that evidence? It's all to be found in the comparisons—that is, the speaker is playing a very neat trick on us: he presents in comparisons with the emotions what is probably the real *cause* of the emotions. If students can be made to sense the complexity and beauty of this apparently simple poem, they will have gone a long way towards understanding what poetry is.

A final poem, also dealing with the relation of life and death:

SONNET LXXIII

William Shakespeare

That time of year thou mayst in me behold
When yellow leaves, or none, or few, do hang
Upon those boughs which shake against the cold,

Bare ruined choirs* where late the sweet birds sang.
In me thou seest the twilight of such day
As after sunset fadeth in the west,
Which by and by black night doth take away,
Death's second self, that seals up all in rest.
In me thou seest the glowing of such fire
That on the ashes of his youth doth lie,
As the deathbed whereon it must expire
Consumed with that which it was nourished by.
This thou perceiv'st, which makes thy love more strong,
To love that well which thou must leave ere long.

Each of the quatrains here describes a metaphor for the speaker's age. What are the differences between the metaphors, and is there any progression from one to the other? Or are the metaphors randomly ordered? What about the time spans suggested by the metaphors? The first refers to late autumn, the second to twilight, the third to the glowing of the last embers of a fire. That is, the time spans seem to narrow. Things seem also to get progressively darker: light isn't mentioned at all and is therefore assumed in the first metaphor, twilight is a time of half light and half darkness, and the glowing embers are a faint glimmer of light amidst black cinders. Also, death becomes more explicit as the poem progresses: not mentioned at all in the first quatrain, used in a metaphor ("Death's second self") in the second, and referred to directly in the comparison in the third ("As the deathbed . . ."). That is, the movement from metaphor to metaphor seems to intensify the sense of impending darkness and death.

The third quatrain concludes with a difficult paradox which requires explanation: "Consumed with that which it was nourished by." What is being consumed is the glow of the fire, which is being used up by the little fuel that remains. If the fire suggests life (the spark of life), what is the fuel, which both nourishes and consumes it? The body? What else might the fire and the fuel be metaphors for? What is the effect of seeing life as a fire that uses itself up in consuming the fuel which nourishes it? Doesn't it make life seem curious, precarious, fleeting, precious?

---

* Choir is an architectural term referring to part of a church or cathedral; here it is a metaphor for a visual effect; the bare boughs look like the skeletal structure of part of a ruined church.

Why does the speaker wish to create this effect? Let's examine the couplet: "This thou perceiv'st, which makes thy love more strong, / To love that well which thou must leave ere long." What is the "this" that the speaker wants the person he's addressing to perceive? And why? To make him love. What does *"thou* must leave ere long" mean? Isn't it surprising that the speaker puts it that way? The first twelve lines of the poem suggest that the speaker's death is imminent; why does the last line suggest that the *listener* might "leave"?

This is a poem that has a specific audience, and it is designed to have a specific effect. We, the readers, "listen in" on a man's address to someone he loves. We see that he has carefully selected and arranged three metaphors in order to make his lover "perceive" something, and that he makes a rather surprising turn in the last line. This poem illustrates that it is often important to pay attention to the speaker's designs on his audience—to the dramatic situation he is in, and how he exploits and controls that situation. We have paid attention to this problem before, but seldom explicitly, and never systematically. Furthermore, although the speaker is an aged man, Shakespeare was quite young when he wrote this poem. How do we account for this? Apparently here Shakespeare is getting out of himself, pretending he is someone else, imagining what it would be like to be in that person's situation, and dramatizing that person's situation for us.

The unit which follows focuses on the frequent necessity for distinguishing the speaker from the author; the students are asked to pay close attention to the speaker's situation—where he is, what he is doing, to whom he is talking—and to how he reveals his character, his values, his interests in that situation.

Poetry for Grade Twelve

The main goal of this unit is to teach the student to distinguish between speaker and author. The focus is on the speaker himself—his values, his attitudes towards the situation he finds himself in. Every poem, the students should be led to see, is the statement of a *character* who may or may not have views similar to the author of the poem, and who reveals enough of himself so that we can get a clear sense of what he is like. The main literary term introduced, defined, and developed in this unit is *irony*; most of the poems illustrate the kind of irony which results from the *author's* skillful manipulating of the *speaker* so that we, the readers, can see more than the speaker sees. Some of the poems illustrate other kinds of irony as well. The unit begins with poems in which it is very easy to distinguish between author and speaker, and ends with poems in which the speaker is ostensibly the author. The main questions, asked again and again, are: What does the speaker reveal about himself? and: What is the main irony in this poem?

We begin with two short poems by Robert Louis Stevenson:

LOOKING FORWARD*

Robert Louis Stevenson

When I am grown to man's estate
I shall be very proud and great,
And tell the other girls and boys
Not to meddle with my toys.

* From *Complete Poems*. New York: Charles Scribner's Sons, 1923. Reprinted by permission.

59

SYSTEM*

Robert Louis Stevenson

Every night my prayers I say,
And get my dinner every day;
And every day that I've been good,
I get an orange after food.

The child that is not plain and neat,
With lots of toys and things to eat,
He is a naughty child, I'm sure—
Or else his dear papaᵃ is poor.

ᵃ last syllable is stressed: papá

Who is the speaker in this poem? A little boy. How do we know? He talks about growing up to "man's estate," and he seems quite interested in toys; we know from our general experience that only little boys talk this way. What is amusing about this poem? The last line, "Not to meddle with my toys." The child wants to grow to man's estate, but he sees that condition in terms of the ability to keep his toys to himself. He wants to be "proud and great," but there's isn't anything very great about keeping toys to oneself; it's hardly something to be proud of. Anything "funny" about the title? Yes, the child in looking forward seems to be looking backward—he expresses the petty selfishness of a child, which is a "backward" rather than a "forward" thing.

A name for the kind of "funniness" in this poem is *irony*. There is a crucial disparity between the child's goal and his understanding of the goal. He sees manhood in terms of childish desires; he looks backwards, not forward; what he sees as an illustration of pride and greatness is actually trivial and petty; and perhaps even his association of pride and greatness with manhood shows a crucial misunderstanding. The important words in this poem have two meanings: the child's meaning, which is a false one, and the reader's meaning, which is true. This doubleness of meaning, in which

* From *Complete Poems*. New York: Charles Scribner's Sons. 1923. Reprinted by permission.

the two meanings working are directly contradictory, produces the effect we have called irony.

The speaker in "System," obviously, is also a child. What irony do you see in this poem? Let's examine the child's understanding of "good" and "naughty." What does he mean by a "good" child? A "good" child says his prayers every night, gets a dinner every day, and an orange after dinner; he is plain and neat, and has lots of toys and things to eat. A child who doesn't fit this pattern is "naughty." Even without reading the last line, we already begin to sense an irony. The child's understanding of goodness seems to be too narrow; the things he mentions may have something to do with goodness, but they are not essential to it. That is, we begin to see an ironic disparity between the child's limited values, and the larger, "truer" values implied by the word "good." What irony does the last line add to what we have seen so far? Notice that the child sees his happy physical condition as resulting from his "goodness." His "goodness," in his mind, *causes* rewards. But he does have a broad enough awareness to realize that there are some people to whom his "system" doesn't apply (the title, on one level, might refer to the child's limited system of values): children with poor fathers. He leaves it at this point: his values work in his world, and not in another. But *we* go a step beyond the child's understanding, and see that the *same* values work in both worlds. The same economic forces—the same economic *system* (the second meaning of the title)—which cause the poor child's poverty also cause the "good" child's rewards. The speaker's affluence, we see, is not the result of his moral condition, as he thinks it is, but of his father's wealth. That is, there is an ironic disparity between the *causes* he sees, and the causes we see.

In both of these poems the voice is clearly not that of the author; rather the author has created a character who speaks. The character has a specific set of values, a specific range of understanding, and the author makes him talk in a way which reveals to the reader the limitations of those values, the narrowness of that range of understanding. This difference between the narrowness and limitations of the character and the broader awareness the poem brings into play in us is the main source of the irony. What is the irony in the following poem, and how is it created?

"NEXT TO OF COURSE GOD AMERICA I"[7]*

e. e. cummings

"next to of course god america i
love you land of the pilgrims' and so forth oh
say can you see by the dawn's early my
country 'tis of centuries come and go
and are no more what of it we should worry
in every language even deafanddumb
thy sons acclaim your glorious name by gorry
by jingo by gee by gosh by gum
why talk of beauty what could be more beautiful than these heroic happy dead
who rushed like lions to the roaring slaughter
they did not stop to think they died instead
then shall the voice of liberty be mute?"

He spoke. And drank rapidly a glass of water

Where is the "doubleness of meaning" in this poem, and how is
it created? One might begin by breaking the poem into phrases
and putting it on the blackboard with clarifying punctuation.
("Next to, of course, God, America, I love you. Land of the pilgrims', and so forth. Oh say can you see, by the dawn's early . . . . My
country, 'tis of . . ." and so on.) Now, what does the speaker's main
subject seem to be? He seems to be an orator (he pauses to drink
a glass of water) who is celebrating the "heroic" deaths of soldiers
who died in battle for America. What does he seem to mean by
"heroism"? Rushing *unthinkingly* into death ("who rushed like
lions to the roaring slaughter. They did not stop to think; they died
instead"). Is this what *we* understand by "heroism"? What is the
speaker's understanding of America? He sums it up in a number of
familiar patriotic phrases, many of which he doesn't even finish.
How do these phrases make us see that his patriotism is unthinking—narrow, superficial? He speaks of beauty. Is what he offers as
an example of the beautiful really beautiful? His last line, "then
shall the voice of liberty be mute?" suggests that he considers him-

self to be the voice of liberty, celebrating the memory of the glorious dead. Does he understand liberty the way you understand it? Were the men who rushed unthinkingly into the slaughter liberated, free men according to your understanding of liberty and freedom? What if they had rushed *thinkingly* into the battle? Now, what is the main irony in the poem? Finally, is this an anti-American poem? No. Then what does this poem attack? Unthinking patriotism. How does it make its attack? By portraying an unthinking patriot in a way which makes us see his absurdity. In contrast, what is real, meaningful patriotism? Does this poem give us any ideas as to what it is?

CLIFF KLINGENHAGEN*

Edwin Arlington Robinson

Cliff Klingenhagen had me in to dine
With him one day; and after soup and meat,
And all the other things there were to eat,
Cliff took two glasses and filled one with wine
And one with wormwood. Then, without a sign
For me to choose at all, he took the draught
Of bitterness himself, and lightly quaffed
It off, and said the other one was mine.

And when I asked him what the deuce he meant
By doing that, he only looked at me
And smiled, and said it was a way of his.
And though I know the fellow, I have spent
Long time a-wondering when I shall be
As happy as Cliff Klingenhagen is.

What is the main irony in this poem? Where is the doubleness of meaning? First of all, Cliff Klingenhagen's action is a mild surprise. A man who voluntarily drinks a glass of wormwood overturns our normal expectations, and to the extent to which our normal expectations are surprisingly overturned, to that extent we experience the effect of irony. But what Cliff does here is only a *mild* surprise; once he poured the two glasses, we half expected

* From *The Children of the Night*, by Edwin Arlington Robinson. New York: Charles Scribner's Sons, 1897.

him to take the bitter drink himself. Hence his action may not seem ironic. The main irony is in the narrator's response: he doesn't understand Cliff's action. He wonders "what the deuce he meant / By doing that?" Do *we* see what he meant? The speaker says, "though I know the fellow," but *does* he know the fellow really? And he concludes by wondering when he will be as happy as Cliff Klingenhagen. He seems to be bewildered altogether by the most striking thing Cliff Klingenhagen does, and he seems not to see a relation between that action and Cliff's happiness. Do we? What is that relation? Why might someone who voluntarily accepts and deals with bitterness be a happy man? Our ability to answer these questions shows that we see further than the narrator, that our understanding is broader than his. He tells us a story, but he doesn't understand its meaning, which is fairly clear to us. This disparity between his failure and our success is ironic. Notice the similar irony in "Charles Carville's Eyes":

CHARLES CARVILLE'S EYES*

Edwin Arlington Robinson

A melancholy face Charles Carville had,
But not so melancholy as it seemed,
When once you knew him, for his mouth redeemed
His insufficient eyes, forever sad:
In them there was no life-glimpse, good or bad,
Nor joy nor passion in them ever gleamed;
His mouth was all of him that ever beamed,
His eyes were sorry, but his mouth was glad.

He never was a fellow that said much,
And half of what he did say was not heard
By many of us: we were out of touch
With all his whims and all his theories
Till he was dead, so those blank eyes of his
Might speak them. Then we heard them, every word.

How is Charles Carville like Cliff Klingenhagen? Both men are puzzles, both men are misunderstood. Cliff Klingenhagen drinks

*From *The Children of the Night*, by Edwin Arlington Robinson. New York: Charles Scribner's Sons, 1897.

bitterness but is a happy man; Charles Carville's eyes are sad, but his mouth is happy—he seems melancholy, but not so melancholy as he at first appears. Both are men with whom the speaker and his conventional friends are "out of touch." Both have mysterious sources of consolation and happiness which, because of their own limitations, the narrator and his group are unable to apprehend.

"Charles Carville's Eyes" takes the situation in "Cliff Klingenhagen" a step further: the message comes to the narrator and his friends, but only after Charles Carville is dead; and this is another irony: while Charles Carville is alive, the narrator fails to read the message in his eyes; when he's dead, the narrator does—too late.

Here is a more difficult poem in which the speaker ironically reveals to us his own limitations and inadequacies:

SOLILOQUY OF THE SPANISH CLOISTER[8]

Robert Browning

Gr-r-r—there go, my heart's abhorrence!
    Water your damned flower-pots, do!
If hate killed men, Brother Lawrence,
    God's blood, would not mine kill you!
What? your myrtle-bush wants trimming?
    Oh, that rose has prior claims—
Needs its leaden vase filled brimming?
    Hell dry you up with its flames!

At the meal we sit together:
    Salve tibi![a] I must hear
Wise talk of the kind of weather,
    Sort of season, time of year:
Not a plenteous cork-crop; scarcely
    Dare we hope oak-galls, I doubt;
What's the Latin name for "parsley"?
    What's the Greek name for Swine's Snout?

Whew! We'll have our platter burnished,
    Laid with care on our own shelf!
With a fire-new spoon we're furnished,
    And a goblet for ourself,
Rinsed like something sacrificial
    Ere 'tis fit to touch our chaps

Marked with L for our initial!
    (He-he! There his lily snaps!)

Saint, forsooth! While brown Dolores
    Squats outside the Convent bank
With Sanchicha, telling stories,
    Steeping tresses in the tank,
Blue-black, lustrous, thick like horsehairs
    —Can't I see his dead eye glow,
Bright as 'twere a Barbary corsair's?
    (That is, if he'd let it show!)

When he finishes refection,[b]
    Knife and fork he never lays
Cross-wise, to my recollection,
    As do I, in Jesu's praise.
I the Trinity illustrate,
    Drinking watered orange-pulp—
In three sips the Arian[c] frustrate;
    While he drains his at one gulp.

Oh, those melons! If he's able
    We're to have a feast! so nice!
One goes to the Abbot's table,
    All of us get each a slice.
How go on your flowers? None double?
    Not one fruit-sort can you spy?
Strange!—And I, too, at such trouble
    Keep them close-nipped on the sly!

There's a great text in Galatians,
    Once you trip on it, entails
Twenty-nine distinct damnations,
    One sure, if another fails:
If I trip him just a-dying,
    Sure of heaven as sure can be,
Spin him round and send him flying
    Off to hell, a Manichee?[d]

Or, my scrofulous French novel
    On gray paper with blunt type!
Simply glance at it, you grovel
    Hand and foot in Belial's[e] gripe;[f]

If I double down its pages
At the woeful sixteenth print,
When he gathers his greengages,
Ope a sieve and slip it in 't?

Or, there's Satan!—one might venture
Pledge one's soul to him, yet leave
Such a flaw in the indenture
As he'd miss till, past retrieve,
Blasted lay that rose-acacia
We're so proud of! *Hy, Zy, Hine* . . .ᵍ
'St, there's Vespers! *Plena gratiâ,*
*Ave, Virgo!*ʰ Gr-r-r—you swine!

ᵃ *salve tibi*: hail to thee. The italicized words in this
stanza are imitations of the kind of things Brother
Lawrence might say. ᵇ *refection*: dinner
ᶜ *Arian*: follower of Arius, who denied the Trinity
ᵈ *Manichee*: one who believes the body is evil, the soul good
ᵉ *Belial*: a devil; ᶠ *gripe*: grip ᵍ *Hy* . . .:
imitation of vesper bells? ʰ *Plena* . . .: Hail,
Virgin, full of grace

This poem is a "soliloquy," the inner musings of a man talking
to himself. Who is that man? Where is he? What is his situation?
He is watching Brother Lawrence, the man he hates ("my heart's
abhorrence!"), tending flowers, and he muses about that man.
What is his attitude towards Brother Lawrence? Look at the second stanza: "I must hear / Wise talk . . . ." Why does he call it *wise*?
Obviously he thinks the talk is foolish and trivial; when he uses
wise, he really means foolish. His use of the word illustrates the
heavy-handed irony we call *sarcasm*. Where else is the speaker
sarcastic? Look at the first stanza: "What? your myrtle bush wants
trimming? / Oh, that rose has prior claims— / Needs its leaden vase
filled brimming?" In what tone of voice ought these lines to be
read? A sarcastic, wheedling tone—a tone which shows that the
speaker is only pretending to sympathize with the view he is expressing, and that in reality he despises it. Notice how the tone
changes in the next line: "Hell dry you up with its flames!" No
sarcasm there, but unveiled malice. Sarcasm is malice veiled in
such a way that everyone can see through the veil. Throughout

this poem the tone varies between malice with the veil, and malice without.

What's sarcastic about the third stanza? How do you account for the speaker's use of "we"? Can you read the stanza so as to give the proper sarcastic tone and emphasis to the "we's"? Where else does the speaker use "we"? Does it always have the same effect? What's the sarcasm in the sixth stanza? What is the speaker implying about Brother Lawrence's motives? (The abbot is the superior of the monastery; he will get a whole melon, each of the brothers only a slice.) Where else does the speaker attribute evil motives to Brother Lawrence? Why does he begin the fourth stanza with the phrase "*Saint*, forsooth!"? Apparently others think Brother Lawrence is saintly. The speaker thinks Brother Lawrence is lustful, lecherous. He describes the alluring Dolores and Sanchicha, and imagines Brother Lawrence's eyes brightening like those of a lecherous pirate—"Can't I see his dead eye glow. . . ." But can he? No. "(That is, if he'd let it show!)" Can we be sure that Brother Lawrence is allured by women? Who is allured by women?

We've begun to see that the narrator's attitude towards Brother Lawrence reveals *his own* petty, malicious nature. Where else in the poem do we find similar revelations? The speaker makes it clear in stanza five that he, unlike Brother Lawrence, always makes a cross with his knife and fork in praise of Christ, drinks orange-pulp (instead of wine?) in three sips, to affirm the trinity. He, unlike Brother Lawrence, is really pious. But what do we think of these actions as examples of piety? Don't they demonstrate a limited, narrow, legalistic, petty understanding of piety, akin to the child's understanding of "man's estate" in "Looking Forward" and the speaker's understanding of patriotism in "next to of course god america i"? Notice how gleeful the speaker is in stanza three when the lily snaps. And why can't Brother Lawrence find any double flower, or any flowers that will bear fruit? Because the speaker, on the sly, has kept them "close-nipped." If we haven't got the point that Friar Lawrence is innocent and good-natured, and the speaker evil, the last three stanzas make it clear. The speaker imagines sending Brother Lawrence to hell by getting him, on his deathbed, to misconstrue a difficult passage in Galatians and prove himself a Manichee. That the speaker thinks

Brother Lawrence might be "Sure of heaven as sure can be" is a clue he may not be as evil as the speaker would lead us to believe. The speaker thinks of opening a "scrofulous French novel" (*he* owns it, not Brother Lawrence—who's the lecherous one?) to a particularly alluring page, and slipping it into Brother Lawrence's sieve (perhaps a basket for gathering fruits and flowers). If Brother Lawrence simply glances at it, he'll "grovel / Hand and foot in Belial's gripe." (Who has already read that passage, and has experienced its power?) The speaker goes so far as to express willingness to make a pact with the devil (it will be a clever pact, with a subtly-worded escape clause—"Such a flaw in the indenture"— so that the speaker can get away at the last minute) simply to blast Brother Lawrence's rose-acacia. And what is the effect of the last two lines? It's the time for vespers, the evening service in which one recalls his sins of the past day and asks forgiveness for them. What's the speaker's reaction to the vesper bells? Who, in the last line, is the "swine"? Notice that the speaker intends the word to refer to Brother Lawrence; coming so soon after "Ave, Virgo," the word seems to label the Virgin a swine; and the speaker's use of this word at this moment of religious introspection reveals his petty malice: no one is as swinish as he. Final question: What is the main irony in the poem?

MY LAST DUCHESS[9]

Robert Browning

FERRARA

That's my last Duchess painted on the wall,
Looking as if she were alive. I call
That piece a wonder, now; Frà Pandolf's[a] hands
Worked busily a day, and there she stands.
Will't please you sit and look at her? I said
"Frà Pandolf" by design, for never read
Strangers like you that pictured countenance,
The depth and passion of its earnest glance,
But to myself they turned (since none puts by
The curtain I have drawn for you, but I)
And seemed as they would ask me, if they durst,
How such a glance came there; so, not the first

Are you to turn and ask thus. Sir, 'twas not
Her husband's presence only, called that spot
Of joy into the Duchess' cheek; perhaps
Frà Pandolf chanced to say, "Her mantle laps
Over my lady's wrist too much," or "Paint
Must never hope to reproduce the faint
Half-flush that dies along her throat." Such stuff
Was courtesy, she thought, and cause enough
For calling up that spot of joy. She had
A heart—how shall I say?—too soon made glad,
Too easily impressed; she liked whate'er
She looked on, and her looks went everywhere.
Sir, 'twas all one! My favor at her breast,
The dropping of the daylight in the West,
The bough of cherries some officious fool
Broke in the orchard for her, the white mule
She rode with round the terrace—all and each
Would draw from her alike the approving speech,
Or blush, at least. She thanked men—good! but thanked
Somehow—I know not how—as if she ranked
My gift of a nine-hundred-years-old name
With anybody's gift. Who'd stoop to blame
This sort of trifling? Even had you skill
In speech—which I have not—to make your will
Quite clear to such an one, and say, "Just this
Or that in you disgusts me; here you miss,
Or there exceed the mark"—and if she let
Herself be lessoned so, nor plainly set
Her wits to yours, forsooth, and made excuse—
E'en then would be some stooping; and I choose
Never to stoop. Oh sir, she smiled, no doubt,
Whene'er I passed her; but who passed without
Much the same smile? This grew; I gave commands;
Then all smiles stopped together. There she stands
As if alive. Will't please you rise? We'll meet
The company below, then. I repeat,
The Count your master's known munificence
Is ample warrant that no just pretense
Of mine for dowry will be disallowed;
Though his fair daughter's self, as I avowed

At starting, is my object. Nay, we'll go
Together down, sir. Notice Neptune, though,
Taming a sea-horse, thought a rarity,
Which Claus of Innsbruck cast in bronze for me!

ᵃ *Frà Pandolf*: the imaginary painter of the picture

What is the situation here? Who is the speaker? Where is he?
Whom is he talking to? Why? What has he done? The speaker is
the Duke of Ferrara; he has just opened a curtain before a portrait
of his last (latest, most recent) Duchess (he makes a point of
emphasizing that only he opens that curtain). He uses the occasion
to talk about the character of the woman, and his attitude towards
it. And what was her character? Notice how the Duke begins; on
the Duchess' face is an "earnest glance" of "depth and passion."
Why is the glance there? Not merely because her husband was
present (here's a hint that the Duke feels such glances should be
reserved for husbands), but probably for some trivial reason; perhaps the painter asked her to expose more of her wrist. Why should
she blush at that? It is innocent flattery—the painter is saying that
her wrist is attractive, and ought to be painted. Or the painter
may have said that the flush on her throat was too beautiful to be
painted. Notice the Duke makes the point that "she thought" the
painter's remarks were "courtesy"; evidently he doesn't think so.
What does he think?

The Duke uses these examples to go on to a more general point:
"She had / A heart—how shall I say—too soon made glad, / Too
easily impressed." In the Duke's mind, what's wrong with the
Duchess? She too easily experiences joy and pleasure in the world
around her. Anything can give her pleasure, anything can make
her joyful. What's wrong with that? She doesn't know how to value
things properly; she doesn't see that some things are more important than others. Obviously, the Duke thinks *he* does value
things properly: he can discriminate the important from the trivial.
And what, for the Duke, is important? He gives us one explicit
example: his "nine-hundred-years-old name"—*his* "gift"—is more
important than any other gift. We are beginning to take sides, and

to sense an irony. The values the speaker affirms, we begin to see, are false, and what he condemns, we begin to see, is valuable.

And what did the Duke do? He didn't explain to his wife what was wrong ("Just this / Or that in you disgusts me; here you miss, / Or there exceed the mark") first, because he has no "skill / In speech" (a falsehood—notice how skillfully he designs his remarks), and second, because explaining oneself to one's wife would be stooping, and he chooses not to stoop. Instead, he "gave commands," and his wife died.

The Duke is exposing himself as a proud, ruthless man, and he seems to be doing it almost by design (notice he says he stopped to open the picture "by design"). Why? Who is his audience? We don't find out until the end of the poem (why not till then?) that he's talking to an emissary from a rich Count, and the two are about to arrange a marriage between the Duke and the Count's daughter. (The Duke, of course, professes to be more interested in the "fair daughter's self" than in the dowry. Do we believe him? Why or why not?) Why would the Duke want the Count's emissary to know (presumably he'll pass the information on to the Count) about the fate of his last Duchess? Why might the Duke want it clear from the outset that he is a proud, ruthless man, who will tolerate only certain behavior from his wife? Notice the reference to Neptune taming a sea horse at the end of the poem. How is the idea of "taming" relevant to what came before? How is it relevant to the Duke's future?

In all the poems we have examined so far in this unit the speaker is clearly not the poet; the poet, rather, has created a character who undergoes some struggle, or faces some problem, or has some point to make. And what the speaker says, ironically, reveals crucial limitations, failures, or weaknesses in his own character. The main point to be made in the discussions of the poems that follow is that even in poems where the speaker is ostensibly the poet, the speaker must be seen as a self-contained character who reveals himself to us *completely* through what he says. The character may or may not be a spokesman for the poet; the point is, he *is* a character, and we can find out enough about him by examining the poem carefully to know all we need to know about him. Another poem by E. E. Cummings:

SINCE FEELING IS FIRST*

e. e. cummings

since feeling is first
who pays any attention
to the syntax of things
will never wholly kiss you;

wholly to be a fool
while Spring is in the world

my blood approves,
and kisses are a better fate
than wisdom
lady i swear by all flowers. Don't cry
—the best gesture of my brain is less than
your eyelids' flutter which says

we are for each other: then
laugh, leaning back in my arms
for life's not a paragraph

And death i think is no parenthesis

Who is being addressed in the poem, and for what purpose?
The speaker is addressing a lady, who is in his arms, and he asks
her to laugh and lean back. Apparently she's crying ("Don't cry,"
says the speaker). Why might she be crying? Let's examine the
speaker's argument. The lady should laugh, he says, "for life's not
a paragraph." Notice, here the speaker rejects a metaphor—and
apparently the metaphor characterizes the lady's point of view.
What does it mean? Where are similar metaphors in the poem?
One is "the syntax of things." What is syntax? Syntax refers to the
conventional rules regulating the relations between words. In this
poem the crucial relation is one between a man and a woman.
What is the "syntax" of such a relationship? "Feeling comes first,"
says the poet. He's asking the lady to give way to her feelings.
What else is he asking? That she be a fool *for "spring is* in the
world," that she surrender wisdom and give kisses. Now, why

might the lady be crying? What does the speaker mean when he says "for life's not a paragraph"? And what does he mean when he adds, "And death i think is no parenthesis"?

In this poem the speaker is urging the lady to make love to him, and his argument, ineptly paraphrased, is that there's something more urgent, something more basic than the conventions that regulate our lives; feeling comes first, and to be faithful to our blood, to the spring within us, and to meet really and truly, we must forget about the rules and regulations; besides, tomorrow we die: and death is an ending—a period, not a parenthesis. But notice the irony in the metaphors: the speaker works against the author. The author is a poet, a man who must always pay attention to the syntax of things (even if he does so by violating it skillfully, as Cummings does here); a poet formulates the world in paragraphs, and translates feelings into words. The speaker, on the other hand, attacks syntax, wisdom, paragraphs, words, gestures of the brain (and "gesture of my brain" might be a good definition for a poem). Ironically, this is a poem against poetry, and in order to gauge its full effect we must distinguish author from speaker, and see the speaker as a witty gesture of the author's brain.

LOVE[10]

George Herbert

Love bade me welcome: yet my soul drew back,
    Guilty of dust and sin.
But quick-eyed Love, observing me grow slack
    From my first entrance in,
Drew nearer to me, sweetly questioning
    If I lacked anything.

"A guest," I answered, "worthy to be here":
    Love said, "You shall be he."
"I, the unkind, ungrateful? Ah, my dear,
    I cannot look on thee."
Love took my hand, and smiling did reply,
    "Who made the eyes but I?"

"Truth, Lord; but I have marred them; let my shame
    Go where it doth deserve."

"And know you not," says Love, "who bore the blame?"
"My dear, then I will serve."
"You must sit down," says Love, "and taste My meat."
So I did sit and eat.

What is the situation here? Who is speaking, under what circumstances, and to whom? The speaker is a guest, invited to have a meal with Love; the two of them engage in a mild argument, which Love wins. What kind of host does Love prove himself to be? He takes charge from the very beginning; the speaker, "Guilty of dust and sin," feels himself to be an unworthy guest; he draws back without saying anything, but "quick-eyed Love" perceives his discomfort, and graciously asks if he "lacked anything." A good host, of course, should be solicitous in this way, and should minister to his guest's needs before his guest expresses them in words. The speaker, at Love's gentle behest, expresses his unworthiness, and the argument ensues. Why does Love say "Who made the eyes but I"? Why does the speaker address him as "Lord"? What is the answer to Love's question "who bore the blame"? Who is Love, and what is this poem really about? Love is God, and the speaker is the unworthy soul aware of its unworthiness. In short, this is a *metaphorical situation* in which the author creates two characters. The "I" in the poem may be a spokesman for the author, or one side of the author's character; but it could be any guilty and contrite soul—it could speak for all of us. And this more general meaning is the crucial one.

In the last stanza Love talks the speaker into staying, but the speaker wants to stay as a *servant* rather than as a guest: "My dear, then I will serve." Nonsense, says Love, sit down and eat— and the speaker does. Why is it appropriate to see God as Love, and Love as a kindly host who insists on serving a reluctant guest? How does this metaphorical situation help us understand the meaning of God's love?

In the two preceding poems it is fairly easy to distinguish speaker from author; now let's examine some poems in which such a distinction is more difficult to make. In each the problem is to define the situation of the speaker, and the emotional and intellectual resources he brings to bear on it.

I SHALL KNOW WHY, WHEN TIME IS OVER*

Emily Dickinson

I shall know why, when Time is over
And I have ceased to wonder why;
Christ will explain each separate anguish
In the fair schoolroom of the sky.

He will tell me what Peter promised,
And I, for wonder at his woe,
I shall forget the drop of Anguish
That scalds me now—that scalds me now!

What is the irony in this poem? What is the speaker's problem?
The speaker is being "scalded" by a "drop of anguish"; she (he?—
we can't be sure) is suffering. But is this suffering really a problem
for her? Apparently not: "I shall know why," she confidently
affirms. What will she know? Probably why she suffers her present
anguish. Christ will explain, and she, wondering at Christ's woe—
probably his anguish and suffering on the cross—will "forget" her
tiny drop of anguish. Apparently the speaker is confident that there
is a reason for her present suffering, and that everything will turn
out satisfactorily in the end.

But can we be entirely sure that she is *really* confident? She will
know why when time is over, but what is the effect of the second
line: "And I have ceased to wonder why"? Isn't knowing why then
too late? What good does it do to know when one has ceased to
wonder? Notice the metaphor "the fair schoolroom of the sky."
What is its effect? Who do you know who might speak in such
metaphors? Isn't it terribly conventional, terribly "cute"? Isn't the
speaker, in using it, echoing a conventional, unsatisfactory, unthinking religious view of life (couldn't you imagine the speaker
in Cummings' "next to of course god america i" using such language?)? The metaphor seems to be an ironic one. What's the
other metaphor in the poem? Doesn't "the drop of Anguish / That

scalds me now" seem to be a more intense and forceful metaphor than "fair schoolroom of the sky"? And why repeat "that scalds me now"? Isn't there a strong hint that nothing can explain away the present suffering, that anguish scalds like boiling water, and that the pain of the scalding (and scalding leaves scars) can't be justified by any conventionally religious view of the meaning of suffering?

There are two meanings then: the poem can be seen as a confident affirmation of faith, or as an ironic expression of profound doubt. One can read the poem aloud to convey either effect, and students might be asked to practice it both ways. Which one is correct? The answer is that one can't tell; a sound case can be made for either interpretation. And in poetry, when we discover something that can be interpreted in two equally valid but contradictory ways, we call the effect *ambiguity*. This poem is an *ambiguous* poem. Is it therefore a bad poem? Is it unclear, uninteresting, invalid because it is ambiguous? Or does the ambiguity intensify its effect, and make it all the more valid and interesting?

HOLY SONNET VII[11]

John Donne

At the round earth's imagined corners,* blow
Your trumpets, angels; and arise, arise
From death, you numberless infinities
Of souls, and to your scattered bodies go;
All whom the flood did, the fire shall o'erthrow,
All whom war, dearth, age, agues, tyrannies,
Despair, law, chance hath slain, and you whose eyes
Shall behold God, and never taste death's woe.†
But let them sleep, Lord, and me mourn a space;
For, if above all these, my sins abound,
'Tis late to ask abundance of Thy grace

* Donne is probably thinking of maps, which often have cupids or angels in the corners.

† *You whose eyes shall behold God, and never taste death's woe*: certain virtuous men may go directly to heaven without tasting death ("Truly, I say to you, there are some standing here who will not taste death before they see the Son of man coming in his kingdom." *Matthew* 16:28).

When we are there. Here on this lowly ground,
Teach me how to repent; for that's as good
As if Thou hadst sealed my pardon with Thy blood.

The poem has two clear parts (the first eight lines and the last six lines), and the question is: What happens to the speaker between them? With what tone of voice ought one to read the first eight lines? The first eight lines consist of a series of commands, and ought to be read in a commensurate tone—perhaps even a slightly pompous tone. Why? The speaker is commanding the angels to blow their trumpets, and all men, the living and the dead, to appear (the souls, freed at death, will reunite with their bodies). What is the speaker calling for? He's calling for judgment day. And why might a man do that? What will happen on judgment day? Apparently the speaker is confident that his fate is assured. He is prepared to meet his God. But is he?

The last six lines show that he isn't. He is aware that his sins might abound "above all these." Why might he realize his sinfulness? What sins might he have committed? Are there any hints in the poem? Look again at the first eight lines. What do we think of a man who commands judgment day to appear? Who ought to give that command? What do we think of a man who is confident that he is sinless, and prepared to meet his God? Isn't he giving God's command, and judging *himself* as if he were his own God? And isn't making yourself your own God the greatest of all sins (notice the first of the ten commandments is "Thou shalt have no other gods before Me")?

Notice the important changes in the last six lines. The speaker now addresses God. And his imperatives are more gentle, more like supplications than commands ("let them sleep, Lord . . . Teach me how to repent . . ."). We see that he is already beginning to repent, that "Here on this lowly ground" he is beginning to earn the salvation which, in the first eight lines, he was sinfully confident of receiving in heaven. What are the ironies in this poem?

In Donne's "Holy Sonnet VII" we see the speaker undergoing an important change. He develops—increases in awareness—as the poem progresses. Notice the many changes the speaker undergoes in Wordsworth's "Surprised by Joy—Impatient as the Wind":

"SURPRISED BY JOY—IMPATIENT AS THE WIND"[12]
William Wordsworth

Surprised by joy—impatient as the Wind
I turned to share the transport—Oh! with whom
But thee, deep buried in the silent tomb,
That spot which no vicissitude can find?
Love, faithful love, recalled thee to my mind—
But how could I forget thee? Through what power
Even for the least division of an hour,
Have I been so beguiled as to be blind
To my most grievous loss!—That thought's return
Was the worst pang that sorrow ever bore,
Save one, one only, when I stood forlorn,
Knowing my heart's best treasure was no more;
That neither present time, nor years unborn
Could to my sight that heavenly face restore.

The speaker begins by telling us that he was "Surprised by joy," and we might think the poem will be about a joyful surprise. But there is a different surprise in store both for speaker and reader: the speaker is surprised, ironically, in the midst of his joy by grief —by a "worst pang," the antithesis of joy. What is the surprise? First he is surprised that the person he expected to be there when he turned to share his "transport" is not there. What else surprises the speaker? Isn't he also surprised by himself? How could he be "so beguiled as to be blind / To my most grievous loss"? And what beguiled him? Joy. Ironically, joy turns to grief, a moment of joyful surprise to a moment of painful recollection and recognition of guilt. "Love, *faithful* love" made him remember—but how strong and faithful could that love be if he forgot his loss, even for a moment? And the pain that arises from his recognition of his forgetfulness of his loss is "the worst pang that sorrow ever bore"— exceeded only by the original sorrow caused by the loss itself. He stands now *doubly* "forlorn"—he's lost not only someone he loved, but something in himself as well.

What does the line "That spot which no vicissitude can find" mean? What are vicissitudes? To what extent is the speaker himself "found" by vicissitudes? What painful vicissitudes are expressed in this poem? Does our not knowing who the dead person is detract from the effect of this poem? How much *do* we know about the dead person on the basis of the poem? What kinds of things do we know? Students should be led to see that the relationship of intimacy, faithfulness, and affection between the speaker and the dead person are clearly revealed, and that we need know no more.

Here is a final poem in which we see a speaker talking about the vicissitudes of life, and going through certain ironic changes as the poem progresses:

TO AN UNBORN PAUPER CHILD[*]

Thomas Hardy

I

Breathe not, hid Heart: cease silently,
And though thy birth-hour beckons thee,
　　Sleep the long sleep:
　　The Doomsters heap
Travails and teens[a] around us here,
And Time-wraiths turn our songsingings to fear.

II

Hark, how the peoples surge and sigh,
And laughters fail, and greetings die:
　　Hopes dwindle; yea,
　　Faiths waste away,
Affections and enthusiasms numb;
Thou canst not mend these things if thou dost come.

III

Had I the ear of wombed souls
Ere Their terrestrial chart unrolls,
　　And thou wert free
　　To cease, or be,
Then would I tell thee all I know,
And put it to thee: Wilt thou take Life so?

IV

Vain vow! No hint of mine may hence
To theeward fly: to thy locked sense

[*] From *Collected Poems of Thomas Hardy*. London: Macmillan & Co,. Ltd., 1930. Reprinted by permission.

Explain none can
Life's pending plan:
Thou wilt thy ignorant entry make
Though skies spout fire and blood and nations quake.

v

Fain would I, dear, find some shut plot
Of earth's wide wold for thee, where not
One tear, one qualm,
Should break the calm.
But I am weak as thou and bare;
No man can change the common lot to rare.

vi

Must come and bide. And such are we—
Unreasoning, sanguine, visionary—
That I can hope
Health, love, friends, scope
In full for thee; can dream thou'lt find
Joys seldom yet attained by humankind!

ª *teens*: sorrows

The speaker here is a man addressing an unborn pauper child, explaining what life is like ("Wilt thou take Life so?"). Life, he says, is full of vicissitude—but what kinds of vicissitude? What does he mean by "Doomsters"? by "Time-wraiths"? Why does he choose those words? What relationship do you see between the verbs in the second stanza ("surge and sigh," "fail," "die," "dwindle," "waste away," "numb")? Isn't he painting an excessively bleak picture of life? Certainly things are always changing, but aren't some hopes fulfilled; doesn't faith sometimes grow stronger? Isn't this an unwarrantedly negative view of things? Isn't there something hopeful?

Let's consider the character of the speaker. What sort of man is he? What is his attitude towards the unborn child? Notice the affection and compassion in the fifth stanza: what is it there that reveals his affection and compassion? He seems to be powerless—is he? What does he hope to do for the child? Does any man have that kind of power? What irony do you find in the last stanza? What do "unreasoning, sanguine, visionary" mean? Are they good traits or bad? How does the poem make us see that they are neither wholly good nor wholly bad? Does the speaker set himself apart from the people who share these traits, or does he identify himself with "humankind"? What does he wish for the child in the last stanza (what does "scope" mean?)? Why does he wish it? (Because he, like all men, is unreasoning, sanguine, visionary.) Isn't it ironic that he does something which he himself mildly condemns? And don't we share his hopeful compassion, despite our knowledge that the cards are stacked against a pauper child? Now, is this merely a bleak, negative poem? What would the world be like if we were all like the speaker here—if we all acted on the basis of the compassion which he displays, and which he has aroused in us? Finally, how many examples of tortured, grotesque use of language can you find in this poem? What makes the examples seem tortured and grotesque? Can you see any relationship between these qualities in the language and the speaker's attitudes?

SUMMARY

As a result of these three sequences, where has the student arrived, and what is he prepared to do next?

The student has learned how to read poems carefully and thoroughly, word by word, phrase by phrase, sentence by sentence. He has learned that poetry can appeal directly and immediately to the common humanity in us all, but that one's awareness of the force, the value, the interest in that appeal is a product not only of the skill of the poem, but also of one's own exertion of energy in reading it. He has learned something that is true of any unified human statement: that it results from choice, that it is made to the exclusion of all other possible statements. He has learned how to apprehend and talk about, in the language of normal intelligent human discourse, two important aspects of poetry: its use of comparisons, and the ironic effects that it sometimes produces.

What next? At least three kinds of study might appropriately follow:

1. The kinds of study that focus on the special effects of poetry— the examination of formal, technical, prosodic aspects of poetry; figures of speech; various kinds of poetic style; and so on. One

might, for example, spend some time on sonnets—define them prosodically, differentiate between different sorts of sonnets, discuss the kinds of subject matter which have been traditionally associated with the sonnet form, deal with the historical development of the sonnet. Studies falling under this general category would introduce students to more of the specialized vocabulary of criticism.

2. Evaluative studies. Little attention has been paid in these sequences to what makes a poem good, and to how poems fail. One might, at this point, appropriately go on to contrast good poems with bad poems, in order to develop in students a sense of critical discrimination.

3. The kinds of studies which emphasize similarities between poems, instead of poems as individual entities. One might study a group of poems by a single author, the poetry of a given historical period, or the development of a genre.

Whatever happens next, if the student going through the tenth, eleventh, and twelfth grade sequences has learned how to read individual poems intelligently, he will be well prepared to undertake any number of more complex projects.

NOTES

1. For critical discussion of "Sir Patrick Spens," see Hazard Adams, *The Contexts of Poetry* (Boston and Toronto: Little, Brown and Company, 1963), pp. 23–28; Charles B. Wheeler, *The Design of Poetry* (New York: W. W. Norton and Company, 1966), pp. 280–87.

2. For critical discussion of "Spring and Fall," see Jerome Beaty and William Matchett, *Poetry: From Statement of Meaning* (New York: Oxford University Press, 1965), pp. 62–65; Elizabeth Drew, *Poetry: A Modern Guide to Its Understanding and Enjoyment* (New York: Dell Publishing Company, 1959), pp. 107–109; *Modern Poetry in the Classroom* (Champaign, Ill.: National Council of Teachers of English, 1959–62), pp. 46–49; I. A. Richards, *Practical Criticism: A Study of Literary Judgment* (New York: Harcourt, Brace and Co., 1929), pp. 77–87.

3. For critical discussion of "Spring," see Francis X. Connolly, *Poetry: Its Power and Wisdom: An Introductory Study* (New York: Charles Scribner's Sons, 1960), pp. 38–40.

4. Cortez was an explorer, a discoverer, a conqueror, but not the

man who discovered the Pacific (it was Balboa). Apparently Keats got the two men confused.

5. For critical discussion of "Holy Sonnet XIV," see Drew, pp. 58–60.

6. For critical discussion of "Tears, Idle Tears," see Cleanth Brooks, *The Well Wrought Urn: Studies in the Structure of Poetry* (New York: Harcourt, Brace and Co., 1947), pp. 167–77.

7. For critical discussion of "next to of course god . . . ," see Norman Friedman and Charles A. McLaughlin, *Poetry: An Introduction to Its Form and Art*, Revised Edition (New York: Harper and Row, 1963), pp. 96–97.

8. For critical discussion of "Soliloquy of the Spanish Cloister" see Adams, pp. 152–54.

9. For critical discussion of "My Last Duchess," see ibid., pp. 145–48; and Beaty and Matchett, pp. 85–90.

10. For critical discussion of "Love," see Reuben Arthur Brower, *The Fields of Light: An Experiment in Critical Reading* (New York: Oxford University Press, 1962), pp. 28–30.

11. For critical discussion of "At the Round Earth's Imagined Corners," see ibid. pp. 66–70; and Richards, pp. 40–48.

12. For critical discussion of "Surprised by Joy . . . ," see Brower, Chapter V.

Part II
SHORT STORY

▨▨▨

Professor Kenneth Johnston's sequence on the short story has two
guiding principles of organization. In the first place he selects his
stories by national origin, with American stories in grade ten,
English in grade eleven, and translations from Continental literature in grade twelve. He then presents a second principle based
on this division, arguing that the American stories may be most
profitably approached in terms of their setting, that the English
stories demonstrate clearly character's point of view, and that the
Continental stories are fruitful sources for examining the use of
symbolism. This is not to say, of course, that these allocations are
absolute and that no American story ever achieves major effects by
symbolism or character, or that English stories never are concerned with setting, or that point of view can never be examined
in a Continental story.

Professor Johnston's approach is worth pausing over, not only
because it describes his methods in this particular sequence, but
also because it exemplifies one kind of pedagogical strategy. (Anyone reading many or all the units in this series will rapidly recognize that many different classroom styles are reflected, with the
only common element the presumption of successful accomplish-
ment.) Although the emphasis throughout this volume is on the
analysis of individual literary works, the sequences also present
problems of arrangement of an entire course. What does a teacher
do when confronted with planning a semester course? Many

teachers have resorted to such unliterary devices as arrangement by subject matter (stories about outdoor adventure, for example). Arrangements of the sort represented by Professor Johnston's are much more viable, since they are founded on literary principles.

Teaching the Short Story
in Grades Ten Through Twelve

KENNETH R. JOHNSTON

Assistant Professor of English
Indiana University

A double principle of organization informs this series of short story explications. The stories are grouped by "national origin" (American in grade ten, English in grade eleven, and Continental translations in grade twelve); and different aspects of narrative technique are emphasized in each grade (scene or setting in ten; the character's point of view in eleven; and parable, allegory, and symbolism in twelve). The combination of these two principles is somewhat arbitrary, but the principles themselves are sound and their arrangement is gauged to counteract the highly arbitrary, unhelpful, and widespread publishing practice of grouping stories according to their real or imagined congruity of subject matter. Teaching literature, at whatever level, is primarily teaching how to read, not what to read. Literary criticism and intellectual conversation may revolve around *what* is important or worthwhile, but the student will have nothing intelligent to contribute or learn unless he has first learned *how*.

Setting. Character's viewpoint. Symbolism. With the mention of these and other of the familiar categories of the analysis of fiction, a certain rigidity sets in, especially among teachers. Most unfortunate is our tendency to put the analytical categories before our experience of the story. We must always keep the story first, using the simple but central questions: Did you like it? Why? Why not? What did it make you think of? What was it about? (The last question usually marks the transition from informal to formal response.) The categories control us and confuse the student if we apply all of them, at random, to every story we assign: What is the plot? What actions occur? What change do they effect? Are the characters realistic or not? What symbols are evident? And so on. This is like diagraming sentences without knowing what our aim is.

Instead, the method here is to present stories that can conveniently be understood by focusing, at least to begin with, on a single aspect of narration, the intention being that as a student learns to pay close attention to successive aspects of narrative craft he will eventually be alert to all. My ordering of the three aspects (setting, point of view, symbolism) is largely gratuitous, as would be any suggestion that other approaches are not possible or necessary to the stories selected for each grade.

An additional presumption I have made is that the bolder strokes of short story art—action, plot, characterization—will have been emphasized in junior high school, along lines suggested by Mary Alice Burgan in her essay, "Action and Narration: An Approach to the Drama and the Short Story."* Setting, character's viewpoint, and symbolism are relatively static entities which require somewhat more maturity to be appreciated, though this is not to say that the stories herein are static—or mature.

Finally, an implicit judgment about the nature of American, British, and Continental fiction has been made in the present sequence—namely, the paramount importance of "the American scene" in American fiction, of the intense interiorization of experience in modern British fiction, and of the skill with which the European mind has expressed itself in symbolic interpretations of its experience. This rationale has a *prima facie* persuasiveness which is elaborated in each section, but no more. Far from being exclusive, it is intended to raise questions, at least in the teacher's mind, which will suggest fruitful ways of comparing similar techniques in fictions of different national traditions—as, for example, the pervasive symbolic aspect of Hawthorne's settings and Lawrence's characterizations.

* This essay is included in *Teaching Literature in Grades Seven Through Nine*, a volume in this English Curriculum Study Series.

A note on study questions: The questions are primarily intended for students, and they are based primarily on the discussion which immediately precedes them. However, to conserve space I have assumed that teachers will readily phrase in question form any points made in my discussions which he deems valuable. This assumption has left me free to include questions and suggestions which are directed to the teacher, questions which point toward different treatments of a story from that undertaken in the explication, and questions which I can't answer, though I know they are important and will yield worthwhile results to the right teacher.

Short Stories for Grade Ten

The five stories considered in this section follow a progression from colonial to modern, urban America. Beyond what is merely historical orderliness in this arrangement, I have tried by it to draw attention to the central importance of setting—place, or land, or frontier—that we have all been taught to recognize in American literature. The historical dimension is not, however, a necessary or paramount dimension for teaching the stories. What the students should learn, primarily, is to pay attention to the many ways in which writers build meaning into their scenery. This is by no means a particularly American technique, yet one may offer as a minimal working generalization the idea that it is more peculiar to American literature than to some other national literatures. One of the technical aims of the section is to disabuse students of the notion that a story's setting is "mere description." Often a story's surroundings are tame in reference to the action that occurs in them, but high school sophomores are mature enough to begin to appreciate the ways in which action is given dimension (that is, meaning) by the background which defines it.

The short story takes a highly individual focus on its main character, and in America our individuality has characteristically been that sense of newness or *self*-creation available to man in a new world. Thus in all of these stories a character is asked to prove himself, to come to maturity, in new or different surroundings, and his actions are in large part determined by the setting or by his expectation and interpretation of it. This is no less true of Hawthorne's Robin Molineux than of Francis Weed in "The Country Husband," by John Cheever. Even though the emphasis of American fiction has, during the last thirty or forty years, begun to shift from the individual's potential in a new scene to his helplessness in an aging one, the emphasis on setting remains constant. This is not to say that our earlier fiction espouses rugged individualism. The rugged individual is our American myth, but artists' visions of "the American Adam" have consistently pointed to the ambiguities and tragic flaws that are inherent in the creation of a self-made man. Such ambiguity is perhaps the central theme of "My Kinsman, Major Molineux."*

MY KINSMAN, MAJOR MOLINEUX
by Nathaniel Hawthorne

The arresting question about Hawthorne's "My Kinsman, Major Molineux" is, of course, what to make of the shockingly comic scene at the end. But the dominant impression before the final shock is of the story's unusual setting, and a teacher might do well to forestall the inevitably lively discussion about Robin's laughter by leading the class with Robin through his confusing evening up to the moment when all becomes clear and he laughs, not least of all, with relief.

As with most fiction over a hundred years old, certain historical factors require explanation, and this is particularly true of Hawthorne, for he is interpreting events "not far from a hundred years ago," which is to say more than two hundred years ago. One might adopt it as a rule, to explain the first paragraphs of all Hawthorne's

---

* This approach to American literature, though by now traditional, need not be taken as orthodox. For a thoughtful analysis of the ways in which American literature has not reflected but rather rejected its immediate milieu, the teacher is encouraged to consider arguments like Richard Poirier's in *A World Elsewhere* (New York: Oxford University Press, 1966). These differences of critical approach are not so far removed from the tenth grade as they might seem to be at first, for sophomores will certainly feel and perhaps resist the heightened archaism of, for example, Hawthorne's story, and their response to the author's style might lead a good teacher with a good class to consider how the story is not set in colonial New England but precisely, by its heightened unreality, in "a world elsewhere." Indeed, the entire unit envisaged by these stories could be treated from the point of view of style. With the exception of Steinbeck, and with the judicious addition of Faulkner, teachers will find themselves with a unit which, despite its diversity, is pervaded by stylistic devices that create one of American literature's classic tones, that of preposterously overstated humor.

stories, word for word, to all classes below the second year of college (see, for example, the introductory essay, "The Old Counting-House," in *The Scarlet Letter*). Once the students understand the political setting of the story and have linked it in their minds with revolutionary acts like the Boston Tea Party, they should be able to discuss intelligently the way Hawthorne sets his scenes to make his final scene at once plausible and shocking.

To create a scene that will reflect as well as abet the ignorance and growing confusion of his young hero, Hawthorne utilizes moonlight, that tried and true element of melodrama: "the ferryman lifted a lantern, by the aid of which, and the newly risen moon, he took a very accurate survey of the stranger's figure." Robin moves through the story in this dusky, indefinite light, not quite night, not quite day. Readers used to electricity and the idea that a town is dark only very late at night will be struck by the extraordinary number of people walking about in the dark, particularly the promenades of the "many gay and gallant figures" in the most prosperous (most Tory) part of town. The oddity of the effect is only anachronistic, but it is an anachronism that works to reinforce Hawthorne's intentions. Hawthorne is quite aware that his setting is weird, and he seems to laugh at his own staginess when he admits the moon itself as a "character" into the final scene: "The Man in the Moon heard the far bellow. 'Oho,' quoth he, 'the old earth is frolicsome tonight!' " The melodrama, however, is quite under control.

First of all, we notice that whenever Robin poses his question, "whereabouts is the dwelling of my kinsman, Major Molineux?" a momentarily brighter light falls upon the scene as though illumination is forthcoming—the light from the barber shop, the tavern's public room, the young prostitute's hallway, the droning watchman's lantern. But instead of being enlightened, he is laughed at, and with each rebuff he is thrust out of the circle of brighter light to continue his moonlight quest. (Laughter, or noise and silence in general, are the oral counterparts to the visual elements of the setting.) When illumination ultimately comes, literally and figuratively, it is again accompanied by laughter, so that our reflection that in some sense the laughter *is* the illumination—that Robin grows toward maturity by laughing at his victimized kinsman—is one of the most profound ways in which Hawthorne's setting is inseparable from his meaning. This paradox is the difficult point of the story, and Hawthorne acknowledges and underscores the difficulty when the brightest illumination in the story—the torches of the demonstrators—becomes a momentary obstruction to Robin's clear vision and understanding: "the unsteady brightness of the latter formed a veil which he could not penetrate." The obstruction is but the final prelude to vision: immediately the cart stands uncovered, and "there the torches blazed the brightest, there the moon shone out like day, and there, in tar-and-feather dignity, sat his kinsman, Major Molineux!" One notes that the moonlight, hitherto not much help to Robin, has here joined the lights provided by the townspeople to make things clear at last.

Much of this kind of detail will prove satisfying to students when they can pursue it themselves. Nevertheless, the teacher will be aware that so far Hawthorne's setting has been analyzed largely as clever staging and lighting, and that a full answer has not been given to the question: What does it *mean* that the laughter is paradoxically the illumination? More than physical light or darkness, more than Robin's confusion or understanding, the setting, as manipulated by Hawthorne, raises the question of appearance and reality which, at the highest level of generalization, is the question ambiguously answered by the story. The major is a heroic, if pathetically defeated, character; the mob, though flushed with victory and laughing enthusiasm, is clearly presented as under demonic influence. If the "moral" of the story is that we must stand on our own two feet and not expect help in making our way in this life, it is a moral severely qualified by the suggestion that we "make our way" in community with cruel and sordid fellows and that the outside help we sometimes hope for (our Major Molineuxs) is at once quite above our deserts and fiercely resented by that community in which we hope to succeed. Whatever we take to be the "good" in this story, the Major's proud aristocratic demeanor or Robin's awareness of the diminished worth of his "shrewdness," both are presented as ambiguous realities—or, to emphasize the paradox again, ambiguous appearances.

The setting points to the discrepancy between appearance and reality in the scene at the corner of the church. Much of this otherwise extraneous and lengthy scene becomes clear when we look closely to see what Hawthorne is doing, and why. The author is intent upon setting almost to the exclusion of every other kind of meaning; words like "scene" and "place" occur half a dozen times in the four long paragraphs devoted to it. What the teacher might notice, though the student need not, is that Hawthorne's first description of the street on which the church stands is a close paraphrase of Coleridge's language in the *Biographia Literaria* when he describes how he and Wordsworth agreed, respectively, to attempt to make the familiar appear strange and the strange familiar: "The sudden charm which . . . Moonlight or sunset diffused over a known and familiar landscape, appeared to represent the practicability of combining both." Thus Hawthorne: "the moon, creating, like the imaginative power, a beautiful strangeness in familiar objects, gave something of romance to a scene that might not have possessed it in the light of day." Hawthorne's submerged allusion to the great Romantic exploration of what is real and what is illusory gives us confidence for drawing our students' attention to his description of the interior of the church. They need not understand the implications of what Robin sees any better than Robin himself, but they should at least realize that the scene is not mere spookiness. Speaking of the solitary moonbeam which "had dared to rest upon the open page of the great Bible," Hawthorne offers two conjectures:

> Had nature, in that deep hour, become a worshipper in the house which man had builded? Or was that heavenly light the visible sanctity of the place,—visible because no earthly and impure feet were within the walls?

These are two profound alternatives and their profundity can be made a function of the meaning of the hilarious final scene.

We must not skip too quickly over the phrase, "which man had builded." Not God, but man. In either alternative there is present the suggestion that man is something that neither nature nor heaven can be immediately related to; they are pure, but he is impure. Or, one may read the first alternative more in man's favor, less in nature's. I think the context denies this, but in either interpretation we remain with the paramount Romantic question of the relation of man, nature, and God. Not to take our sophomores any further afield, we may simply suggest that the question as to man's purity is certainly the question raised by the final scene.

These metaphysical flights, our students might rightly object, are the teacher's not Robin's; yet when we return to the text we find that the scene inside the church immediately gives rise to another scene: Robin's imagination of family devotions at his country home. However, this scene, which he lovingly reconstructs to recall "his thoughts from this uncomfortable . . . evening of ambiguity and weariness," ends by deepening rather than alleviating his confusion, so that he cries, "Am I here, or there?" "But still his mind kept vibrating between fancy and reality," and he imagines himself in the city and in the forest by turns. Robin's confusion in the city has at this point moved from physical to a metaphysical level, and the unreality of every *place* prepares us for the unreality of every moral value in the story's final scene. The homely scene which Robin imagines is, unlike the dream world in which he finds himself, clearly illuminated at its crucial point of meaning: "the good man [his father] in the midst, [held] the Scriptures in the golden light that fell from the western clouds." But when he attempts to rejoin the family, he finds himself barred: "the latch tinkled into its place, and he was excluded from his home." Probably most students will respond to this final detail as Robin's mind's indication that he is dreaming, but the many interpreters of this story who emphasize its psychological aspects are certainly justified by Hawthorne's firmly declarative diction (for example, "excluded") to see in it either Robin's feeling that he has been cast out or more simply his realization that he *is* on his own—thus prefiguring the story's conclusion.*

As to the setting, it has now been seen to be the vehicle of whatever meaning the reader will ultimately assign to the questions

---

* A thorough psychoanalytic criticism of the story is Simon Lesser's chapter, "Conscious and Unconscious Perception," in his book, *Fiction and the Unconscious* (Boston: Beacon Press, 1957). An answer to Mr. Lesser is provided by Roy Harvey Pearce, "Robin Molineux on the Analyst's Couch: A Note on the Limits of Psychoanalytic Criticism," in *Criticism: A Quarterly for Literature and the Arts*, Vol. I, No. 2 (Spring, 1959), 83-90. Both articles are reprinted in the convenient paperback, *Psychoanalysis and American Fiction*, ed. Irving Malin (New York: Dutton, 1965).

raised. " 'Am I here, or there?' cried Robin." Is home home, or not? And if I am here, what is home? With the dissolution of his ties with the Major, Robin has had severed the last of those special ties which we jealously guard to protect our relationship with the world. Whether they are real or not, whether Robin's joining in on the laughter is a good thing or not, whether indeed the "moral" of the story is that we must stand on our own two feet—these are questions that the story leads us to explore, but it provides no pat answers.

It may be objected that approaching "My Kinsman, Major Molineux" primarily through Hawthorne's techniques of scene construction is a rather specialized approach, and I grant it. I point to a further objection, namely that attention to setting in Hawthorne leads us very quickly into the symbolic dimension of his scenes, and indeed to scenes that are almost purely symbolic. But these objections are all to the good, since they keep us from strictly categorical responses to stories and encourage the development of reading flexibility. Perhaps one might do well to preface such an approach as this with a more orthodox discussion, probably the always attractive consideration of the young man away from home for the first time. But attention paid to the story's setting is nevertheless attention directed toward the dominant response that students reading the story for the first time will make to its confused, moonlit scene.

STUDY QUESTIONS

1. Why does Hawthorne have Robin visit so many different sections of the town? In which section does he *not* ask his question or receive any answers? Why not?

2. Trace the word *shrewdness* through the story. With what shades of meaning or tone is it used?

3. What is happening in the town on the night Robin arrives?

4. Why does Hawthorne bring his hero to town at night? Why not on a pitch dark night?

5. How does Hawthorne remind Robin, and the reader, of everything that has happened to him that night? How does this reminder help to make Robin's laughter plausible?

6. The most difficult question: Why does Robin laugh?

THE BLUE HOTEL
by Stephen Crane

Although it is clear from the title on that Stephen Crane means to emphasize setting in "The Blue Hotel," it may be questioned whether he is as successful as Hawthorne in linking setting and meaning. That he probably is not is less a criticism than an entrée to the observation that his technique in creating scene is different from Hawthorne's, and that a different approach to meaning is indicated thereby. To be specific, though several settings are fraught with significance (the startling Palace Hotel itself, the smallish room inside its palatial portals, the saloon bar, and the dazzling winter landscape of Nebraska) the most important scene in the story is an imaginary one: the Wild West barroom existing in the Swede's expectations. This is the setting that not only contains but motivates the story's major action.

In the Palace Hotel, run (by a man whose behavior defines the meaning of proprietor) along domestic lines (Scully's wife and daughters are its staff) with family pride and tenderness (the successful lawyer son and the lamented dead daughter) and with whisky hid circumspectly under the bed, the Swede imagines a Wild West scene and hysterically expects to be ruthlessly murdered at every juncture. The saloon to which he retires in victory is hardly wilder than the blue hotel. The coming progress of civilization—electric streetcars and street lights—is exemplified by the domestication of the Western gambler into a man of "quiet dignity" with "exemplary home life," though he is still engagingly admitted to be a "thieving card-player." Nevertheless, the saloon *is* the vestige of the Wild West, as the blue hotel is a new prototype of the East. Here are bar, whisky, and gambler. Yet in this setting, far from expecting murder, the Swede comes in demanding sociability and small talk, precisely the virtues of Scully's front room. There, sociability and small talk would have stood him in good stead for all their extremity (witness Scully's determined bonhomie), but in the saloon they are his undoing. The Swede, who came to Nebraska expecting to find it both Wild and West, has come a decade or more too late, but from the very strength of his expectations he creates the Wild West and, as he expected, he is killed. ("The Bride Comes to Yellow Sky" is another story in which Crane juxtaposes the Wild West and the real West with withering comedy.)

But how does this imaginary scene relate to the real scenes which Crane evokes? What of the amazing blue hotel, the terrific winter landscape? Or the small front room of the hotel and the conventionally tawdry barroom? One suspects that Crane evokes the grotesque appearance of the hotel only to undercut its significance by the action of the story. A laughable horror to Easterners passing through Fort Romper, for whom it has "no colour in common," the hotel is nevertheless one of Fort Romper's most civilized attractions, at least until the arrival of the streetcars and electric lights. However, for all its startling effect (it turns a "dazzling winter landscape" dull and gray), Crane seems to be saying it is nothing so special after all. Its main room is, surprisingly, small and ordinary. Yet in this small room a tragedy is born: "Such scenes prove that there can be little of dramatic import in environment. Any room can present a tragic front; any room can be comic. This little den was now hideous as a torture-chamber." Indeed, Crane's short story might be called "anti-scenic." Unlike Hawthorne, who seems to attribute a great deal of significance to historical as well as physical setting, Crane is pointing out that we make our own scenes: the power of man's imagination is such that if he wants the Wild West badly enough, he gets it. But a further consideration will show that Crane and Hawthorne are more at one than they might at first seem, for certainly the significant duskiness of the New England village is as much the effect of Robin's frustrated "shrewdness"—that is, of his imagination—as the cause of his confusion, and the same is true of the Swede's Fort Romper. (The imagination creates, in Richard Poirier's words, "a world elsewhere.")

The other scene Crane invests with heavy significance, the winter landscape, also has connections with the meaning he gives or takes away from the blue hotel. The Swede walks through a storm of such proportions that

> one viewed the existence of man then as a marvel, and conceded
> a glamour of wonder to these lice which were caused to cling to a

whirling, fire-smitten, ice-locked, disease-stricken, space-lost bulb. The conceit of man was explained by this storm to be the very engine of life. One was a coxcomb not to die in it. However, the Swede found a saloon.   *12910 O*

These are wonderfully funny sentences, cutting back and forth across each other. The Swede's imagination, or "conceit," misdirected as it is, is here identified as "the very engine of life." Yet what an ambiguous connection, when a heroic quest ends in a saloon!

Still unbroached is the moral dimension of the story; what, by its last section, it seems to be about. This dimension, conjured up in a "fog of mysterious theory" by the Easterner, involves both the responsibility of man for man and the inevitable train of circumstance—"the apex of a human movement"—which man contributes to man's tragic downfall. The dimensions of the story by which Crane means to suggest classical tragedy have been touched on earlier: the unimportance of environment; the mad, lonely, tragic attitudes struck by the Swede; the absurd heroism of man's clinging, louse-like, to this whirling globe. For students to consider for long, as they will inevitably want to, what might have happened had the Easterner made public his knowledge of Johnnie's cheating, is to go astray, like the cowboy, from confronting the real mystery of human existence. For, as the Easterner tartly remarks, "a thousand things might have happened." Still, the startling effect of the Easterner's revelation is not to be dissipated; what most of the story has half-jokingly invoked as tragic is now felt as tragic. And, curiously enough, that constant presence in the American setting, the pressure to prove oneself a man in it, crops up here: "I refused," the Easterner admits, "to stand up and be a man." To ponder this admission and to try to connect it to the meaning which Crane has sought to convey through—or despite—setting, is a stimulating thing. For who then is a man in the story? Who does, as it were, "stand up" above the cash registers, suburbs, and electric street lights of "creeping civilization"? The Swede, of course; yet he is certainly mad. Many things are being said about the American experience, and the continuous transformation of it, by many parts of "The Blue Hotel."

STUDY QUESTIONS

1. Compare Crane's manipulation of setting with Bret Harte's in "The Outcasts of Poker Flat."

2. Since Johnnie, the Easterner, and the cowboy decide correctly about the causes of the Swede's behavior, why do they let things go so far? How do the reactions of each of them to the impending fight affect our estimate of the level of civilization in Fort Romper? Is there a little bit of "Wyoming" everywhere?

3. Compare Johnnie and the gambler as card sharks.

4. What purpose is served by the character of the old farmer who quarrels with Johnnie over cards?

5. Compare Scully's front room with the barroom of the saloon. What similar activity normally goes on in both?

6. Describe the situation of Fort Romper. It is not in the East, or in the Wild West. Where *is* it, metaphorically speaking? What do you make of its name?

THE EGG
by Sherwood Anderson

Unlike Hawthorne's and Crane's stories, the setting of Sherwood Anderson's "The Egg" is neither a central nor obviously helpful way of getting at the story's essence. The central formal elements of the story are Anderson's rough symbolism (the egg) and his subtle manipulation of the emotional involvement discernible in the narrator's tone. The most obvious discussable element in the story is the characterization of the narrator's father, but, though this is a common approach to the story, it seems to me misleading because the story is not "about" the father. Tone and characterization are central in most of Anderson's stories, including the anthologists' favorite, "I'm a Fool," but in all of them the setting carries an implicit weight of significance. This fruitful tension between character and setting is most obvious in Anderson's most famous work, *Winesburg, Ohio*. "The Egg" is worth considering in its setting because important aspects of meaning are conveyed through the narrator's awareness of place, and because it may be valuable for a class to begin to exercise its reading skills by building to conclusions from unlikely beginnings. (Of the more central formal elements, the egg—through Anderson's insistent comparisons of chicken behavior to human behavior—symbolizes the seeds of our great expectations for life and fame, and the final "triumph of the egg" is the way in which these hopes spring eternal in spite of repeated disasters which should convince us to abandon them. The narrator's tone will be considered in what follows.)

America is the setting of this story in much the same way as in Hawthorne or Crane. Though physical scene is less important, awareness of the meaning of the American scene is more explicit: "The American passion for getting up in the world took possession of them." "The American spirit took hold of him. He also became ambitious." The narrator's parents' hopes for their son are motivating factors in "The Egg" as powerful as Robin's confidence in his "shrewdness" or the Swede's expectations about the Wild West. In an oblique, unemphasized manner, this sense of America is connected by Anderson with the process of becoming a man, for it is the birth of their son which transforms the narrator's parents and impels them onto their catastrophic, comic course: "in the following spring I came wriggling and crying into the world. Something happened to the two people. They became ambitious."

Assuming that the comic grotesquerie of the narrator's father is self-evidently enjoyable, let us examine the settings from which its springs. The first scene is the chicken farm, if we ignore the farm on which his father worked before marrying (a most idyllic, irresponsible, and "unAmerican" place: "He had at that time no notion of trying to rise in the world"). Our understanding of the entire story depends on our grasping the metaphorical significance with which Anderson hilariously invests the chicken farm. He says his "tale does not primarily concern itself with the hen. If correctly told it will center on the egg." But in the long paragraph before this he sustains flawlessly the classic American tone of outrageously overstated absurdist humor. His diction alone is subject for an hour's discussion. It is perfectly manipulated between the grandiose and the detailed to support such sudden generalization as, "Most philosophers must have been raised on chicken farms." It is in this grandly comic manner that many of America's greatest writers give their most significant clues to the meaning of their fiction, and Anderson is no exception. (Consider Melville's prefaces to Moby Dick; consider Twain *passim;* consider Faulkner.) High school sophomores may be familiar with very watered-down versions of this style from humor writers like Corey Ford in *The Reader's Digest.* It may indeed be the sophomore's own style, once he has broken away from pure sentiment. Although the narrator says, "I, however, digress," the chicken farm is not a digression but a comic symbolization of the motives—getting ahead in the world—which inform the rest of the story.

The second setting, Pickleville, Ohio, is vintage small-town America, circa 1910. Aside from its silly but altogether plausible name, this scene is handled with matter-of-fact realism, perhaps to contrast with the narrator's expectations of it: he goes "to see the wonders of the world," seeing his family as "a tiny caravan of hope looking for *a new place* from which to start on our upward journey through life." (Italics mine.) This frontier spirit combines, not incongruously, with his mother's desires for his ultimate success, which she phrases as the wielding of control over place: "she may have dreamed that I would some day rule men and cities. . . ." "She wanted me to rise in the world, to get into a town school and become a man of the towns." These representations of hope as a search for a new place and of success as eventual control of it bring us to the story's third important setting, which is not real but entirely metaphorical.

This is the father's bald head:

> the bald path that led over the top of his head was, I fancied, some-thing like a broad road, such a road as Caesar might have made on which to lead his legions out of Rome and into the wonders of an unknown world . . . I . . . dreamed I was a tiny thing going along the road into a far beautiful place where there were no chicken farms and where life was a happy eggless affair.

Students will notice Anderson's repeated references to this bald head, particularly the touching scene in which the mother quietly strokes it to calm the father after his disastrous attempt to enter-tain Joe Kane. It is an odd detail, and perhaps not altogether aptly chosen, but beyond the narrator's childish escapism, its reference to Caesar is important. That broad path, which in reverie he represents on his father's head, is the road to success, and the narrator's longing for "a far beautiful place"—like his expectations for Pickleville and his implicit acceptance of his mother's identification of him with the great figures of history—prepares us to be convinced by the story's closing sentences, in which he involves himself in his family's sorrows.

Throughout the story the narrator's tone has been quietly superior to the events he narrates. This is because of the inevitable sense of mockery involved in telling a comic tale at the expense of one's parents. (Anderson's vignette of the narrator singing "Hippity Hop To The Barber Shop" is doubtless an attempt to counteract the mocking tone with self-mockery.) But in the end he involves himself squarely in his family's American plight: "The question got into my blood. It stayed there, I imagine, because I am the son of my father." The last sentences make us realize that "The Egg" is indeed a family story. Though the story at first centers on "my father," by the end we see the son involved and we get a reason, insofar as one is needed, as to why he told it. The "question," students should be warned, is not the clichéd riddle: Which came first, the chicken or the egg? Rather it is a question of why: "I wondered why eggs had to be and why from the egg came the hen who again laid the egg." Presumably he has learned from his father's experience to avoid pursuing dreams of glory in the business world, but the philosophic dimension of the question has hooked him just as badly: "And that, I conclude, is but another evidence of the complete and final triumph of the egg—at least as far as my family is concerned." Ambition and endless consideration of the meaning or value of ambition—both are equally prominent features of the American scene.

STUDY QUESTIONS

1. Discuss the various ways in which Anderson gives universal significance to the commonest of common places, a chicken farm. Does he do something of the same for Ohio, which like other Middle Western states is often taken to represent the common, average, American way of life?

2. Try to explain the factors in the father's disastrous business experience. The narrator says his father was intended to be a

cheerful man; what went wrong? (It is noteworthy that Sherwood Anderson was a businessman himself until he was past forty. He was relatively successful. Why do you suppose he became dissatisfied and turned to literature instead?)

3. In all three of the stories studied thus far, a character "goes to town." What similarities of treatment of town settings do you recognize in Hawthorne, Crane, and Anderson? What does the town represent?

4. "Every American boy has a chance to grow up to be President." Comment on this national proverb in the light of "The Egg."

FLIGHT
by John Steinbeck

An informal poll of college freshmen reveals that Steinbeck's story, "Flight," is one of the stories most frequently remembered from high school literature. But, curiously, it is recalled by some students as their favorite and by others as the story they liked least. This ambiguity, insofar as it is general, suggests that this story, or others by Steinbeck, may provide a valuable teaching experience; for the ambiguity resides in the story and it is closely related to Steinbeck's emphasis on the story's setting. Perhaps, in some classes, students may enjoy the satisfaction of deciding that the story is not as good as it should be.

What is the story about? What meaning or significance should we attach to Pepé's death? Only two alternatives seem possible. Both involve man and nature—character and setting—interacting in ways characteristic of many American short stories. Has Pepé become a man who pays the full price for his maturity, or has he failed to become a man and therefore pays for his failure? In the first of these interpretations of the story, becoming a man would be something entirely separate from being at home in nature; whereas in the second, to be a man is to be self-sufficient in nature, as Pepé is not. But, on the other hand, the story may not be about maturing at all; it may transcend this large theme to an even larger one—nature's cruel disregard for man. All of these alternatives can provide satisfactory answers for the story; the difficulty lies in relating or reconciling the various possibilities of the story. That the difficulty may be insurmountable makes the story no less instructive than "My Kinsman, Major Molineux" or "The Blue Hotel," where similar difficulties reward us with more and more insight as we pursue them.

Nature functions almost as a character in "Flight." Its action is inexorable: sunrise and sunset, the intense glare of midday, and moon's rise and fall, the succession of mountain ridges surmounting valleys ever more barren and forbidding. It is this relentless power that wears Pepé down—a fact worth noting, since it lessens the importance of nature's more actively ferocious aspects, the mountain lion (almost friendly, ears up "with interest," not "laid back dangerously") and the rattlesnake, which are thus seen as accents or signs of a more general malignity. Although Steinbeck's reputation rests on his delineation of specific social groups, such as the Mexicans of the central California coast in "Flight," his important claim to his title of Nobel Laureate lies in his efforts to suggest a universal significance to his characters' lives. Hence we understand his opening paragraph as a symbolic picture of man's place in an environment which can quickly reduce him to less than man. Man is like the Torres' farm buildings, "huddled like little clinging aphids on the mountain skirts, crouched low to the ground as though the wind might blow them into the sea." Though Steinbeck writes with a realism apparently light-years removed from Hawthorne's brooding symbolic settings, students should recognize that the unstated "drift" of this realism draws our attention to the possible significance of the author's repeated notations of natural fact —the angle of the sun's light, the position of moss on a tree trunk, and so forth. Taken individually, they may be merely accurate and informative—"pure" description—but cumulatively, in a story like this, the details of natural scene add up to a consistent pattern. Two stories that could be used here for very effective comparisons of technique are Jack London's "To Build a Fire" and Ernest Hemingway's "Big Two-Hearted River."

Following this line of the story, the reader can see clearly that nature can turn man into an animal. By the end, speech—that symbolic mode of expression which is purely human (although it has never been Pepé's strong point)—has become a thick hissing and a dog-like whine. Note that Pepé can usually only grin when spoken to, and his physical description is associated with animals: "an eagle nose"; the "lazy cow" or "sneaking lazy coyote" Mama Torres accuses in his lineage; his sheepish smiles; and a knife-throwing wrist which "flicked like the head of a snake." Does this mean that Pepé has been less than a man all along? The teacher will want to spend some time on the characterization Steinbeck employs to give us a picture of Pepé before his flight. Though winning, he is silly, vacant, and useless—much more so than his younger brother and sister.

As to Pepé's becoming a man, alert male students will recognize that Pepé makes many mistakes on his ride into the mountains, but the extent to which this proves his lack of maturity is blurred by Steinbeck, perhaps intentionally. For example, is Pepé eating his jerky too fast? And improperly as well, since he flavors it with bay leaf instead of eating grass mainly and using the jerky to flavor it as Mama recommended? Why are we first reassured that Pepé's flesh wound is not serious, only to discover that it is infecting and becoming indeed the main contributing factor to his weakness and collapse? Is his use of spider webs to stop the bleeding incorrect?

STUDY QUESTIONS

1. Mama Torres says, "A boy gets to be a man when a man is needed." Apply this statement to Pepé's case. She later says he has become a man, but she mourns the fact. How can we reconcile the two?

2. In what ways are the Torres seen to be living a life of naked confrontation between man and nature—that is, without the mediating influence of civilization? (Consider the reference to the truant officer.)

3. How do you respond to Steinbeck's attempt to capture the Spanish dialect of his characters? Why do you think he does so?

THE COUNTRY HUSBAND
by John Cheever

All of the stories considered thus far take place in a historical past or, in "Flight," in a geographically and ethnically limited situation. But John Cheever's "The Country Husband" is about a place, "Shady Hill," familiar to an increasing majority of high school students. The Shady Hill station is on the main line of Suburbia U.S.A. If students do not respond with immediate recognition to the upper middle-class scene at Shady Hill, the teacher need only jog their memories and perceptions for them to draw analogies with their own experience: their father probably drives to the office, or he may take a bus to a factory, but the pattern is the same. (If one feels that Cheever's scene is too remote—as presumably would be John O'Hara's also—a very similar deployment of the American scene is to be found in the more strictly urban stories of Saul Bellow, J. D. Salinger, Herbert Gold, Bernard Malamud, Philip Roth, and, for the small town scene, John Updike. Updike's story, "A Sense of Shelter," would be a very good substitute for Cheever if the teacher feels Cheever's concerns are too "adult" for sophomores.)

Although Cheever's story is in some respects a character study of Francis Weed, the key to Weed's character is not interior but exterior. We are told that "he was not . . . reflective," that "his memory was something like his appendix—a vestigial repository." He is by no means a shallow man, but he has that peculiarly American trait of being very susceptible to shaping by his environment. The action of the story is Francis' struggle—probably his last—to resist the shaping power of his suburban environment. The last section of the story is devoted to a wonderfully convincing series of evocations of scene. We may question whether the details cohere adequately, but we do not fail to recognize that Francis, among them, is very much "the *country* husband," even though possibilities for romance and fantasy are still present on the scene. But for Francis, we feel, the possibilities will remain fantastic and not intrude again as violently into the sphere of real action—where he now pursues, not nymphs, but his new hobby, wood working. And certainly the story is rich enough to support a double response: first, that Francis' last state is better than his first, and second, that he is a faintly pathetic, comic figure both out of and in his lustful phase.

The scene with which the story opens is brilliantly selected from the fantasy life of modern America: What would it be like to be in a plane that is about to crash? Cheever's opening sentence, "To begin at the beginning . . . ," suggests to us that it is this near-catastrophe which shakes Francis Weed out of his normal life pattern, particularly when, due to the vagaries of the weather and the speed of modern transportation, he arrives home to announce his escape to people who cannot quite believe that he was ever in danger. His frustrated attempts to present himself as a man returned from disaster become the representation and perhaps the cause of his subsequent frustration with his entire life. Cheever handles with amusing skill Weed's ego-shattering descent from near disaster back to hum-drum reality; he rapidly details the succession of transports Weed employs, and plops him quickly and perfectly back in "his second-hand Volkswagen." In dramatic terms, this come-down prepares for many subsequent come-downs in the story.

In his description of the falling plane, Cheever plants an arresting bit of detail that does much to prepare us for the story to follow. In the interior of the wildly floundering plane we see "an atmosphere of intense and misplaced domesticity," caused by the combination of "shaded lights, stuffiness, and the window curtains." To underscore these home thoughts from above, Cheever next has Weed's seat partner express, in what he expects to be his last words, that familiar American desire for a place in the country ("a farm in New Hampshire"), away from all the turmoil and responsibility and disaster of industrialized urban life. Students at first reading will take such details as irrelevant, which indeed they are, but they are *perfectly* irrelevant: at once merely realistic and surely significant to them. For example, how much of the story's theme and how many of its characters are summed up in the phrase, "intense and misplaced domesticity"? One should not force students to see significance in every detail, at least not in every story. Hawthorne, one might confidently assert, does not waste a word; by comparison, Cheever and Steinbeck are diffuse. This question has particular relevance in Cheever's case, for one feels that he is sometimes cataloging details for sheer love or laughter—not that this kind of structural irrelevance is not part of one's literary enjoyment. But Cheever's gift of caricature may be subject to question. For example, is the character of Gertrude Flannery necessary to the story, and in such detail?

Between the beginning and the end lies the story. Students

might be asked to enumerate all the scenes that are not part of the story on the realistic or factual level. They are surprisingly numerous. In addition to the consciously remembered war scene, we get Francis' elaborate deliberation on various Lovers' Lanes about the town, his two consciously manipulated dream scenes (Paris and Vermont), and, as reality and fantasy become increasingly confused in his mind, he imagines himself as lost in a specific place—the forest where he actually was lost once on a fishing trip. Now this, too, has a special reality: "He smelled the forest." Does this suggest that being lost is not altogether a bad experience? Through all, of course, Cheever runs a leitmotif of the most fantastic yet most realistic of all places, the unchanging world of mythology. This is evoked largely by the use of names (Jupiter, the dog; "Venus combing and combing her hair as she drifted through the Bronx"), but the mythological place and the suburban place are brought most immediately together in the story's heavily freighted last sentence: "It is a night where kings in golden suits ride elephants over the mountains."

These fantastic, imagined places contrast and comment upon the real scenes in the story—the Weeds' beautiful Dutch Colonial house, "bigger than it looked," with a "burnished" interior; Anne Murchison's small gingerbread house on the other side of the tracks; the city and the commuter trains. What we sense mostly in the contrast is the inadequacy of Shady Hill, whether the imaginary scenes are Francis' escapist dreams, or are worlds, like the mythological one, that impinge on his consciousness almost without his awareness. The dog Jupiter is an instance of Shady Hill's resistance to any heightened sense of reality. As lordly a "rakehell" as the god whom he may incarnate, his days are numbered. Suburbia will cut him down to size, according to its own mode of operation: "The Wrightsons' German gardener or the Farquarsons' cook would soon poison him. Even old Mr. Nixon might put some arsenic in the garbage that Jupiter loved."

The function of the two sharply contrasting settings in "The Country Husband" should not be arrived at inductively, but should be investigated as a way of deepening the overt indictments of suburbia that are made at the Farquarsons' dinner party and by young Clayton Thomas. When Francis realizes that he can tell no one that he once saw the Farquarsons' maid humiliated in extraordinary circumstances, the narration suddenly deepens somewhat beyond his level. Cheever's indictment is indeed sweeping: "In the recorded history of human arrangements, this extraordinary meeting would have fallen into place, but the atmosphere of Shady Hill made the memory unseemly and impolite." For politeness to be the foremost consideration at such a moment is clear evidence how a *form* of living has outstripped the human content of the lives which practice it. Julia is the most obvious prisoner of this dead formalism, but Francis is the most pathetic. The indictment is not consciously his, for the war memory only left him "feeling languid," and his frustration at being unable to communicate it merely becomes a second major factor, along with the crash landing, contributing to his foolish yet understandable romanticizing of his relationship with the baby sitter.

Clayton Thomas' complaint, though petulant and immature, is nonetheless perfectly accurate in its description of the misdirected (that is, frustrated) energy with which a style of life is perpetuated at Shady Hill at the expense of a meaning. "So much energy is spent in perpetuating *the place*—in keeping out undesirables, and so forth—that the only idea of the future anyone has is just more and more commuting trains and more parties." (Italics mine.) To this, Clayton contrasts his determination "to dream great dreams."

One other setting in the story is neither allusive, realistic, nor dreamlike, but stylistic. This is the battlefield created by Cheever's diction in describing the "home front" on which the Weeds principally misdirect their energy. This setting is found mostly in the second section of the story—the dinner scene following Francis' return—where Cheever weaves a tissue of clichés, allusions, and adverbs into a comic but painful representation of the way love has left, or is threatening to leave, Francis Weed's life. "The living room was spacious and divided like Gaul into three parts." Francis happily leaves his warring young children to go upstairs to fetch his eldest; "it is like getting back to headquarters company." "Julia's guns are loaded" for his complaints, and his calling his home a "battlefield" suddenly creates one which Julia leaves in tears.

I leave it to a class discussion to link all the different settings in "The Country Husband" into a coherent whole. Perhaps it cannot be done. The final scene overlooking the suburb's gardens and private lives, though it is highly amusing and even oddly comforting, may raise more questions than it is able to answer. One question is the basic question of the entire story: Is Francis happy or not? Certainly to have returned to a niche in Shady Hill is a most ambiguous kind of happiness, as the weight of scenic contrasts in the story makes clear. Yet Cheever's indictment of suburbia is not Clayton Thomas', and harsh as he is, we must recognize a peacefulness at the end that cannot be all bad.

However these questions are answered, the teacher may successfully approach them by delving into the many settings of the story. Students will doubtless want to focus on the character of Francis Weed, either to attack or defend him as a parent. His character is important, but it does not take us far into the story, since it is a character defined by its reaction to its surroundings. What is true for this Cheever story is true for others, including his earlier, widely anthologized piece, "The Enormous Radio."

STUDY QUESTIONS

1. Cheever does not always feel obliged to announce when Francis is in the real world and when he is in his dream world. Whom does he kiss when he comes home from work the day after meeting Anne Murchison?

2. Try to explain why Cheever expends so much detail on Francis' wartime experience. Why is it never referred to again?

3. Clayton Thomas asserts man's responsibility to "dream great dreams." How is his assertion qualified by his plans for his own life?

4. A puzzler: Why, in the final scene, are there so many references to varieties of dress and undress? (Cowboy suit, space suit, nudity, a cat in doll's clothes, and so forth.)

5. Compare Shady Hill with Hawthorne's colonial town, Crane's Fort Romper, Anderson's Pickleville, and Steinbeck's Monterey. In point of *fact*, these are all very different towns, but as literary *settings* they have much in common. In terms of the author's technique, which town is most different from the others?

6. Cheever calls his story "The Country Husband." What use of "country" is made by the four other writers? What does it mean in Cheever's story?

Short Stories for Grade Eleven

In some of this century's most important studies of the craft of
fiction, narrative point of view has been assigned a paramount
place among the artists' ways of creating meaning and the reader's
ways of apprehending it.* Many anthologies feature introductions
which consider point of view exhaustively, to the disregard of
other analytic approaches.

This is not, however, the method in the following explications.
I believe the importance of narrative point of view has been at once
overstressed and oversimplified in many discussions, particularly at
those points where it is closely related to characterization. Too
often we stress the technical narrative function of a character and
slight his importance as an actor who changes events and is
changed by them. In what follows, questions of point of view and
questions of characterization will be considered with reference to
each other, on the additional presumption that students will have
learned to appreciate "pure" characterization earlier. I am also interested in helping students deepen their understanding of the
technique of omniscient narration in instances where the difference
between the author's voice and the character's consciousness is
slight, even though the pronouns keep us well aware of who is
speaking. To open these questions, I consider first-person narrations like James Joyce's "Araby" and such complex third-person
narrations as Joseph Conrad's "Youth" and "Heart of Darkness"
and Robert Louis Stevenson's "Dr. Jekyll and Mr. Hyde," in all of
which we recognize a modern form—the stream of consciousness

---

* See, for example, Percy Lubbock, *The Craft of Fiction* (New York: Viking Press, 1921); Henry James, *The Art of the Novel* (New York: Charles
Scribner's Sons, 1934), and *The Art of Fiction* (New York: Oxford University
Press, 1948); E. M. Forster, *Aspects of the Novel* (New York: Harcourt Brace,
1927).

narrative—struggling to be born. The section ends with a most difficult case in point, Katherine Mansfield's "Bliss."*

As in the selections from American short stories, a vague principle of literary history informs these English selections. The short story in England naturally has deeper roots than in America. One of the deepest is that which goes back to the criminal fiction of the seventeenth century and to its sibling, the Gothic horror tale of the late eighteenth and early nineteenth centuries. Out of these comes the modern mystery story. Aficionados of the detective story often maintain that the English have little competition in their mastery of the genre, and, making allowance for individual tastes, they are right. The prime ingredient of a good mystery story is plot, and "mere" mysteries can be used to advantage in junior high school when one is first raising the questions of how authors "plot" meaning. But "character is plot," said Henry James, and another descendant of the old criminal and horror fiction is the tale of gradual or sudden revelation of character, of the knowledge of one's own or another's deepest nature, often throwing into confusion normal expectations about the nature of the Self or Man. This revelatory tale is a much more respectable literary type than the murder mystery, but it has obvious connections with the movement of the mystery story's plot which leads toward the exposure of the murderer's identity. As a superficial example of the way in which these two kinds of stories grew up together, one can study the sophisticated use of the Gothic melodrama's machinery of revelation in British fiction beginning with Dickens: magic mirrors, veiled portraits, and dusky vistas hiding yet revealing awful truths. Vestiges of all these gimmicks appear in the stories of Stevenson, Conrad, and Joyce. The revelatory tale is of course a universal type, as are the forms of narration, yet one may suspect—at least for long enough to teach a unit on the short story—that there exists a special congruity between the revelatory tale, the British character, and the progressive interiorizing of narration in British fiction of the late nineteenth and early twentieth centuries. I am

---

* Teachers might want to consider the question of point of view in fiction in connection with the related but different question of *persona* or "speaker" in poetry in general and satire in particular. For example, in what sense might "A Modest Proposal" be read as a short story?

suggesting that sophistication in narration goes hand in hand with sophistication in characterization, and that at certain points one may actually become the other.

Of course, stories of character revelation are prominent also in the American tradition. They are often cited to define the very genre of the short story in any language. Indeed, if revelation is generalized far enough, such stories are the essence of all literature (cf. tragedy). But in the more limited field of short fiction, one feels that stories of inner and perhaps awful revelation are more characteristic of the British than of us, especially when "revelation" is taken in the strict sense of something's being revealed that was not known before. Thus Melville's "Bartleby the Scrivener" is a depth analysis of character, but "Heart of Darkness" is a revelation. The career and writings of Henry James lend an air of plausibility to these speculations: his move to British citizenship, his deep penetrations into the mysteries of character, and, most of all, his genius in the manipulation of point of view. James is doubtless too difficult for high school juniors, but "A Beast in the Jungle" is a story exemplifying the generalizations here set out.

Nothing, however, stands or falls on the truth of these generalizations. They are meant to be suggestive, to encourage disagreement as well as assent—all with emphasis on learning to pay close attention to the myriad ways in which character can define point of view and point of view determine character.

YOUTH: A NARRATIVE and HEART OF DARKNESS
by Joseph Conrad

MARKHEIM and THE STRANGE CASE OF DR. JEKYLL AND MR. HYDE
by Robert Louis Stevenson

If we compare some famous stories by Robert Louis Stevenson and Joseph Conrad with some by James Joyce, D. H. Lawrence, and Katherine Mansfield, our very first observation is that the older writers write much longer stories. All five writers are explorers of the subjective side of human experience. Lawrence and Mansfield sometimes reduce physical setting, so important in American fiction, almost to irrelevance; Virginia Woolf's settings, which exist only in the minds of her characters, are an extreme case in point—illustrative, but too confusing for high school students. There is much more economy in the stories by the later writers. Stevenson's "The Strange Case of Dr. Jekyll and Mr. Hyde" and Conrad's "Heart of Darkness" stretch the limits of the definition of a short story, though in the singleness of their effect there is no doubt that they satisfy the one great requirement propounded by Poe. "Story" value bulks much larger in the two older writers, whereas those of the following generation seem to have stripped the story away to expose with greater clarity its meaning—meaning being defined as the effect of events upon character. Stevenson and Conrad are evidently examining the nature of man at a high level of metaphysical generalization, asking if there is not an inhuman "heart of darkness" lurking within us all. In the later writers the same problem does not admit the same grand formulation. Instead of evil we see folly, lack of feeling, and self-delusion; and, additionally, we see them much more clearly. For there is a good deal of deliberate vagueness in Stevenson and Conrad that depends for its effect on the assumption that we will respond to their stories with a more or less orthodox acceptance of the western, Platonic conception of man's nature: the body and the soul, bad and good, and, by extension, the gross and the spiritual aspects of the soul. This is not true of Joyce or Lawrence or Mansfield.

Yet the recognitions that are achieved in both groups of stories, though more dramatic and profound in Conrad and Stevenson, are of the same order. A large part of the problem of assessing the similarities within their differences lies in answering the question: To whom does revelatory knowledge come? To Kurtz and Jekyll, or to Marlow and Utterson, or (in Conrad) to Marlow's circle of listeners, or to the reader only? While one shrinks from suggesting that Stevenson's and Conrad's stories would be better if narrated in the first person, there can be no question that both their greater length and wealth of detail and their air of greater profundity spring from the latitude given the author by his omniscient stance, *as qualified* by his persistent determination to let the characters speak in their own voice.

In "Heart of Darkness" and "Youth: A Narrative," as in many of his stories, Conrad employs a narrative figure, Marlow, to tell his story. Though not omniscient, Marlow is endowed with remarkable prescience by his creator. In addition, there is in both of these stories a nameless narrator, who is reporting what Marlow said to him and a circle of other middle-aged former sailors, now all successful in business, as they sat listening in the comfort of their club or yacht in England. We cannot call this narrator simply "Conrad," because he is a character affected by the narrative which, in simple terms, *is* the story. So there are two or three narrative "frames" through which we look to the story itself. In "Youth," where Conrad seems to call attention to his technique by his subtitle, "A Narrative," the story is Marlow's account of his momentary, visionary perception of the meaning or essence of youth, and the narrative action is the crude sense of lost youth which Marlow casts upon himself and his auditors. The reflection of youth on age is made explicit at the end of the story when the first narrator records the effect of Marlow's story, but it is implicit throughout in Marlow's refrain, "Pass the bottle," which reminds us of where and to whom Marlow is speaking and suggests that the discrepancy between what he is now and what he was then makes it difficult for him to continue without fortification. I am speaking solely of the effects of technique. There is a great deal more "to" the story in colorful character and incident, but it is by no means true that the story is saying we lose and mourn our youth: the last words of the story connect the appeal of youth with "the romance of illusions." These words are the nameless narrator's. In part they qualify the excesses of Marlow's romance, but they are also a response to qualifications suggested by the mocking ironies of Marlow's own narration.

In "Heart of Darkness," the narrative effect is more complex than this, for here Marlow is at once object and filter of the experiences he records, and the story "happens" to several persons other than himself—and happens in different ways, due to his narration.* At the center of the story are "the horror" and Kurtz, the man who has come closest to it and remained articulate. Other people, like the manager, come close to Kurtz's experience, but they are all limited by their functions; they are not artists with narrative gifts like Marlow's and, instead of passing on Kurtz's experience, they interpret it according to their limitations (the manager, for example, dismisses the meaning of Kurtz's experience as the results of "unsound method"). Marlow is simultaneously narrating other narrations, principally his report to Kurtz's Belgian fiancée. Belgium before and after his trip to Africa is another, partial frame of narrative, and it is important, for it contrasts with the others in that Marlow tells the fiancée a story not of horror, but of love. His narration to the men aboard the *Nellie* is thus one of horror and the extenuation of horror, a compound more unsettling than horror alone. At the end, the nameless narrator recounts another dimension of the story; the moving effect of Marlow's narrative on him. He now sees the "heart of darkness" in the calm English sunset. His response is contrasted by the apparently lesser effect of the story on the "Director of Companies" who notes sharply and suddenly the practical fact that while they have been listening to Marlow they have "lost the first ebb," and we are brought back to the circumstances of the auditors' gathering. The foreground of action in the story is apparently a pleasure excursion, but the gripping narrative has supervened, and the excursion in a pleasant everyday world has, to say the least, got off to a bad start.

As the nameless narrator feared at the outset, Marlow has told "another of his inconclusive tales." Yet Marlow's inconclusiveness is not pointless; nor is a class's examination of the story's narrative frames. One suspects that juniors will enjoy identifying them; the teacher's job is to turn their merely descriptive enjoyment into analytic pleasure by connecting Conrad's complex but obvious

---

* What follows is almost an examination of the "frame" at the expense of the "picture." Teachers who desire a fuller treatment of the story—particularly if they plan to teach it as a *novel*—should see Philip B. Daghlian's "Teaching *Heart of Darkness*" in this volume (pp. 306-316).

techniques to the meaning of the story. The most attractive but most dangerous way to begin a class's reaction to "Heart of Darkness" is to open the floor to speculation on the object of "the horror." Answers will be forthcoming, amazing and banal enough. But even if the teacher struggles through to a coherent statement about the savagery at the heart of Being, he will not have satisfactorily described a reading experience of "Heart of Darkness." Indeed, making such a formulation is precisely the entrée for the bright student, like Conrad's merely bright critics, to protest against the heavy mysteriousness of his style and his pointless multiplication of people telling things to each other, if *that* is all he meant. No, Conrad did not pretend to radically new knowledge about man's basic instincts. Instead, he tells a story, an experience, the donnée of which is an undefinable, nearly unnamable, horror at the heart of man. And, the story is about, not the horror, but the many reactions to, and interpretations of, it—principally Marlow's, the story's main character as well as its narrator. Now, but not earlier, we may lead the class into a generalization about the inseparability of form and content. The various narrative frames *are* the meaning of the story; they do not simply contain it. The main, Kurtzian line, the Belgian line, the *Nellie* line—each of these qualifies and comments upon the others, not to mention the numerous "trunk" lines of individuals' reports and reactions along the way (the chief accountant, the Russian sailor, and so forth). We must maintain constant alertness to see just what conscious or unconscious distortions they contain.

Though it would be pointless to question Marlow's veracity—even if he gives us some warrant—there is nevertheless the question of his or Conrad's narrative style. Specifically, what contribution does Marlow's absurd, existential, or "black" humor make to "Heart of Darkness" or "Youth"? In the latter, the scene of the first mate and crew calmly eating cheese and drinking stout on the burning deck of a sinking ship is priceless, and the former contains one of the funniest sentences ever woven into the texture of serious prose: "My dear boys, what can you expect from a man who out of sheer nervousness had just flung overboard a pair of new shoes!" With so much seriousness in the stories, what is the effect of this constant, almost wacky, comedy of tone and incident?

Lack of humor is one of the things that make Stevenson less a master than Conrad, though he is far from humorless. In "Markheim" and "The Strange Case of Dr. Jekyll and Mr. Hyde," Stevenson invests his theme with a commensurate seriousness of tone. Stevenson is more plainly at work on the quality of man's soul than is Conrad, but his omniscient narration, which allows him much more latitude of statement than Conrad has, is not used to speculate directly on the mystery. Instead he uses a rather large number of devices to remove himself from this responsibility. Obvious enough are the wills, testaments, and letters in "Dr. Jekyll and Mr. Hyde." Less obvious are the extended dialogues, interior monologues, and, in "Markheim," the "interior dialogues."

The last third of "Markheim" is a dialogue between Markheim and his best self disguised as his worst. Technically, it is nicely apt for a story about man's two natures to take the form of a dialogue between them. Conceptually, this works out less well, for if we are to grant any reality to the creature who visits Markheim in the upper room of the murdered pawnbroker's house, we may ask why a real representation of Markheim's evil self is not given equal time. Stevenson evidently felt this weakness, because in "Dr. Jekyll and Mr. Hyde" he twice gives Jekyll's detailed accounts of how it was that his evil rather than his good spirit gained ascendancy. The first third of "Markheim" is likewise a dialogue, the main subject of which is Markheim's terror of a mirror—that is, his horror at seeing himself. But in the last third he is able to face up to himself, though fearfully, and, admittedly, without full recognition that he is talking to himself. Connecting these two sections is a passage of narration the evident purpose of which is to heighten the sense of nervous terror in the story. But students may be asked to consider what is accomplished by the middle section beyond evocation of a mood. Most of Stevenson's narration, and most of the mood evocation, is accomplished not by direct description, but by Markheim's purely interior conversations and speculations with himself. Markheim is a man of strong imagination, and his desire to stop hearing, to be deaf, reflects his desire to quell his imagination, and to stop the dialogue within him that eventually leads him to confess.

Though the story of Dr. Jekyll and Mr. Hyde has become part of our store of proverbial lore, students reading it for the first time will be quite surprised by the form it takes. Most of the story that they are familiar with is in the last two sections—the written testimonies of Dr. Lanyon and Dr. Jekyll. It is almost entirely from these two sections that the many film treatments of the story derive; one of the films is quite good, and all are standard "Late Show" fare.* Certainly, Stevenson's theme and the device of the "magic potion" which he uses to dramatize it have a compelling interest in themselves, but neither is new, and we must suppose there is something in the story that has given it a staying power beyond that of its predecessors and imitators. Mary Shelley's *Frankenstein* is a more famous member of our popular mythology than Jekyll and Hyde, but her book is a dreary reading experience. To some, it is fascinating that her monster's creator, Dr. Frankenstein, should have become identified in the popular mind with his creature, but from the reader's standpoint it is a confusion which could only be entertained as a relief from the tedium of her narrative technique. Stevenson, on the other hand, compels interest precisely because of his narrative skill. He presents the first two thirds of the story through the character of Utterson. Dr. Jekyll is investigating a metaphysical mystery, but our interest in his investigations is captured by Utterson's curiosity about mere mysteries of fact. More than that—and here is where characterization and narration are particularly close—the mystery is heightened and our attention honed by the scrupulous lawyer's refusal to engage in mere curiosity seeking. He never gives in to his curiosity, and only opens a new stage of investigation when he is forced to in dispatch of his legal responsibilities. His restraint is at times maddening, as, at the end, when he rationalizes every move to the distraught Poole; but his restraint is Stevenson's restraint. In the author's refusal to tell his story too fast lies the reason for its continuing power. To put it another way, Stevenson scrupulously re-

* For a detailed analysis of the ways in which stage and film dramatizations of fiction are limited by the necessary removal of the narrator's voice, see Mary Alice Burgan's essay, "Action and Narration: An Approach to the Drama and the Short Story," in *Teaching Literature in Grades Seven Through Nine*, a volume in this English Curriculum Study Series.

strains his omniscience as author to what Mr. Utterson sees and thinks, and does not "leak" any essential information. The things that Utterson cannot possibly have experienced firsthand come to him with unexceptional plausibility, through the post, the press, or report. Thus it is a fitting, rather than an awkward, device that the mystery is finally cleared up in two lengthily reported testaments; the final narration is, so to speak, a "reading" of that which Utterson's position entitles him to read, since he would never indulge in such detail in his own conversation. The reported will or letter can be the deadliest of narrative devices, but though these two contain the heart of Stevenson's story, they represent only a third of the story and nicely satisfy expectations aroused by the first two thirds.

The testaments are finally justified by the character of Mr. Utterson. Going back from the end to the beginning of the story, students may be led to appreciate how their enjoyment depends upon the apparently irrelevant details of Utterson's character and habits. He is the most reserved and reticent of men, yet this very quality, we are told, often made him the last acquaintance of "downgoing man." Furthermore, his walks with Mr. Enfield, besides being the quirky habit of two older bachelors, show how his reticence maintains itself even in the most intimate relationship of which he is capable: though both he and Enfield know perfectly well that each knows that they are speaking about Dr. Jekyll, they carefully refrain from uttering his name and agree never to discuss the matter again.

What is the relationship between narrator and character in Conrad and Stevenson? In Conrad, we may paraphrase James to say "narration is character." Marlow is the only character who vitally interests us; all other characters tend to become more or less caricatures of his view of them. They are interesting and fascinating, but their interest is exterior and the only inner life which is expressed is Marlow's. If character be defined as that to which change and growth occur, then Stevenson's narrator in "Dr. Jekyll and Mr. Hyde" is, like Marlow, the central character in the story. The action of Stevenson's story has effects only upon Utterson the narrator; Jekyll, paradoxically, is scarcely a true character at all— Hyde indeed surpasses him in individuality and vividness. And, as Utterson is the only character in whom growth is evident, so, by the nice congruence of form and content which is one of the sure signs of great artistry, he is the only character in the story with power to change and affect its action. The way in which he elects to do so, given his lawyer's character, is the means by which Stevenson determines the shape of his narrative and guarantees our interest in it.

STUDY QUESTIONS

1. How serious is Marlow? When does he seem to be laughing at what he is telling? Or is he laughing at himself?

2. Why does Conrad make up so many delays for the *Judea*? What effect do the history of the ship and the mishaps of its last voyage have on our response to Marlow's ostensible subject, youth?

3. Are Marlow's requests, "Pass the bottle," inserted at random, or do they break into his narrative at significant points—points at which it is important for us to be reminded of his circle of listeners?

4. For the teacher: Setting and symbol are obviously important in Conrad's stories. Students could be asked to compare the function of his settings with that of American short stories (Grade Ten in this sequence). His symbolism—or Marlow's—seems intentionally heavy, especially in "Youth." The possibility that he is being ironic might be considered, with reference to the discussion of symbolism in Katherine Mansfield's "Bliss," at the end of this section.

5. Is Marlow's tone when he is telling about Belgium different from his tone when he speaks of Africa? How? Why?

6. In both of Conrad's stories, the nameless narrator is something like the reader's representative in the story. Do his responses agree with yours? How does Conrad use this narrator to shape the reader's response?

7. How do we know that Markheim's "visitor" is real? Why doesn't his evil self visit him? (The answer to this question is a criticism of the story, unless we decide the visitor is *both*. Then we could examine the verisimilitude of Markheim's conversation as that of a man talking to himself. But the objective reality of the visitor makes this procedure questionable, rewarding though it may be.)

8. Many students will insist on regarding sensation as more interesting than thought—that is, will regard Jekyll's physical transformations as the "best part" of the story, just as the hapless Wolf Man's transformations are the best part of many a Frankenstein film. It is probably impossible to disabuse them of this notion, but they should be willing—or forced—to argue it in discussion. Sample questions: Would the script of a typical Jekyll and Hyde film make as good a story as Stevenson's? Could a better movie be made, incorporating the character of Utterson?

9. Given the narrative importance of Utterson, is it a flaw in the story that Stevenson does not return to him at the end? Or would such a return be anticlimactic?

10. How is the full title of "Dr. Jekyll and Mr. Hyde" appropriate to the way it is told?

THE ROCKING-HORSE WINNER
by D. H. Lawrence

ARABY
by James Joyce

BLISS
by Katherine Mansfield

Though we find characterization in Conrad and Stevenson where we might not expect to find it, character does not have prime value in their stories. In the stories of England's twentieth-century masters, however, the reverse is true. If for Conrad and Stevenson narration determines character, for D. H. Lawrence, James Joyce, Katherine Mansfield, Dylan Thomas, and others, character determines narrative. That is, individualized, particularized characters are of prime value in their stories, and their narrative points of view are chosen in such a way as to create this value. Marlow and Utterson emerge as characters almost in spite of themselves, but the characters in *Dubliners*, for example, have compelling interest from their first appearance, and it is "in spite of themselves," to stretch the phrase, that they become narrators of their own character.

One reason for the real individuality of Joyce's, Lawrence's, and Thomas' characters is the strongly autobiographical nature of their work. Utterson and Marlow, for all their idiosyncrasies, are types of the lawyer and of the seaman. But in Joyce and Lawrence experience makes its claim to reality and importance by virtue of its atypicality. This does not mean that their themes are merely private and of less general significance than those of the older writers. Rather the reverse, especially in the case of Joyce and Lawrence, who are certainly more significant writers than Stevenson or Conrad in terms of the breadth or level of their insight into human life. An important part of the modern tradition's revolt against Victorianism was its reassertion of the truth that great writing does not mean writing about great subjects, but writing about any subject in a way most calculated to bring out its essential truth.

By way of transition, let us consider briefly one of Lawrence's most famous stories, "The Rocking-Horse Winner." This story is a rule-proving exception to the distinctions just made; the characters are schematic rather than individualized, and the narration is intentionally impersonal. Like "The Strange Case of Dr. Jekyll and Mr. Hyde," "The Rocking-Horse Winner" utilizes a mysterious device to attract our attention, but little of the story's meaning depends upon the device. Just as we do not consider the chemical composition of Jekyll's potion, so we lead our classes away from trying to figure out how Paul's supernatural ritual rides actually work.

The first two paragraphs set the narrative tone for the story: "There was a woman . . . ," and "There were a boy and two little girls." Like a Biblical parable, the anonymity and neutrality of both the narrator's voice and the characters he describes prepare us for a story that will teach a lesson or illustrate a point. The point is that love and immediacy have gone out of modern life because of its solely materialistic definition of value. Lawrence, whose writings are still considered "immoral" by some readers, is perhaps the most determinedly moral of all twentieth century writers. Throughout the story he continues to use definite article and common noun —"the boy," "the mother," "the father"—to point toward the universality he feels in the experience he is describing. As narrator, the other principal technique he uses is a pattern of diction which emphasizes the lack of love he describes—"stonily" is the most frequently used adverb in the story.

Much more in the story deserves attention, but I leave that to the teacher. A satisfactory account of the story must make sure that the focus of the first paragraph, the mother, is never lost sight of, and must attempt to answer the question raised by the final sentence: What kind of a life is it in which one must ride a rocking-horse to find a winner? For our present purposes, however, it is enough to see how Lawrence uses point of view to *deny* characterization.

STUDY QUESTIONS

1. Is Paul lucky? (The question is by no means simple. Oscar Cresswell, definitely a lucky man, is made nervous by Paul's gifts. Though Paul is not always "sure" of his winners, a little reflection will convince us that any method which, when fully operative, works with such rigid and absolute consistency cannot be called "luck.")

2. Is a rocking-horse a horse? (This question, ridiculous at the beginning of discussion, is crucial to accounting for the uncle's final sentence. A rocking-horse never gets anywhere or wins anything; that it must be ridden to find winners is indication of the fundamental sterility and deadness of the life led by Paul's parents.)

3. Unlike the other stories in this section, "The Rocking-Horse Winner" is an examination of a tragic situation rather than a revelation of character. In what sense is it proper to see Paul as a tragic hero?

In Joyce's "Araby," published in *Dubliners* in 1915 but written ten years earlier, we hear the voice that remains the dominant voice of modern fiction, the self-conscious, unheroic but highly sensitive, first-person narrator—a narrator less of events than of emotions. The Dublin boy in "Araby" is, in the line of literary history, the father of Salinger's Holden Caulfield, reflecting in about equal proportion the sensitivity and insensitivity of his popular descendant. Joyce's hero's sensitivity is sentimental and romantic, while Salinger's is cynical and antiromantic, but our perspective on the poignant insufficiency of both characters is shaped by the same narrative technique. For several reasons "Araby" is an excellent introduction to a deeper understanding of this familiar modern voice. First, it describes a quintessentially adolescent experience. Second, it is one of those stories puzzling to adolescents because nothing much seems to happen. Third, it demands close attention to see where and how the author reveals the character revealing himself. The teacher should try to capitalize on the first two reasons to illuminate the third: to show how our immediately felt response to the character is engineered by Joyce's technique.

The key to the young narrator's personality is his excessive emotionalism and romanticizing. This is what the story is about. More than self-revelation of character, it is also self-recognition, for this is the meaning the narrator assigns to his experience at the bazaar. However, the reader, thanks to Joyce, knows more about the narrator than does the narrator himself. This deeper knowledge continues through the last sentence of the story—and constitutes probably the main ingredient in our enjoyment of it.

The question is, will sixteen-year-olds recognize the narrator's romantic excess or will they take it all in with a straight face? The latter reaction is more likely, and it should heighten the teaching-learning experience. A more complex reaction will be that of students who feel Joyce's hero is ridiculous but will not say so because they are used to taking everything in school dead seriously. As an entrée to these problems, I suggest examining the story's sixth paragraph and insisting on honest responses to the narrator's indulgent ecstasy, "*O love! O love!*" From this point one can work backward and forward to see how Joyce is contrasting the narrator's medievalisms and Orientalisms with the shabby realities around him.

The teacher must, however, exercise great tact in this procedure, recognizing that the fantasy life of many of his students is precisely as dramatic and absurd as that of the narrator in "Araby"— or that the students, admiring his emotionalism, will wish it were. And for literary reasons as well, this is, in part, an intelligent response. The city life portrayed is drab and boring, and the narrator is without a doubt the most sensitive actor in this brief slice of the drama of Dublin life. Given the realities of love around him (his aunt's and uncle's stodginess and the stall girl's idiotic flirtations), his imaginative response has nobility in it, and part of his excessive self-derision at the end is unfortunate, for it is aimed at what is best in him.

To speak more technically, we may say that Joyce relies on his narrator's imaginative qualities to tell the story. The boy has a sharp eye, and he is honest. The first paragraph of the story is spoken by an impersonal narrator, Joyce, and its one phrase of interpretation—the houses "conscious of decent lives within them"—establishes the drab middle-class reality against which we measure both the narrator's "naturalism" and his "romanticism." His naturalistic style expresses his disgust with his surroundings, while his romantic style transforms them into something he can appreciate, though we see both the transformation and the appreciation as gratuitous, like his appreciation of *The Memoirs of Vidocq* "because its leaves were yellow." It is hardly necessary to evaluate each descriptive sentence to see if it is excessive, but the range of the boy's emotional life, stimulated by his solitary adoration of Mangum's sister, lies between such descriptions as this:

> The space of sky above us was the colour of ever-changing violet and towards it the lamps lifted their feeble lanterns.

and this:

> We walked through the flaring streets, jostled by drunken men and bargaining women, amid the curses of labourers, the shrill litanies of shop-boys who stood guard by the barrels of pigs' cheeks. . . .

Each description is pushed just a bit too far (the first more than the last), and the "life" of the story exists in the tension between these two styles.

As with most of Joyce's short stories in the *Dubliners*, it is valuable to compare the narrator of "Araby" with Stephen Dedalus in *Portrait of the Artist as a Young Man*. Like Stephen, the boy's healthiest style seems to be his realism, but it is valuably informed and heightened by his romanticism. The story, however, is about the way in which romance or emotion comes between the narrator and everyday reality, heightening his experience but weakening it for an inevitable fall. Note how many times his language un-critically expresses the intermediary distortion caused by his imagination: "I may have stood there for an hour, seeing nothing but the brown-clad figure cast by my imagination . . ."; "in the classroom her image came between me and the page I strove to read." And, most clearly:

> All my senses seemed to desire to veil themselves and, feeling that I was about to slip from them, I pressed the palms of my hands together until they trembled, murmuring: "*O love! O love!*" many times.

Several of the stories from *Dubliners* are anthologized for high school readers, and while Joyce's *Portrait* may be too difficult to use in high school, instructive comparisons can be made between *Dubliners* and chapters of Dylan Thomas' Joycean *Portrait of an Artist as a Young Dog*. These chapters are variously anthologized as stories complete in themselves; also worth comparing are Thomas' separate story, "A Story" (which, like Conrad's "Youth: A Narrative," asks for definition by its title), and *A Child's Christmas in Wales*. The last story in Thomas' *Portrait*, "One Warm Saturday," has the most affinities with the subject matter of "Araby," but the earlier stories, particularly "The Peaches" and "Patricia, Edith, and Arnold," are most instructive comparisons in technique as well as more often available. In these stories, with a younger narrator than the boy in "Araby," Thomas makes apparently simpler thematic statements. Yet they are not mere sketches, any more than is *A Child's Christmas in Wales*, which is far less sentimental than many readers think. In "Patricia, Edith, and Arnold," a girl's heart is broken and the narrator doesn't realize it; Thomas not only limits his omniscience to the intelligence of the young child whose consciousness perceives the events, but he also builds into it the selfish selectivity which determines the attention of the pampered youngster.

Another comparison of character and narrative viewpoint could be made between "Araby" and the classic, "The Open Window" by H. H. Munro ("Saki"). Though largely a joke, "The Open Window" is too cleverly constructed to be dismissed with a laugh.

Many students will laugh at the joke played on Framton Nuttel without stopping to realize that the story is "about" the young girl whose speciality was "Romance at short notice." The care she uses in setting up her victim helps us appreciate the joke; but what gives the joke its punch, so to speak, is the fact that the narration is, though omniscient, very nearly Framton's own. It is he, a nervous wreck, who twice sees the girl, by contrast, as "the self-possessed young lady." For half of the very short story, all niceties of phrasing or irony could as well be Framton's; to first-time readers, his being in the country for a "nerve cure" will not render him immediately ridiculous. But when Framton begins to talk about himself, Munro, as omniscient narrator, takes over and any sympathies or concerns we may have for Framton are modified by our seeing him as both a bore and a hypochondriac. Framton quickly becomes a mere comic object, in flight. The narrator's comment about Framton's "delusion" and the story's final sentence are the only overt interpretive statements in the story, but with them Munro is able to establish the two poles of reference that make the joke both funny and acceptable. This is artfulness of that kind preeminently relevant to the short story, namely, economy.

James Joyce is extravagant company for H. H. Munro; yet the differences in technique may serve to underline the difficulty of Joyce's achievement without pointlessly undervaluing Munro's. Narrative point of view in "The Open Window" keeps us from getting too close to either Framton or Vera, so their characters are subordinated to the joke. The narrator of "Araby" comes to realize that he has played a joke on himself, and this is important to us because we have been so close to him. If this comparison seems too top-heavy, the teacher may want to use the steps outlined in a more "serious" comparison, as between "Araby" and another of Munro's often anthologized pieces, "Shredni Vashtar," in which an adolescent is oppressed and seeks escape like the narrator of "Araby." Munro's celebrated irony is much more obvious in "Shredni Vashtar," but what, we may ask a class, is gained in Joyce's story by leaving all ironies entirely unstated and making them, instead, the very principle of narration—that is, by our understanding from the impersonally narrated first paragraph that the narrator is revealing more than he knows? In particular, how does the difference in narrative point of view affect our response to character?

STUDY QUESTIONS

1. Make a list of about ten phrases in which the narrator of "Araby" describes something in overwrought or inappropriate language (for example, in the bazaar, "I recognised a silence like that which pervades a church after service"). Analyze some of these phrases carefully to see how they do double duty: 1) insofar as they are "too much," they illumine the narrator's character, but 2) they must also be accurate, to have given us such a sense of the complete reality of the surroundings and characters in the story.

2. One element of narrative control in the story not yet touched upon is its verb tense. At two or three points the narrator seems to reveal that his perception of his folly at the end of the story has influenced his "present" situation. Where are these points? How do they affect our confidence in the narrator? (Compare with Conrad's Marlow.)

3. Is the narrator in Thomas' "The Peaches" and "Patricia, Edith, and Arnold" as aware as Joyce's narrator of the meaning of the events he has recounted? How does this difference in narration affect our response to character?

"Bliss" is a story in which characterization and point of view are joined together masterfully, and students should benefit greatly from learning to distinguish the two. Once they have done this, they will appreciate the other technical problem that arises in the story: the often vexing question of symbolism. The story is so highly instructive on both counts the teacher may want to use it twice—once in grade eleven and again in grade twelve, where it might serve as an introduction to the stories of symbolism and allegory which in this series of analyses are reserved until that time.

To clarify students' opinions about the story, I recommend that they be asked to write a one-page statement of what the story is about, to be handed in on the day discussion of the story begins. The assignment need not be graded closely; its purpose is to stimulate affective responses to the story which could lead to thoughtful conclusions. Two stock responses will face the teacher immediately. One will be overwhelmingly positive reactions to Bertha Young's "bliss." For these readers, Bertha Young is a delightful young woman who is cruelly deceived, and her experience in the story will seem rather abrupt and pointless. As in Joyce's "Araby," adolescents will identify with adolescents; as also in "Araby," the honesty in this response is partially accurate and not to be discouraged. The other stock response will see the story as a sexual episode of the *Playboy*-pulp fiction genre: the girl thought she was going to be happy, but she wasn't. Period. Though there is less to recommend this reaction, it, too, isolates an aspect of the story which must be taken into account. Both stock responses are to subject matter, and the teacher will do well to build upon them to show how an understanding of technique—*how* the writer is telling his story rather than *what* he is telling—helps us to understand a story more fully and satisfactorily. Of these two responses, the first is based on a misapprehension of narrative point of view while the second, insofar as it is based on anything other than sexual naïveté, derives from an uncritical acceptance of the symbolism of the story.

At first glance, the story seems to be told by an omniscient narrator; a second glance sees Bertha as narrator; a third scrutinizing glance reveals a combination of two narrative points of view. This combination allows Katherine Mansfield to achieve extraordinarily subtle effects, but appreciating these effects depends on our being able to differentiate between narrators. One might begin by announcing that Katherine Mansfield, being a shrewd and intelligent woman, could not possibly feel as unguarded about happiness as the speaker in the story's second paragraph. However, students will resent and resist this kind of information, and rightly so; indeed, critics of Mansfield's fiction (among them T. S. Eliot) are not at all agreed that such gushings could *not* be hers. A better method is to show the students that there is a difference between the narrator's voice and Bertha Young's. The story opens with someone talking about Bertha Young; the voice is apparently sympathetic, but it is not Bertha's voice, quite. At the end of the third paragraph, the voice asks rhetorically, "Why be given a body if you have to keep it shut up in a case like a rare, rare fiddle?" The fourth paragraph begins with Bertha commenting on the accuracy of the question: " 'No, that about the fiddle is not quite what I mean,' she said."

Insisting on this difference between voices should be enough; we allow that the narrator does at many points choose to identify her voice with Bertha's, or at least, as in the lines just quoted, to "talk" amicably with Bertha. In fact, the distinction is easier than this to establish, since the narrator obviously speaks in the third person and Bertha in the first, but such a simple distinction does not do justice to the subtlety with which Miss Mansfield crosses or blurs the lines between persons. Many points of information and evaluation in the story could as well be Bertha's as the narrator's. It is hardly necessary—or possible—to answer which is which on each point; what is necessary is to keep the question open, realizing that one voice is not the other. In the amazing final sentence and in such sentences as the following—"Came another tiny moment, while they waited, laughing and talking, just a trifle too much at their ease, a trifle too unaware"—one feels, even if one cannot precisely identify it, the difference between Bertha and the narrator: here are the guests, waiting for Pearl Fulton's entrance. Much of the studied artifice of Bertha's life is caught in this brief judgment.

Our assessment of her actions elsewhere in the story and of her highly exterior self-consciousness enable us to say with some confidence that these and other small judgments are not hers, or are much less hers than she may suppose. She is impulsive and irresponsible ("feeling in her bag for the key—she'd forgotten it, as usual"), despite her undeniable attractiveness. Even students quite taken with the apparent excitement of Bertha's life will feel uncomfortable about her behavior with her baby, and most likely they will relate their implicit criticism of her motherliness to her success as a wife.

As these and other details are pondered, students will see more of Bertha's character than they imagined they could. In the first place, with an omniscient narrator we might well expect indications of ways in which the main character is achieving or failing to achieve self-knowledge, but if anything there are fewer indications than in "Araby." Secondly (and this perhaps makes Miss Mansfield's theme more telling than Joyce's), insufficient self-awareness comes to a character who imagines herself to be more honest with herself than her fellow mortals are ("How idiotic civilization is!" is Bertha's refrain on this point), and who furthermore imagines herself questing, indeed attaining, an especially honest and open communication with another fellow mortal, above and beyond the limits of mere civilization.

All of these points bring us to the heart of the story, Bertha's symbolic pear tree—symbol of her beauty, happiness, and transcendence: "she seemed to see on her eyelids the lovely pear tree with its wide open blossoms as a symbol of her own life." (High school students sometimes rebel at the teacher's insistence on searching for symbols in literature. Such rebellion stems in part from the fact that symbolism is one of the most sophisticated modes of understanding, but it also stems from improper, heavy-handed teaching which gaily probes level after deeper level of "hidden meanings" while the student remains behind on the surface, doggedly mistrustful of the enterprise.) In "Bliss" students can learn, relatively painlessly, a good deal about the *im*proper interpretation of symbols. Here for once a symbol is labeled a symbol.

A symbol evokes or connotes more than it could possibly mean if taken literally. Also, a symbol is an exterior sign of some interior, deeply felt reality. To test the adequacy of Bertha's symbol, one asks why the story's last sentence begins with "but." "But the pear tree was as lovely as ever and as full of flower and as still." Why "but"? Good students, whether sympathetic or unsympathetic to Bertha, will realize that her expectation was that the pear tree should be destroyed now that she realizes that her "absolutely satisfactory" life has been destroyed. We need not insist that Bertha literally expected this, for she is not that kind of fool, but the conjunction indicates that she expected it figuratively. There are three ways of interpreting her expectation: either she has forgotten the essential externality of all symbols, or she has created a symbol without an essential tie to an inner reality, or the inner reality has been false. All interpretations provide illuminating perceptions of her character.

Taking the first possibility, we may recall Bertha's persistent response to her surroundings as so many external objects. Her baby is a doll, her husband a pal, her friends are "a decorative group . . . and how they reminded her of a play by Tchekof!" Life is, in short, an artifact, and living is one continuous problem in interior decoration, to be managed with the best taste possible. Taking the pear tree as a symbol is the last step in a continuous series of externalizations. She even dresses like a pear tree, though the narrator tells us that this is unintentional—or is the statement, "It wasn't intentional," Bertha's rationalization? The narrative complexity of the story raises but does not answer the question.

Or, the symbol may be inadequately connected to reality. We notice her selectivity in creating the symbol. Presumably she does feel happy, so the pear tree is partially adequate as a symbol. But she has other deep feelings about life, and one in particular which she refuses to admit to her consciousness or her symbolism: "What creepy things cats are!" The cats, a female and a male, remind Bertha of sexual facts about life which she cannot face, and she turns away from her symbolic picture, actually stammering. Thus the symbol is inadequate, unexpressive. The re-introduction of the gray and the black cats as an image for the exit of Pearl Fulton and Eddie Warren is intentionally obtrusive, and again the two narrative voices are extremely close. It is also a point at which students can learn that symbolism is neither allegory nor algebra. At the end of Bertha's party a "creepy" reality—sexuality and her husband's infidelity—has confronted her, and she rejects it, just as she turned away from the cats earlier. She runs to look at the pear tree, half expecting to see it devastated. A complex of associations has been evoked. To interpret the cats' second "appearance" literally—Miss Fulton as gray cat, Eddie as black—makes no sense, for Eddie is not involved in her momentary perception. The pear tree remains as beautiful as ever because it is not a true symbol. It is not complex enough, and its disappointing endurance reflects Bertha's refusal to admit the complexities which have touched her life. Some students will insist that the pear tree remains a symbol of enduring beauty. If it is so to them, let it be, as long as they agree that it is not symbolic of the enduring beauty of its creator's life.

A last question to be considered as a narrative problem in "Bliss" is the moment of communication which Bertha establishes with Pearl. Here false symbolism and narrative ambiguity achieve their most subtle effect—so subtle, indeed, as to be arguable. When the two women stand side by side looking at the garden, the narration must for several reasons be something very like the stream of Bertha's own consciousness. First of all, the "sign" which Pearl gives is a bland afterdinner remark ("Have you a garden?") which could hardly be less capable of bearing the mystic significance with which Bertha freights it. Second, the rhetoric of the two relevant paragraphs is top-heavy and reflects Bertha's concerns and language entirely: "wondering what they were to do in this [world] with all this blissful treasure. . . ." This is the rhetoric of the opening paragraph of the story, now raised to "symbolic" intensity. The paragraph following it is inserted by Katherine Mansfield precisely to make us question the reality of the moment just passed and see through it: "For ever—for a moment? And did Miss Fulton murmur: 'Yes. Just *that*.' Or did Bertha dream it?" The answer of course is Yes.

STUDY QUESTIONS

1. Do you think Bertha intentionally dresses "like" a pear tree? Present your reasons. She is certainly *seen* to resemble her pear tree: How, and by whom?

2. Bertha's talk is much like the narrator's, or vice versa. What about the other characters? Which ones talk like her and which ones talk differently? Is the story suggesting, in part, that "talk" gets in the way of real experience? (Teachers will probably want to sketch London in the 1920's to provide background for the determinedly liberated, "modern" behavior of the characters.)

3. What is gained, positively, for Bertha's character by making her, so to speak, a partial narrator of her experience?

4. Compare Katherine Mansfield's "non-symbolism" in "Bliss" with Conrad's heavy symbolism.

5. The story is about Bertha. Why is it best told in the way it is? Try to imagine one of the other characters as narrator: what problems arise that get in the way of expressing the story that Katherine Mansfield wants to tell?

Short Stories for Grade Twelve

Any literature in translation inevitably presents a distorted picture of the original, limiting the ways in which critically significant statements can be made about it.* However, in reading European short stories this limitation can be turned to good account, since it forces us to concentrate on an aspect of the genre which is more germane to the European story than to the British or American. This is, simply, the meaning, statement, or "moral" of the story and the several traditional modes of expressing it, from parable to allegory to symbolism. Several other avenues of approach, while they may be important in a story's original language, are quite closed to naïve discussion and should be avoided. Tone and attitude are particularly risky, since "standard" translations reduce wide divergences to a false consistency, and Maupassant, Dostoevsky, and Kafka come out sounding about the same. (The renaissance in the art of translation since World War II has altered this situation.) To a lesser extent setting and character can be equally distorting; important nuances may be lost in translation or may remain unintelligible without lengthy historical explanations. For example, in Stephen Crane's "The Blue Hotel" we recognize both the Wild West of imagination and the not-so-wild West of reality. But can the evocative associations of I. B. Singer's Polish hamlets really come alive for most readers? Can the puns imbedded in the names of many of Dostoevsky's characters be translated felicitously? How much of the atmosphere of the Third Republic, that strange interlude of history in which Maupassant's stories are set, is it worth trying to reconstruct?

* For a teaching unit on the problems of translation, see Edward B. Jenkinson's unit, "Nothing Moves Without Translation," in *What Is Language? and Other Teaching Units for Grades Seven Through Twelve*, a volume in this English Curriculum Study Series.

The short story in America has roots, for better and for worse, in the tall tales of the frontier—tales of man overcoming nature, or being overcome. In England, the short story has strong connections with a background of criminal and horror fiction. In Europe, the short story has been influenced most importantly, among many factors, by the philosophic tradition in Western thought. It is not for nothing that the great figures of Western philosophy have tended to be Italian, French, or German rather than English and American. The English accepted and relished Europeans' designation of them as eminently practical philosophers. Americans have accepted it even more wholeheartedly; the uniquely American philosophy, pragmatism, raises usefulness, the great irrelevancy of European philosophy, to the status of a metaphysical entity. The greatest poets of the Romantic movement were English; the greatest theoreticians of Romanticism were German and French, whereas English Romantic theory is noticeably confused and informal.

This rationale for studying short stories in translation should not suggest that there is more meaning in Continental stories than in stories written elsewhere (a logical absurdity). Rather, it is given to suggest that Europeans have been more ready to make their meaning explicit, or to present their stories as illustrations of discursive arguments. There are countless exceptions, naturally. Yet even the folk tale or fairy tale, the purest of all pure story forms, is often revealed, in its original context, as an illustration of some ancient truth. The European short story, like the "European mind," is preeminently a story of *ideas*. Given this important factor in its tradition of development, it is not surprising that European refinements in the *technique* of the short story have been refinements in the area of allegory and symbolism—the modes of literary understanding which stand closest to nonliterary, or discursive, expressions of meaning, and also the modes which philosophers have most often appropriated to add persuasiveness and suggestiveness to their arguments, from the time of Heraclites' river and Plato's cave.*

---

* Two omissions in the following sequence should be noted. First, the absence of any non-Western short stories. We should attempt to broaden our students' perspectives on the East, but only very modern stories from the

FABLE AND PARABLE

MEMNON THE PHILOSOPHER
by Voltaire

LOVE: THREE PAGES FROM A SPORTSMAN'S BOOK
by Guy de Maupassant

WAR
by Luigi Pirandello

The French, proverbially, are the most rational of the Europeans. Whether the proverb has any truth or not, it is certain that Voltaire is the most rational of rational Frenchmen. He was a philosopher who wrote like a poet, and thus may be taken as a better opening perspective on the European short story than Goethe, a poet who wrote like a philosopher. In Voltaire's "Memnon the Philosopher, Or Human Wisdom" (a miniature of *Candide, or Optimism*), we see clearly the close connection between stated and embodied meanings—that is, between philosophy and literature, between what we are *told* and what we are *shown*. Next, in Guy de Maupassant, Voltaire's countryman a hundred years removed and one of the recognized creators of the short story as a legitimate form of serious literature, we see how literature has taken over, but how, as throughout the Continental tradition, the presence of a "moral" or a definitely assignable meaning remains.

Near East and the Far East (and Africa and Latin America) display more than the most traditional elements of technique, such as fable and parable. Nevertheless, these simple stories, like the fairy story, can be a valuable introduction to the more sophisticated uses of fable, parable, and symbol which are examined in this chapter. Stories from "The Arabian Nights" are useful, as well as parables and "short stories" from the Bible (The Book of Jonah, The Book of Ruth)—which, we should not forget, is a product of Near Eastern civilization. The second omission is of Russian fiction, and it is regrettable. Stories by Chekhov, Dostoevsky, and Gogol would make a particularly valuable supplement to the present selection, for the genius of the Russian masters is precisely their gift for fusing intense realism with intense symbolism.

"Memnon" is properly called a philosophic tale rather than a moral tale. What it satirizes is not man's physical failings, but man's rational weakness which leads him to presume to control or explain away his physical nature. In the Anglo-American Puritan tradition, a story like "Memnon" would emphasize the foolish sinfulness of his lust, gluttony, and mendacity, and some high school seniors, influenced by this tradition, will read it with such an emphasis. But Voltaire has, at least implicitly, a fond regard for human appetites, and saves his scorn for overly rigid attempts to control them. The principal figure Voltaire is satirizing among the "poets . . . who tell us that everything is for the best" is Alexander Pope, reminding us of the radical difference between two national traditions. The target of this philosophic tale is thus philosophy itself, if philosophy is conceived as a system of thought which can account for everything in life.

The most important part of the story, therefore, is Memnon's interview with the celestial spirit, and students should be helped to grasp the irony in the story's last two sentences before they consider the ways in which the form of Voltaire's argument approximates literature. The celestial spirit is voicing the arguments of Leibniz, Pope, and Shaftesbury when he says that the poets and philosophers who tell us that all is for the best are right, "when we consider things in relation to the gradation of the whole universe." Memnon's refusal to believe this, "till I recover my eye again" (that is, never), is a defiant assertion of humanity in the face of philosophy. That such poets and philosophers are "right" may be satisfying to celestial spirits, but their consolations are at best irrelevant and at worst infuriating to men. This interchange exactly parallels the more famous one between Pangloss and Candide at the end of *Candide*. Pangloss gives one last explanation of the necessary causes which led all the events of the book to transpire as they did, and Candide replies in Memnon's vein, though more poignantly: " 'Tis well said . . . but we must cultivate our gardens."

Having understood that the very content of Voltaire's meaning is irony (or philosophical skepticism, as it is tecnically called), students may then enjoy looking over the story again to appreciate the unremittingly ironic tone of everything in it—not least of all that "interesting" moment when Memnon counsels the beautiful niece so closely and tenderly "that neither of them could talk any longer of business nor well knew what they were about."

In what sense is "Memnon" a story? Certainly the setting, action, and characters make no real claim upon our emotions. The oddity of ancient Nineveh's being filtered through the customs of eighteenth-century France should discourage even the most literal-minded student from raising questions of motivation and probability and lead him to connect his experience of the story to his familiarity with parables from the Old and New Testaments. But the story is more than a parable in its *action*. If we have interpreted Memnon's last sentence correctly, then we are justified in feeling that his character has undergone an interior as well as an exterior change as a result of his experience, and that he has come to a realization about life. This change, underemphasized though it be, is what gives the story a more *literary* interest than, for example, the story of Abraham and Isaac. A "pure" parable, somewhat like an allegory, tends to confirm a truth already stated outside the limits of the story; but in *literary parable,* the truth is intrinsic to the story. Memnon's growth in character is what weds the philosophic and literary dimensions of the story together. Without evidence of Memnon's change, Voltaire's philosophic intent would be unclear, though it would be adequate for the philosophic *argument* to end with the angel's last statement.

STUDY QUESTIONS

1. Does Voltaire believe that philosophy is literally impossible and that we should never waste a moment's thought on the meaning of our existence? Or has Memnon made an improper *use* of philosophy, expecting too much of it? (Consider the gradation of worlds of which the angel speaks: apparently, as philosophy diminishes, so does enjoyment.)

2. Though there is not much detail in the story, Voltaire often includes detail to good purpose. What, for example, is the effect of the following sentence: "Having thus laid his little plan of philosophy in his closet, Memnon put his head out of the window." Does the effect relate to the thoroughgoing irony of the story?

3. Use your knowledge of history in explaining the following sentence: "America was not then discovered, and distressed ladies were not nearly as dangerous as they are now."

To recognize a connection between Voltaire and Guy de Maupassant requires that we look at Maupassant in a rather different way. But a special look, while it does less than justice to what is unique in Maupassant, helps us to see ways in which this early master of the genre perpetuates habits of mind that characterize European short stories in general, and French stories in particular.

High school seniors, with few exceptions, will have read some of Maupassant's stories. What is more, they will remember them—maybe not by title (many of his titles are bland, and subject to vagaries of translation), but they will be able to describe an unusual sequence of events, a *plot*, that was immediately interesting to them and, like all things with intrinsic appeal, has stuck in their minds. Their experience is evidence of the genuineness of Maupassant's innovative genius, for his suave facility in plot construction is his primary claim to his position as one of the creators of the modern short story. His gift is real and valuable, despite the nagging persistence of a view of him as a mere entertainer. His plot construction is, at best, not mere intricacy and cleverness of movement—qualities largely irrelevant to the meaning of plot—but the embodiment of meaning in action.

Having recalled students to their earlier enjoyment of Maupassant, we may encourage them to consider it in a new way. His plots suggest meaning; to put it crudely, they make us stop and think. Seniors may also be familiar with the works of O. Henry: can they say that his tricky plots and surprise endings make us stop and think? Without guaranteeing results, I suggest experimenting toward the following conclusions. Will not students recall only the surprise or "jolt" of an O. Henry story, whereas their memory of a Maupassant story will be accompanied by the rudiments of a statement as to the *meaning* of the events? "The Gift of the Magi" defies ready formulation, not because it is so deep, but because the turn of events is so dramatic as to leave us—like its protagonists—at something of a loss. But "A Piece of String" does not. It is true that Maupassant's endings, though abrupt, are not surprises, so the experiment is not entirely fair; but, whether or not it works, it at least suggests that events move toward a meaningful conclusion in his work, though as an artist he naturally does not state it explicitly.

Voltaire's meaning in "Memnon" is not stated, either, but it is built rather obviously into his narrative. My special feeling about many of Maupassant's stories is that they exist within an invisible frame, as though we were to read Aesop's fables without their suggestive titles and inevitable "morals." I hear Maupassant saying, under his breath, "I will tell you a story which shows that . . . ," and muttering at the end, "Thus we see that . . . ." In this he shares the evident motivation of his countryman—to teach.

Any of Maupassant's stories may be used to test out this hypothesis with a class; some of the most familiar ones might be best. However, "Love: Three Pages from a Sportsman's Book" brings an added valuable dimension into discussion, for it is a story whose moral, ostensibly at least, is conveyed symbolically. Voltaire's "Memnon" is not symbolic except in the largest sense—Memnon as Everyman. In "Love," we see vestiges of the philosophic fable, but the meaning is allowed to rise out of events, and our literary enjoyment is heightened at the same time that our merely logical pleasure is clouded. Maupassant was more of a *symboliste* than many of his more popular stories will show, and his sophistication in the mode is evident in "Love," in which, as in Katherine Mansfield's "Bliss," the meaning symbolized by the narrator is not the meaning he actually reveals.

The title suggests a philosophic paper, a definition of a universal truth from an individual point of view. But a humorous tension between "love" and "sportsman" slightly mocks this suggestion. Knowing Voltaire, we smile at the tension caused when we see "philosopher" and "wisdom" linked in "Memnon." The philosophic aura of "Love" is dispelled abruptly when the narrator impatiently rules out all interest in "the drama of passion" beyond the fact that it stimulated him to the recollection which is the story. He has made a predicative assertion, "He killed her and then he killed himself, *so* he must have loved her" (italics mine), but then he throws out agent (cause), effect, and meaning, and substitutes memory. "Their love alone matters to me; and it does not interest me because it moves me or astonishes me, or because it softens me or makes me think, but because it recalls to my mind a remembrance of my youth." Memory in turn is associated not with conclusions of fact and reason, but with the testimonies and miracles of faith: "Love appeared to me, as the Cross appeared to the early Christians in the midst of the heavens."

The illogic of the narrator's reasoning in the first paragraph may have to be pointed out to students, but if they have learned to pay attention to narrative point of view, they will feel that the narrator is confused or confusing, and discussion will quickly bring them to feel he is profoundly inconsistent, hypocritical, or deluded. This is revealed in many ways, the most obvious of which is the clash between the narrator's condescending description of his cousin as "an amiable semi-brute" and the cousin's benevolent concern for the narrator's well-being which prompts the cousin to light a fire even though the blaze will make the hunt less successful. Boys with an interest in hunting and wildlife will feel in addition the inappropriate combination of blood lust and squeamishness in the narrator's attitude toward hunting, and may even make a persuasive case for his poor sportsmanship in his implied reluctance to shoot the drake when, under the circumstances, it is the humane thing to do. The narrator breathes in the sensation of the drake's heartrending cries, while it is left to Karl to finish the job.

Once the narrator's character is well understood, we begin to see that Maupassant is examining the emotionalism, perhaps even the sick emotionalism, underlying the celebrated rationalism of the cliché Frenchman. The narrator says, at the beginning of the second paragraph, "I was born with all the instincts and the senses of primitive man, tempered by the arguments and the restraints of a civilized being." This frank admission of irrational instincts, somewhat winning at first, is seen by the end of the story to express an unrecognized and unhealthy split in his attitude toward life.

The narrator's symbolism may be considered in the light of the extreme contrast between his attitudes. Since students will have taken this symbolism seriously at first and have come away confused, they will be glad to be given an opportunity to tear it apart once the suggestion has been made that there is something amiss in it. Briefly, what are we to make of a judgment that, on the one hand, calls the marsh "the best shooting ground I ever saw," and, on the other, finds in it "the mystery of creation itself"?

> For was it not in stagnant and muddy water, amid the heavy humidity of moist land under the heat of the sun, that the first germ of life pulsated and expanded to the day?

The dichotomy between "shooting" and "life" is the dichotomy of the narrator's personality; it reminds us of the tension between "love" and "sportsman" in the title.

Other excesses and inconsistencies abound: the sadistic (or masochistic?) relish with which the wind and cold are described—violent verbs piled on top of each other to no purpose. And what of the narrator's being seized "by the powerful and singular emotion which marshes cause in me," in light of the fact that "this one was dead, dead from cold" not humid and moist "under the heat of the sun"?

Just as it is difficult to find a coherent meaning in the narrator's symbolism aside from the incoherence of his personality, so it is difficult to assign a meaning to the experience he relates aside from what he unwittingly reveals about himself. We recall that he recalls the experience not to prove anything, but simply because he was reminded of it by a crime of passion. He does not even offer a generalization to the effect that love is violent. Rather, he simply shows that love and violent death are intimately associated in his mind, and that for all his civilized, Parisian rationality he is stimulated by the violence of nature. This is indeed no more than he has admitted about himself, but his excessive indulgence in what he calls "the instincts and the senses of primitive man" shows that his frankness is a ploy to deflect scrutiny. His self-titillation about the mysteries of the marsh and the violence of the wind, not to mention his enraptured audience of the drake's cries, are not primitive instincts at all, but the consciously manipulated enjoyments of an effete city-dweller spoiled by the refinements of "civilization."

It is possible that some students will insist, even after discussion, that the story is to be taken literally, and that its inconclusiveness when so taken is neither here nor there. Then all the narrator's excesses become mere mood evocations, and the connections between love (or life) and death are not odd but plausible or simply gratuitous. If this view is defended by reference to the fact that crimes of passion are still reported daily in our newspapers, then the students should at least be made to see that frequent connection of these two realities has made students as insensitive to the incongruity as is the narrator of Maupassant's story.

Like Voltaire, Maupassant has applied irony to a philosophic enterprise; his narrator fancies himself as wise as Memnon. That Memnon seems to learn while the narrator of "Love" does not is not essential to the meaning of the story; what connects the two is the strategy by which we are shown that our notions of Wisdom and Love are subject to human limitations, either physical or emotional. Maupassant's story is more truly literature than Voltaire's because the meaning depends on attention to the action—especially to actions (like Karl's) which "betray" or qualify the narration—since there is no "celestial spirit" with whom to discuss the meaning of events when they have all transpired.

STUDY QUESTIONS

1. In what ways are setting, character, and action as *un*important in "Love" as in Voltaire's "Memnon"? What sorts of information about these three categories is Maupassant ruling out, and why? What sort does he leave in?

2. Enumerate the ways in which cousin Karl proves himself more than "an amiable semi-brute." In what ways does the narrator's description of his cousin reflect back on himself?

3. Students have probably learned by the twelfth grade that assigning "morals" is an inappropriate response to a story because it truncates the reading experience. This is all to the good, but they might well learn the importance of the lesson in reverse. Ask them to state a "moral" which takes account of all the complexity of the story. (If they have *not* learned the danger of "the moral," let a student give one for "Love" and then subject it to the class's scrutiny.)

4. Another symbol in the story, besides the marsh, is the ice hut, which is compared to "an enormous diamond with a heart of fire." Whose symbol is this, the narrator's or Maupassant's, or both?

What does it symbolize? (Does it connect meaningfully with the narrator's experience, or with our view of his experience?)

The title of Luigi Pirandello's "War," like that of Maupassant's "Love: Three Pages from a Sportsman's Book," suggests a definition to follow. Like Maupassant's, Pirandello's definition is oblique; what is defined is not the general concept but individual versions of it. Being artists, not philosophers, their object is not to tell us what love or war is, but to show us what people think it is; they define the definers. Though both stories may be called philosophic, they are so, like the philosopher Voltaire's, by being antiphilosophic; that is, they are directed against human pretensions to abstract, general knowledge when maintained at the expense of human particularity and weakness.

Actually, war in "War" is less a concept than a catalyst; it is an event in man's existence which demands that he come to terms with it in some way, however inadequate. The conceptual term which is offered by the fat, red-faced man is Patriotism, ideal devotion to King and Country, and it is this concept, rather than war *per se*, that is the subject of Pirandello's examination. Strictly speaking, it is not even patriotism that temporarily soothes the parents, but their acceptance of the fat man's plausible rationalization of patriotism as one among many of the things more important to young men than to their parents. They do not notice the odd company of "illusions" in which the fat man lists it: "girls, cigarettes, illusions, new ties . . . and the Country, of course, whose call we would have answered—when we were twenty—even if father and mother had said no."

The form of Pirandello's story's statement is argumentative; the form of the reading experience it provides is parable-like. Let us consider the parable first. Much less happens in this story than in the previous two. Maupassant's is immediately recognized as a modern short story, while Voltaire's is a philosophic fable. Despite the quite violent actions in the latter, we are clear as to the unreality of the characters who perform or suffer them. Pirandello's characters are fully realized, but the point of his realism is not to involve us deeply in his characters' lives. Rather, it is to give immediacy to their arguments, to make us feel that the story is a tract for our times. The towns, the trains, and the war are all contemporary for Pirandello. If a war is not currently being fought in Italy when one reads the story, a war is being fought somewhere, and that place automatically becomes the setting of the story. Beyond this immediacy, the characters are nothing more than mouthpieces drawn into company by one of literature's oldest organizing devices, the journey. (In its blunt way of lumping characters together, the form of "War" resembles Pirandello's most famous work, the play, *Six Characters in Search of an Author*.) The one way in which he elects to elaborate his characters is to draw attention to their physical ugliness, a corollary, presumably, to the ugliness of their attempts to console themselves for the loss of their sons by viewing it as the loss of so much property, with hardly a word of concern or lamentation for the sufferings of the young soldiers themselves.

The parable takes the form of an argument. Once Pirandello has gathered his speakers together in a plausibly realistic way, he keeps his voice out of much of the rest of the story, leaving the characters to their own conclusions. Their arguments are on two levels. First the various parents bicker back and forth with petty selfishness as to who loses most when sons go to war (again, the sons' losses are never considered). This kind of argument can go nowhere, for it is without objective premises. Nevertheless, the story goes on to imply that such arguments are better than the ones to follow, since they are at least human. The fat man puts the argument on a rational plane, though its rationality is quickly seen to be rationalization. His logic is compelling at first, because he exposes the selfishness of the former stage of the argument with a fine and telling phrase about the relation of children and parents: "We belong to them but they never belong to us." This is small satisfaction for most parents, however, including the fat man, and he quickly blurs his momentarily clear perception with a sleight-of-mind trick which slips love of Country in among those interests like girls and new ties which make young men disregard or forget their parents. He says, in effect, that we do not think of Country but our sons do, because it is one of the things that interests youth. His statement that parents' love for their children is stronger than their love of Country sounds attractive, but we have already seen how largely self-serving love can be. It is on this tissue of illogic, colored by a bourgeois romanticizing of the joys of dying young, that the fat man has the temerity to raise the suggestion that the parents should not grieve but should "laugh, as I do."

This "unselfish" rationality penetrates the bulk of the mother in mourning whose entrance into the carriage provoked the discussion. For three months her husband and friends have been trying to console her, doubtless with all the inevitably inadequate solicitudes which spring up in the presence of grief. But now she sees, or thinks she sees, that her grief was "wrong," and that she was at fault in it because she "could not rise up to the same height of those fathers and mothers willing to resign themselves, without crying, not only to the departure of their sons but even to their death."

The reversals at the story's end are sudden; in them the parable is transformed into a story and the mouthpieces of the argument are revealed as human beings. Pirandello, in attacking patriotism, is attacking the most socially acceptable rationalization of the horror of war. He is certainly "against war," but he opposes it not by direct attack, but by attacking the ways in which war, which everybody hates, is nevertheless made palatable and "necessary." The mother finds herself in "a world she had never dreamt of," but in the next sentence Pirandello makes clear that this world of stoic patriotism is indeed a dream world. The mother asks, "almost as if waking up from a dream," the basic, shocking, human question which tears the fabric of rationalization and plunges the fat man down into humanity and grief: "then . . . is your son really dead?"

Pirandello, like many modern Italian writers, is a much more political artist than we are used to in the Anglo-American tradition. The question of whether we can accept an artist's vision when we do not accept the ideas on which it is founded crops up far more often in European literature and criticism—whether Marxist, Freudian, or whatever—than in English or American literature and criticism. The plays of Bernard Shaw are an illustrative exception to the apolitical Anglo-American tradition, but our difficulty with Shaw's ideas is not nearly so acute as with, say, the ideas in the dramas of Ibsen and Strindberg. Great art transcends whatever limitations of thought inform its origins; great writers need not be great philosophers. Though the political ideology of Luigi Pirandello, as a man, may have been "leftist" and socialistic, "War" is not an ideological story. On the contrary, it punctures the rationalist pretensions of ideology and returns us, less comfortable but more human, to the tragic, insoluble dilemmas of life. Students will find the end of the story sad, but if their attention is directed to the form—parable and argument—which creates it, they should see that grief is more positive, more open, than rationalization, which seeks to avoid pain by closing itself into limiting ideologies which debase human experience into slogans like "King and Country."

STUDY QUESTIONS

1. In what ways does Pirandello seek to present his story in a universal aspect? Why then is he so particular about trains and stations at the beginning?

2. Turn the story into a non-story by overemphasizing its parable-like qualities and altering its dramatic aspects. (One possible non-story would be a piece of narrative propaganda *for* "King and Country.")

3. For better students only: using Pirandello's story as a reference, consider the usefulness of the slogan, "Better Red than Dead." (Or, write a story with this title, making use of Pirandello's devices.)

4. Why does the fat old man twice insist that he is only speaking of "decent boys" in his argument for the glory of dying young in the service of one's country? What effect does this qualification have on the reader?

5. Pirandello's characters are masters of the cliché, and a good translation will capture this. Are his clichés merely realistic, or does he make a heightened use of such phrases as "a world she had never dreamt of," and "words failed him"?

6. A large question raised by the story is this: How do we reconcile ourselves to the need for young men to die defending their country? The question is unanswerable, but inexhaustible.

SYMBOLISM AND ALLEGORY

IN THE PENAL COLONY
by Franz Kafka

GIMPEL THE FOOL
by I. J. Singer

Symbolism has been the dominant mode of literary expression in the twentieth century: the conscious elaboration of the possibilities of symbolism by European writers, especially French and Russian, of the later nineteenth century created what has become the characteristically "modern" literature of all Western nations. Almost every modern short story considered in this three-grade sequence has had a symbolic dimension. It has not been the most important dimension in most of them, but in some, like "Bliss" and "Love: Three Pages from a Sportsman's Book," the pervasive influence of the mode is evident. In these stories the writers not only assume the reader's familiarity with symbolic expression; they build the assumption into the story by creating characters who express themselves symbolically.

In previous explications I have had occasion to mention the difficulty and unpopularity of the symbolic mode among high school students. Every teacher can make his own estimate of how much of this unpopularity results from improper teaching. Heavy-handed symbol hunting can also produce a false enthusiasm on the part of certain students (usually the brighter ones) which leads them to look for the "key" to the "hidden meaning" in every story they read. This is perhaps even more unfortunate than students' distrust of symbols. Recognition of the *limitations* of purely symbolic expression has been urged for almost three decades, but while these processes of intellectual history have been completing themselves, thousands of college graduates with teaching certificates have descended upon secondary schools with the gospel of symbolism, presenting it with an enthusiasm more unbounded than the *avant-gardistes* of fifty years ago. On the other hand, many younger teachers will have graduated from universities where enthusiasm for The Symbol has waned along with other of the doctrinaire aspects of the so-called New Criticism. What is to be recommended in this situation is a certain amount of tentativeness in either the enthusiasm or the distaste that one brings to one's treatment of literary symbolism. Moderation will do much to assuage the distrust of some students and calm the frenzy of others.

My own treatment of "In the Penal Colony" and "Gimpel the Fool" will be tentative, as much for self-defense as for more objective reasons. One winces at the thought of providing a full-scale symbolic reading of Kafka's story for high school seniors; the futility and difficulty of such an enterprise would be too painfully "Kafkaesque." Furthermore, as teachers, our task is not to interpret symbols but to introduce students to ways of reading which will help them respond to symbolic content in a piece of literature. The student who reads "In the Penal Colony" as a true adventure story is not "wrong," but he has radically limited the range of response which it encourages. But so has the student who reads it as "nothing but" an allegory of, say, the decline and fall of Western Christianity. If, however, one finds it difficult to merely elucidate formal technique when teaching symbolism, that is as it should be, for with symbols we are closest to the point where form and content are indistinguishable. A powerful symbol, like the Cross to a Christian, is simultaneously a form and a meaning.

The stories by Maupassant and Pirandello are about recognizably real people doing real things in a familiar world. Though the meaning of each story is large and significant, it does not depend on our translating the action and speeches of the characters to another plane from that on which we first see them. What principally made us aware of the true dimension of these stories is the form—of argument in Maupassant and of parable in Pirandello. Voltaire's "Memnon" is not realistic like "Love" and "War," but everything that happens to Memnon, even the visit of the angel (which comes in a dream), is a recognizably human event. Again the form of the story, especially its archaic setting, calls attention to itself and demands that we see it in a larger-than-literal dimension. Insofar as the entire structure of "Memnon" leads us to generalize the experience it contains, it is a more symbolic story than

"Love" or "War." But no story is "more symbolic" than another because it "symbolizes more" (things, meanings, or whatnot): like any other aspect of the short story writer's art, symbolism is a function of form, not of subject matter.

Thus, "In the Penal Colony" is a more symbolic story than "Gimpel the Fool" not because it suggests a greater scope of meaning (it doesn't), but because it requires for our fullest response to it that we see its characters, events, and actions in a different way from "Gimpel." If we could "translate" everything in the story down to the smallest detail into a nonliterary plane of discourse, it would be an allegory. But it is not, and a great part of its chilling effect depends upon precisely those realistic, plausible factors which resist being taken in any way other than literally. Symbolism is not allegory, though the two modes are closely related *formally*. Purely allegorical meaning is meaning which exists outside the work of art but corresponds, point for point, with everything in the work. It is easy to see that a pure allegory will have little intrinsic interest, since it demands to be taken as something other than itself. The allegorical works which have maintained their attractiveness, like *The Faerie Queene* and *Pilgrim's Progress,* are far from pure; many alloys of strictly literary interest, including symbolism, are introduced by their authors. There has been very little allegorical writing in the twentieth century, but there has been a great deal of allegorical *reading* as a result of misapprehensions in the proper understanding of symbolism, and Kafka has been one of the principal victims of it. Reading symbolically is less definite and therefore is more difficult than reading allegorically. The symbolic writer uses traditional symbols or creates new ones to suggest complexes of association and meaning that cannot be grasped literally. An author would no more say flatly what a symbol "stands for" than he would say what a character, a setting, or an action "stands for," but he might willingly identify an allegorical construction in his work. Meaning *rises out of* a symbol; it is *poured into* an allegory.

Given these strictures, our best approach to "In the Penal Colony" might be to show how its realistic elements cannot profitably be separated from its unreal qualities. No doubt Kafka deplored penal colonies, but it is not the prime intention of the story to get us to pursue the following sequence: there are penal colonies, Commandants to run them, explorers to visit them, but there are not such diabolical machines of execution—or are there? Such a train of thought will make us students of penology, whereas Kafka's intention is not to shock us with the machine but just the opposite. Notice how he does this: it is not the officer's matter-of-fact pride in his mechanism that seduces us (it shocks us), but the explorer's reaction to it. The explorer inwardly objects to all that he sees, so we begin to identify with him and to trust him, never noticing that he is merely expressing reservations (and mental ones at that) about something that should drive him into active protest, shrieking with outrage. Eventually, of course, the explorer's blandly "civilized" objections become part of the absurdity of the story.

It is a paradox that would have amused and terrified Franz Kafka that his nightmare visions of modern man have become so popular. But then, terror and humor are the twin geniuses of his art. His stories are regularly anthologized, but students may "know" Kafka without ever having heard of him. Absurdist humor, from the "sick joke" to black comedy on stage, derives from Kafka's influence to a degree difficult to overestimate. Whether his influence is good or bad is still a subject for debate in some quarters. Two biographical facts that are often cited on one side of the debate or the other seem to me relevant in coming to grips with the paradox of Kafka. One is the consistently humorous response of Kafka's circle of friends when he read them things he had just written: his stories are funny. The second fact contrasts sharply with the first: it was Kafka's request that all his manuscripts be destroyed after his death (he published only one work, *The Metamorphosis*, during his lifetime). Whatever estimate the teacher makes of Kafka, he should be aware that Kafka's stories are not merely repetitive variations on a single theme. Kafka's vision is individual and unique, but it is not monolithic.

Three main strands of symbolic association are woven together in the present story. First, the machine, whose compelling feature is not mechanical but moral: sentence and punishment are identical. The sentence *is* execution, not merely the order for it. Furthermore, the sentence is not a judicial command but a commandment in the moral sense: *"Honour Thy Superiors!"* not "Death by Torture." The paradox at this level is that the condemned man learns "on his body" a rule for life, but at the moment he learns what is, literally, the meaning of his life, he loses all desire to live. (I take it that the beatific vision of "the sixth hour" is the prisoner's recognition of his sentence, and it is just then that he stops trying to eat the warm rice pap provided for him.) All this may be called the moral symbolism of the story.

Second, an evident religious symbolism in the story is the association of Crucifixion motifs with the execution: the archaic notations of time ("the second hour," "the sixth hour"), the transfiguration, and, perhaps, the inscription itself. These associations connect in turn with others from New Testament history: the departed master, the martyrdom of the disciple, and the prophecy of resurrection. The religious symbolism is essentially the link between the story's moral symbolism and what is felt primarily as a political symbolism, the organization of the colony and the attempts of the Old Order to maintain itself against the New. One of several ways in which all three symbolic strands can be seen together is to characterize the Old and New Orders as Justice and Mercy, the convenient summary distinction between the Old and New Testaments. The machine is the means by which the Old Order maintained itself and is the last bastion of its defense; the New Order devotes its attention to subverting its operation. Two qualifications are present, however, which confuse this schematization and warn us of being too confident in it or any other arrangement we make. First, the promised resurrection is associated with the Old Order, not the New, suggesting a millennium of justice instead of mercy. Second, we should not lose sight of the fact that justice and mercy are grotesque caricatures in the penal colony: "justice" is diabolically intricate torture and death, while "mercy" under the New Commandant is imaged in the cloying sentimentality of his Ladies—stuffing the condemned with sugar candy before execution and pressing the fingers of their menfolk to wheedle them into their desires.

The primary *symbolic action* in the story is the association of absurdities: the incomprehensible line drawings of the Old Commandant, the incredibly complex mechanism of "The Designer," the garbled expository style of the officer, and the travesty of justice maintained by the judicial system. What will be noticed about all of these—and it is one of Kafka's most penetrating insights into the life of twentieth-century man—is that it is difficult to distinguish chaos from orderliness. Are the drawings a mess or a miniature masterpiece? The judicial system is unjust, but it could not be more efficient, and if the end of justice is the maintenance of order . . . ? Total chaos is total organization, and vice versa. "Chaos" is usually taken to mean formlessness, but Kafka sees it oppositely and his vision thus penetrates into that deep realm of human experience reported in the fiendish divisions and subdivisions of Dante's Inferno and in the totalitarian efficiency of Milton's Hell.

STUDY QUESTIONS

Note for the Teacher

These questions are largely rhetorical, more to be pondered than answered. They attempt to stay within the confines of the story and thus to demonstrate what can most appropriately be asked of symbolic literature.

1. Why does the officer free the condemned man, and put himself in his place, immediately after he has heard the explorer's decision to inform the Commandant of his disapproval of the machine? (The necessity of faith is evidently being demonstrated.)

2. Is the penal colony safe and free at the end of the story? What explanations can be offered for the behavior of the explorer at the end? for the action of the soldier and the prisoner?

3. The machine falls apart at the end; the significance of this may be clear enough, but what do you make of the fact that, in falling apart, it has failed to write the officer's sentence, *"Be Just"*? Which failure, the mechanical or the moral, most satisfactorily explains why "no sign was visible of the promised redemption" on the face of the corpse?

4. The explorer seems to be the closest thing to a normal human being in the story. Write a one-page analysis of his responses and

motivations. Be sure to comment on the explorer's conviction that in the officer's place he "would not have acted otherwise" (that is, than to execute himself).

5. What is Kafka's purpose in suggesting that the slightest action on the explorer's part—a mere gesture or whisper—will be sufficient to ruin or re-establish the Old Order?

6. The "absurd hero" has been defined as a character whose every effort to understand his situation (his identity, and so forth) embroils him ever deeper in ignorance and confusion. Is there such a "hero" in this story?

7. A fact of Kafka's life which is widely acknowledged to be important in understanding his work is his ambivalent relationship with his father (when a small child, he stuttered whenever he saw his father). Does this fact illuminate "In the Penal Colony" in any way? In what ways could it be used to oversimplify the story?

"Gimpel the Fool" is in its own way as absurd a story as "In the Penal Colony," proving that absurd humor is not necessarily nihilistic. Singer's story is as joyously affirmative about the meaning of man's existence as Kafka's is chillingly negative. Absurdities in the penal colony are fatal if not accepted, but Gimpel gives meaning to his life by his unresisting embrace of one absurdity after another. That these two descriptions are not converse but identical (that is, "accept absurdity to live") is an indication of the fundamentally neutral nature of the techniques employed. It is likely, however, that some readers will object more to "Gimpel the Fool" than to "In the Penal Colony" because of the crude earthiness of character and event in it. Such readers, well-meaning but misdirected, will not notice that Singer's story moves through sweat, immorality, and urine toward God, whereas the cool and perfectly unexceptionable surface of Kafka's language covers a vision theologically black and morally disgusting.

Reflections on the ultimate meaning of either story are probably best pursued privately. A class discussion is more profitably directed toward the ways in which we recognize that symbolic meaning is being presented. "Gimpel the Fool" is more realistic than Kafka's stories, though the life of the Jewish subcommunity in rural Poland at the end of the last century will seem almost as remote as a French penal colony to most American high school students. Nevertheless, even to readers familiar with the setting, the elements of fable in Gimpel's story will be evident. There is no plot, only the sketchy outline of the major events of a lifetime from childhood to the grave. Setting and character are similarly vague. Incident or action, as distinct from plot, is sometimes vivid, but notice how often Gimpel as narrator cuts short the details of an incident with "and so forth and so on," as if what happened, what resulted, from any event were unimportant. And that it is unimportant is not only Gimpel's style of narration; it is the meaning of his life. This happened, and then that happened, and it was always the same. But, says Gimpel, "Let it pass." Like the narrator of Joyce's "Araby," he is not interested in what is unique in his experience; rather, he is struck by what is constant and unchanging in it: he is always deceived.

Through the first three sections, then, the interest of the story lies not in what is objective and concrete in Gimpel's experience but in the pious clichés he uses to rationalize it, which is to say that the interest of the story lies in the main character's attempt to assign meaning to it. His usual response is pious proverb: "Shoulders are from God, and burdens too." But at some points his rationalizations enter into his actions:

> Next to Elka lay a man's form. Another in my place would have made an uproar, and enough noise to rouse the whole town, but the thought occurred to me that I might wake the child. A little thing like that—why frighten a little swallow, I thought. All right then, I went back to the bakery and stretched out on a sack of flour and till morning I never shut an eye.

Action in the story is subordinated to the main character's constant reflections on the meaning or consequences of action; thus Singer shapes our response to what is important in the story.

At the end of the third section, the story is raised to a new level when Gimpel imagines his wife's words: "I deceived Gimpel. That was the meaning of my brief life." To deceive and to be deceived— is the meaning of life only a choice between the two? Immediately Singer expands his scope, by introducing the "Spirit of Evil" into Gimpel's dream. Gimpel has rationalized his existence into a determination to believe even though he knows he's being tricked; life is much less trouble that way, since people are not always angry at you then. But Gimpel's expediency makes him susceptible to the devil's temptation: if the meaning of life is deceit, is not the meaning of death the same? To believe in every deceit makes one deceitful, ultimately—so Gimpel urinates in the bread to have his revenge on all the people of Frampol. If they "believe" in his bread, so much the worse for them! Gimpel always believed them, and what did he get?

By now, students will recognize that the story is an argument about the existence of God, and that Singer has written a story about a fool from the fool's point of view because the essential fact about such a character—to be fooled—and his most foolish reaction to it—to believe—illuminates with striking economy the options available to life seen in any religious perspective whatever. This artistic economy does not preclude in any way the possibility that Singer may have had in mind real persons and incidents which stimulated him to write the story. His ordering of his materials is symbolic, and would be called symbolic even if everything in the story were literally true.

Gimpel is saved by a second dream-vision, in which Elka represents to him almost in his own words the true meaning of folly: to be deceived by deceit. "Because I was false is everything false too?" As Gimpel said earlier, "Today it's your wife you don't believe in; tomorrow it's God Himself you won't take stock in." After this, Gimpel himself begins to behave symbolically, dividing his wealth and setting out "into the world." The last paragraphs of the story are even sketchier than its bulk; their purpose is to generalize Gimpel's experience, to prove that what he learned his last night in Frampol is universally true, and to confirm his belief in belief. His fool's creed, from which he was tempted only once, has been vindicated and Gimpel in gratitude spends the rest of his life wandering from place to place, a fool for God.

STUDY QUESTIONS

1. What elements of traditional fables and parables do you recognize in "Gimpel the Fool"? What traditional symbols and sym-

bolic actions? (For example, the phrase of the Evil Spirit—
"Gimpel, why do you sleep?"—is a form of address often given to
God in the Old Testament. Gimpel's reply comically reasserts the
basic realism on which Singer's symbolism is based.)

2. In what way is the meaning of Gimpel's life seen to give
meaning to the lives of others? Is he a redemptive figure?

3. Can you reconcile Gimpel's discovery "that there were really
no lies" with his desire to be with God where everything will be
"without deception"? What is the difference between lies and
deceptions?

4. Is the symbolic dimension of "Gimpel the Fool" smaller than
that of "In the Penal Colony"? Are there ways of reading "Gimpel"
that would unnecessarily restrict its symbolic possibilities?

5. "Gimpel" has much in common with Voltaire's "Memnon."
Compare the two stories, and try to decide what makes "Gimpel"
"more symbolic," *formally*.

6. In a general discussion of symbolism and allegory, students
may be asked to consider if any events in their lives or in history
have been symbolic (for example, the assassinations of Lincoln
and Kennedy). Have any been allegorical? (Only planned, formal
events—like church services—present "living allegory," since their
meaning is known beforehand. Symbolic meaning arises out of
events, and is not clear until the event is over.)

7. A question that may rapidly go out of date: In the last couple
of years, some rock-and-roll songs have been attacked as disguised
celebrations of drug-taking ("Puff the Magic Dragon" was an
early victim). Students may be asked to analyze such a song to see
if its meaning is literal, allegorical, or symbolic. Or they may be
asked to interpret a popular song as pure allegory. (Some of the
best songs by Bob Dylan and The Beatles are obviously symbolic.
How do we know they are symbolic? How does understanding
the symbolic aspect of a song help us to appreciate it more intelligently?)

Part III
DRAMA

Like the other sequences in this volume, Professor H. James Jensen's on drama is arranged with American works represented in grade ten, English in grade eleven, and European in grade twelve. The plays selected exemplify many different aspects of dramatic literature. The three American plays are good examples of serious non-tragic drama. *Caesar and Cleopatra* is one kind of historical drama. *The Importance of Being Earnest* and *The Misanthrope* are differing examples of the comedy of manners, a mode the beginning student often finds difficult because he still has trouble freeing himself from the notion that great literature has to be tragic. Sophocles' *Antigone* and Ibsen's *Rosmersholm* are outstanding examples of ancient and modern concepts of tragedy.

Perhaps the most unusual feature of Professor Jensen's sequence is his inclusion of Milton's *Samson Agonistes* among the English plays. Although it is one of the acknowledged great works of English literature (whether or not one agrees with Professor Jensen's implied suggestion of its superiority over *Paradise Lost*), it may be surprising to find it in a sequence for the eleventh grade. Yet its inclusion here is appropriate on many counts. In addition to being an important work of a major English poet, *Samson Agonistes* can serve as an introduction to Greek drama; it shows how a poet can work with a Biblical theme; it exposes the student to the genre of closet drama. There are, of course, many other values inherent in the play. Teachers and students adventurous enough to be undeterred by initial difficulties the play may present will be assured of a rich and meaningful experience if they continue their studies to the end.

Teaching Drama in Grades Ten Through Twelve

H. JAMES JENSEN

Assistant Professor of English
Indiana University

The nine plays in this suggested curriculum are good plays whether they are read in privacy or seen on the stage. In the tenth grade Arthur Miller's *The Crucible*, Eugene O'Neill's *The Emperor Jones*, and Tennessee Williams' *The Glass Menagerie* represent American drama. Oscar Wilde's *The Importance of Being Earnest*, George Bernard Shaw's *Caesar and Cleopatra*, and John Milton's *Samson Agonistes* represent English drama in the eleventh grade. Sophocles' *Antigone*, Molière's *The Misanthrope*, and Henrik Ibsen's *Rosmersholm* represent European drama in the twelfth grade. The plays encompass almost all the dramatic genres, such as tragedy, tragi-comedy, comedy, farce, and history plays.

In presenting the plays, I have arbitrarily isolated general areas of discussion which tend to overlap. All areas contribute to the final understanding of a play. *Background* is presented here only where it is necessary for understanding. *Form and meaning* refers to the way in which the author shapes the action to illustrate what he wants to say. *Conventions* are devices a playwright uses which are an accepted part of drama; they may be soliloquy, certain kinds of staging, and so forth.* *Characters* explains subtleties

---

* For a good explanation of conventions, see Gerald Rabkin, "On Teaching Drama," *On Teaching Literature: Essays for Secondary School Teachers*, a volume in this English Curriculum Study Series.

of characterization. *Questions* are a series of questions following the chronological presentation of each play. They are designed to lead to conclusions on all facets of the play expressed in the discussions. Some of the questions deal specifically with ambiguities in the plays which might promote fruitful discussion. Some are designed to include discussions of pertinent and universal problems inherent in our everyday existence.

The plays suggested in this curriculum provide a good basis for any subsequent study of drama and literature. The three American plays represent three important American dramatists, and are mostly serious non-tragic drama. *The Importance of Being Earnest* represents the genre of comedy of manners, and *Caesar and Cleopatra,* besides being a good Shaw play, is a variety of historical drama. *Samson Agonistes* is indicative of our Graeco-Judaic background; it is a Biblical story presented in a Greek form, providing a good, easy introduction to Greek tragedy besides being perhaps the best work of one of the greatest English poets. *Antigone* and *Rosmersholm* represent ancient and modern concepts of tragedy. Sophocles, Molière, and Ibsen, whose plays are studied in grade twelve, are three of the greatest playwrights who ever lived.

Drama for Grade Ten

Form and Meaning

The Crucible is a simple but gripping history play, and like all history plays uses a historical context to illuminate the human condition. Miller mentions in his "Introduction" and in his "Note on the Historical Accuracy of the Play" that he has taken some liberties with historical fact.[1] He has done so simply to make the play more interesting. The parallel to contemporary political situations, specifically the McCarthy investigations of the early 1950's, may have impelled Miller to write the play in 1952, but such a connection is largely incidental. The hysteria and paranoia caused by "witch hunting" is something which has occurred many times in the past, and probably will occur again in the future, as Miller himself says.[2]

The central character of the play is John Proctor. His dilemmas form the conflict on which the play is based. The historical context of witch hunting makes his choices more immediate and striking. The plot concerns him, his wife Elizabeth, and Abigail Williams. If John Proctor were simply a good man wrongfully accused, the play would be merely a melodramatic, barefaced struggle between good and evil, the persecuted and the persecuting. But here we see a struggle in a flawed, yet morally aware, man who takes his sins and their consequences upon himself. The theme of the play is human dignity.

The sin Proctor hides, his "lechery" with Abigail Williams, allows Abigail to be a respected accuser of numerous men and women. By the time Proctor acts, it is too late. The court has gone too far. Its members are too committed to admit their mistakes, whether they want to or not (and they do not seem to want to). Proctor's understandable urge to preserve respectability is so well understood by his wife that she denies his guilt at the last moment he can admit it. And the closing scene of the play dramatizes his dilemma even more. Miller says: "The real and inner theme . . . was the handing over of conscience to another, be it woman, the state, or a terror, and the realization that with conscience goes the person, the soul immortal, and the 'name.'" In other words, if John Proctor falsely confessed and saved his life to preserve himself and others, he would have given up his human dignity and what Miller calls his "immortal soul." He had reason to preserve himself because he thought his affair with Abigail already damned him. At the end of the play he emerges a hero, as he himself recognizes, and the audience supposedly has kept its faith in the nobility of human nature.

Conventions

There are actually two versions of the play: the one to be read with historical notes (or essays) and stage directions; the other to be acted. The notes (or essays) and stage directions fill us in on the background; they make the characters real for the reader. The acting version, what we see on the stage, is a violent, non-illusionary representation[3] of what went on in Salem, Massachusetts, in 1792. It tries to recreate the atmosphere of hysteria and anger. The great danger in staging the play is that there may be too much hysteria. If there is no gradual increase of intensity, if everyone starts out at fever pitch, the play will degenerate into a shouting match. If performed with a delicate heightening of tension, *The Crucible* can be an impressive theatrical experience.

Characters

Much of *The Crucible's* effectiveness is derived from the way we become familiar with the characters. They are easy to understand and although they are types, they are still living people whom we love or hate with equal violence. It is Miller's skill that makes us feel this way. The paranoid Reverend Parris, at first haunted by fear for his job and later haunted by fear for his person, is an uncomplicated character, as are Betty Parris, Susannah Walcott, Mercy Lewis, and Mary Warren, all bewildered or spoiled, conscienceless girls who perhaps, as John Proctor says, need to be punished. Tituba, Abigail Williams' scapegoat, is pathetic. The goodness and respectability of Rebecca Nurse and others like her make us hate their persecutors. Giles Corey, the testy old man who constantly drags people to court, is a slightly comic character who achieves heroism at his death (he is crushed by heavy stones). He is a martyr for the dignity of his family. He dies to protect the property they can inherit. Ezekiel Cheever and Marshall Herrick are low, degenerate types who work for the court and help mold our opinion of it.

Judge Hawthorne and especially Deputy Governor Danforth represent the instruments of an evil which threatens to stamp out man's respectability and integrity. Danforth wavers once, in Act III, when Proctor attacks the court. Miller later changed his mind about Danforth's wavering:

> There is no such swerving on the record, and I think now, almost four years after the writing of it, that I was wrong in mitigating the evil of this man and the judges he represents. Instead, I would perfect his evil to the utmost and make an open issue, a thematic consideration of it in the play. I believe now, as I did not conceive then, that there are people dedicated to evil in the world; that without their perverse example we should not know the good. Evil is not a mistake but a fact in itself.

Putnam represents another kind of evil. He sells himself to Mammon to gain as much land and money as he can. His wife has to find some excuse to explain why her babies died.

We know little about Abigail Williams except that she is beautiful, oversexed, and completely conscienceless. She is the leader of the accusers, a consummate liar and hypocrite. We feel she deserves all kinds of retribution. Elizabeth Proctor is her opposite. Her motivations are explained clearly in the play. John Proctor, the hero, is big and strong, and has to choose between simple, good reputation (keeping quiet about his affair with Abigail Williams) and freeing his wife (indicting Abigail). He tries the latter and fails. He gets another chance: he can choose between life and martyrdom, a life without honor and self-respect and death with its opposite. The Reverend Hale is Proctor's foil (or contrast used to set off another character). He wants Proctor to live, in disgrace if necessary, to ease his, Hale's own conscience. He proves to be the weaker man.

STUDY QUESTIONS

"NOTES ON THE HISTORICAL ACCURACY OF THIS PLAY"

1. Is Miller justified in distorting facts to dramatize history?

ACT I

1. What is the purpose of the introductory essay? What does Miller say in it? What does Miller mean by this statement: "It is still impossible for man to organize his social life without repressions, and the balance has yet to be struck between order and freedom"? What does Miller say the people of Salem are like? Do we need this introduction?

2. What kind of person is Parris? What kinds of persons are Mr. and Mrs. Putnam? Is it natural for Parris, given the kind of person he is, to succumb to the Putnams? How would an actor portray Thomas Putnam to express Miller's description of him? Are the girls ordinary girls whose adventures have gotten them into trouble? Is there anyone in the play we like before the entrance of John Proctor?

3. What conclusions do we come to about John Proctor, Abigail Williams, and the whole idea of witchery after their tête à tête? What is the purpose of the animal imagery (for example, horses) in their conversation? What is the contrast between the people we have seen so far and Giles Corey, Rebecca Nurse, and Francis Nurse?

4. What is the purpose of all the wrangling with Parris, Giles Corey, Putnam, and Proctor? Is it obvious which side the audience is to be on?

5. Why does Arthur Miller descant on witchcraft and demonism? Do we understand his comments better after reading his essay? How would the part of Hale be acted? How does witch fever grow? Can Hale keep his thought on an intellectual level?

Why does Tituba suddenly start confessing and accusing? What is our feeling at the end of Act I?

ACT II

1. Do John and Elizabeth Proctor get along together very well? How is their division indicated? Is Proctor so irritable at Elizabeth's importuning him to accuse Abigail of fraud because he has a guilty conscience, or because she is so patronizing, or both? Explain your answer. How do we react to Mary Warren's account of the proceedings in court? Why is the prosecution's evidence so often described as rock or stone?

2. When Mary Warren leaves, the Proctors are stricken by terror. Is Elizabeth right when she suspects John still likes Abigail Williams? How does John Proctor's "sin" change the emphasis of the play?

3. The scene between Hale, Elizabeth, and John Proctor can be quite effective on the stage. What are their attitudes toward the questioning? How could light and shadow be used to increase the effect? Is it effective to have John Proctor miss the commandment against adultery? Is Hale as firm in his belief as he once was? What do we think of the situation when Giles Corey and Francis Nurse enter? Is Proctor right in calling Hale a coward? Is he right in threatening Mary Warren? Considering his personality, do you think he is acting naturally?

ACT III

1. Why should Danforth be so concerned whether Proctor is attacking the court? It would seem more pertinent to ascertain whether he is telling the truth. What choice does Proctor make when he finds out his wife cannot be executed? Is it a heroic choice? What would we think of him if he withdrew his opposition to the proceedings? Is Giles right in saying Putnam is killing his neighbors for their land? Is the humor about Corey being able to write a deposition as a lawyer very funny at this juncture in the play? What does it do for the scene? For our idea of Corey?

2. Is there too much tension in the play by the time Mary Warren tries to tell the truth? Does Abigail Williams seem to have any good in her? Is she a believable character? If so, why? Do we

really believe that Proctor's accusation of Abigail Williams will ever be accepted? Do we condemn Elizabeth Proctor for lying? Do we condemn Proctor for putting her in a position where she has to lie to save her husband's reputation? Should she have known that if the subject came up it had to be broached by her husband?

3. The scene where Mary Warren goes back to Abigail Williams' side sounds silly, but it can be very effective. What is the effect of such a scene where the audience knows something that only some of the characters know? Explain what Proctor means by this speech:

> A fire, a fire is burning! I hear the boot of Lucifer, I see his filthy face! And it is my face, and yours, Danforth! For them that quail to bring men out of ignorance, as I have quailed, and as you quail now when you know in all your black hearts that this be fraud— God damns our kind especially.

Do we think Danforth believes Proctor? How do we react to Danforth's apparent vacillation? How would we react if he did not vacillate at all? What effect does Hale's departure have on us and on Danforth?

ACT IV

1. How does the degeneracy of the opening scene of Act IV parallel the moral degeneracy of the witch hunts? Is Tituba insane? Why is Danforth so prone to anger? How do we react to Abigail Williams' departure? How do the characters react? Why does Danforth call Parris brainless? What do we think of Danforth now? What does he think he is defending? What do we think of Hale, now that he has returned? Is he right to counsel men to lie, or is he merely trying to ease his own conscience? Is his choice valid, that it is better to live a liar than die for pride? Is pride the issue?

2. It would seem that Elizabeth and John Proctor are more man and wife now than they were in the beginning of the play. Is there an explanation for this change? What is the effect of Giles Corey's heroism?

3. What exactly is John Proctor's dilemma? If he hangs, is he

prideful? Is he an idealist? Or is he realistic? What effect does Elizabeth's confession have on Proctor? Did her silence in the first part of the play produce the catastrophe? Why is Proctor so concerned with his name? Is Hale's last speech the answer, or is Elizabeth's? Or are both true?

4. In "Echoes Down the Corridor," do we get any sense of "poetic justice"; in other words, do we get the feeling that after the catastrophe everyone received his just rewards? Is history different from "poetic justice"?

THE EMPEROR JONES
by Eugene O'Neill

Form and Meaning

The Emperor Jones is a serious, atavistic play about the fall of a Negro emperor of great abilities and dignity. Jones, progressively overcome by fear, loses his grasp of the present; it is replaced by a new reality, that of his ancestors. His fear and his regression increase proportionately to the tempo of the drumming. He goes backward in time, through his own experiences, and then recalls the slave auction of his ancestors and the slave ship that brought them to North America, finally almost succumbing to a hypnotic fixation on a crocodile god which presumably his ancestors once worshiped. In the process of his decline he little by little loses his clothes, vestiges of modern civilization, until he is clad only in a loin cloth. His declining hold on the present depends on his weakening conscious will and his revolver, a symbol of modern technology. As each bullet is fired, Jones degenerates further. At the end, he is lower than Lem and his men, who kill him with a silver bullet, a last testimonial to the power they believe he has.

The Emperor Jones is a tragedy; it produces pity and fear in the audience. Although atavism is a concept difficult to accept rationally, O'Neill succeeds in suspending our disbelief by capitalizing on the fact that everyone is to some extent superstitious. We therefore realize that what happens to Jones could happen to the distasteful Smithers, or to me, or to you. We pity Brutus Jones and fear for ourselves. However, the play is not an Aristotelian tragedy, because Jones has no choice. He perishes not through his own actions but through forces beyond his control, his fears inspired by the drumming. In one sense, this kind of tragedy is medieval, as found in Boccaccio's *De Casibus Virorum Illustrium*, Chaucer's *Monk's Tale*, and the Elizabethan *Mirror for Magistrates*. The formula is this: "He was high and he fell." Brutus Jones falls not because he performs an action but because he is the emperor. In another sense, the tragedy is Aeschylean. In Aeschylus' *Oresteia*, for example, Agamemnon's family is cursed. One horrible event, a murder, starts a chain of reprisals. Crime, pride, and their attendant misfortunes are in the family's blood. Brutus Jones' misfortune comes from his background or blood, if you will, which lives in his memory, a background shared by Lem and his followers. One cannot extend the parallel with Aeschylus too far, but O'Neill's atavism takes the place of the vague but powerful forces which destroy Agamemnon. But atavism is hard to accept. Intellectually, the play is not particularly rewarding, and we have to look elsewhere for its excellences. Outside of what we have already said, the moral of the play is that rats (men like Smithers) will survive when heroes (like Jones) fall. O'Neill has presented us with the shell of tragedy. The kernel is not very meaty.

The play is an illuminating representation of what is going on in someone's mind. The mode is called "expressionism." From the entrance of "the little formless fears" in scene two to the entrance of Smithers and Lem in scene eight we become more and more involved in the workings of Jones' imagination. It is literally true that Jones is in the jungle. But it is not literally true that the chain gang, the "formless fears," and so forth are there. They are real enough to Jones, but they are in his mind. O'Neill's play is in the tradition of *A Dream Play*, *Damascus*, *Easter*, and *Ghost Sonata* (or *Spook Sonata*, as it is sometimes called) by the great Swedish playwright August Strindberg. Another predecessor is Georg Kaiser's *From Morn to Midnight*.

Conventions

Although *The Emperor Jones* is difficult to accept intellectually, it is theatrically successful. Its success depends primarily on O'Neill's manipulation of conventions which in turn manipulate the audience's emotions. These conventions are few and simple. The play starts out as illusionistic representationalism. The characters speak in dialect; we peek into a Caribbean court. The last scene is of the same kind. In the middle of the play, however, we have to accept not only that we can follow Jones through the jungle, but also that we can see into his mind. The skillful use of scenery in coordination with time helps us at least temporarily to believe what we see. The moon progressively changes position in each scene, indicating time lapse, besides providing the lighting. The jungle backdrop keeps us aware of Jones' flight. The primary instrument used to increase our emotional excitement and involvement is the sound of the tightly controlled drum beat which moves faster and faster, closer and closer, and louder and louder as the play progresses. It sets the pace for the action and literally hypnotizes the audience. In conjunction with the foreboding jungle scenery and the action which appeals to that part of us which is inclined toward irrational superstition and atavistic psychology, the persistent drum beats make the play a memorable theatrical experience.

Characters

Jones, a two-time murderer and fast-talking confidence man, rises to greatness in our estimation through his physical appearance, his self-confidence, his sense of style, the breadth and depth of his deception, and his stature compared to Smithers and Lem— especially Smithers. His weakness, indicated in scene i by his superstitious nature, is atavistic in origin. In scenes ii through vii, he loses all the stature he once had. The silver bullet which kills him is superfluous, but is a reminder of his former glory. As Smithers says, "yer died in the 'eighth o' style, any'ow!" Smithers is the foil to Jones; he sets off Jones' greatness. He is lazy, limited in his vision, and servile in his actions, a thoroughly contemptible sycophant, cheat, and bully (when he can get away with it). Lem, despite his ignorance, has more stature than Smithers. He knows he can catch Jones, and his confidence never wavers. He has a knowledge unknown to Smithers and Jones, and perhaps to himself, a knowledge of the processes of thinking inherent in men. Although he puts ignorant faith in his silver bullet, his drumming snares Jones. In the context of the play, his obvious knowledge makes Smithers' last comments effectively ironic: "And I s'pose you think it's yer bleedin' charms and yer silly beatin' the drum that made 'im run in a circle when 'e'd lost 'imself, don't yer? Stupid as 'ogs, the lot of 'em! Blarsted niggers!"

STUDY QUESTIONS

SCENE I

1. The incident with the servant tells us what the natives are up to, but what does it also tell us about Smithers? How does Smithers' treatment of the servant compare with his actions toward Jones? What happens when he tries to bully Jones? What does the comparison say about Jones?

2. Does Smithers hate Jones? Why? Does he feel any other emotions toward him? How do his emotions help characterize Jones?

3. What clues about Smithers' and Jones' pasts do we get in scene i? Are they similar in some ways? What quirks of personality and what kinds of abilities make Jones heroic and Smithers despicable? Why is Smithers not afraid of the drums? What does O'Neill say is the price for being a Jones? For being a Smithers?

4. What purpose do Jones' and Smithers' dialects serve? What is important about Smithers' lower class English accent?

5. Could the play be understood or interpreted if the stage directions were left out? What do the stage directions add?

6. What effect does the beginning of the drum beats have on Jones? What effect does it have on the audience?

7. How does the jungle become alive?

SCENE II

1. Is it "realistic" that Jones should find so many white stones?

2. If Jones feels as if the jungle is his opponent, what does the jungle represent to him?

3. Where do the "little formless fears" come from? What are they?

4. How does the shot scatter the "little formless fears"? If the

fears represent Jones' fears, what does the revolver represent, as it drives those "fears" away?

SCENE III

1. What does Jeff represent? Does the revolver represent the same idea in scene iii that it did in scenes ii and i?
2. What has happened to Jones' clothes? What is significant about this?

SCENE IV

1. Does this scene, even though it seems rather similar in meaning, add anything to scene iii?

SCENE V

1. Why does O'Neill talk so much about Jones' clothes? Was Jones ever sold as a slave? If not, why is the auction scene included?
2. Why does Jones fire two shots in scene v?

SCENE VI

1. What does the silver bullet mean to Jones at this stage of the play? How effective is the pantomime?

SCENE VII

1. What is the significance of Jones' using the silver bullet to destroy the crocodile god?
2. In this scene, what is the significance of the revolver, the state of Jones' dress, and the prayers?
3. How can O'Neill say that the tom-toms have a "baffled but revengeful power"?

SCENE VIII

1. If Jones' revolver is symbolic, does its meaning add significance to the natives' guns?
2. Is it ironical that Lem thinks it is the magic of the silver bullet that gets Jones? What significance do the natives' silver bullets have to them? To Jones? To the audience?

3. Is Smithers the same person he was in scene i? Are his remarks ironical? What effect do they have on the audience?

4. What effect do Smithers' conflicting emotions have on the audience? What is the effect of Lem's lack of speech?

5. Why should the tom-toms stop at Jones' death?

6. Do Smithers' comments show us how we should react to Jones?

THE GLASS MENAGERIE
by Tennessee Williams

Form and Meaning

The Glass Menagerie is about human beings caught by their illusions, their memories, their personal limitations, and the circumstances of their environment. Because it deals with such universal subjects, and because of the skill with which the play is written, we become emotionally involved in the action. The play is, in Tom's words, "sentimental." It is a "memory play." Its characters are too pathetic to be tragic. They are little people overwhelmed by circumstances over which they have no control, circumstances of their environment or of chance. There is little or no action in the play. It is about people, their ugliness, desperation, beauty, and stoical heroism, as they irritate each other in their failure to overcome or escape an environment which is oppressive and sordid. Tom's invitation to Jim O'Connor is of importance only to bring a "gentleman caller" on stage whom Tom, in his opening speech, calls a "symbol . . . [of] the long delayed but always expected something that we live for." Tom's leaving home occurs only after the play proper is finished. It provides the ostensible reason for the play, Tom's sentimental remembrance. The father's action, sixteen years before the play opens, is the reason for the deplorable state of affairs in which the characters find themselves. At the end of the play, when Tom has left, the emotion we primarily feel is that of pity.

Illusion and memory pervade art at all times in all its forms. Modern comparisons to *The Glass Menagerie* might be O'Neill's *The Iceman Cometh*, Gorky's *The Lower Depths*, or Miller's *The*

Death of a Salesman. Pirandello's plays are also good comparisons, especially *Six Characters in Search of an Author* or *As You Desire Me.* Tom's reality is personal reality. It is not fact, because fact is impossible to reconstruct accurately through memory. But to the audience, what appears on the stage becomes real. We receive only the essence of each character Tom remembers, but his relative truth becomes absolute truth for us, by means of the skills of the playwright, the actors, and the director. We see the play; it moves us to belief. We become involved with the characters and the ideas Williams expresses.

Conventions

The first convention we have to accept in this play is that a stage can represent someone's mind. Once we accept this first convention, the rest are easily believable. There is no measurable time, although we know the narrator remembers chronologically ordered events. The use of spotlights, which Williams discusses in his "Production Notes," allows us to see which person in a scene Tom most vividly remembers. Williams first uses "non-illusionistic representationalism" with Tom as narrator, and he keeps us aware of Tom's memory throughout most of the play. Later, he uses "illusionistic representationalism." Tom speaks directly to the audience five times before or after he takes his place in his own memory. There are even times that Tom is absent from the stage, particularly in the extended scene between Laura and Jim O'Connor which takes place while Tom and Amanda are washing dishes offstage. A literalist might object by saying that Tom cannot remember what he never saw or heard. In performance, however, there is no problem. Scene vii is illusionistic, and we are caught up in its realistic atmosphere. At the end of the scene Laura and Amanda are shattered by their failure to capture Jim O'Connor. It is not until Tom's closing speech that we realize we have been watching a scene from a memory play. When we realize that much time has elapsed between the end of the scene and Tom's speech, the pity we feel for Amanda and Laura is considerably increased The interplay of conventions in this scene makes it more powerful.

The scenery reinforces the convention of realism, that serious drama can result from ordinary people living in sordid, urban surroundings. Williams writes within the egalitarian or democratic tradition of American playwrights. The Wingfields live in an alley in St. Louis, in what Williams calls a "cellular living unit" in an "overcrowded urban center of lower middle-class population." The scenery, which is always visible outside the apartment, keeps us aware of the environment. We move in our minds from the surrounding scenery into the house. In an illusionistic representational play we easily adapt to the convention of peeping into someone's house. The curtain (the fourth wall) is transparent, and as we move through it with the narrator, the device becomes believable once we accept the idea of a memory play. Williams explains the convention of music in his "Production Notes." The last convention is Williams' curious, unnecessary "screen device," which Williams also explains in his "Production Notes." Its function is to show what Tom is trying to express, or what he feels about each remembrance, reinforcing the fact the play is a series of memories. It was omitted from the Broadway production because, Williams says, "The extraordinary power of Mill Taylor's performance made it suitable to have the utmost simplicity in the physical production." One can go further than Williams. The device would detract from the characters. The actors should be able to express the same ideas through their performance.

Characters

Tom is the most important but not the central character. He is the narrator, the boy who remembers his sister and mother. We see onstage what Tom thinks is important. At first, we sympathize with him. His mother and sister are holding him back. His shrewish mother nags him continually; he is a young man full of hopes who has to work in a warehouse to support his family. He is a relatively sensitive young man. He writes poetry and has an intense desire to escape his surroundings. He goes to the movies every night to forget his plight and to satisfy his love of adventure. Our sympathy for him wanes, however, when we learn, in scene v, that he could go to night school on his cigarette money (and the money he spends on the movies). When we discover he secretly joined "The Union of Merchant Seamen" instead of paying the light bill, and will leave his helpless sister and mother alone after promising his mother he would not, he becomes even less attractive. When Tom breaks his sister's animals at the end of scene iii, and cuts her with the door at the end of scene vii, Williams is indicating that Tom cannot help but destroy his sister. There is truth in Amanda's statement that Tom is a self-pitying escapist. In his last speech he becomes both odious and pitiable—odious because he abandoned his mother and sister, and pitiable because he is too sensitive to forget them.

The two other male characters are Jim O'Connor and the picture of the father. As Tom says in his opening speech, Jim is a symbol of hope, and also "an emissary from the world of reality." He is a human, likable young man who boasts of his actual and imagined accomplishments. He is charmed by Amanda, and has enough charm himself to depart gracefully from an awkward situation. He is Tom's foil. He sets off Tom's sensitivity, his command of language, and his escapist attitude. Jim's insensitivity allows him to encourage Laura's love. The father, through his picture, is a powerful influence in the play. The picture is onstage at all times, silently expressing the solution of escapism. Williams can even make it say things, as in scene iv where it lights up in answer to Tom's question.

Amanda and Laura are the two major characters. They appear as Tom remembers them. Amanda, bitter, with her tiresome reminiscences of her aristocratic southern background, her forced gaiety, and her shrewish nagging, becomes more than irritating. We cannot help think that both Tom's and Laura's inadequacies are a product of their mother's influence. Amanda almost becomes the villain of the play, but by the end, she comes close to being tragic. We see her debasing herself by selling magazines, and if a director wishes, she can be played as both humorous and pitiable, by her repetitive descriptions, stale jokes, and refusal to see the worst side of Laura's character. Her concern about Laura and her relative lack of concern about Tom are explained as the natural anxiety of a mother for her weaker offspring. As Williams says in the last stage direction, "Now that we cannot hear the mother's speech, her silliness is gone and she has dignity and tragic beauty." The villains become the environment, the father, and by extension, Tom.

Laura is like her glass menagerie, like "blue roses," fragile and
beautiful. She is the purest character in the play. She is sensitive
and oddly beautiful, as Jim O'Connor genuinely notes in scene
vii, and as Williams says in scene vi, scene vii, and the "Production Notes." Williams emphasizes her saintlike, other-worldly
qualities, and she is a complete contrast to her environment. However, she is crippled both physically and emotionally. She is
peculiar, as Tom says in scene v, and it is painful to see her limp-
ing to the victrola whenever she wants to escape the terror the
world forces on her. An actress or director could emphasize either
the limp and the emotional instability or her beauty.

Language and Symbolism

Each character has his characteristic speech. Laura's is simple.
She does not say much. Tom's is terse and vague with undertones
of violence born of desperation at his confinement, hatred toward
his mother, and self-pity. Amanda's language is silly and cliché
ridden, as in her telephone calls and her stock description, in scene
v, of the "little silver slipper of a moon." When Amanda becomes
anxious, her speech becomes silly and frantic. Yet when she confronts a real crisis, her language rises to heights the others cannot
reach, as in her last speech of the play. Jim O'Connor's speech is
the lowest. He is a half-educated, very ordinary human being
who expresses himself in slang and hackneyed phrases he has
learned from speech school. The differences in the characters'
speech and each one's overt concern with language portray the
differences between them as persons. Amanda likes euphemisms,
and Tom tries to break them down; Laura is simple, and Jim is
coarse. A good example of differences in language occurs in the
confrontation in scene iv where Tom and Amanda discuss instinct.

Williams' symbols throw the characters into bold relief. They
are, of course, Tom's, who says in his opening speech that he has
"a poet's weakness for symbols." A woman from "Blue Mountain"
is the mother of "Blue Roses." "Blue Mountain" symbolizes the
gay, carefree, monied, aristocratic existence Amanda Wingfield
perhaps mistakenly feels is ideal. The first legend, "Ou sont les
neiges," which refers to her past life, sets the tone for the whole
play. Williams is referring to the poem by François Villon ren-

dered best in English by Dante Gabriel Rosetti as "Where Are the Snows of Yesteryear." Amanda's dreams come from the past; Amanda comes from the past. Laura's symbols are "Blue Roses," the glass menagerie (which Williams explains in his "Production Notes"), especially the unicorn, and the victrola, her refuge from reality. For Amanda and Laura, both, the "gentleman caller" is a symbol of hope and of escape from their present miseries. Jim O'Connor's symbols are materialistic and coldly pragmatic: the Wrigley Building, television, and so on, all symbols of commercial success and the power it buys. Symbols of Tom, the character, are the shoe warehouse, the "movies," and the moon. The shoe warehouse is symbolic of the environment which is crushing his spirit. He explains his attitude toward the "movies" in scene vi. The moon is adventure, another life. Tom's statement in scene v, that the moon is "rising over Garfinkel's Delicatessen," shows in a single statement the contrast between his dreams and his environment. For Amanda and Laura (see the end of scene vi and the beginning of scene vii), the moon is wishes and hopes. But Williams' moon, just like Shakespeare's moons, is deceitful and fickle (see *Romeo and Juliet*, for example). At the end of the play the moon shines on Amanda's and Laura's blighted hopes and Tom's mistaken illusion that he will be free.

STUDY QUESTIONS

SCENE I

1. In the stage directions, does Tennessee Williams' view of memory reasonably approximate your own experience?

2. What does Williams, in the stage directions, tell us about his attitudes toward people and how they live?

3. What effect will the father's picture have on the audience?

4. What kind of effect does the setting have on the play?

5. In his opening speech, what does Tom reveal about himself? Why does he give the social background of the play?

6. What do we learn about Amanda from the way in which she talks about food, reminisces about her past, and insists that Laura will have gentlemen callers? Is Amanda merely a shrew or is she something else besides?

SCENE II

1. How would Laura act out the pantomime described in the stage direction?

2. Can you sympathize with Laura's feelings about business school and tests? Why would she go to such lengths to deceive her mother?

3. After the legend, "The Crust of Humility," the stage direction has Amanda "hopelessly fingering the huge pocketbook." What are her feelings? How would a good actress use this action to convey these feelings? Is her change of attitude at the end of the scene consistent with her character? Why or why not?

4. What is your attitude toward Laura in this scene? Why does your attitude change as the scene progresses?

SCENE III

1. What is the effect of the opening scene with Amanda? Remember she is spotlighted on a dim stage. How would the scene be acted?

2. In the stage directions and the "Production Notes" Williams says that during the quarrel the brightest light should be on Laura. How would the scene's meaning change if the light were stronger on Amanda and Tom?

3. How does Amanda's appearance affect her argumentative tone?

4. Is Tom's anger justified?

5. What kind of humor does Tom express in the lines starting "I'm going to opium dens"?

6. How do we feel about Tom before he tears his coat and breaks Laura's animals? How do we feel afterwards?

7. Why does Laura cry out "as if wounded"?

SCENE IV

1. What do magicians in general represent? What is the significance of Tom's interest in the magician?

2. Do we sympathize with Laura when we know what she will confront at the delicatessen? Does Amanda's childish "sticks and stones" formula convince us that Amanda believes what she says?

3. In the discussion about instinct, Tom makes man animal-like;

Amanda does not. Compare this confrontation to the eating episode in scene i where Tom's appetite is ruined by talk about animals. Is Tom joking in scene iv? If not, is there consistency with scene i? What does each scene say about Tom's character?

4. Is Amanda justified in calling Tom selfish?

5. Compare this passage of Amanda "spotted" on the telephone with the one in scene iii. How do we react to this one? Is there comedy in the repetition of expression?

SCENE V

1. Why the caption "Franco Triumphs"? What is its connection with Tom's soliloquy on the Paradise Dance Hall?

2. Why does Williams say that Amanda sits on the fire escape steps so gracefully? Why is this action important to the dialogue that follows? What kinds of contrasts does it make evident with Tom's soliloquy, the setting, and Amanda's shrewishness?

3. Do we believe that Amanda's hopefulness is justified? Do we believe her purpose will be successful? If we do not, how do we react to the dialogue between Laura and Amanda at the scene's end?

SCENE VI

1. In Tom's opening lines, why does he call himself dog-like?

2. Scene vi is in three parts: Amanda and Laura; Jim and Tom; and all four together. Contrast the three parts. How do the two groups of characters differ? Does Jim realize how serious Amanda is?

3. What does it say for Tom, when his mother embarrasses him but charms Jim? Is it normal for a boy his age to be embarrassed by his parents?

4. How do Tom's plans for escape contrast to Amanda's attitude toward Jim?

5. How do we feel about each of the characters at the end of the scene? How do we feel about the scene to come?

SCENE VII

1. How does the storm correspond to Laura's feeling?

2. We know why the lights go out, and Amanda soon guesses part of the reason. What effect does this sudden event have on

the audience, who know, as Amanda does not, that Tom plans to run away quite soon?

3. The scene between Jim and Laura is extremely delicate. Williams' stage directions tell us that "Jim's attitude is gently humorous." In other words, he is not very serious, while to Laura "the incident" is "the climax of her secret life." Without the stage directions, how would we know this information? How would they play their parts?

4. Is Jim impressive, foolish, or merely an ordinary mixture of sense and nonsense?

5. What part does the little glass unicorn play? Why does its horn break just when it does? Is it because Laura, at least for the moment, is like other girls, as the unicorn becomes like the other figures in the glass menagerie?

6. Does Jim realize what he has done in leading Laura to hope before letting her down? What does her gift of the unicorn to Jim signify? What kind of feeling do we get when Laura goes to wind the victrola?

7. What is the effect of Jim's putting on his hat in the way Williams says he does? Contrast his actions to Amanda's.

8. Is Tom at fault for not finding out that Jim is engaged?

9. In the following exchange, who is correct? With whom do our sympathies lie?

Amanda: It seems extremely peculiar that you wouldn't know your best friend was going to be married!

Tom: The warehouse is where I work, not where I know things about people!

Amanda: You don't know things anywhere! You live in a dream; you manufacture illusions!

10. What is the effect of the final scene with Tom offstage and Amanda and Laura clasped in each others arms?

Drama for Grade Eleven

THE IMPORTANCE OF BEING EARNEST
by Oscar Wilde

Form and Meaning

The Importance of Being Earnest ridicules people who take themselves too seriously in an absurd world. Wilde, using a ridiculous plot, shallow characters, and a brilliant, epigrammatic style, turns normally accepted beliefs upside down to show how ridiculous or absurd they are. The play is both a farce and a comedy of manners. The stock characters and absurd plot are farcical (as in plays like Molière's *The Doctor in Spite of Himself* and La Biche's *The Italian Straw Hat*), while the witty dialogue and the characterization are in the tradition of comedy of manners. The play is a vehicle for Wilde's clever, pointed, and quotable darts aimed at different beliefs and actions of society. In other words, Wilde is criticizing manners. Even the pun in the name of the play shows the dichotomy between farce and comedy of manners. The young ladies will only marry someone named Ernest (as it is spelled in the play). "Earnest" is also the honorific word Victorians used to describe someone of lofty ideals and a serious, hard-working disposition. The perfect Victorian was "earnest."

The opening lines of the play indicate that marriage is the subject—marriage as a social act and as the basis for society. The central characters are the two young couples. (The gay young couple is often found in comedies of manners, especially in plays such as *Sir Fopling Flutter, The Way of the World, The Rivals, School for Scandal, Marriage à la Mode, The Beaux' Stratagem.*) Wilde indulges in lighthearted fun by gently ridiculing the emotions, training, and minds of young ladies and gentlemen of his time. They are rich, handsome, young, witty, and virtually carefree. If it were not for the intervention of outside pressures, represented by the other characters, the young people would have no problems but that concerning the name Ernest. Wilde exploits, comically, the old battle of men vs. women, which is a central motif of comedy from Aristophanes' *Lysistrata* all the way up to a television show you might see tonight. The women usually win in comedy. Marriage is the end. *The Importance of Being Earnest* is no different.

The characters represent parts of society: Lady Bracknell, the upper class, of which the young people are a part; Lane and Merriman, the lower classes; and the Reverend Mr. Chasuble and Miss Prism, the middle. The criticism of the social structure revolves around the idea of being earnest. The gay young couples ridicule society and are only earnest about each other. The other characters are always earnest, and ironically ridicule themselves every time they speak. The most devastating self-ridicule is by Chasuble, Miss Prism, and the old battle-axe, Lady Bracknell. Chasuble and Miss Prism pretend to be something they are not, and Lady Bracknell mouths platitudes. She expresses the actual, unuttered thoughts of her class. For example, she says:

> I do not approve of anything that tampers with natural ignorance. Ignorance is like a delicate exotic fruit; touch it and the bloom is gone. The whole theory of modern education is radically unsound. Fortunately in England, at any rate, education produces no effect whatsoever. If it did, it would prove a serious danger to the upper classes, and probably lead to violence in Grosvenor Square (Act. I).

The statement is very funny because it runs counter to what we expect to hear. But it is also not funny because many people act as if they agree with what Lady Bracknell says, although they pay lip service to the opposite view. Another example of a funny but all-too-true assumption is Lady Bracknell's *non sequitur:* "Untruthful! My nephew Algernon? Impossible! He is an Oxonian" (Act III). It is in the myriad of comical comments such as these that much of the seriousness of the play lies.

Conventions

Much of the comedy in this play hinges on the illusion of realism. In other words, the play purports to be an illusionistic representation of life as it is. Because of the realism the play seems to be a comedy of manners, but we all know that the action is improbable. No one believes that society is Lady Bracknell. No one believes that Jack Worthing could be left in Miss Prism's black handbag in Victoria Station, exchanged for the manuscript of a three-volume novel. We are in the improbable, absurd world of farce, which forces us to accept its own conventions by overcoming the conventions of the comedy of manners.

We do not really identify ourselves with anyone in the play, as we do in a comedy of manners. If we identify ourselves with anyone it is with Wilde, who we feel is directing the action, commenting on its course, and in general poking fun at the characters he manipulates. In a comedy of manners, we expect selected people of taste to criticize inferior parts of society. We identify ourselves with the people of taste. Here, everyone is being criticized. Wilde creates an absurd world. Wilde is the superior being; therefore, we also are superior and, with Wilde, we laugh at the improbable antics of the characters on the stage. We laugh at first because Wilde's world is absurd and ours is not. On second thought we are not so sure. What we hear on the stage often makes as much sense as what we hear in our everyday lives. As Cecily says to Algernon, "If you are not, then you have certainly been deceiving us all in a very inexcusable manner. I hope you have not been leading a double life, pretending to be wicked and really good all the time. That would be hypocrisy" (Act II). This reversal of moral judgments is also a trick used by George Bernard Shaw. It shows that we pay lip service to platitudes that are no more true than their antitheses. Life is as farcical as the play; the play is an imitation of life.

In acting out this play, one can emphasize the farcical elements, but to succeed best one would have to stage it seriously, in the tradition of the comedy of manners, such as Sheridan's *School for Scandal*. As one can see, much of the entertainment comes through the dialogue and the breaking down of the comedy of manners conventions. If it is played subtly and seriously, the farce will take care of itself.

Characters

The characters are flat, that is, they have no depth. We never understand their motivations except in a most superficial way.

They act to conform to dicta of society, to keep from becoming bored, to respond to natural urges such as hunger, the attraction of young males for young females, and vice versa, or to gain money. Their motivations are reasonable to us, and we see no more of them than we do of people we casually observe from day to day. We do not become involved with such people; we merely see them from a distance.

Lady Bracknell acts both as a mother and as a representative of her social class. Her views of what is right and wrong conform to her society's views. We may not like Lady Bracknell, but we must admire her. She clearly, logically, and magnificently reasons out everything. Behavior is governed by the rules of society. What is funny about her is that she carries to absurdity the views society normally expresses:

Algernon: . . . The doctors found out that Bunbury could not live, that is what I mean—so Bunbury died.

Lady Bracknell: He seems to have had great confidence in the opinion of his physicians. I am glad, however, that he made up his mind at last to some definite course of action, and acted under proper medical advice.

The two young men are always witty, and try to be so. Without wanting to be typical young men, they are. They ridicule marriage, they are attracted by food and young ladies, and they fight boredom by adventures which evade society's rules. They take refuge in a cynicism which they seem not really to believe:

Algernon: I really don't see anything romantic in proposing. It is very romantic to be in love. But there is nothing romantic about a definite proposal. Why, one may be accepted. One usually is, I believe. Then the excitement is all over. The very essence of romance is uncertainty. If ever I get married, I'll certainly try to forget the fact (Act I).

Of course, at the end of the play, they will be married. Their verbal conceits at times become completely absurd, as they try to deceive each other:

Algernon: Yes, but that does not account for the fact that your small Aunt Cecily, who lives at Tunbridge Wells, calls

	you her dear uncle. Come, old boy, you had much better have the thing out at once.
Jack:	My dear Algy, you talk exactly as if you were a dentist. It is very vulgar to talk like a dentist when one isn't a dentist. It leaves a false impression.

Cecily is the conventional ingenue, the pretty young thing who knows nothing of the ways of the world, but who has a natural propensity for charming young men. Gwendolen is more sophisticated merely by being exposed to society and her mother. They are both types.

Unlike the young people, Lady Bracknell, Chasuble, and Miss Prism are not charming at all. We respect Lady Bracknell, but Chasuble and Miss Prism are treated most harshly. Chasuble, however, is at worst a pedantic bore (notice his explanation of his sermon in Act II), while Miss Prism is a hypocrite. She pretends to be serious and trustworthy, yet she has lost a baby in Victoria Station. The older people are all obnoxiously earnest, but Chasuble and Miss Prism both lack taste (witness their ill-chosen metaphors in Act II). The differences between Chasuble and Miss Prism, on the one hand and Lady Bracknell on the other, never come through more clearly than in this passage in Act III:

Lady Bracknell:	Is this Miss Prism a female of repellent aspect, remotely connected with education?
Chasuble (somewhat indignantly):	She is the most cultivated of ladies, and the very picture of respectability.
Lady Bracknell:	It is obviously the same person.

STUDY QUESTIONS

ACT I

1. Judging from the opening lines of the play, what seems to be the play's subject? What are the young men's attitudes toward marriage? Toward society and its demands? What is funny about Algernon's comment on Lane's views on marriage?

2. As the act progresses, what are the different subjects Wilde ridicules or comments on? Are they emotional questions, as viewed in the play? Could they be dealt with "earnestly" in another setting?

3. In the parts of the act which deal with plot (who is Cecily and where is Jack's country house), how does Algernon pursue Jack? How does Jack try to evade revealing his secrets?

4. What does Lady Bracknell add to the play when she enters? What kind of person is she? What are her chief concerns? What kind of person is Gwendolen?

5. How does Act I leave us anticipating Act II?

ACT II

1. What is the contrast between Miss Prism and Cecily? What kind of person is Miss Prism? Is she in any way hypocritical? Is Cecily's abhorrence of study a natural reaction?

2. What are Cecily's feelings as she is about to meet Algernon? Why does she want him to be wicked? What are Algernon's re-actions? How would the scene be played? What effect should their contrasting emotions have on the audience? How witty is the conversation at their encounter?

3. What is the effect of the contrast when the delightful scene between Cecily and Algernon is followed by a much different kind of scene between Chasuble and Miss Prism? Why cannot their scene last as long? Is Jack's entrance effective?

4. What is amusing about the reconciliation between Jack and Algernon? Is Jack as attractive a character when, in his earnestness about Cecily, he tries to drive Algernon away?

5. Why are the vacillations in friendship between Cecily and Gwendolen so amusing? Likewise the muffin incident between Algernon and Jack?

6. How has Wilde led us into looking forward to Act III? Is the reversal of fortunes only a device to lengthen the play?

ACT III

1. At the beginning of Act III, why are Cecily's and Gwendolen's attitudes toward the young men so funny?

2. What is Lady Bracknell like? Are her comments both comical and serious? Why are her comments so interesting?

3. What is the effect of the explanation of Jack's being found in a handbag in Victoria Station? What does it say about Miss Prism?

4. Why is everyone united at the end of the play? Why is the

event arrived at so suddenly? What effect does its suddenness have? What is the importance, if any, of Jack's last statement?

CAESAR AND CLEOPATRA
by *George Bernard Shaw*

Form and Meaning

Shaw is a master of prose as well as of the theater. He has a clear, simple, modern, argumentative style which reflects the clarity and liveliness of his mind. He is an iconoclast. He insults his readers, implying that they are silly, blind, and stupid in not recognizing the self-evident simple truths he expresses. We need not agree with him, but we should think about what he says. He chose to express himself largely through the medium of drama, and his plays are just as fresh today as when they were written over fifty years ago.

Caesar and Cleopatra expounds three theses. The first is that human nature is unchanging. This is the most important idea in the play, and serves as a premise for the other two. The second is that progress as we usually think of it is a delusion. People have not improved in the last 2,000 years; in some ways, they have regressed. The third is "what constitutes a great man." This, Shaw says, is what history can teach us. In his prologue and "notes," Shaw shows and explains these points. The note on baldness shows that people were just as interested in receding hairlines then as they are now. "Apparent Anachronisms" explains Shaw's view of progress. "Cleopatra," "Britannus," and "Julius Caesar" are notes on the characters, and "Julius Caesar" explains the qualities Shaw equates with greatness. Once Shaw convinces us of his theses in his notes on baldness and "Apparent Anachronisms," the character profiles become logical.

Caesar and Cleopatra is Shaw's version of a history play. About conventional history plays he says: "The only way to write a play which shall convey to the general public an impression of antiquity is to make the characters speak blank verse and abstain from reference to steam, telegraphy, or any of the material conditions of their existence." However, Shaw wrote an entirely different kind of play. It is dependent for its success on a comparison with conventional history plays (such as *Henry V, The Crucible,* and *Richard III*). Shaw's protagonist is not an ordinary hero. He is a believable man. He does not express himself loftily in blank verse, but in prose, the language of reason. Shaw deliberately courts a comparison with Shakespeare's blank verse and other heroic plays which employ a similar verse form. His purpose is not to dazzle us but to keep us amused and thoughtful. His play is not great poetry but it is eminently successful in communicating its purpose. Shaw is talking about "then," and "then" is no different from "now." Through the guise of history he talks about important social problems of his own time, such as dependence on inferior statesmen, outmoded attitudes toward smaller countries, and so forth. He says, and he is right, that the British Empire can be compared to the Roman Empire. We in the United States also face many of the same problems. There is much to what Shaw says. By capturing the essence of history, he discusses problems which are universal.

Conventions

We expect certain conventions in a history play, such as a super-hero and much pompous pageantry. Throughout *Caesar and Cleopatra,* Shaw undermines our expectations. A good example of Shaw's reversal of expected pomp and pageantry is in Act II where Caesar meets his Egyptian foes. Most heroes are bold and fearless. They are kind to their friends and bitter to their enemies. The extreme type is found in lesser known plays such as Marlowe's *Tamburlaine the Great* or Dryden's *The Conquest of Grenada, Aureng Zebe,* and *Don Sebastian.* Caesar is Shaw's hero. He is balding, thin, and clever. He does not fight to win honor, but to win. Above all, he is sensible. Shaw's technique is very much like that of Oscar Wilde in *The Importance of Being Earnest.* The opposite of what we expect seems at least as reasonable as what we would ordinarily see.

Shaw also was a great admirer of Henrik Ibsen (see Shaw's *The Quintessence of Ibsenism*). Ibsen's plays were realistic (that is, illusionistic representational plays), but were couched in tragic form. They were primarily social problem plays. Shaw followed Ibsen's lead in writing this kind of play, but instead of tragedy he used comedy as the vehicle. We have then, in *Caesar and Cleopatra*, an amusing social problem history play.

Besides the dramatic conventions we also have conventions inherent in the traditional images of the two major characters, Caesar and Cleopatra. Our expectations are again undercut. Ra sneers that the audience perhaps has come to the theater to see "the serpent of the Nile," the deadly seductress men know as Cleopatra. We are surprised to meet a sixteen-year-old girl, rather young for her age. Shaw implies that he is historically correct in her age, but she was actually twenty or twenty-one (Caesar was fifty-four). Shaw did not make a historical mistake. His reason is that for his purposes he can change her age under the justification of "poetic license." She also went to Rome with Caesar, returning to Egypt after he was assassinated. Shaw, as an artist, recreates history, and what is historically important to Shaw (and to us, by implication) is the truth of human nature. Caesar has something to teach about human nature and the art of governing well. If Caesar and Cleopatra were lovers, Caesar could not teach Cleopatra as he does; while Caesar teaches the sixteen-year-old Cleopatra, he also teaches us.

Characters

Shaw explains his major characters in the short essays at the end of the play. The many other characters show us that Shaw has no use for politicians and soldiers as types; he satirizes them when they try to be something they are not. Rufio is an exception. Although he is a soldier and can kill when his job tells him to, he learns statecraft from Caesar and becomes worthy to govern. Apollodorus is a *fin-de-siècle* dandy, of which Oscar Wilde was a prototype. He announces that his creed is "art for art's sake" (Act III), the rallying cry of English aesthetes of the 1890's. He is Caesar's complement. He is to the world of art what Caesar is to the practical arts of peace, war, government, and civilization (Act V). He is an admirable, accomplished young man who can flatter and amuse with good taste. (For other types of this kind of person see Ibsen's *Hedda Gabler* and Gilbert and Sullivan's *Patience*. The handbook of the aesthetes was Joris-Karl Huysman's *A Rebours*, translated *Against the Grain*.)

Shaw takes great care to show Caesar as just as ordinary man.

Caesar's genius is enhanced by his humanness, and the more believable he is, the more impressive he is. He tries to hide his baldness (Act II), he grows despondent as he becomes hungry (Act
III), and he self-admittedly has a weakness for women (Act I).
But he conquered the world. Through his art, Shaw makes everything seem so simple and reasonable we cannot doubt that he is
right about his characters.

STUDY QUESTIONS

PROLOGUE

1. What are the parallels between the United States and what
Shaw is saying about Rome and England? Has human nature
changed over the centuries? Wherein does Shaw then say we
have made progress? If Shaw is not right, how is he wrong?

2. What kind of person is Julius Caesar? Why do "The Gods"
laugh at man? What kind of gods is Shaw talking about? What
does "spirit of man" mean? Pompey is described as "blood and
iron" (Bismarck's phrase), but why should that be opposed to "the
spirit of man"?

3. Is Ra Shaw? Why or why not? What is his attitude toward
the audience? Why is it effective? Why is Ra so conscious of the
physical audience (the coughing, the seats, and so on)? Why does
he speak in archaic English?

AN ALTERNATIVE TO THE PROLOGUE

1. What would be the difference between using the "Prologue"
and "The Alternative"? Can you give reasons for using either? Do
they both express the same theses?

2. Why does Shaw say Buckingham Palace is ugly? Do we
learn more about Englishmen or about Egyptians from the
passage? Why does Shaw depict the Egyptians as superstitious?
Are their customs any stranger than some of ours (for example,
bad news brought by young noblemen vs. what happens to a
politician predicting the defeat of his own party, even though it is
obvious to everyone defeat is inevitable)? What is our reaction
to Bel Affris' description of the Roman legion? Do we sympathize

with the Egyptians or with the Romans, or are our emotions mixed?

ACT I

1. How does Caesar reveal his knowledge of his greatness in his opening speech? What does Caesar's resentment at hearing himself called "old" explain to us about him? How are we affected by the entrance of Cleopatra?
2. In this act do we feel the massive power of Rome?
3. How does Julius Caesar teach Cleopatra? Is Cleopatra a believable character?

ACT II

1. What does the first paragraph of the stage directions say about the comparison between ancient Egyptians and modern Englishmen? Is Shaw's comparison justifiable?
2. In the meeting, what is the difference between Caesar and the Egyptians? Does Cleopatra play an important role? Why do the Egyptians misjudge Caesar? Why is Britannus such a comical figure, while still retaining dignity?
3. Why does Cleopatra, after the meeting, act toward Caesar in such an overbearing way?
4. Why do Theodotus' grief at the burning of the library and Caesar's reaction have such shock value? Is Theodotus right to have so little regard for Pompey and so much regard for books? What is Caesar's attitude? Is he right? Has Caesar shown much emotion about anything yet? Wherein lies his greatness so far? Or is he merely more clever and self-controlled than the others?

ACT III

1. Is the Roman sentinel any different from sentinels anywhere at any time? How does he help set off Apollodorus? What kind of person is Ftatateeta, from what we have seen so far in the play? Apollodorus, who appears to be expert in all things, leaves what kind of impression on us? How does Apollodorus compare to Caesar?
2. In the beginning of the second scene of Act III, what purpose

does the incident of the dates serve? Compare Caesar and Britannus in the next action. What is funny about Britannus thinking Apollodorus a vagabond professional artist? What is glorious about the swimming incident at the end of the act? What does the scene say about people in general and Caesar in particular? Do you think more highly of Caesar at the end of Act III?

ACT IV

1. At the beginning of Act IV, Cleopatra has matured, and we see her in encounters with different people. How is she different? What do her relationships with the musician, Ftatateeta, and Pothinus show to us? What do we learn from the scene between Pothinus and Ftatateeta? Is the scene in keeping with the tone of the play, or is it more melodramatic?

2. In the second scene of Act IV, what is the purpose of the beginning conversation between Rufio and Caesar? Why is it natural for Caesar to go into the open when secrets are to be told, when someone else would hide? What is the significance of Caesar's words:

> What have I to do with resentment? Do I resent the wind when it chills me, or the night when it makes me stumble in the darkness? Shall I resent youth when it turns from age, and ambition when it turns from servitude? To tell me such a story as this is but to tell me that the sun will rise tomorrow.

What part does style play in the elevation of this passage (such as the parallelism in the analogy)?

3. How do we see Cleopatra and Ftatateeta as they plot the murder of Pothinus? How would Cleopatra be played in the rest of the scene?

4. Notice Shaw's comment on the attitude of the men to Egyptian superstitions: "They feel curious in spite of themselves." Would this be a universal trait? Is it not the same sort of feeling an audience would feel watching *The Emperor Jones?*

5. Why is the murdered man's cry effective at just this moment in the dialogue? What does it say for Caesar when Rufio knows what inebriates Ftatateeta and Caesar does not? Why can Cleopatra neither argue nor charm Caesar into thinking she is inno-

cent? Do we admire Caesar for not being vulnerable to her charms? Or is he a cold fish?

ACT V

1. What is the purpose of the contrast between the Egyptian and Roman soldiers?
2. Considering its length, why is Act V not a part of Act IV? Should there be a space of time between Acts IV and V?
3. Is Caesar overly sentimental toward Rufio and Britannus? How does his sentimentality toward them compare with his forgetfulness of Cleopatra? What does Caesar's attitude toward art say about him, especially by comparison to Apollodorus?
4. How are we to take Caesar's speech about Rome's sons? How are we to take his promise of Mark Antony to Cleopatra? What kind of ending is this? Is it effective? Is it great art, or is it artificial and weak? Is it a parody of other history plays you have read? Or is it serious and a parody simultaneously?

"NOTES TO CAESAR AND CLEOPATRA"

"Cleopatra's Cure for Baldness"

1. Are men still worried about being bald? Why does Shaw include the recipe for baldness if it is incomplete?

"Apparent Anachronisms"

1. What does Shaw consider progress? Is there anything in this passage that appears to be untrue? How would you argue against Shaw, if you disagree with what he says?

"Cleopatra"

1. If Cleopatra was actually twenty or twenty-one, rather than sixteen, when she met Julius Caesar, what do we think of Shaw's essay? Does fact make any difference? Is this another of Shaw's jokes? What is the essence of his essay?

"Britannus"

1. What is funny about the first part of Shaw's tongue-in-cheek analysis of Britannus? What could you say against the essay? Is Shaw convincing or partly convincing?

"Julius Caesar"

1. This is the most serious of the five short essays, and Shaw's virtuosity dazzles the reader. Explain the paradoxes Shaw poses in these lines:
    a. His lies pass for "candors."
    b. "Hence, in order to produce an impression of complete disinterestedness and magnanimity, he has only to act with entire selfishness; and this is perhaps the only sense in which a man can be said to be naturally great."
    c. "Having virtue, he had no need of goodness."
    d. "He was neither forgiving, frank, nor generous."
    e. "Goodness, in its popular British sense of self-denial, implies that man is vicious by nature. . . ."

2. One could produce more of Shaw's quizzical statements. Are they true? Does Shaw demonstrate them convincingly in the play? How would you argue against them? Are you insulted, merely amused, or thoughtful (or a combination of all three emotions)? How does an analysis of a play tell you something about yourself?

SAMSON AGONISTES
by John Milton

Background

Samson Agonistes is a great work of art; it is simple and beautiful in its poetry and as a whole. (Other closet dramas in English literature are Shelley's *The Cenci,* probably the best; Browning's *A Blot on the Scutcheon;* and Swinburne's *Atalanta.*) Milton couches a Biblical story in a Greek form, unifying the two main sources of our Graeco-Judaic culture. He recognizes the debt of his society and culture to the *Old Testament.* It might be a good idea to have students become acquainted with *Judges* 13-16. Milton includes almost everything in the Bible up to the last action by means of the "retrospective glance." The form of the play is most like Sophocles' *Oedipus at Colonus* and *Deianira,* but one can see parallels in any Greek play. In fact, the name of the play is half Greek, half Hebrew. "Agonistes" means "champion" in the sense of muscular prowess, with overtones of the "agony" involved in striving to be a champion. The importance of Greek influence will be seen more clearly in the sections on "form" and "conventions."

There is a striking parallel between Milton's biography and his treatment of Samson. Milton, steeped in Biblical study and very religious, was a Puritan, and the Puritans liked to identify themselves as Israelites, God's chosen people. Milton's Puritan cause had failed; he had made an unsuccessful marriage, he was regularly insulted by his foes, and he was blind. His enemies charged that he was being punished by God. Milton refuted this, but Samson's inner struggle to attain self-assurance might have occurred in Milton himself. The parallel may or may not be true, but it does enhance the drama, and many feel that *Samson Agonistes* is one of Milton's most personal works.

Form and Meaning

Samson Agonistes is a tragedy which, like *Paradise Lost,* tries to justify the ways of God to man. It is about a once mighty man who fell because a flaw in his character—pride—made him vulnerable to women. When the play opens, Samson has already been degraded, but during the course of the play he regains his stature and dies performing his most heroic act. Some argue that the play is not a tragedy because Providence guides the action. They say there are no human choices. But Samson's inner struggle is a triumph of human spirit over adversity, rather than solely a triumph of God over Dagon. In the *Old Testament,* Samson does not act unless he is moved by the spirit of God, but in Milton's play he resolves his inner conflict before he is inspired.

The form of the play is Greek. The opening section corresponding to Act I consists of the Prologue (ll. 1-114) spoken by Samson and the "Parados" or entrance of the chorus (ll. 115-331). Samson does not speak out against God, but bewails his blindness and misfortune, comparing his present state to the time when he was in God's favor. The chorus of Hebrews enters and blames Samson for Israel's woes. Samson rallies and does not admit he alone was responsible. He has avoided the first temptations of losing right reason and falling into despair. The next section, corresponding to

Act II, consists of Episode I (ll. 332-651), Samson's encounter with his father Manoa, and Stasimon I (ll. 652-731), where the chorus comments on the preceding Episode and introduces the next. Manoa presents a new temptation; he wants to free his son by ransom. Samson is neither resigned to his position nor moved to action by God; so he stands firm. It is in this section (ll. 529-33) that Samson tells us his flaw:

> Fearless of danger, like a petty god
> I walked about admired of all and dreaded
> On hostile ground, none daring my affront.
> Then swollen with pride into the snare I fell
> Of fair fallacious looks. . . .

The next section, corresponding to Act III, offers a new temptation. Dalila visits him in Episode II (ll. 731-1002), and the chorus comments in Stasimon II (ll. 1003-61). Dalila tempts him with sensual pleasures, saying she repents and offers to care for him. But Samson remains firm, and Dalila says she is proud of betraying him. Samson shows us that he is forever free of Dalila's influence.

The encounter with Harapha, the giant, serves as Act IV, scene i. It consists of Episode and Stasimon III (ll. 1062-1307). The play starts moving toward a climax. As Samson becomes heated with the conflict of words, he feels the return of his old strength. Harapha fears him. When Samson says, "Come nearer: part not hence so slight informed; / But take good heed my hand survey not thee" (ll. 1229-30), he means, "Come a little closer, Harapha, let me get a grip on you." The moment is dramatic. Samson knows his strength has returned, and he receives a hint of what will happen (ll. 1265-67). When the messenger comes the first time, Samson is still unresolved, but when he returns, Samson feels the spirit of God within him. He will be ready to act if an opportunity presents itself, which, of course, it does. Episode IV consists of dialogue between the officer-messenger, Samson, and the chorus (ll. 1308-1426). In Stasimon IV, the chorus is convinced by Samson that he is an agent of God (ll. 1427-44). Episode and Stasimon IV correspond to Act IV, scene ii.

The last section is the "Exode" (or "exodus"), consisting of the closing episode and chorus. It corresponds to Act V. After the news of Samson's feat arrives, the play ends. We feel pity for Samson, but there is also religious exaltation, since God has triumphed over the Philistines. The ending gives us a cleansed feeling (Aristotle's "catharsis") because Samson has resolved the conflict within himself and subsequently reachieved heroic stature. Just as Greek audiences knew the stories of their tragedies, so we know the story of Samson. The drama does not consist in a surprise ending, but takes place in the mind and body of Samson himself. The resolution of Samson's mental and spiritual agonies produces a feeling of calm in the audience.

Conventions

Samson Agonistes, while being one of the greatest of English tragedies, is a closet drama, presumably written to be read, not performed. It is a performance only in the mind of the reader. However, there are still conventions to be mentioned: the unities of time, place, and action; and decorum of character and style. The purpose of the unities is to promote verisimilitude, or life-likeness. Milton thought that a play was more lifelike if the time was twelve or twenty-four hours, if the play took place on one spot of ground, and if there was only one significant action. He also thought that decorum was important. All parts of a tragedy are elevated and serious. The conventions are rather strict. There are no vulgar, trivial, or clownish characters; all characters must speak in an elevated manner. Therefore, they cannot use ordinary idioms. Milton inverts nouns and adverbs, uses big words, and employs verse (to mention only some important devices). These are conventions of Classic tragedy, and when we go to the theater we expect to hear actors in this kind of play speaking unnaturally. The logic behind it is that Samson is such an extraordinary man and that the subject is so elevated that ordinary speech will not serve to impress us. The method is not strictly necessary, as we can see from Shaw's *Caesar and Cleopatra*; but it works, and that is what is important.

The verse is a complicated matter which I will merely touch on. The basic form is blank verse which Milton varies according to the effect he is trying to produce. In Greek tragedy the choruses were sung and danced. Here, as Milton explains in his preface, there is no need to make the lyric parts regular, since the play is not for performance. Nevertheless, there are some fine lyric sections in the play, as well as other sections written almost in free verse. Notice, for example, Samson's tortured thoughts in lines 606–45. Notice also that when he turns to more philosophic thought, blank verse again takes over. In the semi-choruses in lines 1660–1707, Milton rises to an ecstasy by using wild similes in conjunction with free verse.

STUDY QUESTIONS

LINES 1–331 (ACT I)

1. What is the gist of lines 1–22? What purpose does this introduction serve? Why does Samson, in lines 23–51, relate his history? Do Samson's thoughts lead to the self-incriminations of lines 52–79? What is the importance of his affirmation of God's power in lines 60–69?

2. Why should the verse form change in Samson's great lamentations (ll. 80–109)? What state of mind does Samson express? Why does the verse form change again in lines 110–14? Why does Samson think his enemies are approaching?

3. In lines 115–50, why does the chorus relate Samson's past deeds? What is their attitude toward Samson? What kind of people does the chorus represent?

4. In lines 77–78, why could not Milton say, "I hear someone speaking, but they are too far away for me to understand the words." Why does the chorus keep saying that Samson should not think God is unjust, when we know Samson has already said that He is just? In lines 300–25, does the chorus speak for Milton?

5. What appears to be the purpose of lines 1–321? How far have we progressed in the analysis of Samson and his condition?

LINES 332–731 (ACT II)

1. In lines 340–72, Manoa tempts Samson "to deny God's justice" (see ll. 368–72). How does Samson answer?

2. Manoa then blames Samson for degrading God and elevating Dagon (see ll. 440–47). How does Samson reply (ll. 448–71)?

3. Manoa then tries to convince Samson that he should be ransomed (ll. 472–86). Is Manoa convincing in his attempt to persuade Samson? Manoa follows up his first attempt with a second (ll. 502–20). Why would Manoa want Samson to take the easy way out? What kind of answer does Samson give to Manoa (ll. 487–501 and 521–40)? Is it a clear-cut answer? What important fact does Samson reveal in lines 529–33? Why does the chorus take Manoa's part (ll. 541–57)?

4. Does the fact that we know what is going to happen affect our reaction to this argument between Samson and Manoa? In what way? Why does Milton use regular blank verse in this section of the play?

5. Samson remains firm in staying in Gaza, but what kind of reaction does he have to his father's pleas (ll. 606–51)? In lines 617–22, why does Samson use such grotesque imagery.

6. In lines 667–709, what is the gist of the chorus' prayer? Where is the irony? What is the effect of the change of tone from the prayer to the ornate description of Dalila (ll. 710–31)?

LINES 732–1061 (ACT III)

1. What is the gist of Dalila's arguments (ll. 732–47, 766–818, 843–70, 903, 904)? What are Samson's reactions?

2. In lines 907–27, how does Dalila change her attack? Is Samson's response different (ll. 928–50, and 952–59)? Is Samson tempted?

3. What does Dalila reveal about herself in lines 960–96? Is there a comment here on the theory of history?

4. What is the purpose of the chorus' comment in lines 1003–1007? Has Samson really learned his lesson about women? What is the subject of the chorus' song in lines 1010–60? Is their comment to be taken as truth? Does Milton himself speak through the chorus?

LINES 1062–1307 (ACT IV, SCENE I)

1. Is there a kind of classification of assaults that Samson receives? What is Harapha's purpose in visiting Samson (ll. 1076–90)? Are his excuses for refusing to fight Samson convincing (ll. 1092–1103, 1106–1107, 1130–38)?

2. How does Harapha show his cowardice (ll. 1231–43)? Could this scene be acted out on a stage? Could most of the play? Why or why not?

3. How does Samson's attitude in this scene show improvement (ll. 1139–55)? How is his resolution shown? Why is it psychologically sound that Samson should show more resolution in this scene than he does earlier? How does your answer fit Samson as a man of physical action?

4. In lines 1250–67, who is right, Samson or the chorus? What is the implication of lines 1265–67? Does the chorus sense the full implication of these lines? Does the chorus react as would an ordinary audience or reader?

LINES 1308–1444 (ACT IV, SCENE II)

1. Is Samson's answer to the officer convincing (ll. 1319–21, 1334–42)? How does the chorus express timidity (ll. 1348–53)? How do they compare with Samson? How has Samson changed since Act I (ll. 1354–79)?

2. What is the importance of lines 1381–89, to which Milton has been leading us since the beginning of the play? Is Samson ready now to act if an occasion presents itself? What kind of feeling do we get from the passage?

3. What is the purpose of the chorus' elevated song (ll. 1427–40)?

LINES 1445–1758 (ACT V)

1. In lines 1445–1508, Manoa talks about ransoming Samson, and how wonderful it would be to have him home again. The chorus dutifully replies and answers Manoa's questions about the noise which interrupts his speech (ll. 1472–75). We know, while Manoa does not, that Samson will perform a heroic act. What effect does Manoa's speech have on an audience or reader? What kind of person is Manoa? Is Samson's action made more dramatic by having it performed offstage? Why does not Manoa return to his speech after he hears the "hideous noise" (ll. 1508–20)? What does he hope or fear?

2. We find out by bits and snatches, until the messenger's final speech, what happened offstage. What is the dramatic effect of

Manoa's changing hopes and fears? What is the effect of a bystander describing Samson's final act? The Biblical story says that Samson prayed before he died. Here we only know that "he stood, as one who prayed" (l. 1636). What is the effect of the difference? What things can Milton add which are not in the Biblical account?

3. How could the end of the messenger's speech and the chorus' apostrophe (starting l. 1660) be dramatized?

4. What is the purpose of the imagery in the semi-choruses (ll. 1669–1707)? What effect does the loose verse form have? Is the song effective? What kind of praise does it give Samson? What attitude does Manoa have toward his son's death?

5. What is the meaning of lines 1745–48? What is the meaning of lines 1749–51? Do we learn about "true experience" (l. 1756) in the play? Do we experience "peace and consolation" as the poem says? Are our minds calm after reading the play?

6. Why is the last speech in lyric form? Is it complicated? If not, why not? Does it achieve its ostensible purpose?

Drama for Grade Twelve

ANTIGONE
by Sophocles

Background

Oedipus had four children by his mother, Jocasta: Eteocles and Polynices (boys), and Antigone and Ismene (girls). After Oedipus blinded himself, his sons insulted him, and he cursed them. The curse then worked itself out in the demise of his sons. They decided to rule alternately one year apiece. Eteocles was first, but after his year was up he refused to give up his throne to Polynices. Polynices attacked Thebes with the aid of his father-in-law, Adrastus, and five other young heroes. They all appear in Aeschylus' *Seven Against Thebes*. In the struggle Eteocles and Polynices killed each other. Creon, Jocasta's brother, became the ruler and out of revenge refused to bury Polynices. It is at this point that the play opens.

The problem of fate is important in the play because a play cannot be a tragedy if the characters have no choices in their actions. The characters in this play do have choices, just as anybody does, but their personalities and the influences of their family and blood are such that they determine which choices they will make (their fate). That is why Antigone, a member of the tainted family of Labdakos, will probably die violently. Men cannot predict what will happen unless they have the gift of prophecy. Teiresias had the insight of prophecy given to him by the gods.

Form and Meaning

Both the action and the ideas of the play center around the central conflict, Creon vs. Antigone. Creon is the more interesting character, and therefore the question arises, why is the play called *Antigone?* The answer lies in the didactic purpose of the play: tyrants are bad. Creon is a tyrant, and Antigone is the heroine who stands up for right against evil. Also, this play seems to be part of a trilogy dealing with the story of Oedipus' luckless family: *Oedipus Rex* (430 B.C.), *Oedipus at Colonus* (401 B.C.), and *Antigone* (442 B.C.).

Creon's decline and fall is the form of the play. The play is a tragedy, and Creon is a tragic hero, a man of stature, who falls through his own action. He is an able man whose tragic flaw is *hubris*, or overweening pride. He assumes a god-like position in his judgment of men, and wrongs the gods by his treatment of the dead and by burying Antigone alive. He also refuses to admit he is wrong. But we do not see him as all bad. Every conscientious ruler feels he must uphold the laws of the land, and we can identify with him quite easily and understand his problem. (In Anouilh's *Antigone*—a good comparison to this play—we become even more sympathetic to Creon.) We feel Creon's punishment is more than he deserves; we pity him. Because we can visualize ourselves in his place, we feel fear. Pity and fear are prerequisities for tragedy, according to Aristotle. The working out of the tragedy makes us experience a calmness when it is finished, corresponding to Aristotle's catharsis. Creon is evil not because he upholds the law, but because he goes to an extreme. He is a tyrant, refusing to back down even when it becomes evident he should do so.

Antigone is not entirely admirable. She is right, but she is so extreme in her feelings and actions that we feel she is unbalanced. She is like the irresistible force and Creon like the immovable object. Neither will stop until it is too late. An explosion occurs. When we think of Antigone's actions we wonder if she could not have tried some other method of getting her brother buried. Although she is also a tragic figure, it is harder to identify ourselves with her than with Creon because she is not as human.

There are several themes which hinge on the conflict between the two main characters. The one we see most clearly is public necessity vs. private good. Creon upholds the supremacy of man's political creation, Antigone the duty to the gods and to family. Creon says, "it is best to keep the established laws even to life's end" (l. 1112). Antigone says, "A mortal [cannot] override the unwritten and unchanging statutes of heaven. For their authority is not of today nor yesterday, but from all time" (ll. 452–54). A second conflict is between love and hate. Which is the ruling principle? As Antigone says (l. 523), "It is not my nature to join in hating, but in loving." Creon, on the other hand, tries to carry revenge and hatred too far. They are both extremes. A third conflict is between men and women. Creon says: "While I live no woman shall overbear me" (l. 525); "But I am no man, she is the man, if she can carry this off unpunished" (ll. 482–83); "Let them know they are women, not meant to roam abroad" (ll. 579–80); and "we must not let a woman defy us. It would be better to fall from power by a man's hand, than to be called weaker than a woman" (ll. 678–80). The fourth conflict is that of two strong personalities. If one had backed down the tragedy would have been averted. Neither gives in to the other until it is too late.

Conventions

As in other Greek plays, and in *Samson Agonistes*, there are no acts. The play has no breaks, although it has well-defined parts: Prologue (ll. 1–99); Parados, or entrance of the chorus (ll. 100–55); Episode I (ll. 156–330); Stasimon I (ll. 331–70); Episode II (ll. 371–582); Stasimon II (ll. 583–630); Episode III (ll. 631–780); Stasimon III (781–800); Episode IV (ll. 801–945); Stasimon IV (ll. 946–88); Episode V (ll. 989–1012); Hyporchema, or dance of the chorus (ll. 1013–1152); Exode, or Exodus, or conclusion (ll. 1153–1352). The Episodes are self-explanatory. The Stasima are the comments of the chorus on the preceding episodes. Episode IV includes a Kommos, a lyric lament, spoken or sung by Antigone and the chorus (ll. 801–80). As in *Samson Agonistes*, the method of development shows a steady progress to an expected conclusion. The audience knows the story; the interest is in the way Sophocles saw and handled the events. He interpreted them in his own way.

The unities are kept. The time is one day; the scene is in one place (although characters go to specified places and then return); there is one significant action by Creon (made too late), and there are actions by Antigone, Haemon, and Eurydice, which are all violent. As in all Greek tragedy (and in *Samson Agonistes*), the violence is offstage, which lets our imaginations make the scenes more or less horrible than they are.

The characters speak and act in accordance with their positions in society. Unlike *Samson Agonistes*, however, there is one comic character, the guard who reports to Creon that someone tried to bury Polynices and later brings in Antigone. He is not there for comic relief, however, his purpose is functional. The chorus serves the same purpose as in *Samson Agonistes*.

Characters

Each character, besides being a type, is a person in his own right. Creon is a typical tyrant, slightly paranoid, and determined to uphold the state, which he equates with himself. His first utterance shows the high principles by which he professes to govern (ll. 162–210), but because he is paranoid he thinks that anyone who disobeys the law is actually insulting him (see ll. 653–55, 738). He therefore suspects people of deceiving him before anything happens (ll. 220–21), charges unknown men with thinking subversive thoughts (ll. 288–91), and with no justification accuses the guard of taking a bribe (ll. 292–311, 322). His antagonism toward Antigone stems not only from her disagreement with him, but also from the fact that she is a woman, an inferior being. But Creon's stands are ironical and self-contradictory. He calls Antigone stubborn (ll. 473–78), but he himself is overly stubborn. He says Antigone's first duty is to the state (l. 510), but he tells Haemon that his first duty is to his family (ll. 639–42). When he confronts Teiresias, the irony is that Teiresias, though blind, can see truth. Creon cannot see truth; he is figuratively blind. His blindness and his stubbornness bring on the catastrophe.

Antigone is not a complex enough character to be interesting for long to an audience. She is too singleminded in her duties to her brother. She is also tainted with the blood of Oedipus (as she says in ll. 1–31, 858–70), which influences her to pursue stubbornly a course of self-destruction. She is not a typical girl. She is a heroine. Ismene, an ordinary, feminine girl, is Antigone's foil. Ismene says, "we must remember we were born women, not meant to strive with men" (ll. 61–62). Antigone strives with men, and conducts a heated discussion with an infuriated Creon (ll. 497–525). Her intellectual and moral forcefulness is masculine. However, she utters sentiments very dear to Greek hearts:

> Not for my children, if I had been a mother, nor for my husband, if his dead body were rotting before me, would I have chosen to suffer like this in violent defiance of the citizens. For the sake of what law do I say this? If my husband had died, there would have been another man for me; I could have had a child from another husband if I had lost my first child. But with my mother and father both hidden away in Hades, no other brother could ever have come into being for me (ll. 903–14).

The ties of blood were strong to the Greeks, and we of the modern age put much more importance on romantic love than they did. In fact, a man or woman was to be pitied in the Greek view if he fell into a violent passion. Antigone puts her brother first, but in the Kommos shows how much she regrets not being allowed to live the normal life of a girl, where marriage is important (not love, but marriage). Because of circumstance, Antigone is forced into a situation she does not like.

The guard is a comic contrast to Creon. His earthy humor shows him to be an ordinary man, ready to help others, full of natural sentiments, but always looking out for himself first. He realizes that although Creon is unbalanced, he is a man to be feared and respected. The chorus is also made up of ordinary citizens.

STUDY QUESTIONS

LINES 1–155 (PROLOGUE AND PARADOS)

1. How do Creon and Antigone differ? What kinds of persons are they? What do they debate? What is the purpose of the recapitulation of events? What stand does Ismene take in lines 50–68? In lines 69–99, the division between the two women is greatest. What fundamental kind of stand does each take? Do we admire Antigone? Do we like her?

2. The chorus' reaction to the battle contrasts to Antigone's and Ismene's. If the chorus represents ordinary people, how do the

people of Thebes feel? How do we react to their song (ll. 100–55), knowing also what Ismene and Antigone think?

1. What kind of entrance speech does Creon make? How do we react to it? Is there anything wrong with it (ll. 156–210)? How does the chorus react to Creon's speech (ll. 211–20)? What does line 221 say about Creon?

2. What kind of person is the guard? How can we tell that Creon is impatient with the guard (ll. 237–48)? Why might the chorus think the burial was the work of the gods (l. 278)? How does Creon react to both the guard and the chorus? What does his speech (ll. 280–312) say about himself? Does this speech contrast to his entrance speech? How do we react to the dialogue between Creon and the guard (ll. 312–30)?

3. The chorus praises man, points out his weakness, and condemns the man who scorns good (ll. 331–70). To which man do they refer? Are these lines ironical?

1. How does the guard further characterize himself (ll. 387–440)? What does he tell us about Antigone?

2. The debate between Antigone and Creon is one of the important spots in the play (ll. 450–527). Antigone agrees that the gods demand Polynice's burial, a law higher than man's laws, and that she has to try to bury him because he is her brother, even though she will die because of it. What are Creon's arguments? Who, if either, wins the argument in our eyes?

3. The introduction of Ismene reveals a third point of view (ll. 528–82). What is Ismene's stand? Is her stand more reasonable? How do we react to Antigone's claim to punishment and glory, excluding Ismene? Does Antigone believe she alone deserves recognition because she does not think Ismene is worthy? Or does she merely try to protect Ismene? What is Ismene's attitude toward love, as different from Creon's and Antigone's?

4. The chorus (in ll. 583–630) apparently talks about Antigone and Ismene. But could their words also ironically apply to Creon?

1. Haemon starts out being deferential. What does Creon reveal about himself in his final speech (ll. 639–80)? Is there irony in the chorus' reply (l. 681)? Or is Creon's speech wholly admirable?

2. Does Haemon speak wisely? Why does he bring in the boat analogy? Where is there a previous nautical analogy (ll. 162–90)?

3. The chorus thinks Haemon's speech is wise, but how does Creon react? What do we think of him after his reaction (l. 727)? Is Creon merely trying to shame Haemon or to overpower him with authority for the sake of showing his righteousness, or are these serious arguments? What do we think of Creon after he has resisted the arguments and pleas of his son?

4. Stasimon III (ll. 781–800) is a good statement on how the Greeks regarded great passion. They recognized many kinds of love. Haemon becomes the victim of a mad passion, but, here, is the chorus right in saying that Haemon is angry at his father because he loves Antigone?

1. In the Kommos (ll. 807–80), what kinds of things does Antigone lament? How do we react to the lament? How do we think of Antigone (and Creon)?

2. What do we think of Creon's statement, "Our hands are clean as touching this maiden" (ll. 881–90)? What is the gist of Antigone's moving speech (ll. 891–942), and how do we react to it?

3. The chorus again comments on Antigone's fate as related to other historical events. Wherein lies the irony? Do we know something the chorus does not know? How does our knowledge help the play's dramatic effect?

1. What do we think when Creon accuses Teiresias of being bribed? Who is really blind, Teiresias or Creon? What is the effect of Teiresias' prophecy on Creon? On the chorus? On the audience?

2. Do we have a surge of hope when Creon gives in? Why does

Creon think he may be wrong in changing his mind? Does our attitude toward Creon change?

3. The Hyporchema covers a passage of time. What kind of hymn is this song (ll. 1113–1152)? Is the chorus convinced everything is all right? What kind of dramatic effect is produced?

LINES 1153–1352 (EXODUS)

1. What kind of wisdom does the messenger express (ll. 1153–71)? Why is it more effective to have violent action described rather than acted out (note messenger's speech, ll. 1191–1242)? Do we pity Creon? Is his punishment too severe? Do we think much about Antigone and Haemon?

2. How do we regard Creon's speech, starting at line 1271, in the light of Eurydice's ominous departure? What is the effect of our learning that Eurydice cursed Creon with her dying breath? What is the importance of the chorus' last words? Do we pity Creon? Is his punishment now more than he deserves? Do we feel fear that perhaps we too might some day become involved in circumstances beyond our control? Do we feel better now that the tragedy has worked itself out? What is the role of fate in this play? Are Creon and Antigone doomed before they start, or are their actions products of choice?

THE MISANTHROPE
by Molière

Background

The Misanthrope, one of the greatest of all comedies, was first performed in 1666. It was a product of the corrupt but brilliant court of Louis XIV. Like *Hamlet,* it has been interpreted in different ways. Alceste, the main character, has been thought of as a great hero. The extreme case for Alceste's heroism was made by Jean Jacques Rousseau; others see Alceste only as childish, unreasonable, tactless, vain, and egotistical. The truth lies somewhere in between. William Wycherly's brilliant, bitter, and vicious play, *The Plain Dealer,* is actually a Restoration English adaptation of *The Misanthrope.*

Form and Meaning

The Misanthrope is a true comedy of manners. It consists largely of comments by and about people. The play's universality makes it pertinent to any society, although the society in the play is aristocratic. The plot, which consists of Alceste trying to see if Celimene really loves him, is not very important. The conflict in the play takes place between Alceste and society. Each is satirized: society by the revelations, intentions, and actions of its members; Alceste by his obsession and extreme behavior. It is not Alceste's honesty and sincerity that is amusing, but his carrying them to ridiculous, inconsistent extremes. Occasionally, for example, we may see someone who, when greeted with "How are you?" proceeds to tell us all his real and imagined troubles, in detail. He believes us to be sincere, or he believes we should be sincere. We may admire his principles, but, practically, we find him boring and ridiculous. If we see Alceste as a hero, we see him as standing for truth, virtue, honesty, sincerity, and plain-dealing. Philinte and Eliante are phlegmatic people who debase themselves by excusing, as examples of human nature, the clowns, villains, frauds, and hypocrites which make up society. Celimene is an unforgivable coquette; Oronte and Acaste are pompous fools or even villains; and Arsinoe is the consummate prudish hypocrite.

However, one can look at the play in another way. Philinte and Eliante represent judicious, intelligent, well-mannered people of good taste and breeding. Celimene, a witty, pretty, young widow of twenty, naturally likes to surround herself with admirers and also naturally wants to have a good time. The others are harmless, ordinary people, mixtures of good and bad whom we must expect to be treacherous at times because men are naturally that way. Alceste is an incompetent, ridiculous creature, who can see only two worlds: the court and absolute seclusion. His recreation is to rail. His sole function in society is to criticize it and everyone in it. He thinks he is superior to everyone else without ever having shown it, or proved it. The play seems to point more naturally toward the worse view of Alceste. His impassioned speeches show him to be less judicious than Philinte. Celimene, Acaste, Clitandre, and Oronte are not desirable people to emulate. Philinte and Eliante are meant to provide examples of good sense and normal behavior. *The Misanthrope*, like *Antigone*, propounds the "Golden Mean." It reveals such singleness of purpose that there is not much plot.

Conventions

The most important convention is that of decorum of characters. Each person is the same throughout the play. There is no development or change in Alceste or in anyone else. The play merely unfolds to us the character of each person as he encounters different situations. At the end of the play, the characters leave, one by one, and the play ends in a kind of dying fall. The unities of time and action are not important. Unity of place, however, is kept, as is *liaison des scenes*, a convention of the French theater of the time. It means that the stage is never empty during an act. A new scene occurs when a character enters or leaves the stage.

The other conventions are the usual ones. Alceste and Celimene speak "asides" which the audience, but no one else, can hear. Molière's theater, the Palais Royal in Paris, with both actors and actresses (a relatively recent innovation in the latter part of the seventeenth century), its proscenium arch, and its box stage, lent itself to non-illusionistic representational drama. The play is not realistic because all the characters are types, not actual people. A "comedy of manners," the play deals with codes of behavior, not with personalities; with the appearance of men, not with their complex thoughts and motivations; with society rather than with an individual. To overemphasize Alceste as an individual is to make him into a tragic hero, which he is not.

Characters

A discussion of Alceste as a character is very much a discussion of the play's meaning. Alceste's principles are beyond dispute, but they are absolute ideals which cannot apply to trivial everyday affairs. Alceste's only standard of judgment is sincerity. He criticizes Oronte and his sonnet, allowing no extenuating circumstances such as seriousness of intent on Oronte's part (Act I, scene ii). Oronte's sonnet is full of wordplay, and it is superficial, but it is not bad. Alceste's own poem (which Molière has him repeat twice to show his weakness of mind in doting on it) is just as affected (since it is so out of date) and shows Alceste's removal from his own society. He is a man of extremes. He sees no alternative to life in the king's court but complete isolation. He does not want to act about anything. He will not try to win his case in court nor will he lift a finger to help justice; he would rather complain and be a martyr (Act I, scene i).

Alceste obviously feels superior, but despite his feelings of superiority he is very humanly in love. However, his lovesickness makes his attitude toward mankind no different. He still displays his vanity in these lines: "I wouldn't love her did she not love me" (Act I, scene i). His efforts, in the last scene of the play, to force choices on Celimene are antisocial. He will have her on his own terms or not at all. Is Alceste being self-centered and vain? If society is a common ground where you respect others' wishes and tolerate others' views, Alceste is a vain, self-centered, unacceptable member of a society he rejects. Society, represented by Philinte and Eliante (Act V, scene viii) proves to be more tolerant. It will try to save Alceste from self-destruction not for society's benefit, but for his own. But the principles Alceste stands for are not wrong; he merely carries them to absurd extremes. When one is in society, one abides by society's practices; Alceste refuses to do this. He stands for the dignity of man, but in his failure to be discriminating and in his extreme stand he becomes inhuman, a comic monster. The reason the play gives one an uncomfortable feeling is because many times it is impossible to carry ideals into practical life. This is one of the tragedies of man, and Alceste himself is both tragic and comic.

Celimene is a gay, witty, young widow, the opposite of Alceste (as Philinte points out in Act I, scene i). She is immersed in society, but is much more aware of herself and of others than is Alceste, or any of her suitors, and she is not duped by Arsinoe as is Alceste (Act III, scenes v, vi, and vii). She is a master at describing the essences of people (Act I, scene iv). Her satirical portraits are of boring people whom almost anyone would want to avoid (Act II, scene v). We can see in our minds the bored, shallow, rather sad Viscount for "three quarters of an hour spitting into a well, so as to make circles in the water" (Act V, scene iv).

All the suitors, as well as Celimene, think of Alceste as a bore, which, in his singlemindedness, he is. At the end of the play she makes concessions to Alceste, but does not go so far as to belie her own nature. She knows she cannot exist in isolation. The part of Celimene is a wonderful part for an actress who wants to show off her beauty and acting ability.

None of Celimene's portraits is as comical and revealing as Acaste's portrait of himself (Act III, scene iii). Acaste is an entirely superficial member of society. He is a complete numbskull, who is "his cape and sword" (Act V, scene iv): there is nothing to him but his fashion.

Eliante and Philinte are Molière's mouthpieces. They represent society's golden mean and set off or magnify Alceste's aberrations. Their weaknesses, in turn, are illuminated by Alceste's rectitude. Philinte is the more important character. He is a tolerant, reasonable man, not given to outbursts of emotion. He is ruled by the humor phlegm (Act I, scene i), or is what we call phlegmatic. In fact, he appears emotionally cold. Euphemistically, he could be called a mild-mannered man of reason. There is warmth in the scene between Philinte and Eliante (Act V, scene viii), but hardly the sort of emotion one would expect to find in a triumphal love scene.

Eliante: Were I to offer him this hand of mine,
Your friend Philinte, I think, would not decline.
Philinte: Ah, Madam. That's my heart's most cherished goal,
For which I'd gladly give my life and soul.

In this play of ambiguities we are able to admire both Alceste and Philinte.

STUDY QUESTIONS

ACT I

1. What kind of person is Alceste? What kind of person is Philinte? How does Philinte maneuver the conversation to cover different topics? Is Philinte Alceste's good friend, or is he a kind of gadfly? Does Alceste's love for Celimene sound real? Is there anything peculiar about his attitude toward her?

2. Does Oronte, at the beginning of scene ii, really like Alceste? Is Alceste justified in his attitude toward Oronte? Is Alceste fair in his judgment of Oronte's poem? Is he any less fair than Philinte? Is Philinte's attitude more or less admirable than Alceste's (think of the scene from Oronte's point of view, also)? Is Alceste's poem really better than Oronte's? How would one's interpretation of Alceste influence the manner of his speech on the stage?

3. In scene iii, is Alceste's reaction to Philinte justified? What do you think of someone who in a short space of time insults an acquaintance, makes an enemy, and quarrels with his best friend? Why is there a division between scenes ii and iii?

ACT II

1. In scene i, is Celimene justified in being irritated with the way Alceste speaks to her? What kind of person is Celimene (scenes i, ii, iii, iv)? Does Celimene seem more than naturally concerned with what others think? How is Alceste's attitude toward leaving quite amusing in scenes iv and v?

2. Do the suitors lead Celimene into giving her satirical portraits? Is Celimene vicious, or might another word fit her better? What kind of people does Celimene make fun of?

3. Is Alceste's reaction to the character sketches justified? How are we to take Celimene's character of Alceste? How do we react to Philinte's criticism? When even Eliante disagrees with Alceste, are we convinced that he is in the wrong?

4. What is the effect of Alceste's being called to court?

ACT III

1. Scene i is one of the funniest scenes in the play. What is dramatic irony? How does it fit Acaste's speech? How superficial is Acaste? What one thing is he interested in? How does he compare with Philinte and Alceste?

2. In scene iii, Celimene describes Arsinoe before we see her. Is Celimene's description of Arsinoe carried out in scene v? Aside from Act I, when Philinte and Alceste spoke frankly, this is the first scene where Alceste's principles of sincerity and frankness are displayed. How do we regard honesty in society after scene v? Do we think it is always a good thing? What is a prude, by

Celimene's definition? What is our attitude toward Celimene after scene vi? Do Celimene and Arsinoe understand themselves and each other very well?

3. In Act III, scene vi, why would Molière use such a clumsy bit of stagecraft?

4. In Act III, scene vii, how does Arsinoe get around to penetrating Alceste's skeptical armor? Is Alceste an easy mark for Arsinoe? Would Celimene have fallen for insinuations Arsinoe might make against Alceste? How do we regard Alceste after scene vii?

ACT IV

1. Do we like Alceste better after he is discussed by Eliante and Philinte (scene i)? What does our answer say about our attitude toward Eliante and Philinte? What kind of people are they? How does the contrast of Alceste's rage with the calm reasoning of Eliante and Philinte affect our attitude toward all three characters in scene ii?

2. Is Celimene in the right in scene iii? How do we regard Alceste when he wants Celimene to pretend she loves him? How are we to take Alceste's pronouncement that he would like to see Celimene miserable so he could help her?

3. What is the purpose of the farce in scene iv?

ACT V

1. In scene i, Alceste's view of humanity is quite dark. Is it justified? Has he done anything to prevent injustice and backbiting? Does it appear that Alceste likes to rail at men, that he almost looks for excuses to do so? Why would he say that the loss of his lawsuit gives him the right to rage and storm? Why will he not appeal his lawsuit? Does Philinte like men any better than Alceste? If Alceste places himself above all men, where does Philinte place himself?

2. In scene ii, should Celimene answer Oronte and Alceste?

3. Is it just that everyone turns against Celimene? What kind of people does Celimene ridicule? Can Celimene's letters be defended, except for their wit and entertainment?

4. What is amusing about Arsinoe in scene vi? Is she a believable character?

5. In scene vii, is Alceste only a self-centered, vain, and even cruel person, or is he noble, idealistic, and high-spirited? Is Celimene's attitude rational? Should she give up everything for Alceste?

6. What is the theatrical effect of the characters leaving the stage one by one?

7. Judging by their words and actions in scene viii, are Philinte and Eliante very much in love? What is their attitude toward the world? If they represent society, what is society's attitude toward Alceste? Is Alceste's attitude toward society extreme? What is our final attitude toward Alceste?

ROSMERSHOLM
by Henrik Ibsen

Background

Henrik Ibsen is one of the greatest playwrights of all times and *Rosmersholm* (1886) is one of his best plays. In its use of symbolism and its emphasis on the psychological nuances of characters, it typifies the last productive period of his life, when it was written. *The Wild Duck* is the first play in this period, preceding *Rosmersholm* by two years. It is a much simpler play, although it too is excellent. Other plays of this period include *The Lady from the Sea* (a not so successful play) in 1888, *Hedda Gabler* (a wonderful example of good theater) in 1890, *The Master Builder* in 1892, *Little Eyeolf* in 1894, *John Gabriel Borkman* (a splendid play) in 1896, and *When We Dead Awaken* in 1899.

The political satire in *Rosmersholm* emanates from a political squabble in Norway which took place in the summer of 1885. The disillusioned Ibsen said the country was full of fighting cats. This is why the play starts out to be such a violent satire on politics. But as he conceived the play, Ibsen became fascinated with the characters of Rosmer and Rebecca, especially Rebecca.

Ibsen, although a culmination of eighteenth- and nineteenth-century drama, is the first important modern playwright. As Joseph Wood Krutch says, in "The Tragic Fallacy": "Shakespeare justified the ways of God to man, but in Ibsen there is no such happy end and with him tragedy, so called, has become merely an expression of our despair at finding that such justification is no longer possible."[4] Ibsen precedes the tragic attitude found, for instance, in Miller's *The Death of a Salesman* and *The Crucible*, and Tennessee Williams' *The Glass Menagerie* and *A Streetcar Named Desire*. His conception of a hero as unheroic influenced Shaw's modern conception of Julius Caesar.

Form and Meaning

Rosmersholm is a modern tragedy, as opposed to tragedies like *Antigone* and *Samson Agonistes*. Rosmer and Rebecca must justify themselves to themselves. They are complete in themselves and they complement each other. They are the products of what we would call heredity and environment. There is much in their personalities that they do not will. Rosmer is steeped in conformity and tradition. He lives in the house (Rosmersholm) where no man laughs and no children cry, surrounded by paintings of his ancestors, the continual awareness of his dead wife, and the awareness that although he is incapable himself of action, his name guarantees his ability to influence. Rebecca, who comes from the wild north of Norway, was, because of her illegitimate birth, once a free spirit, aware of no allegiances and capable of any action. The confrontation of the two characters is electrifying and its results are tragic.

The first plane of confrontation is political, and Rebecca conquers. The second concerns passion and Rosmer conquers. Yet another confrontation supersedes these two—the confrontation of two human spirits. Here, Rosmer and Rebecca are united as one; neither conquers. The political confrontation is relatively simple. The liberals (Peter Mortensgard) and the conservatives (Mr. Kroll) are unscrupulous and demanding. They both live in the present, but while Kroll looks backward, Mortensgard looks to the future. It is obvious Ibsen thinks the Mortensgards will win out. Rebecca, once as unprincipled and liberal as Mortensgard, has influenced Rosmer to accept free-thinking. He gives up his religion and many conventions he once held. For example, he is going to chide Rebecca for eavesdropping, but then he realizes he should not because each person is a judge of his own actions (Act

II). This kind of belief works if you have no principles. But, since the members of Rosmer's family have been leaders in the community for two hundred years, he has been brought up with a sense of moral responsibility to others. Rosmer's feelings are that he wants to elevate all people to the level of the best, and he feels that the conservative ways of persons like Kroll are a thing of the past. Kroll is afraid that good people will fall to the level of the bad. Mortensgard merely wants to succeed. Rosmer's idea is noble, but in his case impractical because he has so little confidence in himself that he cannot act. He needs Rebecca to supply this confidence he lacks, and therefore he is easily influenced by her ideas. Politically, Rebecca conquers.

Before the play opens, Rebecca insinuates herself into Rosmersholm because of a great sexual passion for Rosmer. But after living in Rosmersholm (and while imbuing Rosmer with her free thinking) she becomes imbued with its ideals. She acquires a conscience. She assumes the guilt of Beate's suicide and no longer has a free spirit. By the time Rosmer realizes his own passion for Rebecca and proposes to her, she cannot accept him. The marriage cannot be ideal because she cannot tell Rosmer she is guilty without destroying Rosmer's faith in her. Rebecca loses the confrontation of passion. Rosmer (and what he stands for) conquers.

The world surrounding Rosmersholm is a rotten world which will not get any better. Peter Mortensgard, a man with no ideals and no principles, is the man of the future (Act IV). A fine, sensitive man like Rosmer cannot exist in such a world. Ibsen, in essence, is saying that a man can achieve nobility only within himself. If he is to act in the world, he must compromise his nobility with the practical politics of the Peter Mortensgards and the Krolls. The suicide is both a denial and an affirmation. It is a denial of the world; it is an affirmation of the trust and belief Rebecca and Rosmer have for each other. Rebecca, once she has admitted her guilt about Beate's death to Rosmer, can only prove the purity of her love and her belief in him by sacrificing herself. Although Rebecca and Rosmer are admitting they cannot survive as themselves in the world, the suicide also gives them the only possible way to achieve a tragic nobility. The world will not see them as heroic or tragic; their nobility is entirely self-contained.

Conventions

Rosmersholm is a play of "ripe circumstances," as are *Samson Agonistes, Antigone,* and *Oedipus Rex.* The play takes place at the crucial moment of the characters' lives. All previous events lead to the moment of the play. Thus the play opens *in medias res,* in the middle of things. We learn about previous events such as Beate's suicide through the device of the "retrospective glance." The focus on these events is heightened by the unities of time, place, and action. The place is within the one house, there is only one significant action (all the rest lead up to it), and the time (long for an Ibsen play because of the necessity of newspaper publications) is 52 hours.

Ibsen is the first great modern realistic dramatist. We peep through the fourth wall of a house to see represented an illusion of reality. The convention of realism influences the conception of the characters as ordinary people. It also influences other descriptions. Ibsen describes important details in the rooms of the house, such as Rebecca's flowers, the pictures of Rosmer's ancestors, and the view from the window. When someone looks out the window, we know they are looking at the spot where Beate committed suicide by jumping from the footbridge into the millrace. The ghost of Rosmer's dead wife permeates the whole play. Ibsen is also the descendant of Eugene Scribe and his "well-made plays." One of Scribe's devices was the revelation of a mysterious letter at an important moment. It is improbable, for example, that two of Beate's old letters should suddenly come to light on the same day, and so long after she wrote them, but they help us and Rosmer to understand Rebecca's guilty conscience about Beate. In a "well-made play" everything fits; there are no weak links in the play's logic even though probability may be stretched.

Another convention Ibsen uses is that of the *raisonneur*—a character who comments on the action and represents the voice of reason or ordinary common sense. Modern playwrights need someone to comment on the action, to initiate action by advice, to produce irony by misunderstanding an action or statement, and to explain what the audience's reaction should be. The relation of the *raisonneur* to the Greek chorus is functional and obvious.

Examples are Dr. Relling in Ibsen's *The Wild Duck*, Smithers in O'Neill's *The Emperor Jones*, Enobarbus in Shakespeare's *Antony and Cleopatra*, and Ulric Brendel in *Rosmersholm*. In Act IV of *Rosmersholm*, Brendel seemingly raves, but in reality he is a combination Teiresias and Greek chorus. He first tells of his disillusionment, his failure to act until it was too late. We can see the same fate may hold true for Rosmer. His comment on Peter Mortensgard, the man of the future, is splendid in its accuracy and conciseness: "For Peter Mortensgard never wills more than he can do. Peter Mortensgard is capable of living his life without ideals. And that, do you see—that is just the mighty secret of action and of victory. It is the sum of the whole world's wisdom. Basta!" Then, he defines the relationship of Rebecca and Rosmer. Rebecca is the mermaid who will have to sacrifice something of herself. His statements lead Rebecca and Rosmer to contemplate and commit suicide. Brendel's scene is intensely gripping.

Symbolism and Style

Ibsen skillfully manipulates symbols to give his play a tone of mysterious, foreboding disaster. The opening scene sets the tone. We see the room surrounded by the portraits of dead Rosmers, representing the tradition of public service in religion, government, and war. In the midst is Rebecca with her flowers, a life force surrounded by death. Outside the window is the path to the bridge over the millrace where, we shortly learn, Beate, Rosmer's wife, committed suicide. This is where the white horses of Rosmersholm appear. Old Norwegian warriors were carried off to Valhalla by black horses (see Ibsen's play *The Vikings of Helgeland*). The horses of Rosmersholm are less vigorously pure; they are white. Death has a different meaning; the stock has decayed. The symbolism of Act I makes Rosmersholm itself a symbolic force, and it in turn is a part of Rosmer himself. It is the place where seriousness is most important. It is the place where no adults laugh and no children cry (Act III). Rosmersholm represents the world of the past as opposed to the present and the future (Shaw's *Heartbreak House* is a good comparison).

The depiction of Rebecca as a mermaid is an especially poignant and accurate image. A traditional Scandinavian story is of a mermaid who saves the life of a handsome prince and falls in love with him. She loves him so much that she leaves her native habitat, the freedom of the ocean, to be with him and assumes the fetters of the world. The price she pays is three-fold: she cannot speak, she must endure with every step the pain of cutting her feet, and she must observe the prince in his various actions, no matter how painful they might be to her. If she can win the undivided love of the prince she will gain an immortal soul; if he marries someone else, she will die. Rebecca is alien to Rosmer's world. She comes from the north of Norway, from Finmark, a desolate and primitive country (Act III). In Act IV she describes her passion for Rosmer as a winter storm in northern Norway. But Rebecca's life with Rosmer is painfully constricted. She cannot speak or act with her former freedom, and she must watch the man she loves in all his torments. Unlike the mermaid, however, Rebecca wins Rosmer's undivided love. But only with the price of death.

Characters

Kroll and Mortensgard in some ways are two of a kind. Both are unscrupulous in defaming those on the opposite side. Kroll is more of a gentleman than Mortensgard, and his main fault is malicious gossip. Otherwise, he acts like a gentleman—biased, perhaps, but still like a gentleman. Most of his speeches in the play belie his stigma of fanaticism. Mortensgard has no principles and is amoral. Brendel's speech in Act IV condemns Mortensgard, and it can be taken as Ibsen's viewpoint. The Krolls are fighting a losing battle against the Mortensgards.

Ulric Brendel is partially a comic character. He obviously is a drifter and a leech who tries to assume respectability. He is also quite well educated, as seen in his use of foreign expressions. When he reappears in Act IV, we expect another plea for clothes and money; instead, he pleads for lost ideals. Immediately, he ceases being comic and becomes pathetic. His ravings show remarkable insight into people and problems which surround him and precipitate the final action of the play. He is Rosmer's alter ego—the broken man Rosmer would be if he continued living, a man who does not act until action is impossible.

Mrs. Helseth is representative of the views of ordinary people.

She is superstitious, a gossip, and she believes the slander she reads in the newspaper about Rebecca and Rosmer even though she lives in the same house with them.

Rosmer is the last, weak descendant of a strong family. He is easily swayed, as a youth by Brendel, as a man by Rebecca, and finally by Kroll. The guilt about his wife's death has made him virtually immobile. At the end of the play he finally rouses himself to action, a triumph in itself. Despite his melancholic, morbid disposition, Rosmer is a noble, intelligent well-mannered man. But he is useless to the world because he cannot live on the side of either the Krolls or the Mortensgards. Rosmer is a potential hero confined by his conscience, the legacy of his forebears.

Rebecca was born illegitimately in an alien land. She was a free thinker, and there is even a hint that she was involved in incestuous relations with her father (Act III). She, like Mortensgard, has no ideals except self-interest. But she says she has been infected or ennobled (whichever connotation you think applies) by Rosmersholm: "Rosmersholm had broken me. . . . Broken me utterly and hopelessly.—I had a free and fearless will when I came here. Now I have bent my neck under a strange law" (Act IV). She must expiate sin (Act IV), but not in the traditional religious sense. Both Rebecca and Rosmer must expiate for their own sakes, for their own peace of mind, and expiation can only be death. If they did not commit suicide, their lives would have been consumed by morbidity and self-hatred. Rebecca knows this. We never really know if she confesses her guilt about Beate to save Rosmer or if she really is guilty.

STUDY QUESTIONS

ACT I

1. What is the intent of the stage directions? What atmosphere do the stage directions create?

2. What do we feel about the footbridge and its connection with death? What connotation does the conversation about death give to Kroll? What clue do we have to Beate's character when we find out she disliked flowers?

3. Is Rebecca's origin in Finmark of any importance?
4. Kroll's politics have made him *persona non grata* even in his own home. Is Kroll a figure of ridicule or do we feel sorry for him (or both)? Why is Rosmer's father mentioned? What is the signicance of Kroll's comment about him?
5. Why does Brendel use so many foreign phrases? What does his appearance say about Rosmer? Why does Kroll say Rosmer is so easy to influence?
6. Why does Kroll become angry with Rosmer because Rosmer has given up his religious faith? What kind of faith does Rosmer have now?
7. What does Rebecca mean when she says, "There are so many kinds of white horses in the world, Mrs. Helseth"?
8. What is the atmosphere of Act I? What does it reveal to us? Who receives more attention, Rebecca or Rosmer?

ACT II

1. What do you feel about Rosmer when you learn that he knows he acted the part of a coward? Why does Rebecca change the subject so rapidly?
2. Why does Kroll act obnoxiously when he enters? What is his purpose in talking with Rosmer? Kroll and Rosmer are at opposite poles. Kroll says morality cannot exist outside of religion. Rosmer says it can. Is Kroll more moral than Rosmer? Does Kroll sound like a fanatic?
3. What is Mortensgard's tone? Does he sound like an admirable person? Why is Beate's letter important?
4. Is there a parallel between Mortensgard's refusal to answer Rosmer's question about his church membership and Rebecca's defense of her eavesdropping? Why does Rosmer first disapprove and then say that it is all right for Rebecca to eavesdrop?
5. Why does Rosmer say Beate seems to have come again to life? Why does Rebecca say, "Oh, I should never have come to Rosmersholm"? Is this passage in character? Why do Rebecca and Rosmer go over past history?
6. Where does the dialogue between Rosmer and Rebecca lead, and how? Why does Rebecca refuse to marry Rosmer, even though it is obvious she wants to? Why does Rebecca say she will

commit suicide if Rosmer questions her further? Is Rosmer's bewilderment justified?

ACT III

1. The conversation with Mrs. Helseth, which opens the act, seemingly takes a natural course, but it is fraught with drama and information. We learn something about Peter Mortensgard. Why does Mrs. Helseth say Mortensgard set Rosmer and Kroll against each other? Then we learn more about Beate. Why does Mrs. Helseth say Mrs. Kroll is the wicked person who influenced Beate? Why does Rebecca try to justify Beate's death? Is it superstition that says no one laughs or cries at Rosmersholm? What does it say about Rosmersholm and the influence it might have on Rebecca, Beate, and Rosmer? Is it significant that Rosmer cannot stand to see Mrs. Helseth dust?

2. Is Rosmer overly idealistic about bringing love and light to people? Rosmer, after his burst of enthusiasm, becomes despondent. What makes him so? Is Rosmer's comment ironic: "You don't know what guilt means"? Why does Rebecca treat Rosmer as a child? Is she justified in doing so? Why should Rosmer feel guilty about a love for Rebecca he did not know he had when Beate was alive, but which he now thinks he may have felt unbeknownst to him? Do we believe Rosmer will ever try to save the world? Is Rosmer idealistic to think that he has to be pure to win lasting victory in his cause?

3. Is Rebecca justified in deceiving Rosmer to get rid of him? How do we react to the information that even Kroll once loved Rebecca? Does this help explain Kroll's obnoxious behavior in Act II? Is Kroll right about Rebecca's coldness? Is Kroll right about maligning Rebecca because of her birth? What does the discussion reveal? Why does Rebecca react so violently to the information about her birth? Does Kroll argue persuasively?

4. Rebecca says she is going to confess to free Rosmer from guilt. Does she tell the truth, or does she slant what she says to free Rosmer from guilt? Mrs. Helseth thought Mrs. Kroll was the guilty party. Could Mrs. Kroll have wanted to get Rebecca away from Kroll (we know Kroll loved Rebecca)? Is Kroll's love for Rebecca the reason Kroll never visited Rosmersholm for so long?

5. After Kroll and Rosmer exit, Rebecca gets ready to leave Rosmersholm. Why does Rebecca say she caught a glimpse of the white horse? Beate supposedly sacrificed herself. Does Rebecca feel she is in the same position as Beate? How does this affect our belief in her confession?

ACT IV

1. If you noticed, Rebecca has been crocheting the white shawl all through the play. Now it is finished. What is its significance?

2. The opening scene with Mrs. Helseth is comic. Mrs. Helseth believes Rosmer has wronged Rebecca. She thinks they have had a romance, not because she observed it, but because she read it in the newspaper. Why should the newspaper be more real to her than actual life?

3. What is the significance of Rebecca's wanting to return to the North? What does Rosmer's reconversion say about Rosmer?

4. What is the significance of Rebecca's story of her passion and its subsequent submission? Does it give "form and shape" to what she has previously said? What has sapped her strength? How could Rebecca be "infected" and "ennobled" at the same time? Why should Rosmersholm kill happiness?

5. The last secret is probably that Rebecca lived incestuously with Dr. West. Why does Rosmer not want to hear the last secret? The two are at an impasse. Rosmer needs proof that Rebecca has faith in him and Rebecca needs to know how to give that faith. They solve the problem after Ulric Brendel's visit. Therefore, what Brendel says must provide the key to their problem. Comment.

6. What do we think when Brendel says, "Can you grant me a loan"? What do we think when we find out what loan he wants? What is Brendel's tragedy? Can he be compared in any way to Rosmer? What is the significance of Brendel's comments on Mortensgard? What is the significance of Brendel's comments on Rebecca?

7. Rosmer cannot act. Rebecca says he has ennobled her. Rosmer wants proof, or his life in his own eyes will be wasted. Why does Rosmer ask Rebecca to commit suicide? How does the shawl enrich the action on the stage? Why does Rosmer say, "There is a

horrible fascination in this"? What is the significance of Rebecca's statement, "Where I have sinned, it is right that I should atone? What kind of atonement is she talking about? Why should Rosmer's refusal to cross the footbridge make Rebecca's love hopeless? What is the significance of their marriage?

8. Why does the suicide take place offstage? What is the significance of Mrs. Helseth's remarks about romantic love? What is significant about her last statement: "The dead wife has taken them"?

NOTES

1. Arthur Miller, *Collected Plays* (New York: The Viking Press, 1963).

2. Arthur Miller, "It Could Happen Here—And Did," *The New York Times* (Sunday, April 30, 1967), p. D 17.

3. For a discussion of non-illusionary representation, see Gerald Rabkin, "On Teaching Drama," *On Teaching Literature: Essays for Secondary School Teachers,* a volume in this English Curriculum Study Series.

4. "The Supplement of the United States," *European Theories of the Drama,* ed. Barrett H. Clark (New York: Crown Press, 1959).

On Teaching Shakespeare

Shakespeare obviously deserves an important place in the high school curriculum. Universally regarded for more than three centuries as the first author in our language, he has continued to speak through his plays to all kinds of people. Shakespearean titles, characters, quotations, and allusions have become part of the fabric of daily discourse, often used as a matter of course by people who may have only the sketchiest knowledge of the plays themselves. The very universality of his appeal makes Shakespeare difficult to allocate or assign in a curriculum of the sort suggested in this series. For the riches exist not only in the fabulous diversity of the plays themselves but also in the almost bewildering abundance of materials for teaching Shakespeare.

We have prepared analyses of only two Shakespearean plays, *Richard III* and *Henry V*, which have perhaps been taught less frequently in high school than some Shakespearean plays. (These analyses appear in the sequence on history plays—two American and two Shakespearean—in *Teaching Literature in Grades Seven Through Nine*, a volume in this English Curriculum Study Series.) In addition to the two history plays suggested for grade nine, teachers will undoubtedly wish to assign at least one Shakespearean play each year in grades ten through twelve. From the comedies we suggest choices among *Much Ado About Nothing, A Midsummer Night's Dream, As You Like It, Twelfth Night,* and *The Taming of the Shrew;* from the tragedies choices can be made among *Romeo and Juliet, Julius Caesar, Macbeth, Othello,* and *Hamlet.*

Materials for teaching Shakespeare are abundant. There are many paperback series of the plays, all reasonably priced and with varying kinds of editorial apparatus. There are essays and critical analyses both of individual plays and of larger aspects of Shakespeare's work. Some of the more elementarily edited texts will be most valuable to the slow learner, who certainly deserves his try at Shakespeare, too. Definitely there is no lack of Shakespearean matter available to the secondary teacher.

The range of audio-visual aids is also great. Many excellent recordings exist in which the lines are read by outstanding actors. Certainly no class should study a Shakespearean play without devoting considerable time to hearing recordings of important passages. There are also films of some of the plays which can often be used as effective supplements to teaching. Finally, teachers should be on the alert for stage productions of the plays. Taking a busload of students to a nearby university or professional theater to see a play performed will be a most worthwhile experience whenever it can be arranged.

Part IV
NOVELS

▨▨

The novels in this section were analyzed individually by various people, and it is therefore not possible to point out larger patterns in a sequence as we have done with poetry, drama, and short stories. Hence it is all the more interesting that the American novels for the tenth grade meaningfully corroborate Professor Kenneth Johnston's observations concerning the centrality of setting in the study of American fiction. In *The Member of the Wedding* the setting is the American South during World War II; *The Red Badge of Courage* is set in the American Civil War; and *Adventures of Huckleberry Finn* is set on the antebellum Mississippi.

Although the analyses of English novels in grade eleven reflect Professor Johnston's concern with character's point of view, they deal with other matters too. Professor Howard Anderson performs a valuable service by taking a fresh look at *Gulliver's Travels,* a book widely read and frequently misunderstood. He concentrates on the work as a whole, rather than on the individual voyages, and he considers the implications of the fact that Swift was not writing a novel in the ordinary sense. Professor William Madden examines *Wuthering Heights* from the viewpoints of structure and theme, and shows how the former contributes to establishing the theme of forgiveness in the novel. Although other elements necessarily enter his analysis, Professor Philip Daghlian's chief concern is to suggest the many values that may be derived from an extremely careful close reading of *Heart of Darkness*.

The success of Hesse's *Siddartha* and Dostoevsky's *Crime and Punishment* in the classroom is tribute to the customary skill with which Mr. Roy Felsher and Mrs. Virginia Olsen Bush have prepared these analyses, as well as others in the series. Readers may wonder why a sequence stressing world literature should include a work like Paton's *Cry, the Beloved Country*, originally written and published in English, and why the list of suggested additional novels (pp. 369-371) should include others of this kind. The answer goes back to one of the early meetings of the state-appointed committee on literature, when it was agreed that certain books transcend national boundaries in their impact, and that the fact of initial composition in English should not prevent such books from being considered.

Teaching *The Member of the Wedding*

ROY L. FELSHER

Formerly Assistant Director
of the Indiana University
English Curriculum Study Center

THE THREE WORLDS OF MISS ADDAMS

The young heroine of Carson McCullers' novel adopts three names in the course of her adventures. In Part I she is Frankie Addams, a lonely and "unjoined person" who is not a member of anything; in Part II she is F. Jasmine Addams, a "sudden member" who feels "connected" with everything she sees; and in Part III she becomes plain Frances Addams, an older and presumably wiser version of the same person. These names are quite important to the story. At one point her friend Bérenice explains that, "You have a name and one thing after another happens to you, and you behave in various ways and do things, so that soon the name begins to have a meaning. Things have accumulated around the name" (p. 107).*
So many things accumulate about each of these names that it becomes possible to speak of them as three related worlds—the worlds of Frankie, F. Jasmine, and Frances Addams. Taken together, these worlds bridge a gap between innocence and experience and provide a principle of organization for the novel.

The three worlds of the novel are given explicit formulation on the afternoon when Frankie, her cousin John Henry West, and the Negro cook Berenice Sadie Brown attempt to judge the work of

* Page references are to the Bantam paperback edition.

God and imagine ways in which the world could be improved. The Lord God John Henry would create a world with chocolate dirt and rains of lemonade, candy flowers, and an extra eye that could see a thousand miles. John Henry is six years old, and this is a world of innocence. The world of the Lord God Berenice Sadie Brown is of course quite different. "First, there would be no separate colored people in the world . . . and no white people to make the colored people feel cheap and sorry all their lives . . . No war . . . No stiff corpses hanging from the Europe trees and no Jews murdered anywhere . . . No war and no hunger in the world" (p. 92). Berenice is a Negro in the deep South, speaking at the time of the Second World War, and hers is the voice of experience. The world of the Lord God Frankie Addams is a strange combination of the other two. She will agree, for instance, with the main laws of Berenice's creation, but thinks that there should still be wars (little ones) for those who want to participate. Then she could donate blood, if she wanted to, or serve for a while as a WAC in the Air Corps. Frankie's view is neither innocent nor experienced, but somewhere between the two—her own mixture of fantasy and reality. She is too knowing for the world of John Henry, but not old enough or wise enough to accept the world of Berenice.

The main action of the novel concerns Frankie's reluctant admission to this world of experience, which is not quite the same as the adult world. All of us eventually grow up, attain manhood or womanhood, and take our places in society. But not everyone attains that ripeness of experience—experience known and comprehended—that we find in Berenice. Perhaps one must absorb a certain amount of punishment from the world before arriving at this wisdom. As Carson McCullers presents it, the "world" is constantly threatening. From the great affairs of state to the most intimate personal relationships there is the spectacle of pain and disorder. On the international level there are confused reports of the war in Europe; on the social level there are the pressures of racial discrimination which claim a victim in Honey Brown; and on the personal level there is the confusion of Frankie Addams as she tries to order her life in a disordered world. The prevailing sadness of the book comes in part from our awareness of the vulnerability of youth in such a world.

One approach to Frankie's story might concentrate on the disparity between her ideas of the world and her actual experiences. In Part I Frankie complained that she "belonged to no club and was a member of nothing in the world" (p. 1). If we stop to think about this, we realize that the statement is not entirely true. After all, Frankie is a member of her family and her community; she attends the B section of the seventh grade; she corresponds with her brother in Alaska; and she spends long summer afternoons in conversation with Berenice and John Henry. But Frankie thinks of herself as an "unjoined person" and in her own mind that is exactly what she is. She cannot "connect" with anything outside herself, and she turns increasingly to daydream and fantasy as a way of coping with her loneliness. These fantasies may be charming or grotesque, but they have a compelling force for her. She dreams of Alaska as the place most unlike her present home; and with its unspoiled wilderness and snowswept valleys, Alaska becomes an imaginative antidote to the hot, sluggish Alabama afternoons.

There are times, however, when her brother's letters threaten to shatter the dream of Alaska. "For instance, this summer he mentioned that he had been swimming and that the mosquitoes were something fierce. This letter jarred upon her dream, but after a few days of bewilderment, she returned to her frozen seas and snow" (p. 5). It is Frankie's typical response to an unpleasant bit of reality. The heat and mosquitoes are transformed, by a trick of her imagination, to frozen seas and snow. Berenice criticizes Frankie's tendency to enlarge upon the facts.

"This is a serious fault with you, Frankie. Somebody just makes a loose remark and then you cozen it in your mind until nobody would recognize it . . . . You keep building on to any little compliment you hear about yourself. Or, if it is a bad thing, you do the same. You cozen and change things too much in your own mind. And that is a serious fault" (p. 31).

It may not be a serious fault to tamper with the landscape of Alaska; but it becomes increasingly serious as Frankie's fantasies reach out to encompass more significant aspects of her life. The two great disasters of the book follow this pattern. Compare her daydreams about a soldier's life (p. 21 or p. 52) with her actual encounter with the red-headed soldier; or the penultimate wedding fantasy (in Part II) with the actual event. In each case Frankie stubbornly clings to her imagined world—to the point that she is no longer able to deal with the real world. As a result, she is assaulted by the soldier and humiliated at the wedding.

The significant drawback of a fantasy life is that by nature it is a private affair. In Part II of the novel, F. Jasmine tells a number of people about her plan for the wedding, as though it might somehow become more real if she could get someone else to believe it. To be on the safe side she talks to strangers—an old Portuguese bartender, a lady sweeping her porch, a man driving a tractor—and takes comfort in their polite interest. But the real test is to come later in her long conversation with Berenice. This is a pivotal scene of the novel, though there is no significant action except in the minds of the characters.

> The argument that afternoon was, from the beginning to the end, about the wedding. Berenice refused to follow F. Jasmine's frame of mind. From the first it was as though she tried to catch F. Jasmine by the collar, like the Law catches a no-good in the wrong, and jerk her back where she had started . . . . But F. Jasmine was stubborn and not to be caught (p. 73).

Berenice considers herself something of an authority on the subject of marriage, as she has been married four times. Her long monologue on her four husbands almost wins the day. F. Jasmine confesses that she knows nothing of love ("It was a subject F. Jasmine had never talked about in her whole life" [p. 75].) At this point in the novel Berenice seems to speak not for herself alone but for the great common bond of shared experience. She drives her points home with proverbs—the main thing about a wedding is two is company and three is a crowd; you can't make a silk purse out of a sow's ear; you have to cut your suit according to the cloth; and make the best of what you have. ("F. Jasmine always found it hard to argue with a known saying" [p. 73].) By such means Berenice tries to deny the wedding, but F. Jasmine will not let it be denied. F. Jasmine cannot meet Berenice's arguments based on experience; the best she can do is to hold on to her own private vision, which is difficult to articulate. "I see a green tree," she said.

"And to me it is green. And you would call the tree green also. And we would agree on this. But is the color you see as green the same color I see as green? Or we both call a color black. But how do we know that what you see as black is the same color I see as black?" (p. 109).

In her questioning F. Jasmine moves away from a faith in universal vision into a world in which her experiences may be hers alone. Individual distinctions of this sort contrast with the communion she has known with John Henry and Berenice, where the three separate melodies merged into one great harmony:

> they would disagree and start off on three different songs at once, until at last the tunes began to merge and they sang a special music that the three of them made up together. John Henry sang in a high wailing voice . . . . Berenice's voice was dark and definite and deep . . . . The old Frankie sang up and down the middle space between John Henry and Berenice, so that their three voices were joined, and the parts of the song were woven together (p. 116).

The conversation with Berenice, then, distinguishes between private, eccentric meanings and common, shared meanings. In the color images F. Jasmine tries to make a case for the private; but in the music we have a symbol of what is common and shared. She learns at the wedding that the private and eccentric is not respected by others—that all men will not fall into line with your own private fantasies.

In Part III of the novel we learn of a series of disasters. F. Jasmine is humiliated at Winter Hill when she cannot revise her private vision to accord with the fact of the wedding.

> The wedding was like a dream, for all that came about occurred in a world beyond her power; from the moment when, sedate and proper, she shook hands with the grown people until the time, the wrecked wedding over, when she watched the car of the two of them driving away from her, and flinging herself down in the sizzling dust, she cried out for the last time: "Take me! Take me!" —from the beginning to the end the wedding was unmanaged as a nightmare (p. 135).

Back home again, both Frances and Honey Brown are caught by the Law—Frances when she tries to run away and Honey when he breaks into the drugstore for some marihuana. Then, after a sudden illness—though "the word *suffer* was one she [Frances] could not associate with John Henry"—the little boy died. This is a world of dangers and disappointments, and it is not enough to meet such a world with daydreams and fantasies.

"Frances was never once to speak about the wedding," Berenice gave notice to marry T. T., and the kitchen was "not the same kitchen of the summer that now seemed so long ago" (p. 149). To interpret this third world of Miss Addams as one in which Frances finally comes to grips with the world of experience, however, would be a distortion. Overshadowing the happenings of the past months, in the mind of Frances, is her friendship with Mary Littlejohn. "Mary was going to be a great sculptor and Frances a great poet—or else the foremost authority on radar" (p. 150). These are fantasies, too, not far removed from those of F. Jasmine, but Frances has a friend now. She has become a "member."

STUDY QUESTIONS

PART I

1. The opening paragraph of the novel describes Frankie as "an unjoined person. . . . She belonged to no club and was a member of nothing in the world." Is this strictly true? Isn't Frankie a member of her family and her community? Is she "unjoined" in actual fact, or is this really a description of her state of mind? Explain.

2. Who complained about Frankie's "funny smell"? Why does she douse herself with Sweet Serenade perfume? What does this suggest about her sense of her own identity?

3. Why does Frankie daydream about Alaska? Is it simply because her brother Jarvis is stationed there? Or because the summer is hot and Alaska is supposed to be cold? Or does Alaska take on a more special significance in Frankie's mind?

4. Sometimes her brother's letters threaten to shatter the dream of Alaska. "For instance, this summer he mentioned that he had been in swimming and that the mosquitoes were something fierce. This letter jarred upon her dream, but after a few days of be-

wilderment, she returned to her frozen seas and snow" (p. 5). What does this tell us about the world in which Frankie lives? What are the dangers in this sort of world?

5. Frankie's brother is to be married at a place called Winter Hill. How and why do Frankie's thoughts about Winter Hill become associated with her daydreams about Alaska?

6. A large part of this novel describes the conversations that take place between Frankie, her cousin John Henry West, and the Negro cook Berenice Sadie Brown. Here are some random bits of dialogue which suggest the tone of these conversations.

"You jealous," said Berenice. "Go and *behold* yourself in the mirror" (p. 2).

"I don't give a *durn* about it," Frankie said. "It is *immaterial with* me" (p. 4).

"*Less* us have a good time," John Henry said (p. 3).

Carson McCullers has an excellent ear for regional dialect, which she reproduces with considerable accuracy. As these lines suggest, however, the language also assures each speaker a measure of individuality. What qualities are suggested by the underlined words or phrases? Can you find other passages which show Berenice's fondness for Biblical idiom? How does Frankie's mixture of childhood slang with more "grownup" polysyllables reveal her inner confusion? Does John Henry ever use words of more than two syllables?

7. What is the approximate date of the events in the novel? What important world happenings provide a background for Frankie's story?

8. What is the significance of each of these objects: a radio, a lavender shell, a glass globe?

The radio, which has been on all summer, brings news of the war in Europe. Does Frankie listen to it any more? The shell and the glass globe provide food for the imagination. "When she held the seashell to her ear, she could hear the warm wash of the Gulf of Mexico. . . . And she could hold the snow globe to her narrowed eyes and watch the whirling flakes fall until they blinded her. She dreamed of Alaska" (p. 10). What does this suggest about Frankie's world?

9. At one point Berenice criticizes Frankie's tendency to enlarge upon the facts. "This is a serious fault. . . . Somebody just makes a loose remark and then you cozen it in your mind until nobody would recognize it. . . . You keep building on to any little compliment you hear about yourself. Or, if it is a bad thing, you do the same. You cozen and change things too much in your own mind. And that is a serious fault" (p. 31). Is this fair criticism? Can you find examples of such "cozening" in the text?

10. What does Frankie mean when she says, "They are the we of me."

PART II

1. In Part II of the novel Frankie Addams becomes F. Jasmine Addams. Why does she choose the new name? Do the other characters recognize either the new name or the new identity?

2. In Part I Frankie was described as "unjoined" and "not a member of anything"; but now "because of the wedding, F. Jasmine felt connected with all she saw, and it was as a sudden member that . . . she went around the town" (p. 44). Why has she suddenly become a member? Of what? Has there been any change in the attitude of the other people, or is the change only in her own mind?

3. "The old laws she had known before meant nothing to F. Jasmine . . ." (p. 53). What were these laws? Does she deliberately break old laws, or has she simply come to feel that the old laws no longer apply? How does F. Jasmine demonstrate her new freedom?

4. What do we mean by the expression, "once in a blue moon"? Is the Blue Moon that F. Jasmine visits appropriately named?

5. F. Jasmine tells several people about her plans for the wedding. There is her father, an old Portuguese bartender, a lady sweeping her front porch, a man driving a tractor, and a redheaded soldier. Why does she choose to speak to these people? How does each react to her message?

6. Reflecting upon her walk around town, Miss Addams thinks that "she was not trying to trick people and pretend; far from it, she wanted only to be recognized for her true self" (p. 56). Is she successful? What is her true self—is it "Frankie" or is it "F. Jasmine"? Which of these selves do the others recognize?

7. The death of Uncle Charles, a distant relative, prompts these comments by F. Jasmine: "Poor Uncle Charles. That certainly is a pity" (p. 60), and "At one time Uncle Charles was one of the leading citizens. It will be a loss to the whole county" (p. 61). How would you describe the tone of these remarks?

Later, we learn that the death will cause John Henry to attend the wedding, and the narrator notes: "Now that she knew the death of Uncle Charles would in a sense affect the wedding, she made room for it in her thoughts" (p. 71). Is this meant to be a severe or sympathetic criticism of F. Jasmine?

8. Death and marriage are the major topics of conversation on the last afternoon before the wedding. Why does Berenice consider herself an authority on both subjects? How was death a major turning point in her life?

9. F. Jasmine recalls the seven dead people that she knew, but "of all the dead people out of the world, Ludie Freeman was the one F. Jasmine knew the best, although she had never laid eyes on him, and was not even born when he had died" (p. 87). Why did she know him best?

10. Although F. Jasmine admits that Berenice can speak with authority about death, she will not admit that Berenice has superior insight into marriage and weddings. Why not?

11. At one point in the conversation Berenice, John Henry, and F. Jasmine judge the work of God and mention ways they would improve the world. What are the qualities of these three imagined "worlds"? If the world of John Henry (complete with chocolate dirt and lemonade rain) might be called a world of Innocence and the world of Berenice (where there are no wars, no Jews murdered, no segregated races) a world corrected by Experience, then how would you describe the world of F. Jasmine?

12. In Part I the radio, with its news from the battlefield, reminds of the disorder of the world; but now F. Jasmine refuses to listen to the radio. Why?

13. In Part II Mr. Schwartzenbaum, the piano tuner, fills the air with the dissonance and disorder of his trade. Does the untuned piano, perhaps, fulfill the same symbolic role as the radio? Is it possible to shut out entirely the imperfections of the real world?

14. Comment upon this passage: Berenice "raised her chin and drew in her breath in the way of a singer who is beginning a song. The piano tuned and insisted, but when Berenice began to speak, her dark gold voice rang in the kitchen and they did not listen to the piano notes" (p. 95). What does this opposition between melodic voice and dissonant piano suggest? Can you find other passages where music functions symbolically? (See p. 116 and the "special music that the three of them made up together," or p. 128 where F. Jasmine has "to play a duet to a piece she does not know.")

15. Berenice says that all people are somehow "caught," and that maybe we all want "to widen and bust free" (p. 113). How are these characters caught: F. Jasmine, her father, Honey Brown, Berenice, the soldier? Which of them attempts to "bust free"? How? Are any of them successful?

16. Why does F. Jasmine advise Honey Brown to go to Cuba? How does she picture his future life in Cuba? Does her vision of Cuba in any way resemble her vision of Alaska or her vision of the wedding? How does Honey react to her proposal?

17. F. Jasmine frequently confuses her imagined world with the world about her, and she has to pay the consequences. Compare her daydreams about a soldier's life (p. 21 or 52) with her actual encounter with the red-headed soldier. Can you think of other instances where a satisfying daydream interferes with her perception of the real world? When faced with her false image, how does she react?

PART III

1. In Part III of the novel F. Jasmine becomes Miss Frances Addams. Does the new name imply a new sense of identity? Do the other characters adopt the new name or recognize this new identity?

2. Is Frances' disappointment at the wedding surprising? What is her first response to the collapse of her imagined world?

3. On the bus ride back from Winter Hill, Frances is "sitting next to Berenice, back with the colored people, and when she thought of it she used the mean word she had never used before, nigger . . ." (p. 135). In what year was the novel written? Is there

still segregated seating in southern buses today? Is Carson Mc-Cullers' portrait of Negro life in the South adequate to the present-day situation? Can you cite aspects of discrimination in the novel which are probably still present today? Can you cite others which have probably disappeared?

4. After she has run away from home, Frances thinks, "If only there was some one with her! If only she could hunt down Honey Brown and they could go away together!" (p. 144). Why does she choose Honey to run away with? We soon learn (p. 149) that Frances is apprehended by the law, and later (p. 151) that Honey has been arrested and sent to jail. What is the significance of this parallel?

5. The death of John Henry and the imprisonment of Honey Brown are briefly described at the end of the novel. What effect do these events have on Frances? What of her new and exciting friendship with Mary Littlejohn? At the end of the book is Frances Addams finally a genuine "member"?

6. Names are quite important in this story. Berenice says, "You have a name and one thing after another happens to you, and you behave in various ways and do things, so that soon the name begins to have a meaning. Things have accumulated around the name" (p. 107). What things accumulate to give meaning to "Frankie," "F. Jasmine," and "Frances" Addams? Write a theme in which you account for the meaning that attaches to each of these names.

Teaching *The Red Badge of Courage*

VIRGINIA OLSEN BUSH

Formerly Research Associate
in the Indiana University
English Curriculum Study Center

The Red Badge of Courage is both a war story and a story about the initiation of one youth into the world of manhood where this war takes place. The focus is always on the "youth" of the novel, Henry Fleming, and except for the opening scene we are present only at action which Henry observes or participates in. The novel, however, deals extensively with views of war, for Henry must come to a proper understanding of his world before he can truly participate in it. The story of his initiation thus involves an exploration of a series of views of the nature of the world, and of the nature of a war situation in particular, as in the world of the novel Henry's views adjust more closely to life as it really is.

The student should be able to come to an understanding both of the process of Henry's character change as he begins to become a man and of the views and attitudes toward war and life which are involved. He should see how the form of the novel is dependent upon the interaction of the world which Crane has established for his story and the character of Henry Fleming. He should realize finally that the meaning of the novel is developed through its form. These three intimately related elements, then—the world, Henry's character and its change, and Crane's technique—will form the basis for this discussion of the book.

Stephen Crane has frequently been called "anti-romantic" or "realistic," and the world he creates is indeed in many respects a very ordinary one. There is nothing particularly unusual or exotic about it; the fog, mud, sunshine, brambles, and tree stumps all suggest a world which everyone has experienced. People react in ordinary ways: there is a "singular absence of heroic poses"; a wounded officer acts just as if he had "hit his fingers with a tack hammer at home."* This lack of the heroic and extraordinary is all the more remarkable because it occurs in a war story. It indicates that Crane wished to put the emphasis on that aspect of the war situation which it has in common with every other situation that may occur in life.

It becomes clear, however, as the novel progresses, that although this world may be ordinary, it is not without danger. It contains an unpleasant element of hostility and meanness which is threatening to all life: the squirrel perceives this element in the menacing pine cone just as Henry perceives it in the "onslaught of the redoubtable dragons" of the enemy (p. 149). The world contains pain and death. It is an element that must be reckoned with.

Similarly, the world elicits a hostile response from anyone who would participate in it. Henry's mother recognizes that when one goes to participate in a war, a time may come "when yeh have to ...do a mean thing..." (p. 119). Everyone in the story is involved in doing "mean things"—everyone is fighting a war. In response to the world he confronts, each man who fights becomes "a barbarian, a beast" (p. 199), developing the "daring spirit of a savage religion-mad" (p. 224). It is neither a nice world nor an easy one.

The last major characteristic of this world is its moral disinterestedness, an element which compounds the difficulty of taking action. There is a complete lack of reliable sanctions in the natural world. Nature goes "tranquilly on with her golden process" in spite of whatever "devilment" man might create (p. 147). That the squirrel ran when threatened does not provide a sanction for Henry's running: it merely proves that some animals will run in such a situation; the moral dimension is wholly lacking. Even society cannot provide moral sanctions, for despite the general pressure it can apply by exalting courage, it is ultimately too ignorant and unconcerned when it comes to individual cases to be

---

* Stephen Crane, *The Red Badge of Courage and Other Writings,* ed. Richard Chase (Boston: Riverside Press, 1960), 140. All page references are to this edition.

effective. Although Henry receives a modicum of honor and status for his "red badge of courage," his badge is a fraud and his actions have not really been sanctioned. Finally, then, the individual is left to himself to work out his moral and ethical code in accordance with what he understands of life. The better he understands the world, the better and more effective his code will be, but he will not find the code itself in the world.

If we wish, then, to understand the value system which attaches to *The Red Badge of Courage*, we must examine the evidence Crane gives of his own attitudes, which form the standard for the book. These attitudes are best inferred from the words and imagery he uses. Two of the dominant image-patterns are those of the beast and of savage religion which are related early in the novel when the narrator refers to "war, the red animal—war, the blood-swollen god" (p. 135). Religious imagery is associated with the delirium of battle which gives men the motivation to fight, and it is always religion of a barbaric, almost cannibalistic sort.* Animal imagery is abundant and diverse,† but it is significant that the soldiers are associated with various sorts of beasts throughout and only become men when they have lost their self-concern and have successfully fought in such a way as to prove that they are not impotent against the world. Crane's attitude toward war is ambivalent. War is not attractive or noble, he seems to feel, but it is a part of the world we live in and it must be dealt with. It will not do to run, for that is abandonment of life and one's proper role in life. True courage is the quality associated with barbaric religion, but at the same time it is that which leads to assumption of a nonbeastly manhood and which is necessary to participation in life. This is the attitude toward war and courage finally confirmed by the favorable view of Henry given at the end of the book. These values and this world are the background against which Crane portrays the change in Henry's soul.

During the course of the novel we watch as Henry grows from essential innocence and ignorance into experience and knowledge

---

* The "religion of peace" which Henry finds in Chapter 7 is, of course, ironically savage.

† See Mordecai and Erin Marcus, "Animal Imagery in *The Red Badge of Courage*," *Modern Language Notes*, LXXIV (February 1959), 108-111.

and begins to become a man. At the beginning he has the self-centered concern of an infant. He knows nothing outside of his own self, and yet he has great confidence in his "fine mind," and he has an extremely high opinion of himself. By the end of the book, however, this attitude is beginning to change. The experience which he has gained has forced him gradually to expand his knowledge to include more of the world in which he lives and accordingly to adjust the views and attitudes which shape his moral code. There is still a touch of his old vainglory in the last chapters, but the confidence he has in himself now is more legitimate, for it is based on some knowledge. As his knowledge has been extended, he has begun to develop, instead of the selfishness of the infant, the social responsibility of the man. His mind undergoes a "subtle change" (p. 228), and so "it came to pass that . . . his soul changed" (p. 230). The change is not fully completed at the close of the novel, but the line of Henry's development is clear.

There are four major stages in Henry's change, and each quarter of the book deals with one stage. In Chapters 1–6, Henry reacts with fear and terror to the initial shock given his idealism, and his problem in this section is learning to deal with this fear. His picture of war had been one of "Greeklike struggles"—fine, heroic, unequivocally attractive, and remarkably free of meanness and pain. In his first encounter with the hostile element in the universe, he becomes convinced that this element is dominant, and this conviction, closer to the truth but still not quite accurate, produces the fear which makes him run. Confronted by a hostile world and having discovered (p. 147) that Nature is unconcerned with what he does, he is plunged into a moral vacuum where he must rely on himself and his own knowledge of the world for a guide. By the end of the sixth chapter he has discovered that not only has he made the wrong decision according to the traditional morality of society, but the basis for his decision—himself and his knowledge—is what is deficient and at fault. This discovery, made when he learns that the enemy has been held back, leads to the second stage in his development.

The second quarter of the book begins with the statement: "The youth cringed as if discovered in a crime" (p. 153). This stage represents Henry's attempt to deal in his own mind with the two aspects of his "crime" and with the world which elicited this response from him. The movement of the episodes in these six chapters is toward a renewed desire to participate in life and a recognition of the folly of his former conduct on the purely selfish grounds that his lack of a "red badge of courage" deprives him of the honor which is necessary to his self-image. The result is that Henry turns and runs back to the battlefield, an "ironical thing" for him to do, as he himself realizes (p. 157). He wants to make a rallying speech in the midst of the retreat; he seeks to join the men honored by badges of courage; and throughout this section it is continually emphasized that his actions are still selfishly motivated. His great crime this time is his abandonment of the dying tattered soldier in order to rescue himself from discomfort. Two points of revelation occur at this stage in Henry's development. The first is his experiencing of Jim Conklin's death: despite his internalization of his friend's suffering, Henry does expand the sphere of his concern to include another person. The second revelation occurs at the end of Chapter 12, when Henry suddenly realizes that he had not cared enough even to find out who it was that had helped him back to camp.

In the third quarter Henry must deal with his knowledge of the world and his consciousness of his own failings in the context of society. He expects hostility and censure for his cowardly flight, but he discovers that society is ignorant and quite happy to accept his "badge" as valid. He again becomes self-satisfied. Even the pragmatic morality he adopted in the second quarter disappears until he becomes almost totally amoral: he reaches the point where he can consider himself an "individual of extraordinary virtues" merely because he has never had to pay for any of his mistakes (p. 191). The self-centered concern which he had begun to recognize at the end of Chapter 12 increases and in his mind is twisted into "a generous thing" (p. 191). He finds it is "fine, wild, and, in some ways, easy" to fight (p. 199), but he is still fighting only for himself. Although he has developed from the "well-meaning cow" and the "rabbit" of the early chapters into a "wild cat" and an "infernal fool," description in these terms does not imply the author's approval; in Chapter 18 Henry makes the discovery that his fine, wild, and easy fighting hasn't been enough, that he and the rest of the men fight like a lot of "mule drivers." The last fourth of the book shows the outcome of the succession of discoveries which Henry has made. He returns to a morality similar to the idealistic one which he had started with, but one which is capable of realization. He fights, and although his fighting is still partly for personal revenge on the officer who used the term "mule drivers," it is also done out of a sense of moral responsibility. He loses concern for himself, and a totally new emotion—"a love, a despairing fondness for this flag which was near him"—is born within him (p. 208). He now belongs with the rest of the men; he fits in the world; he participates in life. Henry himself feels "aged" (p. 203). When he feels a "quiet manhood" at the end of the book (p. 230), it is manhood in the sense both of maturity and of humanity, and the major part of the change in his soul is complete.

STUDY QUESTIONS

CHAPTERS 1–6

1. The opening of the novel—the opening paragraph describing the two armies and the scene in which the tall soldier brings the rumor that the army is going to move—is the only major part of *The Red Badge of Courage* where Henry Fleming is neither explicitly nor implicitly present while we are reading. Why does Stephen Crane open his novel in this way? What is the function of this scene? Is it only to let us know that this is a war story? Couldn't he have done this just as easily by beginning with Henry saying, "Ma, I've enlisted"? What view of war is established in these first paragraphs? Whose view is it?

How are the armies described? Note such words and phrases as "its eyes," "at the army's feet," "eyelike gleam." Later (p. 135), the narrator refers to "war, the red animal—war, the blood-swollen god." How do these phrases help our understanding of the author's attitude toward war and armies?

2. On page 117 we are told: "There was a portion of the world's history which he had regarded as the time of wars, but it, he thought, had been long gone over the horizon and had disappeared

forever," and "He had long despaired of witnessing a Greeklike struggle." From whose point of view are these statements made? Are they true? Is the time of wars past? Is the time of "Greeklike struggles" past? How does Henry's picture of war contrast with the one examined in Question 1? Which is "nicer" and more idealistic? In the world of the book, which is the correct one?

Throughout the book, but especially in these first six chapters, Henry tries to cling to his own romantic belief in heroic, Greeklike struggles. What incidents shake his faith in this view of war? Is he still holding to this belief by the end of Chapter 6?

3. During the march, the landscape appears "threatening" to Henry. "Absurd ideas took hold of him." He becomes sure that "it was all a trap. . . . They were all going to be sacrificed. The generals were stupids" (p. 134–35). What is happening to Henry; why does he feel this way? How has his view of war as a "Greeklike struggle" changed? Is this new view the correct one? What happens to show Henry that this belief, too, is not wholly correct?

4. The book throughout contains a number of trivial incidents: the horseman bringing orders turns to yell "Don't forget that box of cigars"; a fat soldier tries to steal a horse and is beaten off by a young girl; the commander of the brigade "resembled a man who had come from bed to go to a fire." Can you find other incidents of this sort? Why does the author include such details?

5. For most of the book Henry is bothered by feeling alone and being unable to find anyone who thinks the way he does. Why can't he find anyone with similar feelings? Both he and the loud soldier laughed nervously when Henry asked Jim whether he ever thought that he himself might run; yet when Henry approaches the loud soldier on the matter later, the soldier asserts that, of course, he isn't going to run. Why does this attempt at communication fail? Is Henry worrying about how bad anyone else might be feeling, or is he thinking only of himself?

6. In his first battle, Henry becomes "not a man but a member." He had "lost concern for himself." "It was a mysterious fraternity born of the smoke and danger of death" (p. 143). What sort of a feeling is this? Is it rational? Is this feeling present in Henry in the second battle? Why not? In what elements do Henry's thoughts and actions in the second battle parallel those in the first? How

do they differ? Why does Henry run in the second battle? Does he have good reason? Is he justified? What is the narrator's attitude toward the "mysterious fraternity"? toward Henry's running? Can you be certain?

7. Several of the characters in *The Red Badge of Courage* are known principally by epithets; these epithets give us important clues to their character and their roles in the story. Why is Jim Conklin known as the "tall soldier"? What associations and connotations does "tall" have in this case? Why is Wilson called the "loud soldier"? Why is Henry called the "youth"? Do these epithets apply to these same men by the end of the novel?

8. At the end of Chapter 5 Henry makes two discoveries: (1) "Heretofore he had supposed that all the battle was directly under his nose." Why should this come as such a surprise to Henry? (2) "As he gazed around him the youth felt a flash of astonishment at the blue, pure sky and the sun gleaming on the trees and fields. It was surprising that Nature had gone tranquilly on with her golden process in the midst of so much devilment." How does this contrast with his earlier view of Nature as hostile and threatening? How are these two discoveries related? How are they related to Henry's view of war?

At the end of Chapter 6 the general beams upon the earth "like a sun." How is this sun related to the "gleaming sun" at the end of Chapter 5? What circumstances are different in the scenes they beam upon? How is Henry's situation different? Is the world itself really any different? Does it seem different to Henry?

9. Wishing to be alone with his thoughts after hearing the rumor that they were at last going to fight, Henry goes to his hut, where "the sunlight, without, beating upon it, made it glow a light yellow shade." A page later, in telling how Henry had overcome his mother's realistic and sensible reasons for not enlisting, the narrator says: "At last, however, he had made firm rebellion against this yellow light thrown upon the color of his ambitions." What does the "yellow light" refer to? What has it done to his ambitions? What significance does the color yellow seem to have in this story? Can you find other places where yellow has the same or similar significance?

Stephen Crane uses color symbolically in this novel. Can you find instances of the symbolic use of red? of black? of white? of other colors? What do these colors mean? When reading the book, are you conscious of colors when they appear: are they vivid and startling? Or are they more subtle? How important are they to our understanding of the novel?

10. When and where does the action in this novel take place? What war is being fought? How does a knowledge of the background contribute to our understanding?

The first paragraph in Chapter 1 serves to establish the world of the novel. Why does the author's description include such details as the cold, fog, mud, and earth? Why does he use words like "reluctantly," "purled," and "sorrowful blackness"? How are these details and this manner of description important throughout in the world of the novel?

CHAPTERS 7–12

1. If the central problem for Henry in the first section of the book was whether he would run, his central problem in this second section is that of dealing with the fact that he has run while the rest of the army has succeeded in holding the enemy. Why does Henry "cringe as if discovered in a crime"? What is the "crime" he is "cringing" for? Would he have felt the same way if, at this point, he had found that defeat had indeed overwhelmed the army?

2. "If none of the little pieces were wise enough to save themselves from the flurry of death at such a time, why, then, where would be the army?" (p. 153). This is one of the ways Henry tries to justify his running. Is this justification valid? Is a private supposed to decide for himself what he will do and where he will go? What would really happen to the army if each soldier decided these things for himself?

3. Why does Henry throw a pine cone at the squirrel? Why does he appeal to Nature in this way? Does this experiment prove that Henry was right in running? Why do you think so?

4. Through most of the book Henry and the narrator see the same things in very different ways. First, we are shown how Henry sees something; then, the narrator shows it to us as it really is. This is one of the major patterns of the book.

On page 155 we are told: 'This landscape gave him assurance. A fair field holding life. It was the religion of peace. It would die if its timid eyes were compelled to see blood. He conceived Nature to be a woman with a deep aversion to tragedy." How does this view contrast with that established by the narrator? What discovery does Henry make that contradicts his conception of nature?

5. The place deep in the woods to which Henry has fled is described in religious imagery. Why does Crane use this sort of description? What sort of "chapel" is it?

6. "The red sun was pasted in the sky like a wafer." What qualities is red associated with in this book? What is a wafer? What is the significance in this place of this sentence? How is it related to Henry's feelings and recent experiences?

7. Recall the various incidents in the novel involving Jim Conklin. What sort of man is he? How does Henry see him; what does he represent to Henry?

Why is he looking for a place to die, away from the danger of being run over by artillery wagons? Why does he keep repeating "leave me be—leave me be"? What does this indicate about the author's attitudes about the comparative values of the group and the individual in certain situations? Why is it Jim who dances the "hideous hornpipe"?

8. Chapter 9, in which Henry accompanies Jim Conklin to his place of death and watches his manner of dying, is one of the most startling and moving episodes in the book. How does the author make this scene so vivid? Why does he describe it in such detail?

What is happening to Jim Conklin? How does Henry see what is happening? Is there any implication of a difference between the narrator's and Henry's points of view? What does this indicate about the importance of this scene and its function in the story? In this chapter our eyes are always on Jim, but whom do we think about and sympathize with? Do we experience Jim's death throes primarily from his point of view, or from Henry's? How does Henry react to what he sees? How do we feel towards Henry in this scene? How does the author produce this feeling in us? Why does he do it at this point in the book?

9. Why does Henry wish that he, too, had a "red badge of

courage"? What is a red badge of courage? Late, he does get one. How does he get it?

10. Why does Henry want to join the procession of wounded men? What makes him finally leave it altogether?

11. Twice, while the rest of the army is busy fighting, Henry wants to turn prophet and warn his comrades of impending destruction; in Chapter 12, during the retreat, he wants to make a rallying speech. Why? What does this indicate about Henry's opinion of himself? Is it essentially different from what it was in the first part of the book?

12. What aspect of Henry's character is shown when he reflects that a defeat for the army at this time would vindicate him, in a manner? The narrator comments that Henry "of course felt no compunctions for proposing a general as a sacrifice." How severe a condemnation of Henry is this? How just is it?

13. What significance for the change in Henry's character does the last sentence in Chapter 12 have: "As he who had so befriended him was thus passing out of his life, it suddenly occurred to the youth that he had not once seen his face"?

14. In the first six chapters Henry's greatest "crime" was to run from the battlefield without orders to do so. What is his greatest crime in the second six chapters? How are these two similar?

CHAPTERS 13–18

1. In Chapter 10, Henry had deserted the tattered man because, as the narrator explains, his questions "asserted a society that probes pitilessly at all secrets until all is apparent." Why does this thought bother Henry so much? Is it proved true when he gets back to camp? What is his reaction to this discovery? How does it affect his behavior?

2. "Yesterday, when he had imagined the universe to be against him, he had hated it, little gods and big gods; to-day he hated the army of the foe with the same great hatred." What is the cause of this hatred in Henry? What does the story show to be the immediate result of it in each case? What does this indicate about the author's attitude?

3. Why doesn't Henry give Wilson his packet when he first thinks about it? Later, when Wilson has asked for his packet and

he has handed it over, he thinks "it was a generous thing" (p. 191). What does he think is generous? Is it? How can Henry think it is? In the next paragraph we are told, from Henry's point of view: "He had never been compelled to blush in such a manner for his acts; he was an individual of extraordinary virtues." What has happened to his moral values? What has caused this change?

4. "It was revealed to him that he had been a barbarian, a beast. He had fought like a pagan who defends his religion. Regarding it, he saw that it was fine, wild, and, in some ways, easy." Is this remark meant as approval of Henry's recent fighting; as criticism; or neither? What has the lieutenant just said to him? What does Henry think of his own conduct? In what way is his fighting this time similar to that in the first battle?

5. Henry notices a remarkable change in his friend Wilson. What sort of change has taken place? What may we infer has caused it? Does Henry completely understand and sympathize with this change in Wilson?

6. Henry is given his wound by one of the men in his own army who hits him in the head with his rifle when Henry impedes his retreat from the battlefield. When Henry arrives in camp that night, in order to protect himself from taunts on his running, he tells Wilson: "I've—I've had an awful time. I've been all over. . . . Over on th' right, I got shot. In th' head" (p. 180). Later, while dressing the wound, Wilson remarks: "It's raised a queer lump just as if some feller had lammed yeh on th' head with a club" (p. 182). Does Wilson know, or even suspect, how Henry really got his wound? What do we think when we read Wilson's remark? What purpose does it serve in the story?

After a while Henry grows cocky, finding that no one knows he has run. He declares that "we fight like the devil" and if something is wrong it must be the general's fault. Eventually, a "sarcastic man" remarks: "Mebbe yeh think yeh fit th' hull battle yestirday, Fleming" (p. 194). What does the man mean to imply? Does he know Henry ran from battle? What do we think when we read this remark? Earlier Henry had boldly attacked Wilson by saying, "Day-b'fore-yestirday . . . you would a bet you'd lick the hull kit-an'-boodle all by yourself." How is this remark similar to the one the sarcastic man makes to Henry? In reading it, do we make the same judgment on Wilson that we make later on Henry? Why not? What does this suggest about the way the author has used these statements? Why does he do this? Wilson's remark and that of the sarcastic man serve similar purposes in the story. In what respects are their functions alike?

7. In Chapter 8 we are told that Henry "saw that it was an ironical thing for him to be running thus toward that which he had been at such pains to avoid" (p. 157). Why is this "ironical"? If he were to be perfectly consistent in his actions, where would he run? How does his perception of this disparity between what he had been doing and what he is doing now add to his knowledge of himself?

At the end of Chapter 18, Wilson and Henry regard as an "ironical secret" their "inner knowledge" that their regiment, so proud of itself, so confident of its fine performance, has been called "mule drivers." Why is their knowledge ironical? How is it like the irony of Henry's running toward the battlefield? How does their perception of this irony add to their knowledge of the situation and of themselves?

CHAPTERS 19–24

1. Henry feels he has been "aged" by hearing that the regiment is thought to be no better than a lot of "mule drivers." Is he aged? Why should this knowledge affect him in this way?

Earlier, Wilson said, " 'I believe I was a pretty big fool in those days.' He spoke *as after a lapse of years.*" This indication that both Henry and Wilson have been aged suggests a parallel between the changes they undergo. In what other ways are their changes similar?

2. What symbolic function does the flag serve? On page 208 we are told: "Within him, as he hurled himself forward, was born a love, a despairing fondness for this flag which was near him." Has Henry experienced this feeling before, that we know of?

3. Compare Henry's fighting in the last battle (where he becomes color bearer) with his fighting in the other battles in the book. How is it the same? How is it different?

Note such statements as the following: "There was the delirium that encounters despair and death and is heedless and blind to the odds. It is a temporary but sublime absence of selfishness" (p. 206). "He himself felt the daring spirit of a savage religion-mad. He was capable of profound sacrifices, a tremendous death" (p. 224). What sort of emotion is it that men in war seem to experience at such moments? What is the author's attitude towards it?

4. Animal imagery is abundant in this novel. In the first half of the book Henry is typically described as a "well-meaning cow" (p. 133), a "jaded horse" (p. 149), a "rabbit" and the "proverbial chicken" (p. 150). In the second half he becomes like a kitten, who can "develop teeth and claws" (p. 197); he is a "wild cat," "a beast" (p. 199). At the end, however, "his soul changed" and "he felt a quiet *manhood*" (p. 230). How are these three different sorts of animal imagery appropriate to the corresponding stages in Henry's change? What distinguishes a man from a beast in the world of this novel? When does Henry become a man?

5. "The youth developed a tranquil philosophy for these moments of irritation" (p. 217). "He stood, erect and tranquil . . ." (p. 219). What do these two statements indicate about the change in Henry?

6. On page 228 we are told: "His mind was undergoing a subtle change." What sort of change is occurring?

On page 229 we are told: "From this present viewpoint he was enabled to look upon . . . [his acts] in spectator fashion and to criticize them with some correctness, for his new condition had already defeated certain sympathies." What is Henry's viewpoint now? How close is it to that of the narrator?

7. A great deal of the action in this last section of the book takes place as Henry just looks on. Heretofore, one of his major concerns has been with being a part of things: fighting in battle and not running, joining the procession of wounded men, having a "red badge of courage" like everyone else. In the light of this, what is the significance of Henry's being "*absorbed* as a spectator" (p. 221)?

Teaching *Adventures of Huckleberry Finn*

VIRGINIA OLSEN BUSH

THE MEANING OF *HUCKLEBERRY FINN*

The tendency in a great deal of *Huckleberry Finn* criticism is to apply, unconsciously perhaps, to an interpretation of the novel a modified form of the "thwarted-genius" hypothesis which Van Wyck Brooks first presented in 1920.[1] Brooks dealt with Twain as a man whose genius was inhibited by a genteel tradition and who consequently was unable to achieve complete expression; only in *Huckleberry Finn*, behind the mask of his narrator's illiteracy and disreputableness, did Twain feel free to say what he really wanted to. But even *Huckleberry Finn*, most critics feel, is a flawed masterpiece, and the tendency is to regard the flaws—most notably, the generally disparaged Phelps-farm sequence which ends the book—as Twain's partial return to the confines of popular Victorian taste and values. What Twain "really" wanted to say is to be found primarily in the central, raft-voyage section, and the meaningful moral content of both the beginning and the end is insignificant: this attitude toward the book is current even among the general reading public who are unaware of Brooks' thesis or the scholarly controversy which surrounds it. Private reader and critic alike tend to think in terms of what the book would have meant if its author had not allowed it to become flawed.

There are two cautions that a critical reader of any book must heed, and these are even more essential when the reader is dealing with *Huckleberry Finn*: (1) No work of art has an existence outside of the form in which it was cast by its creator. (2) The elements of a work of art have no existence outside of that work. Speculation on what a novel might have, would have, or should have been has no place in a critical study of what the novel *is*. Similarly, consideration of a character as a real person or a setting as a real place is outside the limits of critical concern. Whatever may be the potentialities of the material of *Huckleberry Finn*, only those actually developed by Mark Twain are relevant to a discussion of the book's meaning; and anyone who begins to speculate on what the book would have meant if a certain potentiality had been developed in a way not contained in the original form of the book is discussing a wholly different work of art.

Ernest Hemingway has said of the novel:

> All modern American literature comes from one book by Mark Twain called *Huckleberry Finn*. If you read it you must stop where the Nigger Jim is stolen from the boys [sic]. That is the real end. The rest is just cheating.[2]

Hemingway feels that the novel's potentiality for tragedy should have been developed by giving the novel a tragic ending; but if one were really to stop reading at the point Hemingway suggests, the form of the novel as Mark Twain wrote it would be wholly altered, and it would be a different work of art. As a critic, then, Hemingway is cheating. Other subtle transformations of the book's meaning would be introduced by the acceptance of any of the other possible alterations which have been suggested to correct the flaw of the ending, such as having Jim and Huck escape up the Ohio instead of floating down the Mississippi, or finding a way to free Jim without going through all the nonsense of Tom's "evasion." The wish seems to be that Twain had avoided the equivocation of the ending as it stands, with its apparent bow to Victorian standards, and had been in some way more "truthful." Yet it is perhaps from this very ambiguity that a large part of our pleasure in reading the book derives; and if it had been given either a decisively pessimistic or a decisively optimistic ending, it might have found far fewer readers and supporters.

In dealing with *Huckleberry Finn* one must look for meaning, not moral. The warning is implicit in the "Notice" with which the author has prefaced his book: "Persons attempting to find a motive in this narrative will be prosecuted; persons attempting to find a moral in it will be banished; persons attempting to find a plot in it will be shot."* A moral tends to be simple, as, "The moral of *Huckleberry Finn* is that one must seek freedom from civilization"; but meaning is something far more complex and less easily stated. The elements of meaning may be self-contradictory or paradoxical, whereas self-contradiction within a moral vitiates the moral's effect. Perhaps it is partly because his novel contains no formal moral, but only meaning, that Mark Twain tacked his "Notice" at the front of the book.

Certainly one element of the book's meaning is the impulse towards freedom. Huck chafes at the petty restrictions to which he is subject at the Widow's—uncomfortable clothes, regular hours, no smoking—and he is glad enough to be free of them when Pap steals him away. But Pap threatens his physical freedom both by locking him in the cabin for days at a time and by attempting to kill him. To Huck, the threat to the freedom to live is more serious than any other and calls for drastic action: he "murders" himself and lights out for Jackson's Island, where he can be free both of the restrictions typified by Miss Watson and the Widow and of those typified by Pap. We might also note that in this first part of the book Huck acts to free himself of yet another sort of restriction, that of Tom Sawyer's romantic imagination, by resigning from the robber gang when he concludes that "all that stuff was only just one of Tom Sawyer's lies. I reckoned he believed in the A-rabs and the elephants, but as for me I think different. It had all the marks of a Sunday school" (p. 14).

The impulse towards freedom acquires added thematic force when Huck discovers Jim on the island and learns his story. Jim, too, has fled because of a threat to his physical freedom—Miss Watson's intention to sell him down the river. Huck seems to identify with Jim's plight, for, having learned from Mrs. Loftus that men are going to search Jackson's Island for the runaway Negro, he rouses Jim, saying, "They're after *us!*" (p. 54; my italics).

---

* Mark Twain, *Adventures of Huckleberry Finn*, ed. Henry Nash Smith (Cambridge, Mass.: The Riverside Press, 1958), p. 2. All page references are to this edition. For other editions, see *Paperback Books in Print.*

Thereafter the need for a place of safety and freedom is always present as a part of the story. The raft becomes for them a haven, a symbol of freedom, as several remarks in Huck's narrative show. "Other places do seem so cramped up and smothery," he says, "but a raft don't. You feel mighty free and easy and comfortable on a raft" (p. 99). Huck always returns to the raft from trips ashore with a feeling of relief; and once it drifts past Cairo, the raft is the only place where Jim has a chance of being free.

After the Duke and the King sell Jim back into slavery, the attempt again to secure Jim's freedom becomes ostensibly the major interest of the book. Throughout the greater part of these last eleven chapters Huck scarcely thinks about his own liberty, although he is now subject to the same social restrictions he suffered at the Widow's; his principal concern is to free Jim. Of course, as it turns out, death has already removed the two persons who had threatened Huck's and Jim's freedom, precipitating their journey down-river. They are both, therefore, nominally free. But Huck begins again to feel the encroachment of "sivilization," and he concludes that he must "light out for the Territory ahead of the rest, because Aunt Sally she's going to adopt me and sivilize me and I can't stand it. I been there before" (p. 245). This is an echo of the very first chapter of the book, in which Huck tells us, "The Widow Douglas, she took me for her son, and allowed she would sivilize me; but it was rough living in the house all the time, considering how dismal regular and decent the widow was in all her ways; and so when I couldn't stand it no longer, I lit out" (p. 3).

In *Huckleberry Finn*, however, "sivilization" does not refer to whole structure of society but only to certain evils which have become associated with it. "Sivilization" includes such petty evils as the necessity to be scrubbed clean and to wear stiff clothes, the lack of freedom to smoke and swear, and the wearisome "pecking" of a Miss Watson. "Sivilization" also means the follies of Tom Sawyer's romantic imagination and the credulity and sensationalism of the populace of the river towns. But the term seems to apply further to an evil which is primitive in its origin, although in the novel it appears in forms in which the "refining" influence of "sivilization" can be seen: the chronic violence that characterizes the river society. It is evident in Pap, in the Bricksville loafers who delight in "putting turpentine on a stray dog and setting fire to him," in the Shepherdson-Grangerford feud, and in the townspeople who tar and feather the Duke and the King and ride them out of town on rails. It is this last brutality, which was very likely to be fatal to its victims, that finally causes Huck to say, "Human beings *can* be awful cruel to one another" (p. 194). A criticism of "sivilization" seems to be implicit in his statement.

The impulse to attain freedom from the cruel and senseless limitations of "sivilization" drives Huck away from society; but a complementary impulse drives him back again. Huck simply is not a loner. Left to himself for any length of time, he soon becomes lonesome. One of his major objections to the restrictions of life with Pap is that when Pap goes off, locking him in the cabin, it is "dreadful lonesome" (p. 22), and even on Jackson's Island he finds that

> by-and-by it got sort of lonesome, and so I went and set on the bank and listened to the currents washing along, and counted the stars and drift-logs and rafts that come down, and then went to bed; there ain't no better way to put in time when you are lonesome; you can't stay so, you soon get over it (p. 34).

Huck likes, and needs, human company. In a very interesting essay on *Huckleberry Finn*, William R. Manierre has pointed out this aspect of Huck's nature:

> Very much a part of his character, along with his pragmatic turn of mind, is Huck's basic adaptability. For all his yen for freedom and the life of slothful ease and dirt, he is a natural born joiner. He "joins" Tom's gang; he "joins" Jim; later, he "joins" the Grangerfords; later still he "joins" Mary Jane Wilks and her cause; finally he "joins" society, presumably for good. In fact, even at the start he was well on his way to joining society. . . . But of course he is adaptable to Pap's ways too; he "joins" Pap; and only breaks with him because of external circumstances: Pap's drunkenness and brutality.[3]

Mr. Manierre's use of the word "join" is significant, for it implies the consent of both parties. Huck could not have joined Tom's gang, for example, unless he had wanted to join and the gang had been willing to accept him. The relationship thus formed is some-thing vital, requiring the active participation of both parties to keep it alive. The epitome of such a relationship is the friendship between Huck and Jim. But the novel also contains examples of another, one-sided sort of relationship, which we may term "adop-tion." In "adoption," one party appropriates another without the other's consent, as when the Widow Douglas takes Huck for her son or when Aunt Sally says she is going to adopt him. The rela-tionship threatens to become not personal but legal, as is that be-tween Huck and his own father. Jim's situation as Miss Watson's slave is of this same type: he is treated as property, not as a human being. Because Huck is not interested in becoming a member of society on just any terms, he tends to flee "adoptive" situations; but he continually seeks the opportunity to "join."

There is, then, a double movement in this novel, both towards society and away from it. From the beginning we find Huck "joining" people and then withdrawing when he discovers in them anything which offends his innate sense of propriety. He resigns from Tom's gang upon discovering that "all that stuff was only just one of Tom Sawyer's lies"; he leaves Pap when Pap's violence gets out of hand; he leaves the Grangerfords to rejoin Jim only after watching the slaughter of Buck Grangerford and his cousin; he attempts to leave the Duke and the King after witnessing their sickening conduct in the Wilks episode. Because Huck is adaptable to a wide range of conditions, he usually waits until events them-selves tend to push him out of an undesirable situation, as happens at the end of his Grangerford sojourn. In fact, the incident which thrusts him out of the Grangerford world is itself that which makes that world no longer attractive to him. Only in extreme circum-stances does he initiate a whole course of action: once at the be-ginning, when he escapes from Pap; once at the end, when he decides to steal Jim out of captivity at the Phelps' farm; and, in a more limited way, when he helps Mary Jane Wilks.

Probably the dominant trait of Huck's character is his longing not for freedom, but for peace. This longing is best expressed in Huck's comments after the difficulty between the Duke and the King about conflicting claims of "rank" has been settled:

The duke done it [took the king's hand], and Jim and me was pretty glad to see it. It took away all the uncomfortableness, and we felt mighty good over it, because it would a been a miserable business to have any unfriendliness on the raft; for what you want, above all things, on a raft, is for everybody to be satisfied, and feel right and kind towards the others (p. 106).

And in the next paragraph he says:

If they wanted us to call them kings and dukes, I hadn't no objections, 'long as it would keep peace in the family. . . .

In these passages, Huck is describing his ideal community, with which the communities he visits along the river contrast sharply. Instead of everyone being satisfied, and feeling "right and kind towards the others," there there is nothing but the unkindness, violence, and cruelty from which Huck has fled. For him, peace is freedom.

The last two sentences of the novel have often been taken as yet another of Huck's bids for freedom, his "final rejection of civilization." But is this really what has happened in the last eleven chapters of the book? Huck has lived for a considerable length of time with the Phelpses, apparently without suffering too great discomfort from Aunt Sally's attempts at "sivilizing" him. In fact, Huck in this section does not seem to need much "sivilizing." When he remarks at the end that Aunt Sally is going to adopt him and "sivilize" him, we may suspect that this process will be quite different from that conducted by Miss Watson, who was trying to transform an independent boy into a well-trained member of society; Aunt Sally means merely to tame down a high-spirited boy who is nevertheless already a part of society—much as Aunt Polly attempts to do with Tom. In this last part of the novel, we find also that Huck has accepted Tom's improbable plan for freeing Jim—with reservations, to be sure; but he never recognizes that this, too, is "only just one of Tom Sawyer's lies" and that there is as great a difference between the "noble prisoner" whom Tom is rescuing and the captive Jim whom Huck is trying to free as there is between Tom's A-rabs and elephants and the Sunday school that Huck sees. Furthermore, Huck has switched his allegiance from Jim to the more socially acceptable Aunt Sally by deciding not to grieve her by going back to Jim and Tom to help Jim get away.

Even Huck's thinking now suggests his integration with society. The perception of dichotomy that was the basis of his decision to "go to hell" is missing. When the doctor who has captured Jim says a few kind words in his favor, Huck tells us:

> I was mighty thankful to that old doctor for doing Jim that good turn; and I was glad it was according to my judgment of him, too; because I thought he had a good heart in him and was a good man, the first time I see him (p. 239).

Huck notices the small good the doctor has done, but he never mentions the much greater good the doctor could have done by letting Jim go. Huck is now thinking like all the rest of his society, which approves small charities but seldom has the courage to consider anything more.

In addition, Huck now thinks materialistically. Earlier, he had burst out passionately against the Duke and the King for selling Jim:

> After all this long journey, and after all we'd done for them scoundrels, here was it all come to nothing, everything all busted up and ruined, because they could have the heart to serve Jim such a trick as that, and make him a slave again all his life, and amongst strangers, too, for forty dirty dollars (p. 178).

Yet when Tom presumes to pay this identical amount to Jim for the time he has spent being a prisoner, a slave amongst strangers, Huck makes no comment. The meanness of Tom's gesture is brought home by the great contrast between the new wealth of the black man and that of the white boy. "Jim has been appropriately served: his physical chains struck off and his psychological chains reaffirmed in suitable financial terms. . . . Forty dollars for Jim and 'six thousand . . . and more' for Huck—a quite proper proportion."[4]

Huck even worries about not having enough money to buy his outfit for the expedition to the Territory. This concern is a significant commentary on his intentions in "lighting out," especially in light of the tendency he has already shown to join society. We must remember that it was Tom who first suggested that they "go for howling adventures amongst the Injuns, over in the Territory, for a couple of weeks or two" (p. 244); and, as Henry Nash Smith has pointed out, "When Huck says he means to set out ahead of the others, there is nothing in the text to indicate that his intention is more serious than Tom's."[5] His concern for his "outfit" confirms the vacation-like nature of this expedition, for Huck has never before worried about being properly equipped in a serious situation. Furthermore, Huck never says anything to indicate that he intends to stay away longer than the suggested two weeks. That Huck says he is going to light out *ahead* of the rest means very little. It is just a game he is playing: he is making believe that it is a serious business in order to mask the fact that he is now only pretending to escape from civilization. Like Tom, he knows they will be returning.

By the end of the novel, then, Huck has found relative peace and freedom. Both he and Jim have now acquired the status in society which assures them society's protection against the cruelty and inhumanity which could otherwise be turned on them, as on a stray dog. Jim is a freed man; Miss Watson, who represented the inhumanity which had threatened him, is dead. And, similarly, Huck can now be free of fear, for Pap, who represented the cruelty threatening him, is also dead. Huck has no compelling reason to light out, except perhaps some small worry lest Aunt Sally secure too great legal control by adopting him.

The burlesque treatment of events in the last eleven chapters of the novel and even the tediousness of this section beguile us into accepting Huck's initiation into society. The lack of seriousness in the style of writing makes us less critical of what happens. Throughout the Phelps-farm sequence we have been, perhaps disturbingly, aware that Huck is not now so independent as he was, floating down the Mississippi, and it is with a sense of relief that we find him saying that he must "light out." But we are also aware that this is a clever ending, that it goes just so far and no further, that it is unquestionably "right." And it is "right" precisely because it is ambivalent, affirming both the value of independence and the value of society. The length and style of the concluding chapters of *Huckleberry Finn*, so very different from the preceding section, constitute something of a flaw, for they make this part of the book seem boring and anticlimactic; and yet the concluding chapters are very important to the book's meaning, for they prepare the necessary background, both in tone and in incident, for Huck's final statement:

> But I reckon I got to light out for the Territory ahead of the rest, because Aunt Sally she's going to adopt me and sivilize me and I can't stand it. I been there before (p. 245).

Mark Twain has aroused in us the desire for freedom, has satisfied it, and has given us the pleasing illusion that the impulse is still operative, while in fact we are safely at peace.

ON TEACHING *HUCKLEBERRY FINN*

When teaching *Huckleberry Finn*, the teacher will not want to give his students an interpretation—either that in the preceding essay or any other—but will want them instead to develop their own from their own examination of the book. High school students will of course be unable to formulate a complete idea of the novel's meaning, but they should be able to recognize the social criticism and the movements toward and away from society which are at the heart of the book. Probably the best way to help students understand the novel is to have them study the way in which the story is told, concentrating on the character of Huck as narrator, for the body of the novel's meaning is contained in and developed through him. In this way they will discover the importance of the first-person narration and of the language used in writing the book, and they will discover also something of the origins of the abundant irony and humor which it contains.

Huckleberry Finn assumes the dominant position in the book because of his double role as narrator and central character and because of the relative unimportance of a conventional plot in this novel. The numerous incidents of which the novel is made up are given unity first of all by the single consciousness—Huck's—which has observed and reported them all. Huck's observations on all that takes place put the incidents into perspective and indicate links in meaning between them. Furthermore, Huck himself is always unobstrusively present, as spectator if not as participant, to provide us with a standard by which to judge the other characters. Huck's responses to what he sees form a second layer of action in the novel: indeed, Huck does relatively little to affect the physical action, but his private reactions tend to define the meaning of the actions of others. Thus, when he says that it made him sick to watch the killing of Buck Grangerford, or that the carrying-on of the King and the Duke about their "poor brother" was "enough to make a body ashamed of the human race," or that it made him sick to see what the townspeople had done to the Duke and the King in tarring and feathering them, the meaning of these incidents is made clear and we see the links between them. The student should see that Huck's commentary is important to the way in which we look at what happens.

Twain's use of a thirteen- or fourteen-year-old narrator with relatively little formal schooling allows him to write in language not usually used in literature. This language, in its simplicity, informality, and freshness, is peculiarly suited to the novel and is one of its great beauties. Huck's description of the summer storm in Chapter 9 and of dawn on the river in Chapter 19 illustrate well its lyric potentialities. Its suitability for accurate and specific description is evident in such passages as that in which he speaks of the stars as having been laid by the moon, just like frogs' eggs (p. 101); or that in which he says that Mary Jane Wilks "had more sand in her than any girl I ever see; in my opinon she was just full of sand. It sounds like flattery, but it ain't no flattery" (p. 161). The student should see that it would be difficult to write a more effective description of the multitude of stars or the character of Mary Jane Wilks.

Huck's naïveté is the basis of the novel's irony and his lack of humor is the basis of its humor. Huck reports seriously and honestly on what he observes, without intending or seeing the implications of all that he says. These implications are very apparent, however, to the reader, and most of Twain's social criticism in the novel is attained in this way, through his ironical use of Huck as narrator. The Grangerford episode shows Twain at his best. The naïve Huck always appears sincerely impressed by the furnishings of the Grangerford establishment. He respectfully tells us of Emmeline's pictures: "They was different from any pictures I ever see before; blacker, mostly, than is common." The understatement of this remark is humorous; and the lack of judgment in it prompts us to make our own judgment. This principle operates throughout the description of the Grangerford house. Although Huck is sincere in his admiration of the "cultured" furnishings, it is evident to us from the details he gives in the description that their "culture" is superficial, tasteless, and overly sentimental. The irony of description from Huck's point of view is far more effective in conveying this impression than would be a direct description in Twain's own voice. The teacher may help his students to see this by having them read the "House Beautiful" section of *Life on the Mississippi,* in which Twain attacks the Grangerford type of culture directly.

By approaching the novel through these narrative devices and through the structural pattern indicated in the discussion of the novel's meaning, the teacher should be able to lead his students to see something of what it means and to understand why *Huckleberry Finn* is such an effective and enjoyable book.

STUDY QUESTIONS

CHAPTERS 1–16

1. Huck begins his book by referring to *The Adventures of Tom Sawyer:*

> That book was made by Mr. Mark Twain, and he told the truth, mainly. There was things which he stretched, but mainly he told the truth. That is nothing. I never seen anybody but lied, one time or another, without it was Aunt Polly, or the widow, or maybe Mary (p. 3).

What does Huck think of *Tom Sawyer?* What do you think the "stretchers" are that he says it contains? After reading the first paragraph, do we expect *Huckleberry Finn* to be essentially the same sort of book as *Tom Sawyer?* Why or why not? Do we expect to find any stretchers in *Huckleberry Finn?* Why or why not? Do we expect to find more or fewer than in *Tom Sawyer?*

2. In Chapter 1 Huck states that he doesn't "take stock in dead people." Why? What does this indicate about his character?

3. What sort of person is Miss Watson? What does the phrase, "a tolerable slim old maid," add to the description of her in Chapter 1? Why is it important that these are Huck's words? How would the meaning be changed if we thought that it was Mark Twain calling her a "tolerable slim old maid"? Would the humor be lost?

4. What is Huck's attitude toward Jim in Chapter 2? Is Jim portrayed as an individual or as a type? Defend your answer.

5. Why does Huck finally decide to run away from Pap (Chapter 6)?

6. In Chapter 6, Pap rails against a government that would let a free Negro vote. On what grounds does he make this objection? Contrast the free Negro Pap speaks of with Pap. What is the effect of this contrast? Why does Twain choose to have Pap rail against the government on this account?

7. In Chapter 7, when Huck plans and executes his escape from Pap, does he act like a typical boy who is "running away"? In what ways is his behavior different? Why?

8. After meeting Jim on Jackson's Island, Huck remarks, "I was ever so glad to see Jim. I warn't lonesome, now" (p. 36). How lonesome a boy is Huck? Why? Find other evidence of his loneliness. How great a motivation is loneliness for his actions? Explain.

9. What is Huck's first reaction to Jim's announcement that he has run off? At this point, why does Huck declare he won't tell on Jim?

10. Reread Huck's description of the summer storm in Chapter 9 (p. 42). How effective is this description? Why? By specific. What is unique about the language used? Is this language a strength or a weakness?

11. What is Huck's reaction to the corpse in the house floating downstream (Chapter 9)? How do you account for this reaction?

12. What sort of a person is Mrs. Judith Loftus (Chapter 11)?

13. After learning that men are going to search the island for the runaway slave, why does Huck tell Jim, "They're after us!" (Chapter 11)? What is the significance of his use of "us"? Is anyone after him?

14. How does Huck feel about the death of the gang on the

Walter Scott? Is he sentimental about it? Would the widow and "good people" have reacted as he did? Why?

15. Why do you think Twain named the wrecked steamboat the *Walter Scott*? Who was Walter Scott?

16. In Chapter 14 Huck says of Jim, "Well, he was right; he was most always right; he had an uncommon level head, for a nigger." What does this tell us about Jim? What does it tell us about Huck? Why is the statement more effective coming from Huck than if it had come from an omniscient narrator?

17. What does Huck learn from Jim's response to his practical joke (Chapter 15)? What does Jim's response add to our impression of him? Why is it so difficult for Huck to "humble himself to a nigger"? Why does he finally do it?

18. Why does Huck feel so miserable in Chapter 16, realizing that he has helped to free Jim? Jim speaks of buying his wife and then getting the children, stealing them if need be. Why does Huck say, "It most froze me to hear such talk"?

19. Why does Huck protect Jim and lie to the men looking for runaway slaves?

20. What is Huck's reasoning in deciding not to "bother no more" about learning to do right (Chapter 16)?

CHAPTERS 17–31

1. In Chapter 17 Huck describes the Grangerford house. What do its furnishings tell us about the Grangerfords? What does Huck think of the house and the culture it represents? What does Mark Twain think of it? Would the criticism have been more or less effective if Twain had stated in his own voice exactly what he thought? Why?

2. What in Emmeline's poetry and art is Twain satirizing? What does Huck's remark that "They was different from any pictures I ever see before; blacker, mostly, than is common" indicate about her art?

3. What is Huck's reaction to the feud and the killing of Buck Grangerford? How does his reaction influence the way we regard the feud?

4. How long do you think Huck spends with the Grangerfords? Why does he stay there? What makes him leave?

5. In Chapter 18 Huck says: "We said there warn't no home like a raft, after all. Other places do seem so cramped up and smothery, but a raft don't. You feel mighty free and easy and comfortable on a raft" (p. 99). Explain the thematic significance of this passage.

6. What is the effect of the contrast between the first part of Chapter 19, describing life on the raft, and the chapter immediately preceding it?

7. In Chapter 19 Huck says he and Jim were glad to see the King and the Duke shake hands, "for what you want, above all things, on a raft, is for everybody to be satisfied, and feel right and kind towards the others." In the next paragraph he adds, "If they wanted us to call them kings and dukes, I hadn't no objections, 'long as it would keep peace in the family . . ." (p. 106). How are these passages an explanation of Huck's way of life? Why do he and Jim take the two rogues in? What is the significance of Huck's speaking of "the family"? Has he ever had a family?

8. How appropriate are the following passages of narration or conversation to the fourteen-year-old, ill-schooled narrator of this novel: Huck's comments on the Shakespearean rehearsal in Chapter 21; Sherburn's speech to the lynch mob in Chapter 22; Huck's conversation with Jim about kings in Chapter 23. Consider the language used, the factual knowledge involved, and the point of view displayed.

9. What does Jim's story in Chapter 23 about the way he treated his deaf-and-dumb daughter tell us about him?

10. In response to the conduct of the Duke and the King in the Wilks episode in Chapter 24, Huck says, "It was enough to make a body ashamed of the human race." Why does he feel this way? In what way are their actions now worse than anything Huck has seen before?

11. In Chapter 27 the King and the Duke sell the Wilkses' slaves, separating the family. What parallels to this incident can you find in the book?

12. How effective is Huck's description of Mary Jane in Chapter 28 (p. 161) as the girl with the most "sand" in her? Why?

13. In Chapter 31 Huck says, "You can't pray a lie—I found that out." Throughout the book there has been a great deal of talk

about lies: for example, in the first paragraph of Chapter 1; in Chapter 3, when Huck decides that the A-rabs and elephants were "only just one of Tom Sawyer's lies"; and in Chapter 28, when Huck decides that it will actually be safer to tell the truth to Mary Jane than to tell a lie. After rereading these passages and any others you can find referring to lying, explain what the significance of lying is in this book.

14. In Chapter 31 Huck finally decides to steal Jim out of slavery and, after a long battle with his conscience, says: "All right, then, I'll *go* to hell." Explain the importance of this incident to the story as a whole and to the growth of Huck's character.

CHAPTER 32–CHAPTER THE LAST

1. What is the significance of the mood established at the start of Chapter 32?

2. When Tom agrees to help free Jim, Huck exclaims, "Only I couldn't believe it. Tom Sawyer a *nigger stealer!*" Why is this so difficult for Huck to understand?

3. Is Huck's attitude toward Tom in this last part of the book consistent with all that he has learned and been through? Why or why not? What is his attitude?

4. In Chapter 40 Huck says: "When me and Jim heard that [Tom was wounded], we didn't feel so brash as what we did before." Contrast the way Huck and Jim act here with the way Tom has been acting throughout this section of the book.

5. Tom gives Jim forty dollars for being a prisoner for him. Is this a good and admirable thing for him to do? Why or why not? Forty dollars is also the sum for which the King had sold Jim to Silas Phelps. Is the similarity of these amounts perhaps a commentary on Tom's action? What does it suggest?

6. In Chapter 41 Huck decides not to grieve Aunt Sally by leaving to go back to Jim and Tom to help Jim get away. Why does he make this decision? Is it the right decision? Defend your answer.

7. In the last paragraph of the novel Huck says: "But I reckon I got to light out for the Territory ahead of the rest, because Aunt Sally she's going to adopt me and sivilize me and I can't stand it. I been there before." What is the significance of this remark?

Compare this "lighting out" with his lighting out earlier from Pap. Which is more serious? Does Huck intend to stay away forever both times? How good an ending do you think this is for the novel? Why?

NOTES

1. Van Wyck Brooks, *The Ordeal of Mark Twain* (New York: E. P. Dutton, 1920).

2. Ernest Hemingway, *Green Hills of Africa* (New York: Charles Scribner's Sons, 1935), p. 22.

3. William R. Manierre, " 'No Money for to Buy the Outfit': *Huckleberry Finn* Again," *Modern Fiction Studies*, X (Winter 1965), pp. 341–42.

4. Ibid., p. 348.

5. Smith, p. xxi.

Teaching *Gulliver's Travels*

HOWARD ANDERSON

Assistant Professor of English
Indiana University

The encounter of an ordinary Englishman and a rapidly shifting series of little men, big men, madmen, apes, and horses—all of them fascinating in themselves and all the more so for the resemblances they bear to the mankind we know—makes *Gulliver's Travels* immediately appealing and consistently absorbing. It is a book worth a great deal of study, for the questions it raises about nearly every aspect of the lives which human beings lead together constitute a thorough criticism of common assumptions about how those lives are lived and how they should be lived. Dealing with politics, education, laws, professions, marriage, parenthood (to name only some of his more recurrent concerns), Swift never loses sight of the fact that they are aspects of *human* relations and are of the greatest importance anywhere and anytime. Fantastic faraway worlds may unexpectedly reveal the truth about the commonplace world back home; and while Swift may refer to particular embodiments of, say, political relations in early eighteenth-century England, those embodiments are only particular local examples of recurrent, even universal, human behavior. For this reason, although the local and topical references in the book are frequent and interesting—so that it may be a good idea to read a well-annotated edition*—mere familiarity with these references should not be taken for a full understanding of the book. The con-

---

* The Riverside Edition, ed. Louis A. Landa (Boston: Houghton Mifflin, 1960) is one example of a number in paperback. All page references are to that edition.

cern of *Gulliver's Travels* is with human nature and human conduct that change little from one century to another.

Throughout the book Swift's aim is to lead the reader to assess his assumptions about himself and the rest of mankind. To do so, he makes use of whatever methods will most effectively force into question the ridiculous, irrational, and trivial on the one hand, and the harmful, cruel, and destructive on the other. This whole range of mistaken uses of human powers constitutes, for Swift, multifarious manifestations of *pride*—all the result of mistaken self-assurance and self-concern. Swift's purposes are, I should say, moral and rhetorical in a more direct sense than is true of the writers of most novels. While the worlds created in most novels may allow us considerable insight into our own world—as is true, certainly, of both *The Red Badge of Courage* and *To Kill a Mockingbird*—the relationship that first of all concerns the writers is that between events in the world of the novel and the people who occupy it. *Gulliver's Travels,* however, aims to keep the reader constantly alert to direct relations of one kind or another between the fantastic places Gulliver visits and the world the reader himself inhabits. Swift aims to give us new and often shocking insight into the ways of our world, and to persuade us on the basis of that insight to think and act more consistently in keeping with our own best interests and those of our fellow men. To do so, he creates characters and places for them to live and act in—this he shares with the novelists. But this similarity should not lead us to forget the difference in aim and thus in manner of proceeding.

The book is, then, throughout, an attack on the misuse of human capacities, often a very funny attack—a good joke that makes us laugh even though we more and more ruefully acknowledge that the truth we are laughing at hurts. Reading through it once makes us realize that we are in the hands of a writer whose humor is matched by his intellectual and ethical rigor, who is extraordinarily willing and able to put his finger on what is wrong with the way we live. In Book I, the attack is directed at those in power: politicians, social leaders—those whose arms, authority, and prestige (if not their inherent abilities) are such as to keep even so powerful an embodiment of common manhood as Gulliver in subservience to their petty, willful and finally destructive ambitions. In Book II, in case the reader has begun to feel smug about the virtues he shares with the admirable Gulliver, the attack switches directions: the ordinary man himself is implicated in the viciousness which was the prerogative of the great in Book I. In Book III, the abstraction of learned men is attacked as we see how far they are from devoting their brains to what really matters in human life. And in Book IV, the focus again enlarges and we have before us the vanity, greed, and bestiality of all men shown up through their identification with the Yahoos and by contrast with the Houyhnhnms.

But if we are confident after reading the book of the soundness of Swift's values, if we put our trust in his unfailing concern with justice, honesty, and the other virtues traditionally most highly valued in Western thought, we also come to realize that his *methods* of dealing with his reader are scarcely such as to make us confident; in fact, they may have made us very nervous indeed. For while *Gulliver's Travels* champions most of the highest values that have developed through the centuries in our culture, it does not present them in anything like a straightforward sermon. On the contrary, Swift seems determined from the start not to *present* them at all, but to make us see them for ourselves. He works throughout to make us think for ourselves. Like Socrates, who comes in for praise in Book IV, Swift implies that the unexamined life is not worth living; and, like Socrates, he is determined that the reader's examination should be thorough and honest. To look into the most important of the various techniques he uses to accomplish this aim, we had better be prepared to read the book a number of times and spend a good deal of time studying it.

Perhaps the most generally inclusive way to describe Swift's method in *Gulliver's Travels* is to call it a technique of surprises—provided we keep in mind that surprises can include shocks and betrayals. Varying surprises keep us alert and thinking as we read. The first of them are benign enough: the Lilliputians, scarcely bigger than insects in contrast to a man, quickly turn out to have characteristics and customs that correspond, despite the difference in scale, to those of Englishmen. Swift makes us see this for ourselves although his narrator Gulliver is so unfamiliar with centers of political and social life that he can only describe what goes on in Lilliput, naïvely unaware of parallels at home. But the reader, who presumably reads the newspapers and knows what goes on in the capitals of the world, recognizes that Lilliput has a wider reference than is apparent to Gulliver. The effect of our discovery that beings six inches high carry on like full-sized human beings is inevitably to diminish the importance of human beings: it's like being imitated by an ant. But Swift's use of the Lilliputians does not follow a single established line. The uncomplimentary effect on our judgment of the great in our world may result from the fact that the Lilliputian systems of education, of reward and punishment, are clearly superior to those at home; the Lilliputian king, miniscule as he is, is a more dignified figure than George I and a number of other national leaders to whom we inevitably compare him; and so on. But then much of their wisdom is unexpectedly canceled by Gulliver's consignment of it to the past; we are suddenly made aware of the vanities of the pursuit of honors in high places, and of the treachery of European politics, by seeing them identified, not contrasted, with Lilliputian habits. What looked at first like an amusing pleasure trip to a never-never land of charming little people, turns out, in these several unlooked-for ways, to bring us back home.

Swift's shifting use of the Lilliputians in Book I makes us aware that we had better not rely on easy assumptions about what is going on around us; it is clearly a mistake to take for granted that because the Lilliputians sometimes look innocent they will therefore be consistently exemplary. But he waits until Book II to jolt us with the discovery that the unreliability extends to the center of the narrative—to Gulliver himself. From the opening paragraph of the work, Gulliver has seemed a good, honest, ordinary man; he is well equipped by education and profession to observe facts and record them carefully. Through the first book he stands for simple moral virtues; above all in his refusal to support the Lilliputians' cruel ambitions against their neighbors he wins our respect. He is not immune to some of the more harmless vanities— he is obviously pleased, for example, with the high title he wins in Lilliput, while we have to smile at the incongruity of a Lilliputian title on gigantic Gulliver—but he shares none of the serious vices of the Lilliputian (and European) nobility. The respect,

mixed with just a little amused condescension, that we have come
to feel toward Gulliver continues well into Book II. We may smile
at his efforts to maintain his dignity among people who handle
him like a pet mouse, and at his struggles revealing the pettiness
of all human attempts at dignity and grandeur. But as Gulliver
says, "the King of Great Britain himself, in my condition, must
have undergone the same distress." And the more serious satire
in the earlier parts of Book II is directed at the Brobdingnagian
farmer's inhumane treatment of a helpless dependent. Then without warning, in his conversations with the admirable King of
Brobdingnag, Gulliver turns from a sympathetic mouse into a
vicious rat. While he seems, in the bland brutality of his speech
on the glories of gunpowder, quite as unaware of the implications
of his words as he had been in Book I, it is a new kind of unaware-
ness. He has changed suddenly from a character whose innocence
protects him from the malevolent ambitions that characterize the
great of the world, to one who is merely unconscious of his own
depraved addiction to destructive power. He is himself fully a
member of "the most pernicious race of little odious vermin that
nature ever suffered to crawl upon the surface of the earth."
Gulliver betrays our trust: after his talks with the King, we can
never put our confidence in him again.

But this is not to say that he continues to sound the way he does
in the conversations with the King; on the contrary, through much
of Book III he resumes the role he played earlier. He is usually
a noncommittal reporter of the odd antics, the more or less inhumane detachment, of the rulers in Laputa and the learned men
in Lagado. He records it all, largely without comment, and his
own character plays a part in our judgment of what he records
only in that we must again, as in Book I, be aware that his mind
is not such as to make for us the necessary connections between
that world and our own. And much of our pleasure, here as earlier,
derives from the inappropriateness of Gulliver's coolly reportorial
tone to the preposterous actions he describes. We have no reason
to think that Gulliver has developed into an evil character in Book
II and that he will remain so through the rest of his travels. In
fact, we have no reason to think of him as a character in the sense
of one who *develops* through traceable causes at all. Rather, he

moves back and forth between different roles depending upon Swift's judgment of how he may best be used to throw light upon the vanities and vices of the reader and the world he lives in.

These roles, which Swift manipulates with the ease of a puppeteer using one puppet and then another, are not consistent with one another; Gulliver does not develop or grow to something better or worse as a character in a good novel does on the basis of the experiences that confront him. If he did so, we should expect him to praise the Laputans for their sophisticated grasp of power politics, just as he criticized the King of Brobdingnag for his failures in that line. And we should certainly not expect from him the kind of ideal hopes for human fulfillment which he expresses at the prospect of meeting a Struldbrugg. Swift uses him in this rhapsody on the possibilities of eternal life on earth for the purpose of demolishing such optimism. Gulliver here is in another role: neither the accurate but limited reporter nor the uncomprehending exponent of destructive power, but a naïve and enthusiastic believer in man's generous and creative instincts. And our attention, in each case, is intended to center not (as it would in a novel) on how Gulliver comes to be as he is, but rather upon the existence of what Gulliver is talking about in the world within and around us.

In Book III, then, the shock that Swift has in store for us does not involve further disappointment in Gulliver's own moral character; rather, it centers in the amazing distance between the intellectual ingenuity of the powerful and the learned and their failure to put that ingenuity to practical use for their own true well-being and that of mankind. And in the Struldbrugg incident, the shock centers between the commonplace assumptions about the benevolent possibilities of human nature and the very real physical and spiritual limitations that reduce man to whining, grasping futility. In Book IV, Swift enlarges the contrast between good sense and the various perversions of the intellect that is so noticeable in the voyage to Laputa. "Horse sense" based in experience, in common observation of what is valuable in ordinary daily life, is the dominating faculty of the Houyhnhnms. We share Gulliver's surprise when he finds that this admirable possession makes the horses superior not only to the Yahoos, who painfully resemble human beings, but indeed to human beings themselves. And our sense of shock deepens as we find just how closely the Yahoos do in fact resemble us: each of their traits and habits, described in revolting detail, shortly turns out to have an analogue in our own species. At last, to his horror (which we share, though we may also find it funnier than he does), Gulliver has to admit that if there is any difference at all between men and Yahoos, it is the Yahoos that have the advantage: they have not lost the physical power of beasts nor have they acquired some of the more sophisticated vices which men, in their endless lust for pleasure, have invented. The good sense of the Houyhnhnms makes them immune, of course, not only to these pleasures but also to some which may appear to the reader more legitimate sources of human satisfaction and concern. But if we are not inclined to envy the horses their cool love life, their refusal to mourn the death of those close to them, and a few other such stoic virtues, we cannot deny that their conduct is in most important ways an ideal that we admire and should aspire to, but that the dirty, destructive, and lively Yahoos are a fair picture of the way we look without any clothes on.

Only one more surprise is in store for us. As Gulliver leaves Houyhnhnmland, the focus shifts once again from the various human vices represented in the Yahoos to one represented in Gulliver. Beastly as men have been shown to be, Gulliver's violent rejection of them and, worse yet, his assumption that he alone is immune from the worst of their vices, constitutes in itself a despicable human failing. Gulliver speaks of the human pride which blindly arrogates to itself a position of superiority of which it is utterly unworthy. Ironically, attempting to divorce himself from his own kind, failing to recognize even Houyhnhnm-like virtue when he confronts it in the Portuguese sea captain who generously helps him get home, Gulliver is himself more like a Yahoo than like the Houyhnhnms whom he thinks he is imitating. *Gulliver's Travels* ends with the ultimate vain and vicious human delusion: a portrait of a man who proudly asserts that he alone is without pride. The distance between what Gulliver means to say about himself as he concludes, and our awareness of what Swift means to say about blind mankind, is the final irony of this totally ironic book of travels—which ends, where it began, with the ordinary, individual traveler.

STUDY QUESTIONS

BOOK I

1. We can assume that since first impressions are important, a good writer will take care with the opening of his book. Study the first paragraph of Book I. Just what do we learn about Gulliver and why is this information important? (1) What social class does Gulliver seem to belong to? How can you tell? Why is Swift interested in having such a man tell us the story? (2) What are the various elements of Gulliver's education? Why is Swift interested in having a man educated like this tell us the story? (3) Is there anything in the letter of the publisher to the reader which precedes the *Travels* (p. 7) that contributes further to the effect of this paragraph in building the character of the narrator? (4) Does the map of Lilliput and Blefuscu that faces the first chapter in most editions contribute further to the effect on us achieved by Sympson's and Gulliver's descriptions of Gulliver?

2. Notice the careful detail with which Gulliver describes the tiny size of the Lilliputians, the vast quantities of their food which he eats, and so forth (p. 17 ff.). What contrast is Swift emphasizing here? Find other places in the opening chapters where Lilliputian dimensions are effectively contrasted with European ones.

3. What is our response to the King of Lilliput as he is described on page 24? He is of course tiny, but what do you think of his looks, his dress, and his way of speaking? Why does Swift have Gulliver include the fact that the King "held his sword drawn in his hand, to defend himself, if I should happen to break loose"? How does the little King's appearance and way of handling himself compare with that of most important (full-sized) men you have seen? What do you think Swift is up to in describing a little man as he does; that is, what do you think he intends us to think of? How does his emphasis on the contrast in size between Lilliputians and Europeans begin here to be at once humorous and an instrument of Swift's criticism of the actual world? How does the humor serve satiric purposes?

4. If the description of the admirable little King of Lilliput reflects by contrast on world leaders whom Swift (and we) could name, what is the effect of the description (pp. 31-32) of the Lilliputian competition for big political jobs and honors? In what way is its effect on our judgment of actual great men similar to that achieved by the description of the King, and in what way is the *method* by which it is achieved different?

5. What kind of comment does Swift make on political parties by having the chief difference between those in Lilliput a matter of the height of their heels? What kind of comment does he make on political and international disputes by the Lilliputian quarrel over how to crack an egg? Of the methods of satire investigated in questions 3 and 4, which is he using here?

6. What picture do we get of the Lilliputians from Gulliver's extended description of their laws and customs in Chapter 6? Do these laws and customs seem entirely consistent with the actual deeds of the Lilliputians who treacherously attempt to destroy Gulliver in Chapter 7? That is, for example, would we expect men who hold the ideas about ingratitude described on page 48 to treat Gulliver as they do? How does Gulliver explain the disparity between the institutions and the men? If the institutions no longer operate as he describes them (at such length), and if they do not explain the actions of Lilliputians at the present time, why does Swift bother to describe them in such detail?

7. The account of the council's consideration of Gulliver's "treason" in Chapter 7 satirizes the notorious ingratitude of those in power; at the same time it hits at a related topic—the debasement of friendship in such circles. Notice Swift's method: (1) What is our expectation when we are told that Gulliver's friend Reldresal was called on to give his opinion on whether Gulliver should be executed? (2) In precisely what way is Reldresal's response unexpected?

BOOK II

1. Study the account of Gulliver's first encounter with the Brobdingnagians (pp. 70–71). How is Gulliver handled by the farm worker who picks him up? To what is he compared? What does this comparison suggest about human beings? How does

Gulliver act when the farmer puts him down and examines him? What do his actions suggest about human beings?

2. On successive pages (pp. 74–76) Swift dwells at some length first on the ugliness of the Brobdingnagian nurse's breast and skin and then on Gulliver's need to urinate and defecate. What would you say is Swift's satiric purpose in these passages, and how do both subjects serve a similar purpose? Be sure that you see, however, the different methods by which he accomplishes his satiric purpose in these two passages.

3. How would you say that Gulliver's actions in a scene such as the one in which he is first shown to the public (p. 79) affect the reader? How do we feel about what he does here? Can you express your response in one word, or does it take several? How do Gulliver's actions here reflect on human actions in the ordinary world? Does our response to him in this scene affect our way of looking at what people do in the world around us? That is, what does Swift accomplish by placing Gulliver in a world of giants? Find other comparable passages which support your answer to the last question. How is the judgment Swift leads us to make of human actions here similar to that which he led us to in Lilliput? Compare this passage (p. 79) with the one about Lilliputian rope dancing (p. 31), for example. How would you contrast the *methods* by which he leads us to these similar conclusions?

4. If Gulliver's funny performances lead us to reconsider our pride in our importance as human beings, what does his master's treatment of him lead us to see? What aspect of human nature and inclination is focused on in the Brobdingnagian farmer's treatment of Gulliver? While neither Gulliver's actions nor his master's reflect very flatteringly on human nature, how would you characterize each and which would you say embodies the more reprehensible human potentials?

5. If Gulliver is a kind of side-show freak to the Brobdingnagian farmer, what does he become to the Queen? What does the King assume Gulliver is when he first sees how the Queen treats him? What is your response to Gulliver's description of the box the Queen orders for him (pp. 84–85)? Again, how does his position here (though far more comfortable than with the farmer) lead us to reconsider our pride in the importance of human beings?

6. Chapter 5, on various mishaps Gulliver suffers in Brobding-nag, is one of the funniest in the book. What makes it so funny; what are the common characteristics of all the mishaps? While these adventures have little of the specific satiric reference to particular aspects of life in the ordinary world that characterizes a passage like the one on Lilliputian rope-dancing, would you say that it is entirely without satiric implications? What is its reference to common human experience?

7. Notice Swift's repeated attention to apparently random bits of information about customs or habits that conflict with our own. Gulliver remarks incidentally that the Brobdingnagian sabbath is Wednesday and that the King shaves just twice a week; he pays a lot of attention to the foreign names for familiar things, and so on. All of these "facts" seem to have little importance in themselves; why does Swift have Gulliver bother with them? (1) What effect does their presence have on our judgment of Gulliver as an observer and narrator of his experience? (2) What effect do they have upon our way of looking at things we take for granted in our own everyday experience?

8. If we define verbal irony very generally as a statement in which there is some important difference between what seems to be said and what is actually meant, we can see by now that *Gulliver's Travels* is almost constantly ironic. This is true of the work as a whole, and of its details. Using this definition, and bearing in mind that Demosthenes and Cicero were the greatest orators of Greece and Rome, tell precisely what is ironic about the last paragraph on page 102.

9. Swift focuses his satire on quite different objects and his method becomes considerably more intense as we move from Chapter 5 to Chapter 6. Just what is the difference between the subjects Gulliver speaks of in this chapter and what he had spoken of in Chapter 5? And how would you describe his method? Notice the roles that Swift has Gulliver and the King play: what is the relationship between what Gulliver says and the King's response? What is the effect of having the King begin with a series of *questions* and only gradually work up to the powerful assertions with which he concludes his evaluation of Europeans and their institutions?

10. How do you begin to feel about Gulliver as he talks about the glorious advantages of gunpowder in Chapter 7? (1) To what extent does Gulliver here sound much the way he has sounded earlier—notably in his speech to the King in the preceding chapter? (2) And in what ways does he sound different? How would you describe the way that he seems to feel about the bloody and brutal destruction he describes? Is this how you would expect him to feel? Consider the attitude he took toward the Lilliputians' desire that he destroy Blefuscu and the Big-Endian refugees. Can you find other examples in which he stands for moral values that we would expect would make it impossible for him to take the attitude he does toward gunpowder?

11. If this attitude does not seem entirely to fit the character of the Gulliver we have known so far, what does Swift accomplish by having Gulliver talk this way? Would you say that the horrors of gunpowder are more or less vivid to us because Gulliver describes them all in a rather childishly elementary, untechnical way, and without apparent awareness of the possible inhumanity of the processes he describes?

BOOK III

1. How would you describe the relationship between the fact that the men of Laputa employ flappers to draw their attention to conversation (p. 127), that the clothes made for Gulliver do not fit (p. 130), and that their wives are dissatisfied with them (p. 133)? What characteristic of the Laputans is responsible for all? Is this characteristic revealed in other ways in this chapter? Why is it appropriate that such men should occupy an island that flies high above the earth?

2. Remembering that the inhabitants of Laputa are the rulers of the continent below, tell what their habitation of a flying island implies about the relation between rulers and ruled? How does the description on pages 137–38 contribute to our understanding of that relationship?

3. (1) How would you describe the relationship between the various experiments and inventions Gulliver observes in his visit to the Grand Academy of Lagado (Chapter 5)? That is, what do they all have in common? What aspect or tendency of science is Swift satirizing here? Is there any relation between this tendency

of science (or scientists) and the tendency of rulers satirized in Chapter 2? (2) What is Gulliver's manner in describing these crazy projects? Does he talk as if he thinks they are crazy? How does his attitude toward them make the satire more effective than it would be if he spoke very critically of them?

4. But notice that Gulliver's tone changes suddenly as he *does* speak critically of a project in the opening paragraph of Chapter 6. What are the differences (in type and value) between this project and all those described in Chapter 5, and what is gained by having Gulliver disapprove strongly of this one? Notice that this project, which Gulliver criticizes as the work of men "wholly out of their senses," bears a close resemblance to the state of affairs which Gulliver wanted the King of Brobdingnag to believe existed in England (Book II, Chapter 6). There he spoke of such conditions as actual and admirable; here he laughs at them as impossible and senseless. But if Gulliver's attitude toward such governmental policies shifts inconsistently, what *is* consistent about *Swift's* attitude toward them? What is he interested in showing about policies of governments in our world?

5. How does Swift use the past to criticize the present in Gulliver's visit to Glubbdubdrib? Would you say that he always presents the past in the same way, or does he use it differently in different passages? Compare, for example, his treatment of politics in Rome in the paragraph beginning at the bottom of page 163 with his treatment of old English country men in the preceding paragraph on page 163. Do Rome and Old England have the same kind of relation to the present?

6. Gulliver's tone contributes a good deal to the satire on royal presumption and cruelty in Chapter 9. What phrases in particular establish the cool, somewhat noncommittal tone which makes the satire in his account of the King of Luggnagg's receptions at once more amusing and more cutting than outraged disapproval could make it?

7. If Gulliver's tone in the passage just mentioned was cool and largely noncommittal, how would you describe the tone (or attitude implied by the way he talks) when he hears about the Struldbruggs and goes on to talk about what he would do if he could live forever (Chapter 10)? What words would you use to describe the way he sounds and a person who might talk like that?

Why does Swift find it useful here to use a Gulliver who is different (in just this way) from the noncommittal reporter that Gulliver is most of the time? Precisely what has Gulliver ignored about the human condition and about human nature that allows him to speak as he does in describing the possibilities available to one who could live forever? Does human life exemplified in the Struldbruggs seem to you a full and fair picture of our existence? What aspects of our existence is Swift focusing on and forcing us to bear in mind?

BOOK IV

1. Although Gulliver feels that he has "never beheld in all my travels so disagreeable an animal" as the Yahoo, we may be quicker than he to notice some resemblance between this repulsive beast and the species to which Gulliver himself belongs. What parts of the description of his first meeting with them lead us to suspect this similarity?

2. The resemblance of the Houyhnhnms to human beings, on the other hand, has little to do with their appearance and everything to do with their actions; this resemblance is not lost on Gulliver, who thinks they must be magicians only posing as horses. What is your response to the Houyhnhnms in Gulliver's first encounter with them? Would you say that you have different kinds of responses, resulting perhaps from the incongruity of their appearance and their actions?

3. We have become aware of the role of verbal irony in the satire of *Gulliver's Travels,* but we should also recognize an irony of situation, where the real situation is very much different from what someone involved in it supposes. Just how does this kind of irony play through Gulliver's meetings with the Yahoos and the Houyhnhnms in Chapter 1? (Notice particularly such indications of his suppositions about the situation as his repeated reference to his stock of beads and knives.)

4. Irony of situation plays a part in sharpening Gulliver's shocking recognition of the fact that the Yahoo, upon close examination, bears "a perfect human figure" (p. 186). Here it is the pair of Houyhnhnms who are not so fully aware of the true situation as Gulliver. What is it that they do not know which contributes to the pain of Gulliver's growing awareness?

5. What opinion do we form of the Houyhnhnms as we come to know them? (1) What do you think of the way they eat and the manner in which they entertain guests (p. 187); their treatment of Gulliver (p. 188); the status of lying in Houyhnhnmland (pp. 190, 193); the status of other vices (p. 197), especially as this is contrasted with conditions in Europe in Chapters 5 and 6; the status of reason among them (pp. 215–16); their most-valued virtues (p. 216); the values they teach their young (pp. 217–18); their literature and architecture (pp. 220–21)? (2) Do you find that you respond somewhat differently to them, however, on the basis of such things as the opinion of themselves implied by the name they have taken (p. 190); the description of their sex life (p. 216); of their attitude toward the death of loved ones (p. 221); of their awkwardly and elaborately human gestures (pp. 185, 221)? What faculty or characteristic seems to dominate everything they do? Would you say that the picture we get of them is largely admirable or not?

6. And what of the Yahoos? What is their relationship to human beings? We have seen in question 4 that Gulliver soon is forced to recognize that the "deformed" creatures toward whom he felt so much "contempt and aversion" in fact look very like human beings. But is this uncomplimentary resemblance the only blow Gulliver's human pride has to suffer? (1) When the Houyhnhnm makes a close comparison of the physiques of the Yahoos and of the human being in Chapters 4 and 5, what turns out to be their relative merit? (2) In what other direction does he carry his comparison in Chapter 7? In what ways are the results just like those of the physical comparison?

7. On the basis of your answers to questions 5 and 6, how would you characterize the relationship between man and Yahoo on the one hand, and man and Houyhnhnm on the other?

8. We might expect that Gulliver's experience with the exemplary Houyhnhnms would lead him to be just about an ideal human being. But what do you make of his actions when he gets back to our world, particularly his behavior toward Don Pedro and toward his family? How does Gulliver justify his conduct? How does he apparently see himself; does his picture of himself leave anything out? How do his assumptions about himself make the last two paragraphs of the book ironically humorous?

Teaching *Wuthering Heights*

WILLIAM A. MADDEN

Professor of English
Indiana University

That *Wuthering Heights* is an unusual novel is evident from its structure: it contains not one, but two stories, told consecutively and involving two generations—the generation of Heathcliff and Catherine in the first story and the generation of Hareton and Cathy in the second story. The key to the novel is to be found in the relationship between the two stories.

Both stories are set in the narrative frame established by Lockwood and Nelly Dean in the opening chapters (a point to which we will return later). Both stories oscillate between the poles of Wuthering Heights and Thrushcross Grange. Both contain a love-triangle: Heathcliff-Catherine-Edgar Linton, and Hareton-Cathy-Linton Heathcliff. In each triangle the "dark" figure (Heathcliff-Hareton) is an orphan and an outcast, subject to the power of others; in each triangle the "light" figure (Edgar Linton-Linton Heathcliff) enjoys ostensible "security" and exhibits the manners of "polite" society; in each triangle the woman (Catherine-Cathy) moves between the attractions of the dark and the light male figures, marries the "light" figure but loves and seems destined for the dark figure. Both Heathcliff and Hareton are humiliated, later confront their humiliators in a dramatic scene, and triumph over them; both Edgar Linton and Linton Heathcliff are isolated; and both Catherine and Cathy are thrown back upon themselves and confront similar trials by drawing upon inward resources.

The numerous and pointed parallels between the Heathcliff-Catherine and the Hareton-Cathy stories suggest that Emily

Brontë wanted readers to see the two generations as, in some sense, commentaries upon one another. With so much in common, the question of how do the two stories differ therefore becomes an important one. One way of calling attention to the difference is to compare the symbolic juxtapositions that occur in each generation. To this end it is helpful to provide a simple diagram which outlines the main contours of the double plot and at the same time indicates in a graphic way the contrast between events in the first generation and those in the second generation.

Heathcliff-Catherine   Hareton-Cathy

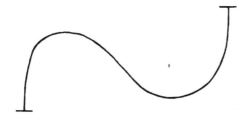

Such a graph not only calls attention to the reversal in the rhythm of the main action, but also implies something about the nature of the action in each part. The first half of *Wuthering Heights* involves either the death or expulsion of the major figures, and may therefore be seen as conforming to the tragic pattern of rise and fall; the second half ends with the hero/heroine's assimilation into society, and may therefore be seen as conforming to the comic pattern. Such a device also will alert students to the fact that the quieter Hareton-Cathy story in the latter half of the novel contains as much "action" as the more tempestuous Heathcliff-Catherine story in the first half, although it is clearly action of a different kind.

The difference between the fate of Catherine Earnshaw and that of Cathy Linton can be explained by the nature of Emily Brontë's central concern. Her sister, Charlotte Brontë, remarked that Emily "held that mercy and forgiveness are the divinest attributes of the Great Being." The double rhythm of *Wuthering Heights* centers around the moral agency of forgiveness: without the power to forgive, without mercy, men are doomed; with it, they can transcend outward circumstances and inward tension and arrive at the moral and psychic maturity upon which civilization rests.

So viewed, *Wuthering Heights* becomes an astonishingly detached exploration of the moral agencies through which the major characters succeed or fail in attaining psychic integration. The Heathcliff-Catherine story is a story of hate, vengeance, isolation, and death; the Hareton-Cathy story is a story of forgiveness, love, integration, and life.

In presenting this double parable *Wuthering Heights* not only asserts men's need to give and accept forgiveness, but also discriminates between those forms of behavior which masquerade as forgiveness and the true thing. In a moment of temporary happiness, for example, Catherine Earnshaw claims: "I'll take no revenge on his [Edgar's] folly—I can afford to suffer anything hereafter" (p. 100),* and later tells Heathcliff in a moment of self-pity, "I won't upbraid you! I forgive you. Forgive me!" (p. 158). But she does not, in fact, forgive either man; rather, torn between Heathcliff and Edgar, she withdraws from the conflict which they provoke within her by regressing, in her final delirium, to the security of a remembered childhood world when the dark Heathcliff impulses and the light Edgar impulses had not yet become fatally separated within her. Unable to blend them in maturity, Catherine obtains revenge by destroying herself, just as Heathcliff will later exact revenge by destroying others. "You and Edgar have broken my heart, Heathcliff! And you both come to bewail the deed to me, as if you were the people to be pitied! I shall not pity you, not I" (p. 155). Catherine's beauty in death testifies to the reality of the integration she had known in the childhood world to which she returns—"No angel in heaven could be more beautiful" (p. 161)—but its inadequacy is likewise evident: in her death mask there is the peace of inexperience and stasis, not of moral maturity.

For moral maturity we must turn to the second generation and especially to the younger Cathy, offspring of Catherine Earnshaw

* Page references are to the Signet Classic edition (CD10), published by The New American Library.

and Edgar Linton, who can forgive both Heathcliff and the wretched Linton Heathcliff. Of the latter, she says: "I felt I must forgive him: and though we should quarrel the next moment, I must forgive him again" (p. 243). She likewise confronts and triumphs over Heathcliff's campaign to make her hate. "I don't hate you," she tells him at one point; "I'm not angry that you struck me. Have you never loved *anybody* . . . ?" (p. 262). Through her capacity to forgive, Cathy finally succeeds in redeeming the brutalized Hareton. "Say you forgive me, Hareton, do! You can make me so happy, by speaking that little word" (p. 299). The theme of forgiveness reflected in these passages permeates the entire novel—its action, its characterization, its symbolic structure, and its manipulation of point of view.

The first story begins with the appearance of Heathcliff, an outcast waif, without Christian name, who has been rescued from the slums of Liverpool by Mr. Earnshaw and who is presented by him to the family at Wuthering Heights "as a gift of God, though it's dark almost as if it came from the devil" (p. 40). Nelly Dean (the narrator of these early events) reports (p. 41) that she was frightened by a "peep at a dirty, ragged, black-haired child," that Mrs. Earnshaw "was ready to fling it out of doors" (the child at this point is referred to by everyone as "it"), and that Hindley and Catherine, the Earnshaw children, instinctively see "it" as a rival, their resentment having been increased by the loss of the gifts, promised by their father, which Heathcliff's arrival has occasioned. Catherine, "grinning and spitting at the stupid little thing," is struck by her father as a consequence. Everyone refuses to have "it" in their rooms on the first night, so Nelly "put it on the landing of the stairs, hoping it might be gone on the morrow."

So the first story opens. Heathcliff, the "dark" element in life, occasions fright, dislike, and cruelty; the fear and bitterness caused by his introduction into the family, though later meliorated to some degree by Mr. Earnshaw's protective care and Catherine's growing sympathy for him, persist. For a time, it is true, there seems to be hope for the dark child in Catherine's growing fondness for him, but when, at fourteen, Heathcliff resolves, in order to make himself worthy of Catherine, to "be good," and asks Nelly to help him to be so, his resolve is promptly snuffed out by the malicious cruelty of Hindley, by an unintended insult of Edgar, and by Catherine's toleration of their treatment of him. A terrible exchange between Heathcliff and Nelly follows:

> On my inquiring the subject of his thought, he answered gravely—
> "I'm trying to settle how I shall pay Hindley back. I don't care how long I wait, if I can only do it, at last. I hope he will not die before I do!"
> "For shame, Heathcliff" said I. "It is for God to punish wicked people; we should learn to forgive."
> "No, God won't have the satisfaction that I shall," he returned. "I only wish I knew the best way! Let me alone, and I'll plan it out: while I'm thinking of that, I don't feel pain" (pp. 63–64).

When Catherine a few years later deceives herself into thinking that she can have Edgar as well as Heathcliff and marries the former, Edgar is added to Heathcliff's list of enemies and his rage eventually destroys first Catherine, then his own wife and son, and later threatens Edgar, Cathy, and Hareton. Heathcliff's resolve to get revenge is thus sustained with destructive fury for some two hundred pages of the novel. The day on which he made that resolve was Christmas.

The counterthrust to Heathcliff's unforgiving rage appears in the second generation. The action begins with the appearance of Cathy at Thrushcross Grange. Once there, she soon encounters the dark figure of Hareton at Wuthering Heights, but now the processes of the first half of the novel are reversed. Brutalized by Heathcliff as Heathcliff had earlier been brutalized by Hindley Earnshaw, Hareton nevertheless continues to love Heathcliff. Disgusted by Linton Heathcliff as Catherine had earlier been disgusted by Edgar Linton, Cathy nevertheless forgives Linton and looks after him. The difference in the moral quality of Hareton's and Cathy's responses explains how the almost identical circumstances and events of the two generations issue in such radically different results. The action in the second half of the novel is no less intense than in the first half, but it is action of a rarer kind. When Heathcliff, hoping to awaken in Cathy the hatred for his son Linton which he himself feels, confronts her with the fact that Linton's malice is prevented from injuring her only by his impotence, Cathy replies:

"I know he has a bad nature; he's your son. But I'm glad I've a better to forgive it; and I know he loves me and for that reason I love him. Mr. Heathcliff, *you* have *nobody* to love you; and, however miserable you make us, we shall still have the revenge of thinking that your cruelty arises from your greater misery!" (p. 273).

Cathy's "revenge" thus takes the form of an insight that leads her to understanding. Her recognition that Heathcliff's cruelty arises from his misery and loneliness ultimately disarms Heathcliff and frees Cathy from his destructive hate. When Heathcliff later sees in the younger Cathy the image of the Catherine whom he had loved and lost, he cannot bring himself to destroy her; at the same time, crippled by his rage, neither can he bring himself to forgive her. He lives out his last days in increasing withdrawal, awaiting reunion with the one good thing he had known in life.

The symbols of light and dark which dominate both the plot and the characterization of *Wuthering Heights* are basic. The forces and figures of darkness take on symbolic dimension through their affiliation with the value of energy and the threat of chaos; the forces and figures of light are likewise ambiguous, symbolizing both the value of order and the threat of sterility. In this respect Emily Brontë's use of "light" and "dark" point to what Nietzsche later called the Apollonian and Dionysian impulses in life. Pure light makes for sterility and stasis; pure darkness makes for destruction and anarchy; psychic integration depends upon the human capacity to blend the Apollonian and the Dionysian in a life of ordered energy. Socially the two elements are represented by the "dark" Wuthering Heights of the Earnshaws and the "light" Thrushcross Grange of the Lintons, each having its own strengths and its own weaknesses, and our sense of the individual characters is determined by their places on this light-dark scale of values. Heathcliff, "dark" in nature and cut off from the "light," becomes pure destructive energy; Linton Heathcliff, "light" in nature and cut off from the energy of "darkness," becomes frozen in sterile impotence. Between these extremes, ranging from darker to lighter but possessing something of the quality of both, are Hareton, Catherine, Cathy, and Edgar. Hareton, we are told, has Catherine Earnshaw's eyes; Cathy has the Earnshaw eyes, but the Linton complexion; Edgar is light-haired and soft-featured, "pensive and amiable," "sweet," and "almost too graceful"; and Linton has Isabella's Linton-eyes, "only morbid," and is portrayed as looking like Edgar's younger brother, only sickly.

Another symbolic extension of the light-dark imagery can be traced in Emily Brontë's use of locks of hair. Just after Catherine dies, the integration which she had vainly sought in the naïve expectation that she could have both Heathcliff and Edgar on her own terms is symbolized by Nelly's weaving together and placing in a locket, which is to be buried with Catherine, a lock of dark Earnshaw hair and a lock of light Linton hair. The desired "integration" remains external, a state piously wished for but unachieved. At the end of the story of the second generation, on the other hand, we see Cathy and Hareton together, already on the road to mutual love, "her light shining ringlets blending at intervals, with his brown locks" (p. 292) as she bends to help Hareton with his studies. The blending of the locks becomes an outward sign of an inward state of psychic balance and health, the state which is the necessary basis of civilized society.

The point is reinforced by equivalent symbols drawn from nature. The presiding celestial light in the first half of the novel is the moon, which eerily illuminates a harsh demonic landscape of moorland wilderness populated by gnarled oaks and thorn trees, wolves, predatory dogs, and snakes. The presiding light in the second half is the sun, which illuminates a "comic" landscape of gardens and parks populated by larch trees, lambs, doves, lapwings, and larks. At the end of the novel, Lockwood, walking the path between Thrushcross Grange and Wuthering Heights, finds himself in a twilight that transfigures the entire landscape; "the glow of a sinking sun behind, and the mild glory of a rising moon in front, one fading, and the other brightening" (p. 291). As he arrives at a point halfway between the two worlds of darkness and light, he observes: "all that remained of day was a beamless, amber light along the west; but I could see every pebble on the

path, and every blade of grass by that splendid moon" (p. 291).
Sentimentally moved by the moonlight, Lockwood characteristically romanticizes and falsifies the scene. What we feel is that
sun and moon have reached a momentary balance which serves as
a cosmic endorsement of the community of forgiveness and love
tentatively established by Cathy and Hareton.

Finally, there is Emily Brontë's brilliant manipulation of the
point of view from which we see events in *Wuthering Heights,* perhaps her greatest contribution to the development of novelistic
technique. The plot graph suggested earlier omits this element,
and a more adequate diagram of the novel might therefore be
something like the following

with the dotted circle representing Lockwood and his values and
the solid circle Nelly and her values. At the beginning of the novel
Lockwood and Nelly appear to the reader to be "civilized" persons
who must tell terrible, seemingly incredible, things of which they
were merely the spectators. Their conscious "respectability" and
their "common-sense" directly appeal to equivalent characteristics
in the average reader, who looks in his reading for what will confirm his own sense of things. While their very ordinariness seems
to guarantee their reliability, and thereby guarantees the authen-
ticity of events which might well seem improbable if presented
directly, it is nevertheless exposed, as the novel progresses, as a
fatal triviality of mind and character. Thus Emily Brontë woos the
complacent reader into a "willing suspension of disbelief" that

enables her gradually to move us into the strange (but far more real) world of Wuthering Heights and Thrushcross Grange. One of the most effective ways to alert students to Emily Brontë's irony is to invite them to examine the reliability of Lockwood and Nelly as informants and commentators.

We learn that Lockwood, for example, is in flight from the very faint possibility of real involvement with another person, more specifically, that he is escaping from a possible sexual encounter, and that he seeks instead the less dangerous company of a fellow "gentleman." After his first meeting with Heathcliff, he believes for a short time that he has found what he was searching for: "A perfect misanthropist's Heaven—and Mr. Heathcliff and I are such a suitable pair to divide the desolation between us. A capital fellow!" (p. 9). But by the end of Chapter 1 he has been awakened to the facts: "It is astonishing how sociable I feel myself compared with him" (p. 14). Even Lockwood's misanthropy turns out to be superficial and self-regarding. His self-deception, not only about Heathcliff but more importantly about himself, is revealed by his dreams. Under the impact of his encounter with Heathcliff and Wuthering Heights, Lockwood undergoes—really suffers from— two terrifying dreams, both precipitated by his reading of Catherine's diary. The first is a vision of a dingy chapel in which a sermon on the four hundred and ninety-first sin—the unforgivable sin—by the Reverend Jabes Branderham stirs him into challenging the preacher and thereby provoking a battle which eventually involves the preacher and his entire congregation, until "every man's hand was against his neighbor" (pp. 28–29). We are in this way introduced to the theme of forgiveness, and to the sustained violation of it which will occupy the first half of the novel. The second dream, which immediately follows the first, concerns the ghost of Catherine which attempts to enter the window by Lockwood's bed. Lockwood tricks her and, made cruel by fear, defends himself by rubbing her wrists on the broken window pane. The "sociable" Lockwood, an outwardly complacent and respectable figure of light, reveals the latent aggressiveness and destructive fear which he censures in Heathcliff, but which also resides and works unconsciously, beneath the surface of his "civilized" manner, in Lockwood himself.

Through Lockwood we are introduced to Nelly Dean. Though by background, temperament, and habit much closer than Lockwood to the world which we are about to encounter, Nelly nevertheless prides herself on possessing a realistic, "common-sense" view of life very much akin to Lockwood's, although in her it is tricked out in a superficial piety to which Lockwood does not pretend and which generally conceals Nelly's essential superstitiousness. She thus mediates for the reader between the utterly shallow and self-deceived view represented by Lockwood—which Emily Brontë quickly exposes for what it is—and the frightening world of undisguised dark and light impulses which dominates the inner story. The marvelous irony at work in Emily Brontë's handling of the "frame" enables her to expose the limitations of the very personae through whom she has lured us into accepting the hard truth which she wishes to convey. Only the Lockwoods and the Nelly Deans of the world can at the end of the novel accept the former's sentimental and the latter's matter-of-fact superstitious response to the events they have witnessed. Nelly concludes: "I believe the dead are at peace, but it is not right to speak of them with levity." Lockwood, visiting the graves, wonders "how anyone could ever imagine unquiet slumbers, for the sleepers in that quiet earth" (p. 320).

Thus, the last voices that we hear, like the first, are those of Nelly and Lockwood, and their comments ease the reader back out into the world of normality, but their complacency will not deceive the attentive reader regarding what has happened in between. From the moment in the third chapter when we hear the Reverend Jabes Branderham's sermon during Lockwood's dream-vision and witness its results, we are aware that the novel has forgiveness as its central theme. Through dreams, letters, and speeches that expose the inmost feelings of her characters, Emily Brontë explores the timeless world of psychic impulse where the springs of forgiveness and revenge reside. Civilization, Emily Brontë suggests, rests ultimately upon the maturity of individual men and women, but their maturity in turn depends upon the health of the civilization into which they are born. Heathcliff, the stray waif, is the embodiment of an undifferentiated power for good or evil which it is in civilized society's hands either to channel and make creative or to thwart and make destructive. The tragedy is that civilization in 1785 was unable to channel his exceptional energy into creative action.

Christian as well as seasonal imagery is brought to bear upon the double rhythm of *Wuthering Heights*—Heathcliff's alienation is finally determined on Christmas and Hareton's integration commences on Whitsuntide*—but Emily Brontë is not writing a Christian parable. Rather, through the sophisticated use of point of view, irony, symbol, and circumstantial realism, she is translating into the novel form the aspiration toward wholeness. This aspiration, the novel affirms, can be realized through recognizing that the only unforgivable sin is the refusal to forgive. While to be able to forgive is, for Emily Brontë, a sign of redemption and the badge of psychic maturity in the novel, she does not attempt to tell us what the ultimate sources of grace, of psychic health, are —*why* Catherine should be unable to forgive, and as a result should regress, is no more explainable than Cathy's capacity to forgive. But the symbolic genealogy of the younger Cathy indicates the conditions for such forgiveness: the blending of the dark Earnshaw energy with the impulse for order represented by the Lintons. Of the two perhaps the former enjoys priority, since it is better to act than simply to exist. But when we do act, whether we love and forgive or hate and seek vengeance—and both are always possible—entails predictable social as well as personal consequences. Such is the law of psychic and social existence, a law which Emily Brontë bases not upon faith but upon experience. Students who vicariously experience the inner nature of hate and love, of revenge and forgiveness, as rendered in the two stories in *Wuthering Heights,* may perhaps come away with at least an obscure sense of what, in Emily Brontë's view, it means to "grow up."

STUDY QUESTIONS

CHAPTERS 1–9

1. Lockwood narrates the events in Chapter 1. Why has he come to a remote part of England? Why is he at first attracted to Heath-

---

* The Christian liturgical season celebrating the descent of the Spirit upon the Apostles.

cliff? Does his attitude change during the course of the chapter? In Chapter 2, Lockwood compares himself to King Lear: is this comparison appropriate or not? Defend your answer.

2. Who owns Thrushcross Grange? How far is it from Wuthering Heights? How old is Heathcliff? How is he related to Hareton and Cathy? How old is Cathy? What does she think of the servant, Joseph? Do you think that Joseph is meant to be a comic character? Why, or why not?

3. In what kind of book has Catherine Earnshaw kept her diary? What date does it bear? What does Catherine's listing of various possible last names for herself—Earnshaw, Heathcliff, and Linton—suggest about her? What does she think of her brother Hindley and his wife?

4. What were Sundays like at Wuthering Heights? Had they always been that way?

5. Who is Lockwood's "guide" in his first dream? Is there any connection between the two dreams he has? What do they suggest about him? Is there a natural explanation for his having these dreams at this time? Why does Lockwood ask Nelly Dean to tell him the story of Wuthering Heights?

6. How long has Nelly Dean been living at Thrushcross Grange? According to Nelly, what is Heathcliff's main interest? Where did Mr. Earnshaw find Heathcliff? How does the family at Wuthering Heights respond when Mr. Earnshaw brings Heathcliff home? Nelly reports that Heathcliff generally told the truth when he was a child, and yet "bred bad feeling in the house." What do you think of Nelly's evaluation of Heathcliff?

7. Why does Emily Brontë use Lockwood and Nelly as narrators?

8. What is Mr. Earnshaw like? How does Catherine treat him? How does he treat her? How do Heathcliff and Catherine respond to Mr. Earnshaw's death?

9. What do Heathcliff and Catherine think of Thrushcross Grange when they look through the window? What do they think of the Lintons? What is the name of the Linton dog? What is old Mr. Linton like?

10. What effect does Catherine's stay at Thrushcross Grange have upon her? What is Nelly's advice to Heathcliff after Catherine

returns to Wuthering Heights from the Grange? Is it good advice?
What happens to Heathcliff's resolution to "be good"? Why? What
is the next resolution? What day is it?

1. What is the effect of Heathcliff's return upon Catherine's and
Edgar's marriage? What was Heathcliff's original reason for returning? Why does he change his mind? Why does he become
interested in Isabella?

2. Trace carefully Nelly's role in the quarrel between Heathcliff and Edgar and during Catherine's illness. Would you say she
is a servant to be trusted?

3. Words relating to vengeance and forgiveness occur fairly
frequently in the speeches of Catherine, Heathcliff, and Edgar.
Discuss the attitude of each character towards forgiveness. Why
does Catherine die? What do you think of Nelly's comment upon
Catherine's death?

1. Nelly is the same age as Hindley. How old is Hindley when
he dies?

2. What is Heathcliff's motive for raising Hareton as his son?
How does Hareton reenact Heathcliff's earlier humiliation? What
causes the quarrel between Cathy and Linton? How do their
"heavens" differ? Does the confrontation between Hareton and
Linton remind you of any earlier scene in the novel?

3. Compare the Catherine-Edgar and Cathy-Linton relationships. How are they alike and how do they differ?

1. What is Edgar's attitude during his last years towards Heathcliff? Compare Edgar's death to Catherine's and try to explain the
difference.

2. How does Cathy respond to Heathcliff's brutality? Does her
response differ from Linton's? Nelly's? Lockwood's? Trace the
history of Cathy's locket. Is there any symbolic significance in this
history? What "revenge" does Cathy take on Heathcliff?

3. How does Hareton's relationship to Cathy change? Does Emily Brontë offer any reason for this change?

4. What does Heathcliff think of the "conclusion" of his campaign? How do you account for his feelings? What would he like to do with the property he owns? Why? Compare Heathcliff's death-mask to Catherine's. To Edgar's.

5. What is Nelly's final view of the events? Lockwood's? Are their comments adequate?

Teaching *Heart of Darkness*

PHILIP B. DAGHLIAN

In addition to being a richly complex story, Joseph Conrad's *Heart of Darkness* is of an excellent length to demonstrate the value of close reading as a means of studying prose fiction. The teacher who is fully aware of the advantages of reading closely a poem, or even a short story, may well quail before the problem of reading a novel in the same way. *Heart of Darkness* is long enough to demand some kind of sustained treatment in presentation, yet not so long that it cannot be handled in from four to five class meetings. Reminders of the values to be derived from close and careful reading might then carry over into longer works, even though class time may not permit extended treatment. Since *Heart of Darkness* reflects so many complexities of meaning and significance, a case can be made for studying it rather late in the high school curriculum.

Although the information is not particularly important in terms of literary analysis, the fact remains that Conrad spent six months in the Congo in 1890 and made the long inland voyage which supplied much of the material for the externals at least of *Heart of Darkness*. He later called the development of the Belgian Congo "the vilest scramble for loot that ever disfigured the history of human conscience and geographical exploration."

Although its complexity makes *Heart of Darkness* difficult to summarize very satisfactorily, there are various levels at which it may be read. One could present it as rather fuzzy melodrama and travelogue, except that it is not a very successful story in this light. Some might be tempted to treat the story as an impressionistic account of the evils of exploitation attending the early ivory trade in the Congo. A powerful objection to this approach is that it is nonliterary. Artistic effect would rapidly be lost under the impact of sociology and history. A much more plausible level of approach would be to read it as a story of the jungle's effect upon a man of extraordinary potentialities for good and for evil (Kurtz). It may be possible to develop a further broadening of the significance of this reading at the end of the study, depending on the immediate classroom situation at that time.

The first matter to establish about the story is the matter of narration.* There is a fairly elaborate frame device which is maintained throughout. A group of former mariners, all inactive on the sea now except Marlow, are on a sailing yacht in the Thames estuary at sunset, waiting for the tide to change. The story is told by Marlow to his companions; there are several reminders of an audience throughout the story (pp. 95, 103, 120†), and a return to the scene on the yacht at the end. There is a conscious intent to widen the scope of the story, "to evoke the great spirit of the past upon the lower reaches of the Thames" (p. 66). It is against the meditation evoked by the role of the Thames in the history of civilization that Marlow observes that "this also has been one of the dark places of the earth" (p. 67).

In addition to knowing how the story is told, we must recognize aspects of Marlow's character in order to understand his narrative method. In the first place, Marlow was not an ordinary matter-of-fact Englishman. He was still an active sailor, with the mark of the East upon him: ". . . he had the pose of a Buddha preaching in European clothes and without a lotus-flower" (p. 69). Then, unlike many sailors, to Marlow "the meaning of an episode was not inside like a kernel but outside, enveloping the tale which brought it out only as a glow brings out a haze, in the likeness of one of those misty halos that sometimes are made visible by the spectral illumination of moonshine" (p. 68). Equally untypical was his attitude toward colonization:

> The conquest of the earth, which usually means the taking it
> away from those who have a different complexion or slightly

---

* See also Kenneth R. Johnston's treatment of this matter in his sequence on the short story in this volume (pp. 115-118).
† Page references are to the Signet Classics edition (CD4).

flatter nose than ourselves, is not a pretty thing when you look into it too much. What redeems it is the idea only. An idea at the back of it; not a sentimental pretence but an idea; and an unselfish belief in the idea—something you can set up, and bow down before, and offer a sacrifice to . . . (pp. 69–70).

Two other traits of Marlow are crucial to the story—his attitude toward women's unrealistic view of life and his violent hatred of lies.

It's queer how out of touch with truth women are. They live in a world of their own, and there has never been anything like it, and never can be. It is too beautiful altogether, and if they were to set it up it would go to pieces before the first sunset. Some confounded fact that we men have been living contentedly with ever since the day of creation would start up and knock the whole thing over (pp. 76–77).

You know I hate, detest, and can't bear a lie, not because I am straighter than the rest of us, but simply because it appalls me. There is a taint of death, a flavour of mortality in lies—which is exactly what I hate and detest in the world—what I want to forget. It makes me miserable and sick, like biting something rotten would do (p. 94).

Marlow views the entire journey into the heart of darkness in the light of these attributes, and tells his story so that a listener must consider it in the same way. The omniscient narrator observes "that we were fated . . . to hear about one of Marlow's inconclusive experiences" (p. 70). There is a constant intent of a universalizing quality throughout the whole story.

The "haze" enveloping Marlow's experience is objectified in seven scenes: (1) The account of Fresleven, Marlow's Danish predecessor, who was killed by the natives in a pointless scuffle provoked by an argument about two black hens (p. 72). (2) The knitting women and the map of Africa in the Company offices (p. 73). (3) Marlow's examination by the doctor, with his interest in the changes Africa brings about in individuals (pp. 75–76). (4) The shelling of the bush. "In the empty immensity of earth, sky, and water, there she was, incomprehensible, firing into a continent" (p. 78). The first benefit of civilization is to call the natives

Enemies. (5) The chain gang, who are dignified with the title of Criminals. Marlow realizes that he will encounter in this land "a flabby, pretending, weak-eyed devil of a rapacious and pitiless folly" (p. 81). (6) The grove of dying Negroes, Workers, who had been recruited "in all the legality of time contracts" and are now cast off to die (p. 82). (7) The chief accountant (pp. 83–85). The first three of these scenes reflect a sense of vague unreality, appropriate to a city of the whited sepulcher, of hollow men (p. 73). The four remaining are marked by a much harsher irony, as Marlow gets to Africa. With the accountant's last words to Marlow (p. 85) we gradually begin to see the plot developing: Kurtz, a remarkable man, is to be the goal of Marlow's journey up the Congo.

With Marlow's arrival at the Central Station three factors begin to sharpen his interest in Kurtz: (1) In contrast to the evil natures of the manager's group Kurtz is presented as an emissary of progress. (2) Marlow becomes aware of an active plot against Kurtz. (3) Suspected by the manager of belonging to the idealistic set in Europe responsible for Kurtz's appointment, Marlow is forced to think of himself as being on Kurtz's side.

During Marlow's uneasy interview with the manager (pp. 87–89) there is much talk of Kurtz. The manager's appraisal of the time needed to repair the boat is very nicely estimated. Kurtz should be dead in three months or so. Marlow learns more about Kurtz in the conversation with the manager's agent, the brickmaker waiting to make bricks (pp. 89–95). Kurtz is an artist and an emissary of progress. Marlow, "of the new gang," is supposedly connected with him. Marlow remembers his conversation with his aunt (p. 76), when she talked to him of his mission as "an emissary of light, something like a lower sort of apostle." Marlow, despite his great dislike of lies (p. 94), lets them think he is on Kurtz's side. This action is related of course to the great lie Marlow has to tell in Part III to lay Kurtz's ghost forever. At this stage in the story Marlow finds himself, as in a dream, forced to take sides with a person of whom he knows nothing.

The talk of rivets (pp. 95–97) in connection with repairing the steamboat represents Marlow's desire for tangible things, his way of keeping up, "against the great demoralization of the land," like the accountant's starched linen (p. 83). As Marlow observed, "rivets were what really Mr. Kurtz wanted, if he had only known it" (p. 96). By using his supposed influence with the powers back home, Marlow forces the agent to write for rivets, despite the veiled warning that no man in the jungle bears a charmed life.

With the last sentence of Part I, expressing curiosity about Kurtz, Marlow still thinks of him as an emissary of progress, a "man who had come out equipped with moral ideas" (p. 99), perhaps the only man in Africa with "an idea . . . something you can set up, and bow down before . . ." (pp. 69–70). Up to this point the reader knows little about Kurtz except that he has become Marlow's goal, and that he possesses great powers for good.

Part II of the story presents Marlow's trip up the river, culminating in his finally getting to Kurtz. Overhearing the manager and his uncle discussing Kurtz (pp. 99–102), Marlow realizes the manager's great fear of Kurtz, and he identifies himself with Kurtz, who seems to be a person of immense potentialities for good and therefore a threat to the manager and his kind. It is only at the end of this section that we discover the actual degradation to which Kurtz has sunk.

The universal aspect of the trip is stressed from the start: "Going up that river was like travelling back to the earliest beginnings of the world . . ." (p. 102). Marlow manages to escape "the stillness of an implacable force brooding over an inscrutable intention" (p. 103) because of the demands of running the boat, what he calls "mere incidents of the surface." Yet there is the constant awareness of the pressing fascination of the jungle, the temptation to respond to the appeal of savagery which lurks in us all (pp. 105–106), what Marlow had earlier called the "fascination of the abomination" (p. 69). Only through the "surface-truth" of having to cope with keeping the boiler fired or avoiding snags in the river can an ordinary person like Marlow maintain his equilibrium (pp. 106–107). The book on seamanship is presented as another example of the "singleness of intention" (p. 108) that can save a man in the jungle. We gradually realize that Kurtz has yielded to the temptation of the heart of darkness, whereas Marlow did not.

Through the early stages of the journey Marlow records his increasing interest in Kurtz: "I was then rather excited at the pros-

pect of meeting Kurtz" (p. 102); for Marlow the river seemed to
crawl toward Kurtz (p. 104); Marlow would watch a tree ahead
"to measure our progress towards Kurtz by . . ." (p. 109). "The
approach to this Kurtz grubbing for ivory in the wretched bush
was beset by as many dangers as though he had been an enchanted
princess sleeping in a fabulous castle" (p. 114).
During the attack in the jungle Marlow realizes that he had
been looking forward to a talk with Kurtz. At this point Marlow
breaks his narration to describe Kurtz as he actually saw him (pp.
119–22). He remembers Kurtz chiefly as a voice: " 'My Intended,
my ivory, my station, my river, my —' everything belonged to him"
(p. 121). He had literally "taken a high seat amongst the devils
of the land" (p. 122). Marlow tells of reading Kurtz's report to the
International Society for the Suppression of Savage Customs: "a
beautiful piece of writing," but essentially false, with the only true
part of the pamphlet the scribbled postscript, "Exterminate all the
brutes," which must have been written at some time after Kurtz had
succumbed to "certain midnight dances ending with unspeakable
rites, which . . . were offered up to him . . ." (p. 123). Marlow's
commentary on Kurtz is that "he had no restraint" (p. 124). To
the tattered Russian sailor, however, Kurtz's effect was to "enlarge
the mind" (pp. 126–28), to impress the impressionable.
In the final section of the story the moral conflict comes to the
issue and is resolved. Now Marlow must side with Kurtz against
the manager not because of external circumstances as before, but
by a conscious act of moral volition.
The actual picture of Kurtz when we see him at last belies all
his advance notices. Marlow sees the heads on the stakes (p. 132),
the heads of Rebels against Kurtz. During the rites attending the
celebration of Kurtz by the natives, "they would crawl" (p. 133).
Everything about Kurtz was a lie, including his name (p. 135).
All the tributes to Kurtz had come to Marlow at second hand. We
never see Kurtz as a powerful figure, and we have only the evidence of all with whom he came in contact, including Marlow
himself. Kurtz was completely hollow, but in a special way. He
had many talents, including music, journalism, poetry, but he
failed to realize any of this potential because he lacked the final
core of belief, of something real.

The barbarically attractive jungle woman (pp. 136–37) is in contrast to Kurtz's Intended. She is equal to The Intended in her devotion to Kurtz, but she is opposed to The Intended, as representing the primeval attraction of the heart of darkness. She is so attractive because she signifies the spell of the jungle (pp. 105–106). And Kurtz had yielded to this spell.

During Kurtz's attempt to escape into the jungle (pp. 141–44), *he* crawled now, even as the natives had crawled before him. In trying to break "the heavy, mute spell of the wilderness" over Kurtz, Marlow is inspired to tell him, "You will be lost . . . —utterly lost" (p. 143). Finally, he gets Kurtz back by unspecified means.

Marlow was the only person on the boat who saw anything of the dying Kurtz as the trip down the river started. He watched with fascination as the last moment came, and he heard the final cry, "The horror! The horror!" (p. 147). These words, together with "Exterminate all the brutes" (p. 123), were the only true things Kurtz ever said.

By now we must address the question why a free man like Marlow should have had to choose between the two evils of the manager and his gang on the one hand, and Kurtz on the other. Presumably it is part of Marlow's price for dealing at all with the heart of darkness, as he did by taking the job in the first place. Throughout the experience Marlow finds himself confronted by a choice of nightmares and by the need of remaining loyal to the nightmare of his choice (pp. 138, 141, 146). Marlow finally chose Kurtz because Kurtz had summed up: "The horror!" It was a completely evil summation, but Kurtz had forced himself to make it and had thereby achieved a kind of victory (p. 149). But this victory does not absolve Kurtz, because he cannot be absolved.

Marlow finally lays the ghost of Kurtz and discharges the obligations of his loyalty to him by a lie to The Intended. He must suffer some taint since, like Kurtz, he has made a voluntary choice of moral evils. Marlow's act must be considered against the twin facts of his violent hatred of lies (p. 94), and his conviction that women live completely out of touch with reality (pp. 76–77).

During his interview with The Intended, Marlow discovers in her "a mature capacity for fidelity, for belief, for suffering" (p. 153). "For her he [Kurtz] had died only yesterday" (p. 154).

Eventually Marlow finds himself telling the great lie to The Intended: "The last word he pronounced was—your name" (p. 157). The experience has finally worked itself to an end. The final paragraph returns the story to the Thames estuary, and there is a universalizing quality related to the scene at the opening of the story.

Depending on the reaction and interest of a given class, a teacher may sometimes find it feasible to suggest a further level of significance for the story. He may wish to suggest that we have here a meditation on the exceedingly thin margin that divides what we call civilization from primeval savagery. Early in the story Marlow talks of living in a flicker of light where the darkness was only yesterday (p. 68). He describes the experience with Kurtz as "the farthest point of navigation and the culminating point of my experience" (p. 70). At this point in the story Marlow, looking back, can see the full significance of his trip.

Though most of us respond occasionally, or at least potentially, to the primeval sides of our natures, most of us also manage to keep out of danger. Convention, laws, policemen, what the neighbors might say, and so on, keep us from succumbing in most instances. Only where these external inhibitions do not apply, as in the jungle, does the ultimate and true test come. And even here the results are not foreordained. In terms of this story there are three ways in which individuals can respond to the temptations of the heart of darkness, wherever they are encountered (p. 122): (1) An individual may be so foolish and so innocent that he does not know that he is in danger and is therefore unharmed. The tattered Russian sailor exemplifies this position in the story. (2) He may be so noble and so exalted a creature "as to be altogether deaf and blind to anything but heavenly sights and sounds." Kurtz's Intended falls readily into this category. (3) Finally, there are ordinary people, like Marlow, for whom the earth "is a place to live in, where we must put up . . . and not be contaminated." Here man survives through "powers of devotion, not to yourself, but to an obscure, back-breaking business."

The power of evil, in other words, is not something that comes to us only out of the jungle. It is always around us, but most of the time it is neutralized by the conventions of the world we ordinarily live in. It is only in the acid test of an isolation like Kurtz's that the individual is called on to face up to surviving or succumbing to the power of evil.

Note for the teacher

Robert Kimbrough, ed., *Heart of Darkness*, Norton Critical Edition (N307), includes, along with an authoritative text of the story, miscellaneous background material and critical selections. The teacher should understand that this volume is much too advanced for high school students, and that it can not take the place of the teacher's own carefully developed analysis.

STUDY QUESTIONS

PART I

1. What is the purpose of Marlow's meditation on the Roman conquest of Britain? Point out the places where the author makes it clear that Marlow is telling the story. What effect does this knowledge have on the reader?

2. What is the significance of the account of Fresleven? of the two knitting women and the map of Africa? of the Company doctor?

3. By what means has civilization come to dignify African natives as Enemies, Workers, Criminals?

4. What is the significance to Marlow of the Chief Accountant?

5. Clearly explain Marlow's attitude toward women, and toward telling lies. How are these attitudes related to the way in which he tells the story?

6. What does Marlow learn in his interview with the manager?

7. Indicate clearly what Marlow learns about Kurtz in Part I. By the end of this section Marlow is curious about Kurtz, but does he have any reason to think that Kurtz is anything other than the prodigy he has been described as?

PART II

1. What does Marlow learn as he overhears the conversation between the manager and his uncle?

2. What is the effect on Marlow of the trip up the river? Is

there any relationship with the Romans on the Thames centuries earlier? What kinds of things occupy Marlow's attention on the trip? What connection is there between these matters and the discussion of rivets in Part I (pp. 95–97)?

3. What is the relevance of the tattered copy of *An Inquiry into some Points of Seamanship?*

4. How is the passage on pages 105–106 related to the term "the fascination of the abomination" on page 69?

5. Pick out the many places in this section where Kurtz is Marlow's goal, the object of his increasing interest, despite the fact that we come more and more to realize that Kurtz is not what he is cracked up to be. Why should Marlow, an intelligent observer, continue nonetheless to be attracted to Kurtz?

6. What does Marlow report about Kurtz when he starts talking about him in the midst of the account of the attack in the jungle? What does Marlow mean by saying that Kurtz was a voice? Explain the importance of the report to the International Society for the Suppression of Savage Customs—and of its postscript.

7. Who was the Russian sailor? What relationship does he have in the story to the manager? to Kurtz? to Marlow?

PART III

1. What is the significance of the heads on stakes to Kurtz? to Marlow? What is the point of referring to the natives as Rebels?

2. Compare in some detail the actuality of Kurtz with all the reports we have had about him.

3. What is the significance of the savage woman? Why is she so barbarically attractive?

4. Give an account of Kurtz's attempted escape and Marlow's successful attempt to bring him back. How did Marlow manage to engage Kurtz's attention? How important is the fact that the precise means of getting Kurtz to return are not specified?

5. Describe and comment on Kurtz's death. Why does Marlow determine to remain true to Kurtz's memory? Does this mean that Marlow forgives Kurtz? Can anyone forgive Kurtz?

6. Describe Marlow's visit with The Intended. Why does he tell her a lie? Does he merely want to spare her feelings? Bear in mind Marlow's attitudes toward women and toward lies.

GENERAL QUESTIONS

1. Where is the heart of darkness? How does it operate on people like Kurtz? like Marlow? like The Intended? like the Russian sailor?

2. Is this only a story about life in the jungle, of the evils of colonization? What is the story *about*, in its broadest sense?

3. Can a Kurtz be found only away from civilization?

4. In what ways is *Heart of Darkness* a moral story? Is this the same thing as a story with a moral? Why, or why not?

Teaching *Siddhartha*

ROY L. FELSHER

AN ASIAN TALE

Siddhartha is a young Indian living at a time of great religious ferment (the sixth century B.C.). Dissatisfied with the quality of life in his village, he sets out on a lifelong quest for spiritual happiness. Hermann Hesse's novel is the story of this quest, told with a combination of dignity and simplicity reminiscent of the finest Biblical prose.

Siddhartha encounters many teachers: the wandering Samanas, ascetic pilgrims who preach a traditional Hindu doctrine; Gotama, the Buddha, who excites all India with the promise of a new path to salvation; and Kamaswami, the merchant, who shows the pleasures of worldly success. Siddhartha learns to venerate each of his teachers, but he cannot remain with them, for he is driven by a need to find his own truths and his own personal salvation.

Inspired, perhaps, by the successful works of Rudyard Kipling and Joseph Conrad, many American and European authors have set their novels in the exotic East. *Siddhartha* was among the first and most successful of these recent works.

The Asian setting has certain advantages for a novelist. It allows a more searching account of manners and customs than popular taste will permit in novels with more familiar settings. In recent novels set in Asia—Maugham's *The Razor's Edge*, Greene's *The Quiet American*, and Forster's *A Passage to India*—we see that at least one of the characters functions as a spokesman for Western civilization. There are dramatic possibilities in the confrontation of East and West that we respond to. In *Siddhartha*, of course, all of the characters are Asian, but the principle remains the same.

Discussion of the novel, then, might center upon the ways that the author manages to make this Asian story serve as a critique of both East and West.

Students will appreciate Hesse's favorable view of the East. All of the characters are Indian, and together they have an impressive array of talents, manners, and values which show Asian society at the time of the Buddha at its most attractive. The omniscient narrator registers approval when it is merited, and one feels that, on the whole, he admires the people appearing in the story.

Situations that are representative of the East, however, lead the reader to imagine comparable situations in the West. Much of the novel's charm resides in these comparisons. When Siddhartha applies to the merchant Kamaswami to be his assistant, he is asked what talents he possesses. "I can think, I can wait, and I can fast," says Siddhartha (p. 66).*

> "And of what use are they? For example, fasting, what good is that?"
> "It is of great value, sir. If a man has nothing to eat, fasting is the most intelligent thing he can do. If, for instance, Siddhartha had not learned how to fast, he would have had to seek some kind of work today, either from you, or elsewhere, for hunger would have driven him. But as it is, Siddhartha can wait calmly. He is not impatient, he is not in need, he can ward off hunger for a long time and laugh at it. Therefore, fasting is useful, sir" (p. 67).

Granting that the ability to fast may be of value to an Asian living at the time of Buddha, would it be of any value to a European or American living today? Would students reconsider their answers if we interpreted the word "fasting" to mean self-denial or fortitude? It is characteristic of *Siddhartha* to pose questions like this. Most readers will be interested first by what is different and exotic in the Asian setting; but the good reader will be able to see parallels between typical Eastern and Western situations.

CRITICISM OF EAST AND WEST

There are no Europeans in this novel, but the main character, Siddhartha, is essentially a Western personality. He upholds the

---

* Page references are to the New Directions paperback edition.

values of independence and freedom of speech and thought that we like to think of as basic to modern Western civilization. Where the other characters are submissive, Siddhartha is domineering; where the others are passive, Siddhartha is active—even aggressive —in his role as spiritual explorer. By contrasting these character-types, the author can criticize both East and West.

Siddhartha is frequently the author's spokesman, especially when one of the other characters is to be rebuked. Thus we learn from Siddhartha that the ordinary Brahmin tends to be "a wicked sly priest, or just a good stupid sheep amongst a large herd" (p. 4); we are told that the doctrine of the Samana pilgrims offers "consolation" but also "tricks with which to deceive oneself" (p. 20). Even the illustrious Buddha, who has reached the goal of salvation in his own lifetime, is judged unable "to communicate the secret in words and teachings" (p. 36) to his horde of disciples. The common theme running through all these judgments is a major criticism of the East. Siddhartha condemns abject submissiveness, the tendency to place total faith in doctrine—any doctrine—and to dispense with all criticism. For doctrine hardens into dogmatism, and the individual becomes a slave to inherited traditions and beliefs. By contrast, Siddhartha's personal credo is clear. "I must judge for myself," he says. "I must choose and reject" (p. 37).

Throughout the novel, as Siddhartha moves from one teacher to the next, there is a continual emphasis on choice, judgment, and the reasons for each decision. Siddhartha resembles the scientist in his attitude toward the facts of experience; and at such moments his mere presence is an implicit criticism of the East. Most readers will be sympathetic to the fervor and singlemindedness with which Siddhartha pursues his goal; but they may fail to see that at the end of the novel, after a lifetime of inquiry, Siddhartha returns to his original beliefs.

The teacher might want to emphasize Siddhartha's return to original beliefs by having students compare the climactic moment in the novel, when Siddhartha achieves his personal salvation (p. 138), with earlier passages which describe the younger man's conception of what that salvation must be like. The ideas, at least, are the same. And this should give us pause before we conclude that the novel is simply a celebration of Western attitudes at the expense of a sluggish and dogmatic East.

The criticism cuts both ways. Although the novel begins with Siddhartha, as the author's spokesman for the West, setting an example for the degenerate East, it concludes with the opposite situation. In Part I, Siddhartha is something of a philosopher who likes to believe that "thought alone" can show the way to salvation; but in Part II, he is repeatedly forced into situations in which he is intellectually helpless and in which he must rely upon other sources of strength to survive. No philosophical theory required that Siddhartha become a merchant. No logical argument was needed to arouse his interest in the beautiful Kamala. In his youth he had had altogether too much of philosophy and abstract argument; now he thirsts for experience. Siddhartha would have agreed with the poet John Keats that the axioms of philosophy have to be proved upon our pulses. "Nothing ever becomes real till it is experienced," wrote Keats. "Even a proverb is no proverb to you till your life has illustrated it."

Up to this point Siddhartha still upholds values that we are likely to think of as "Western." In youth he is the determined philosopher, in middle age the romantic adventurer; but through all this he remains committed to the idea of a personal salvation that must be achieved through personal explorations of life. However—and this is the grand irony of the book—no amount of exploration is sufficient. Siddhartha's attempts at philosophical truth lead only to confusion; they lead him to forsake philosophy altogether. His commitment to experience and the life of the senses leads to another kind of dead end; now he becomes so disillusioned that he contemplates suicide. It is only at the end of his life, when he befriends the old ferryman Vasudeva, that he gains illumination.

Vasudeva functions at the end of the novel as Siddhartha functioned at the beginning: against him we measure the failings of the other characters. Vasudeva is a simple man who is not a thinker; in fact, he is the opposite of all that Siddhartha has stood for in the novel. If Siddhartha stands for the values of the West, then Vasudeva represents the wisdom of the East. It is through his example that Siddhartha learns the power of meditation and submission. The lesson is simple:

> When someone is seeking . . . it happens quite easily that he
> only sees the thing that he is seeking; that he is unable to find

anything, unable to absorb anything, because he is only thinking of the thing he is seeking, because he has a goal, because he is obsessed with his goal. Seeking means: to have a goal; but finding means: to be free, to be receptive, to have no goal (p. 141).

If Siddhartha made a mistake, it is simply that he tried too hard. So intense was his desire for salvation, so single-minded was he in the pursuit of his goal that he soon lost patience with any path that did not offer an immediate reward. It was for this reason that he left the pilgrims, that he rejected the Buddha, that he fled, finally, from his friends in the village. Only in Vasudeva's hut does he learn that "in every truth the opposite is equally true" (p. 144), that the truth of the restless seeker must be balanced by the truth of calm submission, that the values of the West must be balanced by the virtues of the East.

STUDY QUESTIONS

PART I

1. Why is the Asian setting important to this novel? Could the incidents described here take place in Europe or America? Why or why not?

2. What is the nature of Siddhartha's quest? To what extent is the quest determined by the Asian setting? Do you think the same *kind* of quest would be possible in Europe or America? Why or why not?

3. Siddhartha's father becomes angry when he is told that his son wishes to leave the village, but he remembers that "it is not seemly for Brahmins to utter forceful and angry words" (p. 11). Rather than argue, father and son engage in a silent battle of will. Siddhartha will not let anything—not even father—stand between him and his goal. The father decides to sacrifice his own interests to please his son. Who do you think emerges from this conflict with most honor? Why?

4. Why does Siddhartha join the Samanas? What value does he find in practicing their ascetic code? At one point Siddhartha tries to identify with all the things in the universe, living or dead: "he became a dead jackal, lay on the shore, swelled, stank, was dismembered . . ." (p. 16). To a high school student this may seem

morbid; but what value is ascribed to such practices in the text?

5. Why does Siddhartha leave the Samanas? What has he learned from them?

6. Why does Siddhartha admire the Buddha? Does it seem reasonable that Siddhartha should admire the Buddha and still reject his teaching? Why or why not?

7. Comment on the Buddha's distinction between the "thirst for knowledge" and the "goal of salvation" (p. 36). Would this correspond to a contemporary thinker's distinction between science and religion? Why? Does Siddhartha confuse the two?

8. Comment on the Buddha's parting advice to Siddhartha: "You know how to speak cleverly my friend. Be on your guard against too much cleverness" (p. 38). Can you find an instance where Siddhartha is led astray by his own cleverness?

9. There is no dramatic action in the chapter called "Awakening." Siddhartha is the only character to appear and the "action" consists entirely of his thoughts. How does the author manage to hold our interest? Cite specific examples of his use of contrast, analogy, imagery, and metaphor.

The chapter abounds with images of birth (or rebirth). What is being born in Siddhartha? Is the birth joyous or painful?

10. The novel is divided in two parts. What is the unifying theme in Part I? Does the conclusion of Part I mark a significant turning point in the development of plot or character?

PART II

1. In Part I, Siddhartha had been something of a philosopher. He recognized the need for thought and for the investigation of causes; "for to recognize causes, it seemed to him, is to think, and through thought alone feelings become knowledge and are not lost, but become real and mature" (p. 39). In Part II, this philosophical stance will be put to the test. As you read, consider whether the important decisions made by Siddhartha are really the result of thought, or whether they have some other cause.

2. After Siddhartha, who are the most vivid characters in the book? What is there in the characterization which makes them so memorable? Do some characters emerge as striking personalities? If so, describe the traits which give them this identity.

3. Which characters are so generalized that they tend to repre-

sent important social types? What is the difference between a *generalized character* and a *stereotyped character?*

4. Siddhartha's experiences with Kamala and Kamaswami seem to follow a roughly parallel course. In each case enjoyment and satisfaction were real up to a point, but in each case these were followed by disillusionment. What conclusion does Siddhartha draw from these experiences? Does he conclude that love and money are unworthy aims in life? Or is it rather his own attitudes toward these which are at fault? Explain your answer.

5. "Most people," says Siddhartha, "are like a falling leaf that drifts and turns in the air, flutters, and falls to the ground. But a few others are like stars which travel one defined path: no wind reaches them, they have within themselves their guide and path" (p. 74). Is there, perhaps, something arrogant in this distinction? Siddhartha obviously considers himself one of the fixed stars.

Write a theme in which you consider Siddhartha's attitude toward ordinary people—the falling leaves—in most of this book. Consider, in your theme, Siddhartha's change in attitude toward ordinary people. Explain how this change came about.

6. There are several important dreams in the novel. How is the reader supposed to interpret them? Are they symbolic, or prophetic, or merely entertaining?

At one point Siddhartha dreams of a small rare songbird which Kamala kept in a golden cage. Here is the dream: "This bird, which usually sang in the morning, became mute, and as this surprised him, he went up to the cage and looked inside. The little bird was dead and lay stiff on the floor. He took it out, held it a moment in his hand and then threw it away on the road, and at the same moment he was horrified and his heart ached as if he had thrown away with this dead bird all that was good and of value in himself" (p. 83). What is the meaning of this dream? The songbird is mentioned again on pages 87, 99, and 100. Do these references clarify the symbolic meaning of the dream?

7. In what respects does the quarrel between Siddhartha and his son resemble an earlier quarrel between Siddhartha and his own father? What has he learned from the previous experience?

8. What does Siddhartha learn from the river? Could he have learned it without the help of Vasudeva?

9. Siddhartha claims to have discovered only one great truth:

"Knowledge can be communicated, but not wisdom. One can find it, live it, be fortified by it, do wonders with it, but one cannot communicate and teach it" (p. 144). Consider these methods of teaching that the reader finds in the novel: (a) the indoctrination of traditional beliefs; (b) the method of rational argument; (c) teaching by example.

Write a theme in which you take one of these methods of teaching and explain which characters use the method and why the method is or is not successful. Does the method you have selected communicate knowledge or wisdom? If you think it communicates either, you will need to define what you mean by knowledge or wisdom. Finally, consider Siddhartha's generalization on knowledge and wisdom. What does it teach you?

Teaching *Cry, the Beloved Country*

VIRGINIA OLSEN BUSH

Alan Paton's *Cry, the Beloved Country* is a moving account of life in twentieth-century South Africa. It deals with death and rebirth, destruction and rebuilding, in a society so divided against itself that fear rules, making rebirth and rebuilding difficult—and almost impossible. It paints the portrait of this world in the numerous characters that people the book, in the descriptions of the beauties of the land, and in the invocations of it which begin, "Cry, the beloved country. . . ." There is also a story, telling of death and rebirth, destruction and rebuilding in the lives of two men. But the whole is so worked that this story cannot be separated from the portrait of the society nor this portrait from the story; the two are fused, and the meaning of the book is to be found only in the combination.

It is the country, the land of hills that are "grass-covered and rolling, and . . . lovely beyond any singing of it," that dominates this novel. Its presence is felt in the very title of the work and thereafter from the first page until the last. The whole of the first chapter is an incantation of this land, creating in us a knowledge not only of its beauties but also of the passionate love which it evokes. The whole of the first part of Chapter 1 is then repeated almost word for word at the beginning of Book II, and sentences of this same section are echoed in the last paragraph of the book. This repetition creates of the land a frame which holds together the parts of the book—a frame within which they are set off and may be viewed.

This use of the land is perhaps understandable in light of the nature of South Africa itself. The contemporary South African writer Nadine Gordimer discusses in "The Novel and the Nation in South Africa" the South Africans' lack of any real identity as a nation. She contends that geography and a common sphere of economic activity are the only two of the eight points in Reinhold Niebuhr's definition of a nation that apply to South Africa. Of other common sources of identity for a nation she says:

> Our common historical experience is not one of fighting together, but against one another—white man against black, Afrikaner against Englishman. We have no common frame of political thought, but a clash of bitterly opposed ideologies. As for fear of a common foe—the foe we fear is each other.[1]

It is not surprising, then, that the land—that geographic unit which is one of the few things all South Africans hold in common—should assume the importance it does in *Cry, the Beloved Country;* for this book deals with precisely that fighting, that clash, and that fear of which Miss Gordimer was speaking and with the attempt to build something better. Stephen Kumalo telling over the "deep melodious names" of his homeland or watching the sun rise from the mountain over the great valley of the Umzimkulu, James Jarvis standing on that same mountain above his farm, looking out and brooding on the great valley, and presumably all men—white, black, Afrikaner, and Englishman—can love this one thing. It is the one foundation upon which rebuilding may begin.

The voice of the narrator comes out of this land, and its appeal is to the land. When we examine the various parts of the book, we find that the narrator shifts in and out of the minds of the different characters and often shifts to a point of view which, though not precisely that of any one of these characters, is not completely divorced from any of them.

> Cry, the beloved country, for the unborn child that is the inheritor of our fear. Let him not love the earth too deeply. Let him not laugh too gladly when the water runs through his fingers, nor stand too silent when the setting sun makes red the veld with fire. Let him not be too moved when the birds of his land are singing, nor give too much of his heart to a mountain or a valley. For fear will rob him of all if he gives too much.*

* Alan Paton, *Cry, the Beloved Country* (New York: Charles Scribner's Sons, 1948), p. 80. All page references are to this edition.

Who speaks this invocation? Is it Stephen Kumalo, his brother John, Arthur Jarvis, James Jarvis, Msimangu? the white population, the black population? Perhaps any of these could have spoken this passage, given the occasion and the ability to think in these terms, but none of them *is* given the occasion and the ability. This passage is an articulation of the fear which all of these people inarticulately feel, and in this it is like many passages in the book. Nor is the narrator Alan Paton himself, even in the sarcasm of many of the sketches in Chapter 12, where he seems to come closest to speaking in his own voice. For here too one can hear the voice of the land speaking, this time in indignation, and the whole of this section is framed by two lyric passages, one of them quoted above, describing fear in the land. It is the lyricism of the writing throughout the book that finally distances the narrator from the author. Who then is it that speaks in this book? Perhaps we may regard this narrator as the soul of the country itself, a self which the author has assumed in order to tell his story.

If the land of South Africa is the frame, the society is the very material and substance of the picture. Chapter 9, about Shanty Town; Chapter 12, about fear; Chapter 23, about the discovery of gold; and various other parts of the book deal explicitly with this society. Life in the black townships of Johannesburg, the setting for the greater part of the book, is shown to be for the most part squalid and unbeautiful, lawless, amoral, lacking the old restraints and customs, dangerous and full of fear. The injustices and inequalities result from the fear which infests even white Johannesburg, driving people like Harrison and the anonymous white citizens of Chapter 12 to intolerance and hatred. This is a society split in pieces, divided against itself, one in which even the pieces are breaking down. Here the customs are such that the greatest meaning comes when they are broken in such a way as to fashion a piece of something new, as when the young white man "breaks the custom" and helps Kumalo out of court after the trial. Yet Alan Paton's portrayal of South African society is not an indictment of it. As one critic has expressed it, his "powerful, realistic descriptions [are] tempered only by a vein of unsubdued tenderness."[2] This tenderness is basic to the tone of the book, and its effect can be seen when one realizes that, of the numerous characters that people this world, the overwhelming majority are kind and compassionate people who have managed to conquer their fear or who at least have it under control. In fact, after having experienced the evils of South African society in Johannesburg, Stephen Kumalo still concludes that nowhere else has he met with such kindness.

It is the story of Kumalo—and secondarily that of Jarvis—that gives specific shape to this portrait of a society, just as the society gives substance and background to the story. Like the rich green hills which have broken down into red, barren earth, and like the society which has split apart into unproductive factions, Kumalo has "lived [his] life in destruction" (p. 255). Book I is principally the story of his gradual realization of the storm which has been gathering over his head and of the extent of the destruction when it finally breaks. Book II tells the same story of James Jarvis, for he too has lived his life in destruction. Book II also sees the beginning of the process of rebuilding for both men, as they begin to understand what has happened and what is now needed— Jarvis by discovering what his son had been working for and Kumalo by discovering why his son became a thief and then a murderer. Thus, from the deaths of these two young men, something new is born in their fathers, giving them new life and leading to a hope of new life in the society and new life in the land: from death, rebirth; from destruction, a rebuilding. In Book III we find the first concrete results of this process in the increased happiness and peace of both Kumalo and Jarvis and in their co-operation to rebuild Ndotsheni. The story of these two men is inseparable from, and in many respects is the same as, that of the society they live in; but it is through the specific story that our feeling for the whole is crystallized.

Our knowledge of the world of a novel is fundamental to our understanding of its story since it is this world that determines which actions will be possible and which will not and which will be invested with the greatest meaning. It is necessary for the reader to understand the South Africa that is the setting for *Cry, the Beloved Country* in order that he may understand the fear that forms so great a part of Kumalo's own breaking-down and the great meaning that lies in Jarvis' acts of friendship. The story of a father who loses a son and gains wisdom through his suffering is, on its own level, of universal significance, but the passionately South African voice through which this story is told raises it to another level as well, that of the breaking-down and rebuilding of a society, and this too is not limited to South Africa but is of universal significance, for society is always in a process of change.

STUDY QUESTIONS

BOOK I

1. Why has Alan Paton begun his book with the description of the land that comprises Chapter 1? What are the principal qualities of the language of this description? How are they important? What does this first chapter tell us about South Africa? How does it prepare us for the story that follows? What themes does it introduce? What mood does it establish for the book?

2. What do we learn about the Reverend Stephen Kumalo in Chapter 2? From this first impression, what do his main character traits seem to be?

3. In Chapter 3, the paragraph of Kumalo's reflections as he waits for the train (pp. 11–12) tells us something of what he thinks of Johannesburg, although he has never been there. What is this paragraph intended to show us about Kumalo? How accurate a rendering do you think this is of such a person's thoughts about something he has never experienced? Is it stereotyped, in the way that Indians saying "Ugh" and expressing amazement at the white man's inventions have often been stereotyped in our own culture? Defend your answer.

4. Before Paton actually moves the setting of the story to Johannesburg he has already given us some idea of what the city is like. From whom do we get these first impressions? Are they definite or vague ideas? Why? Are these first impressions confirmed or altered when we see Johannesburg itself? What does this city mean to the people in the book? Does it mean different things to different persons? How does Kumalo's attitude toward it develop and change during the course of the novel?

5. In Chapter 5, Msimangu says: "The tragedy is not that things

are broken. The tragedy is that they are not mended again" (p. 25). What does he mean by this? What things are broken? Why are they not mended again? How is this talk of "broken" and "mended" related to the conversation Msimangu has just had with Kumalo? It is also Msimangu who says: "It is fear that rules this land" (p. 26). Why does he say this? How much of what he is saying does Kumalo understand at this point?

6. On page 29 we are told: "There is laughter in the house, the kind of laughter of which one is afraid. Perhaps because one is afraid already, perhaps because it is in truth bad laughter." What is "bad laughter"? What are its qualities? What does it indicate? In what ways is it characteristic of Johannesburg? Why should fear be connected with this kind of laughter?

When Kumalo fetches his sister the neighbors discuss the affair, "some with approval, and some with the strange laughter of the towns" (p. 32). What does this suggest that these latter neighbors think of the matter?

7. Why does the narrator tell us that Gertrude's hand is "cold and wet, there is no life in it" (p. 29)?

8. What sort of person is John Kumalo? What descriptive words and phrases does the author use to characterize him? What in his conversation and in his behavior supports or adds to this impression?

John says, "It is true that the Church speaks with a fine voice, and that the Bishops speak against the laws. But this they have been doing for fifty years, and things get worse, not better" (p. 36). Later we learn that John, too, speaks with a fine voice but goes only so far and no further. Does he himself perceive this parallel? What does this tell us about John?

9. John Kumalo and Msimangu are speaking (p. 37); Kumalo says:

It is hard to explain in a letter. Our customs are different here.
And Msimangu said, are there any customs here?
John Kumalo looked at him. There is a new thing growing here, he said. Stronger than any church or chief. You will see it one day.

What is it that is growing? Are there any customs here? If not, why? If so, what are they and what do they mean?

10. The words "afraid" and "sullenly" occur often in the episode at Mrs. Mkize's house, and they are also used frequently throughout the book. Why? Which characters are afraid? Which are sullen?

11. Why does Msimangu break out bitterly against the girl, "Perhaps you will find another man," while Kumalo is moved to compassion (p. 68)? Later, Kumalo himself speaks bitterly to her. Why? Are the causes of these two outbursts similar?

12. What truth about power does Msimangu tell to Stephen Kumalo? How does his brother John illustrate this truth?

Love, Msimangu says, is the "only one thing that has power completely" and he sees love as the only hope for his country. His only fear is that "one day when they are turned to loving, they will find we are turned to hating" (pp. 39–40). How can love be the one thing that has power completely? Does the change from loving to hating happen at all in the novel? Does it seem likely to happen?

13. In Chapter 10, Kumalo tells his small nephew about Ndotsheni. What is there about "deep melodious names" that should give him great pleasure and make even a little child "listen solemnly" and "gaze out of wide and serious eyes" (p. 61)? To what extent does the author use words that are deep and melodious to make the reader "listen solemnly" to his story? Cite specific examples. How successful is he?

In his Author's Note to the Scribner's edition, Alan Paton says:

> For the benefit of readers I have appended a list of words at the end of the book, which includes by no means all the strange names and words that are used. But it contains those, a knowledge of the meaning and approximately correct pronunciation of which, should add to the reader's enjoyment (p. viii).

Why does he think that a knowledge of both meaning and pronunciation of these words should increase the reader's enjoyment? Does it? How? How does the continual use of a word such as "umfundisi" add to the total effect of the book?

14. How would you describe the phrasing and the rhythm of the sentences in this book? Sentences such as the following are common:

The grass is rich and matted, you cannot see the soil (p. 3).

It is well-tended, and not too many cattle feed upon it; not too many fires burn it, laying bare the soil (p. 3).

Cry for the broken tribe, for the law and the custom that is gone. Aye, and cry aloud for the man who is dead, for the woman and children bereaved (p. 73).

Of what literary work do sentences such as these remind you?

15. In Chapter 13, the narrator asks: "What broke in a man when he could bring himself to kill another?" (p. 87). How would you answer this question? Does the book suggest any answer?

16. At Ezenzeleni, Kumalo sits for a long time, thinking.

He turned with relief to the thought of rebuilding, to the home that they would fashion, he and his wife, in the evening of their lives, for Gertrude and her son, and for his son and the girl and the child. After seeing Johannesburg he would return with a deeper understanding to Ndotsheni. Yes, and with a greater humility, for had his own sister not been a prostitute? And his son a thief? And might not he himself be grandfather to a child that would have no name? This he thought without bitterness, though with pain (p. 88).

Later, Msimangu comes to him and says, "And what have you found?" to which Kumalo answers, "Nothing." Is this true? What has he found? And what is it that he is looking for that he has not yet found?

17. Why does Kumalo react as he does to the news that what he feared is true? Contrast his reaction with his brother's. Contrast the behavior of the two brothers after they have seen their sons.

18. Father Vincent tells Kumalo, "But sorrow is better than fear. For fear impoverishes always, while sorrow may enrich" (p. 108). How may sorrow enrich? Why does Father Vincent say "may"?

19. In the interview between Kumalo and the girl in Chapter 16, she says, "Quietness is what I desire," and the narrator comments, "And the word, the word desire, quickened her to brilliance." What does the word "quicken" mean? Why does the author use it here? What significance does this word have for the rest of the book?

20. Who is the narrator of this novel? Is it the author himself, an

assumed self, one of the characters in the story, someone outside of the story, or none of these? Is there only one narrator or does the narrator change frequently? To help you decide who the narrator is, examine the following passages: Chapter 1; the last paragraph in Chapter 11; the various parts of Chapter 12; the third paragraph in Chapter 3, beginning, "It is interesting to wait for the train at Carisbrooke. . . ."

21. Paton devotes several chapters or parts of chapters to descriptions of South Africa and life there. Chapter 9, dealing with the construction of Shanty Town, is one of these. How important is this chapter to the book? In what ways?

BOOK II

1. Why does Paton begin Book II with the same words as Book I? Why doesn't he make it a separate chapter, as he did in the earlier section? What is the effect of the repetition?

2. What is our first impression of James Jarvis?

3. How well did Jarvis know his son before his death? How well did Kumalo know his? How well does each come to know his son afterwards? How does this knowledge come to each? For whom is it easier? Does this knowledge of the son lead to any other knowledge?

4. The book is peopled with many fairly well-sketched minor characters. Why does the author use so many? Choose any three of the minor characters and discuss their functions in this book.

5. Why should Jarvis find it necessary to tell Harrison, "I was very fond of my son . . . I was never ashamed of having him" (p. 138)?

6. What does the conversation between Harrison and Jarvis in Chapter 19 (pp. 138–41) tell us about the South African situation as seen by the white population?

7. On page 141 we are given a picture of Kumalo and his church and school as James Jarvis remembers them:

> A dirty old wood-and-iron church, patched and forlorn, and a dirty old parson, in a barren valley where the grass hardly grew. A dirty old school where he had heard them reciting, parrot-fashion, on the one or two occasions that he had ridden past there, reciting things that could mean little to them.

Has Kumalo ever before been pictured as a "dirty old parson," or have we ever been prompted to think of him as such? How accurate do you think Jarvis' memories probably are? How well acquainted with what he is remembering is he? Why has the author waited until Book II to give us a portrait of Kumalo as a "dirty old parson"? Does it change our impression of Kumalo, or does it add to it? How? Does our feeling for Kumalo change?

8. What is the significance to the story of the following passage?

> And so he told her in low tones all he had heard. She marvelled a little, for her husband was a quiet silent man, not given to much talking. But tonight he told her all that Harrison had told him (p. 142).

9. What sort of views does Harrison express to Jarvis the night after the funeral? How does Jarvis react? Does he agree, disagree, or does he perhaps not know just now? Why does he say he could have wished to hear his son argue with Harrison? Compare what Harrison says about the mines with what John Kumalo and others have said in Book I. Who do you think is right? Why?

10. Why does it give Jarvis "increasing knowledge of a stranger," his son, to read Lincoln's Second Inaugural Address?

11. How effective do you think the last words of Arthur's manuscript, "Allow me a minute," are in the context of the rest of the novel? Do they seem natural in the context of the manuscript itself? Why? Is there anything to justify the use of these words?

12. Does Absalom tell the truth in court? Why do you think so? What is his attitude now?

13. Recalling what has been said earlier about justice (Chapter 22, pp. 157–58), do you think the judge's decision with respect to Absalom and the two others is justice? Is it just?

14. What is the significance of the young white man's "breaking the custom" by helping Kumalo out of court after the trial?

15. What significance is there in Absalom's wish to name his son Peter? Who was Peter in the Bible? What does this suggest may be Absalom's symbolic role? Could this role also be fulfilled by Arthur Jarvis? How? What else in the book supports this symbolic identification? Who was Absalom in the Bible? What does the name mean in Hebrew?

BOOK III

1. Kumalo laughs at many things in Chapter 31. What kinds of things does he laugh about? Why does he laugh?

2. In Chapter 35, when Kumalo and the young agricultural demonstrator are speaking together, the young man says:

> We work for Africa . . . not for this man or that man. Not for a white man or a black man, but for Africa.
> —Why do you not say South Africa?
> —We would if we could, said the young man soberly.

What does he mean? Why can't they say "South Africa"?

Another South African writer, Nadine Gordimer, in discussing South Africa's lack of real unity as a nation, has said that geography and economics are the only two things that all South Africans have in common. Of some of the other things which commonly give identity to a nation she says:

> Our common historical experience is not one of fighting together, but against one another—white man against black, Afrikaner against Englishman. We have no common frame of political thought, but a clash of bitterly opposed ideologies. As for fear of a common foe—the foe we fear is each other.

What significance does this statement have for *Cry, the Beloved Country?* Does it help you to understand the young man's remark?

3. Of what do you think Kumalo's vigil on the mountain is intended to remind you?

4. In what ways are the experiences of Kumalo and Jarvis parallel? In what ways are their reactions to these experiences similar?

5. Why does the book end as it does? What is the function of the last paragraph? What is the tone at the conclusion of the book?

NOTES

1. Nadine Gordimer, "The Novel and the Nation in South Africa," *Times Literary Supplement,* August 11, 1961, p. 520.

2. Fred H. Marcus, "*Cry, the Beloved Country* and *Strange Fruit:* Exploring Man's Inhumanity to Man," *English Journal,* LI (1962), p. 612.

Teaching *Crime and Punishment*

VIRGINIA OLSEN BUSH

Crime and Punishment, because it is a massive and complex work, is recommended only for academically talented students in grade twelve. These students, most of whom will soon be entering college, can be expected to read the book twice and to respond to the more careful and sophisticated examination which it demands. The first reading should be fairly rapid and should cover a period of approximately two weeks, during which time the class would be concentrating its study on other matters. During this first reading the student should be permitted to experience the novel and become caught up in Raskolnikov's suffering with a minimum of reflection on it. Care should be taken, however, that everyone does read the novel at this time. Perhaps ten to fifteen minutes of every class period might be spent in a brief discussion of questions of the type given at the end of this essay in the section, "Study Questions for a First Reading." The very few questions asked at this time should concentrate primarily on the psychological aspect of the novel in order to make sure that everyone understands basically what is happening. The teacher might give the class an occasional, short quiz to ensure that everyone is keeping up with the reading. However, the art of the novel is so compelling that, on a first reading, the reader becomes completely involved in what he is experiencing and has little desire to analyze it, and there is therefore little point in a teacher's trying to overcome this involvement and enforce analysis at first; he would do better to use it as the base for a more analytic second reading.

The second reading should cover a period of from one to two weeks, during which time the class would be concentrating its study on *Crime and Punishment.* The reading assignments should now be larger—one part of the novel at a time. Some students will of course not reread the book, but they should still profit from the detailed classroom examination of it. The purpose of the first reading is to acquaint the student with the book well enough that he will have a perspective from which to view its many parts. Thus, on the second reading the teacher will be able to move from specific questions about what is happening to problems of psychological interpretation, ideas, and artistic structure, as suggested in the section, "Study Questions for a Second Reading."

Art, character, and idea provide three valid and valuable approaches to the teaching of *Crime and Punishment,* and we shall discuss each in some detail. All three aspects of the novel, however, are so closely interrelated that it is impossible to examine one without making some use of the other two. Conversely, no one approach can be wholly adequate. The teacher should combine all three, while concentrating on the one which will work best with his particular class.

ARTISTIC STRUCTURE

Boris Pasternak has been quoted as saying, "It is the art of *Crime and Punishment* that moves us deeply rather than the story of Raskolnikov's crime."[1] This statement is important, for it prompts us to consider the artistic merits of the novel. All too often readers and critics has discounted Dostoevsky's skill as an artist, praising him instead as a philosopher and psychologist in the belief that the power of the novel lies in its philosophical and phychological insights. The art of the novel, however, permits the expression of these insights with full force, and it deserves respect. Dostoevsky masterfully controls both the way we look at what happens and the ordering of the details we perceive. In this largely nonrealistic novel, the measure of his success is our complete belief in the inevitability of what happens.

The chief characteristic of Dostoevsky's technique in *Crime and Punishment* is his use of an essentially dramatic form adapted to the special conventions of the novel. There is scarcely any authorial intervention for the purpose of speculation, commentary, or moralization. The author's thoughts are instead particularized and presented in dramatic encounters, from which his thoughts must be inferred. The presentation of action is almost totally scenic, with only a few paragraphs of panoramic presentation in Part II, when Raskolnikov is unconscious for several days, and at the start of Part VI, when several days pass during which Raskolnikov is confused about events and their order of happening. A great part of the most important action is presented either in dialogue or in Raskolnikov's "soliloquies." The novel attends in detail to every episode, giving us the impression that we could accurately account for every hour Raskolnikov spends during this period of his life, from the time he gets up until he goes to bed again. With a dramatically objective narration, Dostoevsky imparts a sense of immediacy to his fantastic account of crime and ensuing punishment and, by the narration's very objectivity and attention to detail, renders the account more realistic, much as a similar attention to time and detail on the stage tempts us to believe in what we see happening, no matter how nonrealistic it is. The great advantage which Dostoevsky has over the stage play, in casting his tale as a novel, lies, however, in the massive accretion of detail which prose narration permits and which is largely denied to drama because of the limitations of time and the exclusive use of dialogue.

The dramatic nature of the novel, however, creates for the reader the same problem which he faces when he attempts to read a play: he must learn to stage the action in his mind's eye. He must become the director and interpret the speeches, deciding how each is to be acted. All novels contain this problem to a certain extent, but in *Crime and Punishment* it is more acute than in most, and for this reason it is a novel demanding a higher degree of literary sophistication from the reader.

The special implications of this problem can be seen if we examine one scene from the book. Part III, Chapter 5 is devoted to the first meeting between Raskolnikov and Porfiry Petrovich. Raskolnikov, preparing to sound out Porfiry, has just engineered a "natural-appearing" entrance for himself and Razumikhin in his own "hearty-seeming" laughter at his friend's discomfiture. We are told enough about Raskolnikov to judge with fair accuracy how he actually appears. The problem of interpreting Razumikhin is negligible, for he is a very frank and open person, even to the others in the book. But what are we to do with Zametov, who "*seemed* a little disconcerted" [emphasis added], or, even more importantly, with Porfiry himself? Dostoevsky doesn't let us inside these characters, and hence they remain something of a mystery for us. Yet we must come to some decision on what they are thinking and doing, not only if we are to know them, but also if we are to know Raskolnikov; for the way we perceive these characters will influence the way we perceive Dostoevsky's hero. Consider the following passage:

> "That doesn't matter," answered Porfiry Petrovich, receiving these financial explanations with some coldness; "if, however, you prefer it, you may write direct to me, to the same effect; that is, having learnt of so-and-so, and offering the information that certain things are yours, you request . . ."
> "Can this be done on unstamped paper?" hastily interrupted Raskolnikov, once more interesting himself in the financial side of the matter.
> "Oh, yes. Stamped paper is not necessary at all!" Suddenly, with an openly mocking expression, he screwed up his eyes as if he were winking. Perhaps, however, this was only Raskolnikov's imagination, for it lasted only for a moment. At any rate there had been something, and Raskolnikov could have sworn he had been winked at, God alone knew why.
> "He knows!" flashed through his brain like lightning.[*]

Anyone who has read this far in the novel will recognize that Raskolnikov's remark (like his laughter earlier and much else that he says in this scene) is extremely uncharacteristic of him: despite his poverty, Raskolnikov is neither penny-pinching nor thrifty, and his usual attitude toward his financial position is one of fierceness and pride, not embarrassment and humility. But does Porfiry recognize that this is a false note? The author insists upon this question, forcing us to deal with it by the more obvious question raised by the narrative: does Porfiry really wink, or doesn't he? The narrative doesn't tell us. In our own staging of this scene we

---

[*] Feodor Dostoevsky, *Crime and Punishment*, tr. Jessie Coulson, ed. George Gibian (New York: Norton, 1964), p. 240. All quotations are from this translation.

must decide whether or not we see him deliberately "screw up his eyes." Of course, Dostoevsky has established his main point—Raskolnikov's extreme susceptibility to panic and fear—no matter which way we make our decision; but whether or not we regard the wink as real will determine whether or not we regard Raskolnikov as half-mad, whether we see his reaction as unnecessary or, on the contrary, vitally necessary for his self-preservation. It is a problem of interpretation. The ambiguity is deliberate, and so it is perhaps not necessary for us to make a final decision one way or the other; but the choice is open to us and we must come to terms in some way with the question it poses.

Related to the objectivity of Dostoevsky's use of dramatic form is the effect of his use of oblique statement to express meaning.[2] Neither the narrator nor any one character in the book iterates exactly what the author himself is trying to say. We soon learn that Raskolnikov is wrong in his theory on crime and in many of his conscious thoughts. Sonya is wise, but when she speaks, she communicates feelings and beliefs, not intellectualized ideas. Both Razumikhin and Porfiry hint at acceptable ideas on crime, but neither expands on his ideas, and when we hear that they have been arguing about the matter, we are no longer sure what the position of each is. Similarly, no one character expresses in his actions all that Dostoevsky wants to say. Meaning must instead be inferred from a synthesis of characters, actions, and ideas. "Truth emerges from the whole complex structure instead of from one outright affirmation or abstract statement," George Gibian says, comparing *Crime and Punishment* with Plato's *Symposium* in this respect. "A simple, unequivocal statement . . . would release the reader from the salutary, in fact indispensable task of smelting down the ore for himself."[3]

Through dramatic form and oblique presentation Dostoevsky has taught us to view his world comprehensively, taking all of its elements into account; through his handling of point of view he focuses our sight in such a way that the comprehensive view, taking shape, becomes clear and meaningful. His use of point of view is very careful. His notebooks indicate that he had at first considered telling the story exclusively from Raskolnikov's point of view as a "confession" or "diary of a murderer." By the time of the final draft, however, he had revised his plan. The novel as it stands is narrated in the third person and is limited for the most part to Raskolnikov's point of view. As we noted above while examining the scene between Raskolnikov and Porfiry Petrovich, we are made aware of all that goes on in Raskolnikov's mind, but we are not allowed very much inside the other characters. The intimate knowledge we thus gain of Raskolnikov is very important in establishing rapport between the readers and the murderer which would be lost with a more distanced narration. Point of view, however, slips occasionally to that of the impersonal narrator or one of the other characters. In this way we are brought away from Raskolnikov's often distorted view of the world in order that we may be given a more normative view which will establish proper perspective. Each time that we see Raskolnikov and his crime as Sonya, Razumikhin, or Dunya does, we gain a more sure understanding of what Dostoevsky is trying to say; this device guards against our falling into the mistake of agreeing completely with Raskolnikov. The use of Svidrigaylov's point of view in large sections of the second half of the novel has a similar effect, although it functions in the converse manner. By allowing us inside the consciousness of this highly articulate, amoral man, Dostoevsky gives us knowledge of an extreme form of one of Raskolnikov's tendencies and prompts us to judge against it.

Dostoevsky further clarifies the nature of his universe by carefully ordering all of its elements so that interrelationships are made visible, falling into definite patterns which are continually reordered to give fresh insights. Something of this technique can be seen in the way he expresses the motives for the murder. At the beginning of the novel, even before we know specifically what Raskolnikov contemplates doing, we are given hints of all his motives, although there is no clear indication which are the most important or how they are all interrelated. We know that he is poor, that he feels he must help his mother and sister, that he is proud and loathes all the humanity around him, that he is concerned with speaking a "new word" (his theory on crime, as we later find out). As Raskolnikov himself searches for the real motive for the murder, we see now one, now another of these reasons coming into prominence. It is not until the end of the book, when we have been shown all possible combinations of motives, that we can understand Raskolnikov's motivation in its full complexity, for it lies not in one, but in all of the motives considered.

The most important patterns in the book are those which draw various of the characters together, emphasizing similarities. Concepts of crime, sacrifice, and suffering, and intellect, spirit, and will are all developed in this way. Each is manifested in several characters, but they all center in Raskolnikov and are related to each other through him. We shall examine the way in which each of the above concepts is patterned and then consider how they are used as a whole to structure the book.

If we look through *Crime and Punishment*, we shall find many examples of crime and attempted crime. We must first realize however, that, as is frequently pointed out, the word "crime" is an inadequate translation of the Russian "prestuplenie," which signifies a "stepping across (some barrier)," or "transgression"; that is, the word which Dostoevsky used refers to actions in the religious as well as the legal sphere. Thus, there are two aspects to Raskolnikov's crime: "It is the civil line of the accepted that Raskolnikov believes he crosses in murdering Alyona and Lizaveta; it is the religious line which he also crosses."[4] Others who step across the line of permissible behavior are Sonya, in prostituting herself (she is called by Raskolnikov "a great sinner"); Luzhin, in falsely accusing Sonya of theft in order to win back Dunya; and Svidrigaylov, in committing repeated sins of seduction and sadism for his own sensual gratification. Not all of these acts are legally crimes, but they are all transgressions: they are all unpermissible acts of aggression directed either against the self or against others in an attempt to secure power and use people as a means to an end. Raskolnikov's act of murder, however, is the epitome both of aggression against the self and aggression against others.

Acts of sacrifice, and particularly self-sacrifice, are numerous. Sonya sacrifices herself for her family; Lizaveta, with her incessant hard work, does the same for her sister; and Dunya is about to sacrifice herself in marriage to Luzhin for her mother and brother. The Marmeladovs, Alëna Ivanovna, and Pulkheria Alexandrovna, all of those to whom sacrifices are made, with the exception of Raskolnikov, accept the sacrifice, and by their acceptance participate in it. But it is Raskolnikov who makes the greatest sacrifice of all, when he murders the old woman and his better self, all for the sake of a theory. In general, Dostoevsky emphasizes the ironic ineffectuality of the sacrifices that are made, with Raskolnikov again the major example.

The third concept is suffering, which, along with crime and sacrifice, is one of the major components of the complex of behavior which Dostoevsky is examining in his study of Raskolnikov's commission of murder. That part of the St. Petersburg population which is represented in *Crime and Punishment* is poor and miserable; almost without exception, they suffer, as if suffering were the natural condition of mankind. What is of greatest interest for us, however, is that the author emphasizes that these people seem to *need* to suffer. The experience and acceptance of suffering acquire religious force in Dostoevsky's writing; they are related to the passion, or suffering, of Christ. This connection is made as early as the second chapter of the book, when Marmeladov declares in his conversation with Raskolnikov:

> "Crucify, oh judge, crucify me, but pity your victim! Then I will come to you to be crucified, for I thirst for affliction and weeping, not for merriment! . . . Do you think, you who sold it, that this bottle of yours has been sweet to me? Affliction, I sought affliction at the bottom of it, tears and affliction, and I found them, I tasted them. But He will pity us, He who pitied all men and understood all men and all things, He alone is the judge" (Part I, Chapter 2).

The connection between suffering and piety can also be seen in both Sonya and Lizaveta (Raskolnikov himself recognizes this relationship in his first meeting with Sonya in her room, in Part IV, Chapter 4) and in the painter Mikolka, who confesses to the murder from a desire to "accept suffering." It is worthwhile examining the case of Mikolka in some detail, since it is chiefly through him that Raskolnikov's connection with this group of sufferers is made clear.

Most of our knowledge about Mikolka comes from what Porfiry tells Raskolnikov in Part VI, Chapter 2. We learn that Mikolka was a "schismatic," a member of a religious sect that "run away to settle out of the reach of all authority," that he had once even intended to become a hermit, that he had been a bookish sort. These details alone are enough to establish the analogy between Mikolka and Raskolnikov, for Raskolnikov, too, has been a bookish person; he has isolated himself from the rest of humanity for months, just as a hermit does, and he has sought by his theory of the extraordinary man to put himself beyond the reach of all authority. When we remember that a schismatic is a "raskolnik," the word which is the root of Raskolnikov's name, and that the peasant with whom Raskolnikov identifies himself in his first dream is also named Mikolka, the identification of the painter Mikolka with the corresponding aspect of Raskolnikov's character is complete. (Note: some translators consistently translate the painter's name as Nikolay, apparently to avoid confusion of the painter with the dream-figure; but this, I believe, defeats the author's intention.) The connection with suffering is made by Porfiry Petrovich in this same speech. "Do you, Rodion Romanovich, know what some of these people mean by 'suffering'?" he asks. "It is not suffering for somebody's sake, but simply 'suffering is necessary'—the acceptance of suffering, that means, and if it is at the hands of the authorities, so much the better."

That Raskolnikov suffers is evident enough, but that he needs to accept his suffering, at least with one part of his being, is not so obvious. We can recognize the compulsion, however, in his return to the old woman's flat, when he rings the bell and asks about blood, and in the fact that he does not run away, but instead stays where he will be continually tormented by the police. Furthermore, Porfiry, who makes many perceptive remarks in his final visit with Raskolnikov, says that he is convinced that Raskolnikov will confess:

> ". . . suddenly . . . you will volunteer a confession, perhaps quite unexpectedly even to yourself. An hour beforehand you will not know that you are going to come forward with a confession. You see I am convinced that you will 'resolve to accept your suffering'; you don't believe my word now, but you will come to the same conclusion yourself" (Part VI, Chapter 2).

The compulsion, in Raskolnikov, is submerged in the subconscious and dominated by both the intellect and the will, which fight against it. Raskolnikov's "softer" emotions—those of love and compassion, both of which have religious overtones in a Christian society—also have their origin in the subconscious and meet with the same opposition: Raskolnikov impulsively gives the Marmeladovs some money but then immediately *thinks*, "What a stupid thing to do." The religious nature of his suffering is never made any more explicit than this, and in fact it could not be, given Raskolnikov's character; but the analogies with Marmeladov, Sonya, Lizaveta, and especially Mikolka are designed to imply the connection and make clear this very important part of Raskolnikov's nature.

We come now to the last three concepts: intellect, spirit, and will. These are the three parts of Raskolnikov's soul, which is split in two, with intellect and will for the most part together opposing spirit. Intellect, the power of conscious thought, is very highly developed in Raskolnikov. It is that part of him which is responsible for his theory on crime and the extraordinary man and for most of the statements which he makes in the book. In Raskolnikov, thought is completely divorced from feeling, which is a power of the spirit, resulting in the cynicism, coldness, and inhumanity of his ideas. Of the other major characters, the one who is most like Raskolnikov in this respect is Luzhin. He, too, within the limits of his ability, has thought things out and developed his theories. Very early in the book (Part II, Chapter 5) we find how similar the thinking of the two men actually is. Soon after Luzhin has explained how the greatest good will come from loving one's self alone and looking only to one's own advantage, Raskolnikov very perceptively remarks to him, "Carry to its logical conclusion what you were preaching just now, and it emerges that you can cut people's throats. . . ." This is precisely what Raskolnikov himself has done. Throughout the book there are numerous other references as well to utilitarian theories. They are usually attacked, occasionally by Raskolnikov himself in one of his "Schilleresque" moods.[5]

The parallel between Raskolnikov and Luzhin, however, extends to one further, most important point. Both men, when their projects fail, blame the failure on a "blunder," a mere mistake in tactics, and see nothing else blameworthy in what they have done.

Luzhin, having been dismissed by Dunya, reflects that if he had only given her expensive presents, she could never have gotten away from him; his theory—to tie Dunya to him with bonds of gratitude—remains the same. Similarly, Raskolnikov, we are told (Epilogue, Chapter 2), even in prison "could find no particularly terrible guilt in his past, except a simple *blunder,* that might have happened to anybody." Intellectually, he can still find nothing wrong with his theory. The major characteristic of Luzhin, then, and of the intellectual side of Raskolnikov's personality is that pure intellect predominates, unalloyed with the softer human feelings which are the basis of a Christian sense of morality.

The concept of will is represented in both Raskolnikov and Svidrigaylov. Svidrigaylov is an example of a man whose life is devoted almost entirely to self-gratification; he does as he wants to. The force of his will is strong enough that he can overcome all obstacles without trouble to himself. The one exception occurs when he gives in to Dunya, for had he willed it, he could have taken her by force, getting as much pleasure as he was accustomed to get from life. Raskolnikov's crime, like all of Svidrigaylov's, is committed through force of will. Although he knew beforehand that he was "a louse like everyone else," Raskolnikov was trying to *will* himself into the class of extraordinary men: his intellect provided the idea, but his will provided the force necessary to go through with the murder. After the murder it is his will which is frequently the most vital and active part in him. The intellect virtually ceases to function as a living force, remembering still the old ideas, which, as Porfiry notes, he no longer even believes in (Part VI, Chapter 2), but developing nothing new. As with Svidrigaylov, the will comes in to fill up the near-vacuum in Raskolnikov's soul and provide him with the motivation to go on living. Raskolnikov never consciously reflects on why he is trying to evade the police; he very simply and desperately wills that he live, and live free. This will, which is most frequently expressed in the novel as fierce pride, is almost all that gives him the energy to struggle with his torments for as long as he does.

Spirit, the third aspect of the personality, is most purely represented in Sonya. Faith, compassion, and love she feels intuitively, without constructing theories to explain or justify them. When

Raskolnikov asks her what God does for her, "in a rapid whisper" she replies, "He does everything" (Part IV, Chapter 4). The response of the rationalist Raskolnikov to Sonya's intuitive and emotional approach to life is clear when he tells her, "You must judge things seriously and directly at last, and not weep like a child and cry that God won't allow it." Throughout the novel, those who are deeply religious are characterized as being "childlike," although Dostoevsky, unlike Raskolnikov, gives the word a favorable connotation. The connection between Sonya and Lizaveta in piety and childishness, in particular, is made very strong, especially when they both react to Raskolnikov with the same childlike gesture of fear—Lizaveta when he approaches to kill her, and Sonya when he confesses the murder. The attitude which they take to him is itself invested with religious overtones of submissiveness and turning the other cheek.

It is the childlike part of his personality that Raskolnikov has subordinated to the intellect and the will, but we can still trace through the book numerous instances where it crops up and achieves expression despite all that he can consciously do. In the first and thematically the most important of these incidents, Raskolnikov is himself a child: he dreams he is a boy of seven going with his father to a church service in memory of his dead grandmother; he is devout and reverent, and he loves the church with its ancient icons. When he sees Mikolka beating the old mare to death, he responds with weeping, anger, and love without ever understanding why. He kisses "the poor eyes and mouth" and then asks, "Papa, why did they kill the poor horse?" Significantly, when he awakes from this dream he prays, "Lord! . . . show me the way, that I may renounce this accursed . . . fantasy of mine!" (Part II, Chapter 5). Nowhere else in the novel does he sincerely pray.

This same part of Raskolnikov is also seen in frequent impulsive acts of charity—as when he tries to save the drunk girl from a would-be seducer, or when he gives the Marmeladovs almost all of his money—acts which his intellectual consciousness despises as soon as he has had a moment to reflect on them. Occasionally, Raskolnikov even "softens" and experiences feelings of love for brief moments with his sister, with his mother, but especially with Sonya: after he has confessed to Sonya and received her response

("There is no one, no one, unhappier than you in the whole world!"), "Long unfamiliar feelings poured like a flood into his heart and melted it in an instant. He did not withstand them; two tears sprung into his eyes and hung on his lashes" (Part V, Chapter 4). This is the part of himself which Raskolnikov kills along with Lizaveta—unintentionally and as a necessity that he had not foreseen—and which must be resurrected.

A device which Dostoevsky often used in his novels, which frequently deal with a split personality in the hero, is that of the "double"—alter egos given to the protagonist corresponding to the different sides of the split. We have seen that each part of Raskolnikov's split personality is repeated in at least one other character in a purer and more intense or startling form: these other characters are his doubles. Most critics discuss Raskolnikov in terms of a dualistic split, with Svidrigaylov the double for one side and Sonya the double for the other. Maurice Beebe, however, has suggested a "reinterpretation" of the novel, in which he recognizes three doubles—Luzhin, he says, represents the intellect, Svidrigaylov the senses, and Sonya the spirit.[6] The interpretation I have suggested differs slightly from this in making Svidrigaylov the representative of the will, but there is little point in arguing about labels, as such, for Dostoevsky is not using his characters allegorically. Luzhin, Svidrigaylov, and Sonya, while subordinate in importance to Raskolnikov, are all complex characters, and the student should be led to see their complexity as well as their thematic relationships to Raskolnikov, so that he will not be tempted to think of the novel in terms of a simplistic formula. Sonya is not disembodied spirit, but a human being in whom the soul's spiritual part is especially strong and predominates; in Svidrigaylov will predominates; and in Luzhin intellect predominates. Furthermore, none of these characters precisely equals the part of Raskolnikov's personality to which we have said it corresponds; rather, they express the basic concepts of intellect, spirit, and will in variant and individual forms. Thus, Dostoevsky uses the doubles to explore the parts of Raskolnikov's soul in the varying forms which it might take and, by emphasizing the common elements, to define and make clear its nature.

He uses the incidents of crime, sacrifice, and suffering in the same way. As we have seen, the acts and experiences of many of the characters are parallels and analogues of those of the central character, Raskolnikov. They are used by Dostoevsky to expand the meaning of what Raskolnikov is doing and going through, while at the same time defining it more closely.

Because the story of *Crime and Punishment* is essentially one of inner conflict—Raskolnikov's struggle to reconcile the various aspects of his being—the author is faced with the problem of rendering a very private life both interesting and intelligible to his public. His skillful handling of point of view solves half of the problem by carefully controlling the way the reader looks at the material being presented; the other half of the problem is that of controlling the material itself so that it is meaningful when perceived, and this Dostoevsky achieves by his structuring of crime, sacrifice, and suffering, and intellect, spirit, and will—the principal abstract elements involved in Raskolnikov's experience.

Dostoevsky dramatizes the conflict within his hero by having him come into conflict with people who are the embodiment of the warring elements within him. The "Schiller" in him, the spirit, opposes Svidrigaylov in all their encounters, as Svidrigaylov is quick to recognize and point out to him. Raskolnikov's dislike of Luzhin, which has its origin in this same Schilleresque part of his soul, is also obvious. And in the interviews with Sonya, we can see both the intellect and the will hurting her and struggling to withstand her influence. Raskolnikov's crime, sacrifice, and suffering are all presented dramatically in encounters with other people. All of the characters are involved, for the most part, in dramatic conflicts only with Raskolnikov, and not with each other. Svidrigaylov, for example, does not oppose Sonya, although he does oppose the Sonya-like part of Raskolnikov. And although Luzhin and Sonya do come into conflict when he accuses her of theft, this is not really a battle of Intellect against Spirit in this first stage; only when we realize that the incident is actually a part of the larger conflict between Raskolnikov and Luzhin can we grasp its full significance as such a battle. The ordering of the dramatic action thus precludes the simplicity of allegory, in which Sonya as Spirit would have been directly in conflict with Svidrigaylov as Will, and so forth; and it consequently leads to the subtlety and massive complexity which characterize the book.

Finally, it is interesting to note that Raskolnikov is almost always able to perceive the faults of others, even when they are also his own. He very perceptively comments on the mistakes and sins of everyone from Sonya to Svidrigaylov and Luzhin, including his own mother and sister. His ability to recognize his own faults, at least when they appear in others, is, of course, essential to the pattern of the dramatic action, which lies in the warring of the parts of Raskolnikov's soul with the various characters in whom each part sees faults it abhors. In conclusion, therefore, to all we have said about the structuring of the dramatic action, we must agree with Pearl C. Niemi, who says: "Blind to the beam in his own eye, the murderer of two people serves as righteous, passionate judge of moral disorder in the world around him. Herein resides the central irony of *Crime and Punishment* as well as the virtue of its structural tightness and unity."[7]

If we turn for a moment to consider the Epilogue, we find that it lacks almost all the features that characterize the first six parts of the book. The style of writing is totally different. The presentation is panoramic, rather than scenic; direct and expository, rather than oblique and dramatic. The narration is neat, precise, and unambiguous. In contrast to the intense and detailed treatment given to the two weeks covered in the first six parts, the treatment of the many months covered in the two chapters of the Epilogue is cursory almost to the point of superficiality. The point of view is that of the impersonal narrator, never that of Raskolnikov.

The demands of the Epilogue of course differ from those of the main part of the book. In ending the book, Dostoevsky had to lead the reader gradually way from the world of the novel, tapering off the intensity of the emotions hitherto portrayed and evoked, so that the reader's return to the "real world" would not be so great a shock as to destroy the credibility of the whole book. Dostoevsky also wanted to carry the story beyond the point reached at the end of Part VI, where Raskolnikov has confessed, but where his regeneration is still only a possibility which is not yet assured. He seems accordingly to have adopted the plan of using a distanced narration to tell of Raskolnikov's first conscious act of love, when he clasps Sonya's knees and weeps.

By abandoning his earlier style of narration, however, Dostoevsky has forfeited the sense of immediacy and reality which it gave to his story. By telling us, rather than showing us, that the process of Raskolnikov's rebirth has begun, he weakens the effectiveness of this most important event; it does not carry the force of conviction. When Raskolnikov thinks to himself, "Could not her beliefs become my beliefs now? Her feelings, her aspirations, at least . . . ," we regard the thought as insufficiently motivated. We have been too much accustomed to knowing everything that goes on inside Raskolnikov to be able to accept an isolated thought without further proof. For this reason, some critics have considered the Epilogue to be logically unsound as well as artistically poor; they feel that there has been no previous indication that Raskolnikov was tending, or could tend, in this direction. While a careful reading of the main section of the novel will reveal that the spiritual element does exist in Raskolnikov's soul and that it is capable of being evoked (especially by Sonya) and is thus capable of resurrection, Dostoevsky does not manage to convince us that the resurrection has been effected precisely as he says it has. The problem of the Epilogue would thus seem to be one of artistry rather than logic or psychology; and, in an effective but very unfortunate manner, this last part of the book throws into high relief, by its lack of the features which made the first six parts so successful, Dostoevsky's great skill as an artist in the greater part of *Crime and Punishment*.[8]

CHARACTER

A comparison of Raskolnikov's feelings and behavior before and after the murder points up the subtle change which he undergoes at that crisis. Before the murder, Raskolnikov is a monomaniac who is nevertheless a whole human being, free to respond to life in any way he wishes. Once he has definitely decided to commit the murder, however, he has irrevocably committed himself to one way of life, excluding much that had formed a part of his former existence; by the act of murder, he has committed himself to belief in his theory and behavior in accordance with it. He is the condemned man who has been given, in lieu of execution, a "hand's-breadth of ground" to live on and who comes to feel the meanness of his position in the universe. He longs for "air, air, air" and the freedom of action and response which he had formerly enjoyed.

Part I of the novel gives a remarkably full portrait of Raskolnikov as he is before the murder. Each of the six incidents which precede the crime presents Raskolnikov with an opportunity to decide what he is going to do, and each time his response is slightly different. It varies from loathing and a sense of the ridiculousness of the crime, to a desperate need to act, to cynical consideration of "percentages," to religious horror, to the final acceptance of "fate." The variety of these responses to his problem impresses us with the large degree of freedom which he still possesses: he can move easily from one extreme to the other and contradict himself without feeling compromised. The opposed aspects of his character, which give rise to the different responses, can coexist in relative peace, and, at this point, love for mother and sister is equally as important as poverty or depression or a theory in determining his course of action.

The pressures to which Raskolnikov succumbs in finally deciding to commit the murder also tell us a great deal about the sort of person he is. Economically, he, like Sonya, has reached the point where the few kopecks it is possible to earn by honest labor are no longer enough. He is the only hope of his mother and sister: in order to help them, he must finish at the university and get a good job; and until then, he not only is unable to help them but even is a drain on their own resources, for they must support him. This latter aspect of the financial problem becomes especially important for Raskolnikov when he learns that unless he can do something to improve the situation, Dunya will sacrifice herself for her family in essentially the same way that Sonya has for hers. None of this problem is new, but Raskolnikov's need to find a solution for it has now become desperate. He has reached the point where he can understand completely what Marmeladov had said earlier, "Every man must needs have somewhere to turn to. For there comes a time when it is absolutely essential to turn somewhere" (Part I, Chapter 2). The theory of crime and the extraordinary man gives

Raskolnikov somewhere to turn to, even though he realizes from the start that it will do no good. Faced with an almost insuperable mass of problems, Raskolnikov longs to be able to give the master-stroke which alone can solve them all and thus prove himself one of the class of "extraordinary men." In fact, Raskolnikov's sense of impotency has gnawed at him for so long that being an "extraordinary man" has become extremely important to him as an end in itself, and not just as a means to another end. His intense loathing at times for all the world results from his extreme dissatisfaction with all aspects of his position—in the world, in his family, and in his own private ambition and self-respect—and it culminates in the desire to establish a new moral order, which would do away with all such concerns and bothers. All this his theory would do for him, by permitting him to step across all obstacles without a twinge of conscience; it has the lure of a panacea. All he has to do is dare, and all his problems will be solved. Thus, pressured from all sides, Raskolnikov succumbs to a temptation which has all the inevitability of fate.

Once, however, he has accepted the devil's challenge, he becomes not a man whose life is about to be renewed by a panacea but one who is condemned to death. Immediately after he learns that Alëna Ivanovna will be alone at seven o'clock, he goes to his lodgings:

> He went in like a man condemned to death. He did not reason about anything, he was quite incapable of reasoning, but he felt with his whole being that his mind and will were no longer free, and that everything was settled, quite finally (Part I, Chapter 5).

Later, on his way to murder the old woman, he compares himself to a man going to execution. The condemned-man motif also appears again after the murder. Just before his encounter with Zametov in the tavern, Raskolnikov thinks of a condemned man who,

> just before he died, said, or thought, that if he had to live on some high crag, on a ledge so small that there was no more than room for his two feet, with all about him the abyss, the ocean, eternal night, eternal solitude, eternal storm, and there he must remain, on a hand's-breadth of ground, all his life, a thousand years,

through all eternity—it would be better to live so, than die within the hour? (Part II, Chapter 6).

And Raskolnikov goes on to agree with this man, saying, "Only to live, to live! No matter how—only to live!" Later, he discovers that it has indeed been his fate to be given the "hand's-breadth of ground," for, after helping the Marmeladovs, he is "full of a strange new feeling of boundlessly full and powerful life welling up in him, a feeling which might be compared with that of a man condemned to death and unexpectedly reprieved" (Part II, Chapter 7). The condemned-man motif points, therefore, to the death-in-life to which Raskolnikov has condemned himself by daring to commit murder.

The "condemnation" results in the striking contrast between the variety of Raskolnikov's actions and responses before the murder and the single-mindedness of his behavior afterwards. Once he has committed himself, no other course but that of his quasi-utilitarian theory seems open to him, for this theory is all that can fully justify his crime. Love, which had been important in pressuring him to act, has no place in the theory and consequently now has no place in his life if he is to be consistent and avoid compromising himself. Impulses of love, compassion, and religion are never consciously major moving forces in Raskolnikov after the murder, although such impulses do crop up from time to time, as it were illicitly. In its inhumanity, the theory cuts him off from all that is human, and Raskolnikov must either accept the isolation—the "eternal solitude" of the "hand's-breadth of ground"—or reject the theory, standing exposed as one who has acted in intellectual error, one compromised. In his pride, he accepts isolation. The acceptance is expressed symbolically in Part II, Chapter 2, when he flings into the water the twenty-kopeck piece an elderly woman had asked him to take "in the name of Christ": "He felt that he had in that moment cut himself from everybody and everything, as if with a knife"; and he returns home, "shuddering like an overdriven horse," like the old mare beaten to death in his dream, and falls dead asleep. The limited range of actions of which Raskolnikov is capable is made clear later in the novel when he must find some way to protect Dunya from Svidrigaylov: "All this time, throughout the whole month, Raskolnikov had been so weary that now he could resolve a problem like this in only one way: 'Then I shall kill him,' he thought with cold despair." The strange attitude of loathing, bitterness, and despair which Raskolnikov brings to his theory-dominated life is understandable only if we realize that he is chafing at the limitations which he has imposed on himself, that he longs to be free to take a different course. The following words which Porfiry speaks to Raskolnikov in their last interview are thus very important:

> "You invented a theory, and you were ashamed because it went wrong and because it turned out to be not even very original! It proved mean and base, it is true, but that does not make you hopelessly mean and base. You are not mean and base at all!" (Part VI, Chapter 2).

The crisis at which Raskolnikov chooses to murder has thus widened the split in his personality and brought the two sides into open warfare. This warfare is his "punishment," and the pressures which it imposes on him lead to the final crisis, at which Raskolnikov turns in the opposite direction and elects to "accept his suffering." Just as the moment in the Haymarket when he learns that Alëna Ivanovna will be alone makes him a "condemned man," the moment there when he kisses the earth destines his eventual resurrection. But whereas the first crisis was the result of external pressures and came in accordance with his own will, the last is the result of internal pressures and comes against his will, demonstrating the great power of the forces now acting on him.

The dominant motif for this second phase of Raskolnikov's experience is the Lazarus story. The first mention of Lazarus occurs in Raskolnikov's first interview with Porfiry, in one of a number of curious questions which Porfiry asks, "A-a-and, do you believe in the raising of Lazarus?" and Raskolnikov replies, "Y-yes. Why are you asking all this?" (Part III, Chapter 5). Later Raskolnikov will ask Sonya to read to him the raising of Lazarus, and Dostoevsky will give us the story almost in full. Like the earlier, condemned-man motif, it suggests significant interpretations for a body of events; this time, however, the emphasis is on life-in-death rather than death-in-life. Lazarus was a man who was sick and died, and whom Christ raised to life again, thereby dispelling the unbelief of Jews who were there. Raskolnikov, too, has been sick, and in a sense he has died of his sickness, for this sickness is directly related to his crime and it is the commission of the crime which kills the most vital part of him. When Raskolnikov chooses utter isolation from all humanity, he chooses a kind of death; and it is interesting to note that for four days after he throws away the money given "in the name of Christ," he is like a dead man, lying unconscious for fully three of those four days. It is on the fourth day that the encounter with the Marmeladovs leaves him "full of a strange new feeling of boundlessly full and powerful life": Lazarus, too, was brought to life on the fourth day. Dostoevsky, however, cannot ask us to believe in so stark a miracle as the complete resurrection of Raskolnikov in one moment; he makes the renewal of life in Raskolnikov a gradual process, saving the final moment for the Epilogue. Until then, Raskolnikov is still virtually a dead man, one not executed but nevertheless restricted to a "hand's-breadth of ground," or a man raised to life but still restricted by the winding sheet of the tomb. Because a state of death is impossible to dramatize, Dostoevsky dwells on the state of death-in-life and life-in-death in order to make the fact of death perceptible to us and the necessity of resurrection evident. Therefore, despite the psychological reality of the process, the resurrection in the Epilogue has finally the force of a miracle, creating belief in even Raskolnikov.

The complexity of Raskolnikov's character is such that it cannot be adequately explained: it can only be understood from a reading of the novel. No one interpretation is likely to be wholly satisfying, and most are likely to contain at least a grain of truth. A comparison of Raskolnikov's character before and after the murder is valuable because it can lead the students to see the basic movement in the development of his character and permit them to draw their own conclusions. And, by concentrating on both phases of the development, it can lead them to see how very complex his character actually is.

IDEA

The third approach to *Crime and Punishment* is a study of the ideas it deals with. Crime and punishment constitute the principal theme of the novel, and one of the ways this theme is developed is through an exploration of ideas of morality. "What is crime?" The novel presents many examples of it and a great deal of explicit consideration of the question by the various characters. The search for the answer is one major aspect of the book.

The morality espoused by those who adopt "the latest ideas" tends to condone crime for a variety of reasons. The first discussion on the morality of crime, which is coincident with the first explicit mention of murdering the old woman, occurs in the tavern conversation between the student and the officer. In a brief but important passage the student touches upon a major tenet of Utilitarianism: the greatest good for the greatest number of people. For him, morality becomes a matter of "arithmetic": "thousands of good deeds will wipe out one little, insignificant transgression" (Part I, Chapter 6). Raskolnikov echoes this idea in thinking how much good he could do by committing a murder which would be, after all, "no crime" and then using the money he would steal. Both Raskolnikov and the student further excuse the murder by saying that the old woman deserves to die.

A second excuse for crime is that a person has the right to dispose as he likes of his own property. Lebezyatnikov urges this argument to Luzhin in defense of Sonya's prostitution, saying, "And even now she had the right to act as she did; she was suffering, and that was her stock, so to speak, her capital, which she had a perfect right to dispose of." Similarly, Mikolka, in Raskolnikov's dream, yells, "She's mine, she's my property," whenever someone in the crowd admonishes him for beating the mare.

The morality which Luzhin expounds in Raskolnikov's room is yet another of the variations in which crime (or transgression) is condoned. Luzhin argues against sharing one's cloak with one's neighbor; he advocates loving one's self alone: "If you love yourself alone, you will conduct your affairs properly, and your cloak will remain whole . . . and the more, so to say, whole cloaks there are in a society, the firmer will be its foundations and the more will be undertaken for the common good" (Part II, Chapter 5). He is seeking to justify a dog-eat-dog policy by saying that it will promote the greatest good for the greatest number. Such a morality condones Luzhin's behavior towards Dunya and his false accusation of Sonya, as well as a great deal else, as Raskolnikov realizes: "Carry to its logical conclusion what you were preaching just now, and it emerges that you can cut people's throats . . ." (Part II, Chapter 5).

Still another sort of excuse for crime is voiced by Lebezyatnikov as he speaks with Luzhin about Sonya. "Everything depends on environment and circumstances," he says. "The environment is everything, and the man is nothing" (Part V, Chapter 1). Thus, if a man commits a crime, it is not he who is to blame, but his society. The pressures of St. Petersburg life on the poor cause Sonya to walk the streets and Raskolnikov to murder, and, from this point of view, exonerate them. This same argument comes up in the discussion of crime when Razumikhin and Raskolnikov visit Porfiry. The Socialists, Razumikhin declares, "explain everything by the 'deleterious influence of the environment' "; and in summary of their position he says they believe that "crime is a protest against the unnatural structure of society—and only that, nothing more, and no other causes are admissible . . ." (Part III, Chapter 5).

Despite the variety of the specific arguments used, these four excuses for crime have their basis in a common morality. They view life mathematically, as if it were nothing but a matter of quantities which can cancel each other out. Man is but one of these quantities and has no special or sacred importance. His intangible and immeasurable qualities, the most human of his attributes, such as the capacity for love and compassion, are discounted and disregarded. The individual is insignificant, expendable; and the useless or destructive individual even more so. And while the voiced concern for the Common Good seems altruistic enough in theory, in practice the morality tends to be strongly self-centered.

The kinship of Raskolnikov's theory with this group is easily seen. His theory, as he explains it to Porfiry and Razumikhin, states that mankind is divided into two groups, the ordinary and the extraordinary, and that each of these latter, who have the gift of "saying something new," "has the right in himself, to permit his conscience to overstep . . . certain obstacles, but only in the event that his ideas (which may sometimes be salutary for all mankind) require it for their fulfillment" (Part III, Chapter 5). It is made clear later that an adjunct of the theory is the belief that a human being is a "louse." Raskolnikov's theory is every bit as ruthless and mathematical as the other forms in which the "contemporary morality" appears. All humanity is divided into two groups, and there is a discoverable law of nature which governs the number of "extraordinary men" that are produced. Again the individual is nothing, a louse. No allowance is made for the intangibles, the nonmaterialistic part of life. And while the theory abstractly stated appears disinterested and concerned only with Truth, in practice it is seen to be self-seeking and self-centered.

Raskolnikov, however, goes beyond the other holders of the latest ideas. They provide excuses for crime—rationalization and justification—but they do not deny the concept of crime. The Socialist considers crime a "protest against the unnatural structure of society" and excuses the criminal on that account, but he does not deny that a crime was committed. Mikolka seems to recognize that, under most circumstances, his act of violence would be considered a crime, but he defends himself by shouting, "My property!" Only Raskolnikov is unconcerned with excuses, for the "ordinary man" may not step over any obstacle and there can be no excuse for the crime he commits; and the "extraordinary man" may step over any obstacle and the overstepping will be *no crime.* Raskolnikov denies the validity of the concept of crime for a certain class of men. This denial is what so shocks Razumikhin:

> "but what is really *original* in it [the theory]—and what I am sorry to say, belongs only to you—is that you uphold bloodshed *as a matter of conscience* and even, if you will forgive my saying so, with great fanaticism . . . This, therefore, is the main idea of your article. This *moral* permission to shed blood is . . . seems to me more terrible than official, legal, licence to do so . . ." (Part III, Chapter 5).

Thus, while Raskolnikov's theory is far more terrible in its implications than all the other theories in the book, it has actually far more integrity than most of those presented, for it does not seek to excuse what it knows to be wrong. Raskolnikov acts honestly in accordance with the premises of the theory; the great trouble is that those premises turn out to be "mean and base."

The moral standard in *Crime and Punishment* is a Christian one. Its representatives in the novel are Sonya, Razumikhin, and Porfiry, but it is never stated directly and fully by any of them. It is left to be inferred from the events. Dostoevsky, however, clearly sanctions this morality and not the many other theories of crime, with which it contrasts sharply. The Christian morality recognizes crime or transgression and finds no excuse for wrongdoing. No class of men is exempt. It asks man to assume a sense of responsibility. But it is not hard and cynical: it attends to the non-materialistic side of life, and it includes love and compassion as the most important of its principles. It is in comparison with this standard that Raskolnikov's theory is finally found to be hopelessly inadequate and incomplete.

STUDY QUESTIONS FOR A FIRST READING

PART I

1. Consider the introductory pages of Chapter 1 up to the point where Raskolnikov reaches the house where the old woman lives. What is our first impression of Raskolnikov?

2. What does Raskolnikov do as he leaves the Marmeladovs' flat in Chapter 2? What does he think of his own action?

3. With what emotions does Raskolnikov react to his mother's letter at the end of Chapter 3?

4. What other two women does the drunk girl in Chapter 4 cause Raskolnikov to think of? What is the connection among the three?

5. With what emotions does Raskolnikov react to his dream of the mare in Chapter 5?

6. How does Raskolnikov react to the information that the old woman will be alone (Chapter 5)?

7. When did you first realize exactly what Raskolnikov is thinking of doing?

8. In Chapter 6, to what extent does Raskolnikov have his mind under control after the first murder?

PART II

1. What is Luzhin trying to say with his metaphor of the torn cloak in Chapter 5? Who disagrees with him? Whose thinking is most like Luzhin's?

2. How does Raskolnikov feel after helping the Marmeladovs in Chapter 7? Why? What does he ask Polenka to do for him?

1. How does Raskolnikov act towards his mother in Chapter 3?
2. What is Raskolnikov's theory on crime (Chapter 5)?

1. With what emotions does Raskolnikov react to Svidrigaylov's desire for an interview with Dunya (Chapter 1)?
2. What does Raskolnikov ask Sonya to read to him from the Bible in Chapter 4? When had the incident which she reads about been mentioned before? By whom?
3. What is Raskolnikov's mood at the very end of Chapter 6?

1. Why does Luzhin accuse Sonya of theft in Chapter 3?
2. What reasons does Raskolnikov give Sonya for the murder in Chapter 4?
3. How does knowledge of Sonya's love for him affect Raskolnikov (Chapter 4)?
4. How does Raskolnikov feel towards his sister in Chapter 5?

1. What ways does Raskolnikov think of to protect Dunya from Svidrigaylov in Chapter 3?
2. What is the immediate reason for Raskolnikov's bowing down and kissing the earth in Chapter 8?

1. What is Raskolnikov's attitude towards his crime in the greater part of the Epilogue?

STUDY QUESTIONS FOR A SECOND READING

1. What is the setting? In what ways is the setting important? Why would a small provincial village be inappropriate to the story? Why is the period important?

2. In Chapter 2, Marmeladov speaks to Raskolnikov at some length about what it is like to "plead without hope for a loan":

". . . Nevertheless, knowing in advance that he will give you nothing, you turn your steps towards him and . . ."
"But then why go" put in Raskolnikov.
"But if you have nobody else, no other place to turn to! Every man must needs have somewhere to turn to. For there comes a time when it is absolutely essential to turn somewhere."

Does Raskolnikov as yet understand the full importance of having some place to turn to? When does he begin to feel the need for such a place? How important is this need in determining Raskolnikov to murder?

3. In Chapter 2, in one of his most eloquent speeches, Marmeladov declares: "Do you think, you who sold it, that this bottle of yours has been sweet to me? Affliction, I sought affliction at the bottom of it, tears and affliction, and I found them, I tasted them." Examine this remark in the context of the rest of the paragraph. Why does Marmeladov seek suffering? To what is this suffering related? Elsewhere in the novel much is said about the need to "accept suffering." Who is the most notable example of this need? Does Raskolnikov need to accept his suffering? Explain. What others accept their suffering?

4. Dostoevsky frequently uses phrases such as "Later the young man more than once recalled this first impression . . ." (Part I, Chapter 2). Why?

5. Why does his mother's letter have such a marked effect on Raskolnikov?

6. Why doesn't Raskolnikov want Dunya to sacrifice herself for him? Is he thinking only of her happiness?

7. Reread Part I, Chapter 5—the dream of the mare beaten to death. What is the significance of this dream? What connections are there between the characters in the dream and those in the main part of the book? Write a short essay to answer these two questions. The following questions should help you; first work out in detail the answers to them.

Who in the novel, like Mikolka, kill? What similarities exist in the manner of killing? in the attitude toward that which is killed?

Who in the novel are killed? What similarities exist between the nag and Alëna Ivanovna? between the nag and Lizaveta? Remember that at this time Raskolnikov has no thought of killing Lizaveta. Why then is she clearly related to the old mare? Why is it significant that both she and her sister are represented in the one animal? What characters in the novel, like the mare, fail to pull the burden they are supposed to or would like to pull?

Raskolnikov consciously identifies himself with the seven-year-old boy in the dream. What are the child's outstanding character traits? Are these same traits found in Raskolnikov? When? What traits does Raskolnikov have in common with Mikolka? When do these traits appear in Raskolnikov? at the same time or in the same mood as the childlike characteristics? What significance does this finding have for our interpretation of Raskolnikov's character?

What is Raskolnikov's waking reaction to this dream? After a few moments' reflection on it, he prays. Is prayer characteristic of the child or of Mikolka? Does Raskolnikov ever again in the novel seriously pray?

8. After learning that the old woman will be alone, Raskolnikov returned to his lodgings and "went in like a man condemned to death. He did not reason about anything, he was quite incapable of reasoning, but he felt with his whole being that his mind and will were no longer free, and that everything was settled, quite finally" (Part I, Chapter 5). Why is the image of the condemned man appropriate?

9. Why does Dostoevsky introduce the explicit consideration of the murder through the conversation between the student and the officer in Part I, Chapter 6?

PART II

1. In Chapter 2, Raskolnikov asks himself why he never even looked inside the purse, if he had indeed murdered for money. The narrator notes that this was not even a new question for him. Why hadn't he looked inside it?

2. Why does Raskolnikov throw away the money the woman gives him in Chapter 2? Why is it significant that it is given "in the name of Christ"? The narrator says that Raskolnikov "felt that he had in that moment cut himself from everybody and everything,

as if with a knife." Explain the significance of the incident in the light of this remark.

3. Raskolnikov says to Luzhin in Chapter 5: "Carry to its logical conclusion what you were preaching just now, and it emerges that you can cut people's throats . . ." Is this true of the theory Luzhin was "preaching" with the metaphor of the torn cloak? Defend your answer. How much alike is the thinking of the two men on this subject? Compare Luzhin's false accusation of Sonya and Raskolnikov's commission of murder: in what ways are the two acts similar? Does either man regard what he has done as a crime? What do they both think was wrong with what they did?

4. In Chapter 7, Raskolnikov is again compared to a condemned man, this time to one who has been "unexpectedly reprieved." How is this image appropriate to what has just happened to Raskolnikov? Also at this time, Raskolnikov asks Polenka to pray for him, although it is clear that he no longer believes in prayer, as he did just after his first dream. Why does he make this request of her? Why is it significant that this incident should follow so closely the image of the condemned man unexpectedly reprieved?

PART III

1. Speaking of Raskolnikov with his mother and sister in Chapter 2, Razumikhin says, "Really, it is as if he had two separate personalities, each dominating him alternately." How valid is this statement? What are the two separate personalities Razumikhin sees in Raskolnikov? Find several incidents in the novel to illustrate the domination of each. What are the major characteristics of each?

2. At the beginning of Chapter 5 Raskolnikov comes into Porfiry's presence in a burst of laughter. How characteristic of him is this laughter? Why does he stage his entrance in this way?

3. Consider the following passage from Chapter 5. Porfiry has been explaining how Raskolnikov should go about making the request to get back the items he had pawned.

"Can this be done on unstamped paper?" hastily interrupted Raskolnikov, once more interesting himself in the financial side of the matter.

"Oh, yes. Stamped paper is not necessary at all!" Suddenly, with an openly mocking expression, he screwed up his eyes as if he were winking. Perhaps, however, this was only Raskolnikov's imagination, for it lasted only for a moment. At any rate there had been something, and Raskolnikov could have sworn he had been winked at, God alone knew why.

From whose point of view is this passage narrated? Are we told definitely what Porfiry is doing and thinking? Why? How do we react to the episode? How does the point of view build up our sympathy for Raskolnikov? Is this point of view used in the book as a whole or only in this passage?

4. The following conversation takes place between Raskolnikov and Porfiry in Chapter 5. Raskolnikov speaks first:

"Hunt out your thief! . . ."
"Well, and if we find him?"
"It serves him right."
"Logical enough. And what about his conscience?"
"What concern is it of yours?"
"Well, on the grounds of humanity."
"Any man who has one must suffer if he is conscious of error. That is his punishment—in addition to hard labour."

Does Raskolnikov suffer? Does he have a conscience? Is he conscious of error? of sin? Is he subconsciously aware of sin? Defend your answer.

5. Summarize Raskolnikov's theory. What in the theory so shocks Razumikhin? Attack or defend the theory. Be sure to make your argument as tight as you can. What do you think Dostoevsky thought of the theory? What does the novel suggest as an alternative "theory"? How do you know?

6. In Chapter 6, Raskolnikov says, "I killed not a human being but a principle!" What does he mean? What truth is there in this statement?

PART IV

1. What is the significance of the story of the raising of Lazarus in Chapter 4? Why does Raskolnikov ask Sonya to read that particular story? What parallels exist between the story of Lazarus and that of Raskolnikov?

2. In Chapter 4, Raskolnikov says to Sonya:

"You will understand afterwards. Haven't you done the same? You too have stepped over the barrier . . . you were able to do it. You laid hands on yourself, you destroyed a life . . . *your own* (that makes no difference!). You might have lived by reason and the spirit, but you will end on the Haymarket . . ."

The Russian word which is translated into English as "crime" actually means something closer to "transgression," that is, "stepping across a barrier." (Look up the etymology of "transgress" in a dictionary.) He is thus saying that she too has committed a crime. In what ways are their crimes similar? How are the origins of their crimes similar? He also tells her in this chapter, "That you are a great sinner is true . . . but your greatest sin is that you have abandoned and destroyed yourself *in vain*." Is this true of both of them? Explain.

PART V

1. What effect does Sonya's love have on Raskolnikov in Chapter 4?

2. In Chapter 4, Raskolnikov says: "Did I murder the old woman? I killed myself, not that old creature! There and then I murdered myself at one blow, for ever! . . . But it was the devil who killed the old hag, not I . . ." What does he mean? How true is this statement? What part of himself does he believe he has killed? Later Sonya says to him, "You will destroy yourself, destroy yourself." Does this mean he has not yet killed himself? What part of him does Sonya mean he will destroy? In what sense are they both right?

PART VI

1. Reread Chapter 2. In general, how accurate is all that Porfiry says in this chapter? What does he mean when he says, "This is . . . a contemporary case, something that could only happen in our day, . . ."? Is he correct?

2. Compare and contrast Mikolka the painter, as Porfiry describes him in Chapter 2, and Raskolnikov. How deep and extensive is the similarity?

3. In this same chapter, Porfiry says to Raskolnikov:

> "You invented a theory, and you were ashamed because it went wrong and because it turned out to be not very original! It proved mean and base, it is true, but that does not make you hopelessly mean and base. You are not mean and base at all!"

How accurate is this estimation of Raskolnikov's character?

4. In Chapter 3, Raskolnikov asks himself what he could possibly have in common with Svidrigaylov. What do the two have in common? How are they similar in character?

5. In Chapter 5, Svidrigaylov tells Raskolnikov: "The Schiller in you is always getting into a muddle." What does he mean? "Schiller" has been used as a descriptive term many other times in the novel. Who else have been called Schillers? The reference is to Friedrich Schiller. Who was he? Why does Dostoevsky use his name as a term to describe certain people? What do these people all have in common? What does "Schiller" mean in this novel?

6. In Chapter 7, Raskolnikov thinks to himself: "Oh, if only I were alone and nobody loved me, and if I had never loved anyone! *All this would never have happened!*" Is this statement true? Explain.

EPILOGUE

1. Do you believe Raskolnikov in Chapter 1 when he states that he confessed out of "sincere remorse"? Why? What is the significance of Raskolnikov's betraying "a desire to magnify his guilt"?

2. Explain the meaning of Raskolnikov's dream of the intelligent microbes in Chapter 2. What does this signify about his thinking?

3. How satisfying is the ending? Do we believe in Raskolnikov's resurrection? Why or why not? Has it been adequately prepared for in the main part of the book?

4. Compare the narrative technique in the Epilogue with that in the first six parts of the book. Consider use and treatment of time, point of view, and types of events narrated, as well as any other points you find relevant. Which do you think is more effective, the main part of the book or the Epilogue? Why?

NOTES

1. Quoted by Pearl C. Niemi in "The Art of *Crime and Punishment*," *Modern Fiction Studies*, IX (1964), p. 291.

2. See George Gibian, "Traditional Symbolism in *Crime and Punishment*," *PMLA*, LXX (1955), pp. 979–96.

3. Ibid., pp. 931, 980.

4. Edward Wasiolek, "On the Structure of *Crime and Punishment*," *PMLA*, LXXIV (1959), p. 136.

5. Friedrich Schiller, the German romantic poet, came to represent in the nineteenth-century Russian mind the whole Western romantic movement. Dostoevsky often describes as "Schillers" people in whom feeling is stronger than reason.

6. Maurice Beebe, "The Three Motives of Raskolnikov: A Reinterpretation of *Crime and Punishment*," *College English*, XVII (1955), pp. 151–53.

7. Niemi, p. 299.

8. For a defense of the Epilogue, see Gibian, "Traditional Symbolism in *Crime and Punishment*," and Paul Marx, "A Defense of the Epilogue to *Crime and Punishment*," *Bucknell Review*, X (1961), pp. 57–74.

GRADES 10-12

Additional Novels for Class Reading

Teachers may wish to have all students in a class read and discuss one or more of the following novels in addition to, or in place of, one or more of the novels in the suggested novel sequence. The novels listed here were recommended by pilot-school teachers, members of the state-appointed committee on literature, or the staff of the English Curriculum Study Center because their literary merit and their appeal to students could justify their being taught to entire classes.

The novels are divided into three categories: American, English, and world literature. As was pointed out in the Introduction to this volume, the study of American literature is recommended for grade ten, English literature for grade eleven, and world literature for grade twelve. As was pointed out on page 234, the study of world literature is not limited to those works that we study in translation but includes works that were originally written in English.

AMERICAN

Clark, Walter van Tilburg. *The Ox-Bow Incident.* (Paperback editions: Signet Classics, Vintage Books.)

Hawthorne, Nathaniel. *The Scarlet Letter.* (Paperback editions: Airmont, Bantam, Barnes & Noble, Bobbs-Merrill, Collier Books, Dell, Dolphin Books, Holt, Rinehart & Winston, Modern Library College Editions, Norton Critical Editions, Perennial Library, Pyramid Books.)

Hemingway, Ernest. *The Old Man and the Sea.* (Paperback edition: Scribner Library.)

Knowles, John. *A Separate Peace.* (Paperback editions: Bantam, Dell.)
Melville, Herman. *Moby Dick.* (Paperback editions: Airmont, Collier Books, Dell, Holt, Rinehart & Winston, Library of Liberal Arts, Modern Library College Editions, Norton Critical Editions, Perennial Library, Regents, Signet Classics, Washington Square Press.)
Rolvaag, Ole. *Giants in the Earth.* (Paperback edition: Perennial Books.)
Salinger, J. D. *The Catcher in the Rye.* (Paperback editions: Bantam, Signet.)
Steinbeck, John. *Of Mice and Men.* (Paperback editions: Bantam, Compass Books.)

ENGLISH

Conrad, Joseph. *Lord Jim.* (Paperback editions: Airmont, Bantam, Barnes and Noble, Collier Books, Dell, Holt, Rinehart & Winston, Houghton Mifflin's Riverside Editions, Pocket Books, Perennial Library, Signet Books, Washington Square Press.)
Dickens, Charles. *Hard Times.* (Paperback editions: Dutton Everyman Paperbacks, Holt, Rinehart & Winston, W. W. Norton & Co., Perennial Library, Premier Books, Signet Classics.)
———. *Tale of Two Cities.* (Paperback editions: Airmont, Barnes and Noble, Collier Books, Dell, Houghton Mifflin's Riverside Literature Series, Modern Library College Editions, Perennial Library, Scholastic Book Services, Signet Classics, Signature Books, Washington Square Press.)
Greene, Graham. *The Power and the Glory.* (Paperback editions: Bantam, Compass Books.)
Hardy, Thomas. *Tess of the D'Urbervilles.* (Paperback editions: Airmont, Dell, Houghton Mifflin's Riverside Editions, Modern Library College Editions, Norton Critical Editions, Perennial Library, Signet Classics, St. Martin's Library, Washington Square Press.)
———. *The Return of the Native.* (Paperback editions: Airmont, Bantam, Barnes and Noble, Collier Books, Dell, Dolphin, Holt, Rinehart & Winston, Houghton Mifflin's Riverside Editions, Scholastic Books Services, Scribners, Signet Classics, St. Martin's Library, Washington Square Press.)
Orwell, George. *1984.* (Paperback edition: Signet Classics.)
———. *Animal Farm.* (Paperback edition: Signet Classics.)

WORLD *

Camus, Albert. *The Plague*. (Paperback edition: Modern Library College Editions.)

———. *The Stranger*. (Paperback editions: Random House, Vintage Books.)

De Unamuno, Miguel. *Abel Sanchez & Other Stories*. (Paperback edition: Henry Regnery Co.)

Joyce, James. *Portrait of the Artist as a Young Man*. (Paperback edition: Compass Books.)

Mann, Thomas. *Tonio Kroger*. (Paperback edition: Appleton-Century-Crofts, Inc.)

Remarque, Erick Maria. *All Quiet on the Western Front*. (Paperback editions: Crest Books, Premier Books.)

Silone, Ignazio. *Fontamara*. (Paperback edition: Dell.)

Warren, Robert Penn. *All the King's Men*. (Paperback edition: Bantam.)

---

* An excellent teachers' guide to world literature is Robert O'Neal's *Teachers' Guide to World Literature for the High School*. Champaign, Ill.: National Council of Teachers of English, 1966.